THE MIDDLE ATLANTIC COAST

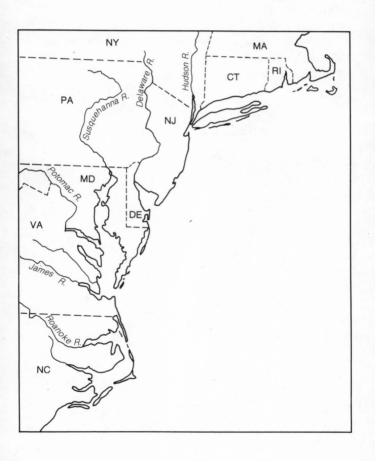

Other Sierra Club Naturalist's Guides

The North Atlantic Coast
  Cape Cod to Newfoundland

Southern New England

The Piedmont

The North Woods
  of Michigan, Wisconsin, Minnesota, and Southern Ontario

The Sierra Nevada

The Deserts of the Southwest

A Sierra Club Naturalist's Guide to

THE MIDDLE ATLANTIC COAST
Cape Hatteras to Cape Cod

by Bill Perry
Illustrations by Casey French Alexander

SIERRA CLUB BOOKS *San Francisco*

The Sierra Club, founded in 1892 by John Muir, has
devoted itself to the study and protection of the earth's
scenic and ecological resources—mountains, wetlands,
woodlands, wild shores and rivers, deserts and plains. The
publishing program of the Sierra Club offers books to the
public as a nonprofit educational service in the hope that
they may enlarge the public's understanding of the Club's
basic concerns. The point of view expressed in each book,
however, does not necessarily represent that of the Club.
The Sierra Club has some fifty chapters coast to coast, in
Canada, Hawaii, and Alaska. For information about how
you may participate in its programs to preserve wilderness
and the quality of life, please address inquiries to Sierra
Club, 530 Bush Street, San Francisco, CA 94108.

Copyright © 1985 by Bill Perry

Library of Congress Cataloging in Publication Data
Perry, Bill.
    A Sierra Club naturalist's guide to the Middle
Atlantic Coast.

    Bibliography: p.
    Includes index.
    1. Natural history—Atlantic Coast (U.S.)
I. Sierra Club. II. Title. III. Title: Middle Atlantic
Coast.
QH104.5.A84P47 1985   508.74   83-18691
ISBN 0-87156-810-1
0-87156-816-0 pbk.

Cover and book design by Drake Jordan
All photographs by the author unless otherwise credited
Illustrations by Casey French Alexander (except where
otherwise credited)
Maps and diagrams by Nancy Warner
Printed in the United States of America
10 9 8 7 6 5 4 3 2 1

TABLE OF CONTENTS

ACKNOWLEDGMENTS

I AM INDEBTED to more persons than it is possible to name for making the preparation of this book easier and more enjoyable than it would have been without their contributions. My field work was greatly facilitated by the cheerful cooperation of the managers and their staffs in the National Wildlife Refuges, the National Seashores, the Sandy Hook Unit of Gateway National Recreation Area, Cape May Point State Park (New Jersey), and Seashore State Park (Virginia). Special thanks are due the managers and rangers of Assateague Island and Fire Island national seashores for providing me with transportation and accommodations; to Marcia Keener for reading parts of my manuscript and offering many valuable suggestions; and to Bill Cary for volunteering to fly me over Assateague Island so that I could photograph it.

I am also grateful to my wife, Bernice, for accompanying me on many field trips and for tolerating my absence at other times.

Most of the drawings in this book were executed by Casey French Alexander; a few, by Michael Graham, originally appeared in *Discovering Fire Island,* published by the National Park Service in 1978.

Introduction

An Atlantic Coast Overview

The part of the Atlantic coast covered by this book extends from Cape Cod, Massachusetts, to Cape Hatteras, North Carolina. It differs noticeably from the coasts to the north and to the south of it. Between Cape Cod and New Brunswick, Canada, a rocky shoreline dominates, with scattered mainland sand beaches occurring less and less frequently as one moves northward until, beyond southernmost Maine, the sand beaches almost disappear. Thereafter an irregular, intricate, island-studded land-sea interface prevails, with deep, narrow inlets reaching miles inland, separated by long, narrow necks of land. Those inlets are the flooded lower valleys of rivers that flowed to the ocean when sea level was much lower; the many islands along the Maine coast were once the high points on that earlier mainland landscape.

South of Cape Cape Ann, Massachusetts, the coast embraces Massachusetts Bay, a broad embayment open to the ocean and unprotected by offshore islands. The southern bight of this embayment is called Cape Cod Bay; it is quite shallow and is largely cut off from the open sea by a long peninsula, shaped like a bent arm, that extends eastward for about 30 mi. (48 km), then northward for about 20 mi. (32 km), with its extremity a handlike hook that curves again to the south. Cape Cod roughly separates the rockbound shores of northern New England from the sandy shores that predominate south of the cape to the Florida Keys. And the extensive barrier beaches characteristic of the Middle Atlantic coast begin to dominate the scene on the outer (ocean) side of the forearm of the cape.

The long, slightly curved line of Nauset Beach and Monomoy Island forms an almost unbroken 20-mi. bar-

1. The protective barrier of Nauset Beach shields much of the ocean-facing arm of Cape Cod from Atlantic storms. Massive rocks left by the glacier dot the marshes and uplands of the cape.

rier on the east side of Cape Cod. Monomoy was formerly a long sand spit attached like a spur to the elbow of Cape Cod. Though not strictly a barrier beach, since it does not lie parallel to the mainland coast and does not separate the ocean from a lagoon or other protected body of water, Monomoy is typical of the sandy, linear spits and islands that are the predominant land forms fronting the ocean waves from Nauset Beach to Cape Hatteras, and beyond. They occur not only off the mainland shores but also bordering large islands, such as Martha's Vineyard, Nantucket, and Long Island.

These lines of coastal barrier are interrupted by bays, such as Buzzards Bay and New York Harbor, and by estuaries, such as Chesapeake Bay and Albemarle Sound. On a map these embayments, absent from most of the coast north of Cape Cod, are the most conspicuous coastal landforms from here to Cape Hatteras. Beyond Hatteras, the deep embayments disappear. The great chain of barrier beaches called the Outer Banks, off North Carolina's mainland, is the single most conspicuous shoreline feature of the U.S. Atlantic coast.

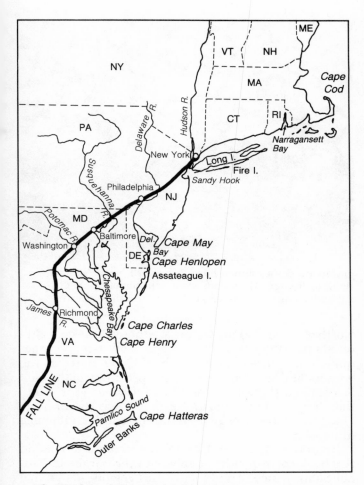

2. The Embayed Section of the Atlantic coast of North
America. The fall line is the boundary between the
Atlantic Coastal Plain and the higher Piedmont Plateau
(see Chapter One).

The Embayed Section, as the coast between Cape
Cod and Cape Hatteras is called by earth scientists, is
different from the northern New England and southeast coasts biologically as well as physiographically.

An Atlantic Coast Overview

3. Canada geese, shown here in Eastern Neck National Wildlife Refuge, Maryland, are a conspicuous part of the fall and winter wildlife of the Middle Atlantic coast.

North of Cape Cod the waters are those of the cold Gulf of Maine—though shallow Cape Cod Bay becomes quite warm in summer. South of Cape Hatteras the winter climate is tempered by the proximity of the Gulf Stream and the waters tend to be warmer year round than they are to the north. North of Cape Hatteras the Gulf Stream veers away from the coast and its influence diminishes.

To biologists, the Middle Atlantic coast as defined in this book corresponds roughly with the Virginian Faunal Subprovince. The biota of this region—its animal and plant life considered as an entity—differs to a considerable degree from that of the Carolinian Province south of Hatteras, and from that of the Acadian Subprovince to the north.

This middle section of the U.S. Atlantic coast, including its estuaries, sounds, open bays, and adjacent terrestrial environments, embraces the geological features and processes and biological communities that are the concern of this book.

Seashore Ecology

The subject matter of this book falls into two main categories: the physical (such as geology, physiography, and meteorology) and the biological (botany, zoology, and ecology). The emphasis is on life systems; however, an explanation of the shaping of the coastal landforms and of the physical forces that continue to mold them is needed in order to understand the dynamics of the life communities. Following a chapter on *geomorphology*—the science of the configuration and evolution of landforms—these communities are discussed in roughly the order one would encounter them when moving from the inshore subtidal waters of the open coast to the upper reaches of the estuaries.

Biological Systems

Because of the great complexity and diversity of life in the seashore environments, this book does not attempt to describe them in detail, or to identify more than a sampling of their key species. Rather, the emphasis here is on the functioning of communities in terms of the interrelationships of organisms and their relationships to the physical habitat. How the organisms live—their food habits, habitat requirements, production of young, harboring of parasites and commensals, alteration of the immediate surroundings by their activities, size relationships, etc—are explained by discussing a few representative and conspicuous plants and animals in each major community. The serious student of seashore ecology will want to refer to field guides and study reports, many of which are listed in the Bibliography. For use in the field, identification manuals will be essential; there are several thousand kinds of mollusks and crustaceans alone that are native to the region covered by this book.

An important aspect of seashore ecology is the adaptation of plants and animals to life in salt and brackish water and to life in those terrestrial habitats on the margin of the sea where salt spray, storm surges, and shifting substrates create especially severe conditions for survival. Of the some 200,000 known species of plants and animals that live in marine environments, the vast majority are found in the intertidal zone or in the *photic zone* (the region of light penetration) of the Continental Shelf. Particularly rich in diversity of species—and of enormous significance to humans—are the eelgrass beds, intertidal mud and sand flats, and salt and brackish marshes. These communities are also relatively easy of access for the amateur naturalist, and they are treated here in some detail.

In terms of number of species, animals are by far the major component of these communities. The densely vegetated marshes and eelgrass beds contain plants of only a few species; the intertidal flats have even fewer, and those are mostly microscopic. Hence animals are given more attention in the discussions of marine and brackish environments.

Beaches and shoals of nearly pure sand support the least varied life communities. However, the normally spare diversity of these habitats is greatly increased when an unusual abundance of a prey species attracts an influx of predatory species. Examples of such abundance occur when flocks of shorebirds come to the beach to feed on mole-crabs, and when in early summer large numbers of gulls, shorebirds, and ibises feast on hordes of breeding horseshoe-crabs' eggs.

In general, animal species are discussed in the context of the trophic level to which they belong—that is, the animals' position in the food chain. The explanation of how a plant-and-animal community functions focuses largely on "who eats whom." A species occurs in an ecosystem not by happenstance but by virtue of its adaptations. It must be equipped not only for survival under the conditions of the physical environment but for acquiring the available food and the means of protecting itself from those that would feed upon it. The adaptation for protection from predators may be primarily a high reproductive capacity—survival for the species rather than for the individual.

Organisms are divided into two main groups according to their trophic, or nutritional, requirements. *Autotrophs* are plants or plantlike animals that are capable

6   INTRODUCTION

4. Laughing gulls feeding on horseshoe-crab eggs as they are being deposited, at Brigantine National Wildlife Refuge.

of manufacturing their own food. *Heterotrophs* are the other plants and virtually all animals; they cannot manufacture their own food, and they must obtain it from organic substances. The heterotrophs include *herbivores*—feeders on living plants; *carnivores*—animals that eat other animals; and *decomposers*—organisms that utilize dead plant and animal material. (Larger animals that feed on dead organisms are called *scavengers*.) There are some specialized animals, the *parasites* and *commensals*, that are not so easily pigeonholed; they, too, are discussed in the pages of this book. However, none of these above categories of animals is conveniently neat and distinct. Where, for example, would one place human beings? Calling them *omnivores* hardly fits them into a trophic slot. Like many other animals, they can be classified in more than one trophic division; like few others, humans are always at the top of the food chain—unless one considers mosquitos and other animals that feed upon humans externally and internally!

Habitat and Niche

An animal in nature has six basic needs: food, oxygen, water, living space, shelter, and protection. The habitat,

5. The bay scallop larva is part of the zooplankton; the young scallops growing their shells are sedentary, often attached to a blade of eelgrass. When mature they are essentially benthic animals; but they are able to swim and thus are part of the nekton.

or home, of an animal is the place that provides these needs. This applies equally to the marine and the terrestrial animals of seashore environments. An association of animals and plants living in a common habitat is called a *community*.

Many species migrate back and forth between communities, in response to the rhythms of the tides, of day and night, of seasons, and of reproduction, feeding, and migration patterns. Many others are restricted for their entire lives to one habitat. Some—such as the bay scallop *(Aequipecten irradians)*, which in its early stages typically lives attached to a blade of eelgrass but in its adult form is mobile—spend part of their lives in one community and the remainder in another.

A basic principle of the life community is that every plant or animal in it affects every other plant and animal, either directly, as through predation or commensalism, or indirectly, as through alteration of the habitat

8 INTRODUCTION

or competition for food. Thus, any action by humans that reduces or increases the population of any species in the community will affect every other organism in the community, in one way or another.

The role of an animal or plant in its community structure and function is its *niche*. The term refers not merely to the physical space a species occupies but to its position as defined by what it eats, what preys upon it, what commensals it harbors, how it alters its own environment, and other factors. A species' niche can logically be equated with the role of an individual or a group of persons in a human community—defined in terms of jobs, social and economic position, use and alteration of the environment, and food habits. An interesting aspect of niche in ecology is that similar niches in two different habitats may be filled by unrelated and quite different species.

The term environmental niche is applied to the particular specialized habitat or microhabitat a species utilizes. Closely related or unrelated species may occupy adjoining substrates that differ only in the ratio of mud to sand, or in the length of time they are exposed by the tides. The mollusks, for example, can be divided into three major ecological groups according to the environmental niches they occupy: the *benthic* forms (collectively, the *benthos*), which burrow into, creep on, or attach to the bottom; the *planktonic* forms *(plankton)*, which as adults or larvae float about at the mercy of the currents; and the *nektonic* forms *(nekton)*, which are strong enough swimmers to control their own movements.

Only about 2% of the mature water-dwelling species of the seashore are free living; the rest dwell on and in the bottom deposits or attached to living plants, rocks, shells, pilings, or other structures. This lopsided ratio does not apply to numbers of individuals, however, nor does it apply to the larval and juvenal stages of animals; for uncounted billions of minute plants and animals exist in the plankton. Most of the animals in that vast assemblage are larval stages of species that spend their adult lives as benthic organisms; many others are larvae of fishes or other forms that spend their entire lives as

6. The flipper of this humpback whale, feeding on sand lances off Cape Cod, is parasitized by barnacles, which as larvae are part of the plankton.

free-swimming animals (the nekton). Accordingly, knowledge of the geographic range of an animal is not enough to assure that one can find it; knowing its environmental niche is often necessary to locating a species, and is of great help as well in identifying found specimens.

Carrying Capacity

The concept of *carrying capacity,* so central to the management of terrestrial habitats (including cropland), is equally applicable to marine environments. Carrying capacity—the limit of density of a given species in a particular habitat—depends primarily on the supply of available food, pressure of predation, and competition with other animals for living space and food. In seashore environments as well as on the uplands, the carrying capacity of a habitat with respect to

INTRODUCTION

a "desirable" species can often be improved by management techniques. For example, oysters depend on locating hard substrate suitable for the *spat* (larval oysters ready to begin forming a shell) to settle on, for if they settle directly on the bottom they risk being smothered by siltation. Management practices for extending the natural substrate have ranged from spreading oyster shells on the bottom to dumping old automobile bodies. The carrying capacity of oyster habitat is also affected by the presence of predators, such as sea stars. Two kinds of management techniques have been adopted to improve the oysters' chances for surviving predation: removal of sea stars; and provision of floating rafts with poles or other hard substrate materials that are suspended beneath the raft but well above the bottom (where the sea stars dwell).

Many human practices have severely reduced the carrying capacity of areas by drastically changing the nature of the habitat. Deposition of dredge fill, or siltation due to disturbance of the bottom from dredging operations, may reduce or eliminate a population of an economically desirable species. Pollution of a habitat by organic materials that use up excessive oxygen in decomposition lowers its capacity to support animal life that requires a good supply of oxygen.

Conversely, man's activities occasionally have increased the carrying capacity of an area for some species, even when wildlife management or habitat enhancement was not the intent. The use of dredge-fill islands by colonial nesting birds is a notable example. (Such sites frequently are merely substitutions for natural habitat destroyed or usurped by humans elsewhere, as on the barrier islands.)

Distribution

The geographical distribution of a plant or animal species is limited by its biological and physical requirements and by the opportunities for dispersal to suitable habitats. Among the factors determining suitability of habitat are the nature of the substrate; water temperatures; salinity range and patterns of changing salinity; the presence of predators; transport of planktonic larval stages, eggs, and seeds by oceanic and estuarine currents; turbidity; pollutants; seasonal conditions; migration routes; competition from other species with similar requirements; habitat size; exposure to sun and desiccating conditions in the intertidal zone; and of course availability of food in sufficient supply. With so many factors in the formula, it is not easy to determine why a species present in one habitat is absent from another that appears to be identical.

Occasionally, even frequently, a species of plant or animal is found well beyond its normal range—even in a habitat that does not seem to supply all of its basic needs. An example is *Donax variabilis,* the *coquina clam,* which is sometimes found on Long Island barrier-beach shores after currents carry the larvae from its usual southern habitat. Another aspect of distribution to be kept in mind is that like almost everything in nature the range of an animal or plant is quite likely at any period to be changing—becoming more contiguous or more spotty, expanding or diminishing. The *common periwinkle, Littorina littorea,* is a case in point. A European species originally, it is believed to have arrived on North American shores centuries ago, perhaps even before the first Europeans, the Vikings, reached the continent. It probably drifted across the North Atlantic on a log or a piece of seaweed and established itself on the shores of Newfoundland. The periwinkle appears to have reached Maine more than a century ago; since then it has extended its range to Maryland.

Unusual circumstances sometimes drastically reduce or expand the range of a species. An example is the disappearance of the bay scallop from much of its normal range when the East coast was struck by the eelgrass blight in the early 1930s (see Chapter Five). Other influences that can cause temporary reduction or extension of the range of a species are warming or cooling trends at either extremity of the range; unusual short-period cold snaps or heat spells; strong desiccating winds in the intertidal zone; onshore winds that bring oceanic floating animals to coastal waters; pollutants

INTRODUCTION

from oil spills or mainland sources; and alteration of normal ocean-current regimes. Man's introduction of plant or animal species into areas not formerly occupied by them, either by accident or intention, is frequently the cause of changed distribution patterns. A recent controversy arose over an attempt by commercial shellfish producers to begin a mussel-culture operation in Cape Cod waters. Others in the shellfish industry, in the business of harvesting clams, objected on grounds that the introduction of mussels into the area would hurt production of their shellfish.

Plankton and Nekton

The plankters are the most abundant organisms in most brackish environments, and they constitute the low trophic levels of most food chains. Plankton, as they are collectively called, is the group of aquatic organisms, both plant and animal, that are incapable of making major horizontal movements independently. These organisms are captives of the tides and currents and rely on them for transport. Some do make efforts at swimming, but these efforts are negligible in relation to the movements of the medium in which the organisms exist. Many, however, are capable of controlled vertical movements, which in the case of plants are related to photosynthesis and in the case of animals are often related to feeding. Since protoplasm is heavier than water, and some planktonic organisms additionally bear the weight of shells or skeletons, many have special devices that aid flotation or permit vertical migration.

Since eating and being eaten are the essence of existence in these and other environments, relative size is a factor in the functioning of the community, and a system of classifying plankton by body size is helpful in ecological studies. One such system is the following:

Ultraplankton	5 microns
Nanoplankton	5–60 microns
Microplankton	60–1,000 microns
Mesoplankton	1–5 mm
Macroplankton	5 mm

An additional category, *megaplankton,* includes larger drifting animals, such as jellyfish, and some comb jellies that are not minute enough to be lumped with the macroplankters.

The first and smallest two categories above consist mostly of one-celled organisms—the producers (diatoms and other algae) and the decomposers (fungi and bacteria)—and the microscopic eggs of some vertebrates. The next two categories, the microplankton and mesoplankton, are mostly herbivorous larval and juvenile crustaceans, protozoans, and *appendicularians* (primitive invertebrate chordates). The eggs of fishes are also a major component. The macroplankton consists of fish larvae, small crustaceans, and the small comb jellies.

PHYTOPLANKTON

This group is the plant plankters. The most prominent are diatoms, unicellular organisms with silicate skeletons, occurring in a great variety of forms that include chains and spirals. A population of diatoms not fed upon or otherwise depleted can double once a day. Diatoms are drifters with no motile capacity. They are most abundant in relatively cold waters. *Dinoflagellates* are also widespread, and are more common in warmer seas. These are one-celled plants, most of which have cellulose cell walls and whiplike "tails" that enable them to swim. They exhibit a great array of adaptations that enable them to live off of dissolved organic substances or to ingest dead organic matter, and thus have the ability to live in deep or turbid water where little sunlight penetrates. The infamous "red tide" plagues are massive concentrations of certain dinoflagellates— literally hundreds of millions of the plants occurring in a cubic meter of sea water—that cause mass mortality of other organisms, including economically valuable fish and shellfish.

Some of the *blue-green algae* are phytoplankton; needing sunlight for photosynthesis, they must be able to remain near the surface, and for this function they exhibit a variety of adaptations. Nonplanktonic mem-

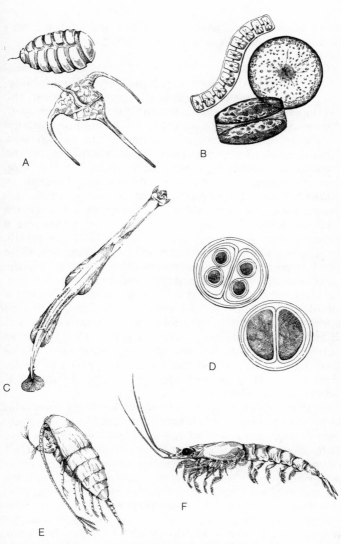

7. *Phytoplankton:* **A.** Dinoflagellates. **B.** Diatoms. **C.** Blue-green algae. *Zooplankton:* **D.** Arrow worm. **E.** Copepod. **F.** Horned krill shrimp.

Seashore Ecology

bers of this plant division are discussed under Plants Associated with *Zostera Marina* in Chapter Five.

ZOOPLANKTON

The minute drifting animals are generally nonbuoyant, but can float or maintain a vertical position in the water mass because each has some control of movement. Some also have a limited ability to move horizontally.

The zooplankton can be divided into two groups. The *holoplankton* are permanent members of the plankton community, remaining there in the egg, larval, juvenile, and adult stages. Members of the *meroplankton* spend only part of their lives—generally immature stages—as plankton. In the latter category are oysters, which broadcast their eggs (100 million at a time) in the water, producing larvae that are totally unlike the adults and live a planktonic existence. (The adult oyster is a benthic organism that is strictly *sessile:* permanently attached, not free moving.)

There are advantages for an organism in having a planktonic stage. A planktonic population can be spread around the ocean and estuaries relatively easily. If the animal is a fish, oyster, or other nonplanktonic species as an adult, it is not in competition with members of its own species that are in the juvenile stage. And for small organisms, the food supply is bountiful where the planktonic stage occurs.

The most common zooplankters are the Copepoda; they are members of the holoplankton. Typically, they make up 50% to 80% of the zooplankton community. Not all copepods are planktonic, however—not even all oceanic species. Some are benthic organisms, and some are parasites. Most, primarily herbivorous, feed by straining phytoplankton from the water. A number, however, are carnivorous or omnivorous. *Calanus finmarchicus* is probably the most abundant species in the northern part of the Middle Atlantic range—in southern New England waters. It sometimes occurs in such numbers as to give the water a yellow or red color. It is fairly large as copepods go, measuring about 1/6 in.

(4 mm). This copepod is an important food for herring and mackerel.

Some larger zooplankters are the Chaetognatha, or arrow worms, which occur to 1/2-in. (12 mm) in length; and the euphausiid crustaceans, of which the most common on our shores is *Meganyctiphanes norvegica*, the horned krill shrimp. This euphausiid measures as long as 1.5 in. (38 mm) and can swim, and thus almost qualifies as a member of the nekton. The chaetognaths and euphausiids are holoplankton.

The phylum Cnidaria (including, for example, jellyfish, anemones, and medusae) includes both holoplankters and meroplankters. Most members of this phylum, in fact, are plankton during at least one stage of life; and some are extremely large, though having only limited motile ability.

Although most of the phylum Mollusca (including gastropods, bivalves, and squids, etc.) are meroplankton, a few spend their entire lives in the plankton community. The so-called *sea butterflies*, or *pteropods*, are gastropods specialized for a life as swimmer-drifters. the bulk of the meroplankton is made up of larval stages of mollusks along with crustaceans and fishes.

Since plankton exists in abundance to well below a depth of 100 meters, its members are by no means to be considered shore animals. Their existence in great numbers in the estuaries and coastal waters reflects the bountiful supply of nutrients there.

NEKTON

The strong swimmers—as opposed to the plants and animals that live at the mercy of the currents—are the *nekton*. This group includes squids; cartilaginous fishes (sharks and allies); true, or bony, fishes; and the sea turtles. One might also consider the marine mammals to be part of the nekton—if not the partly land-dwelling seals and walruses, at least manatees and cetaceans, which are confined to the supporting medium of water. The larger crustaceans that swim about in the water column rather than living exclusively on the bottom are also nekton. Many members of the nekton are discussed in the chapters on estuaries and the eelgrass community (Chapters Three and Five, respectively).

Life Cycles

Most benthic animals produce free-swimming larvae that, not being large or powerful enough to be independent of the currents, are part of the plankton. Mortality among these is so high, owing to predation, that maintenance of the population demands a high rate of reproduction. In most species, the larvae are strikingly different from the adults; metamorphosis comparable to that in butterflies and beetles is almost universal in these marine animals. In many cases, the differences within a single species between larval stages and between larvae and adults have caused different life stages to be designated mistakenly as separate species, or have resulted in failure to recognize relationships between species. The student of seashore life will quickly discover that classification of marine invertebrates is far from stabilized. Discrepancies among identification manuals

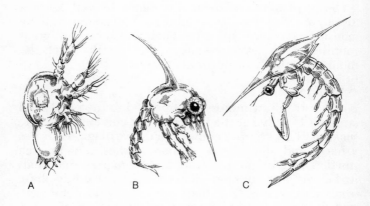

A   B   C

8. *Larval stages of some marine crustaceans:* **A.** Copepod. **B.** Crab. **C.** Mantis shrimp.

INTRODUCTION

are frequently evident. In this book, for the most part, nomenclature and taxonomic position (classification) follow those in the Peterson Field Guides.

More detailed information on reproduction, the phenomenon of metamorphosis, and subsequent growth of marine animals, including fishes, can be found in *The Ecology of the Seas,* edited by D.H. Cushing and J.J. Walsh. For other references on littoral (shoreline) and shallow-water animals, most of which contain some information on reproduction and life cycles, see the Bibliography. Books listed under Field Identification Manuals will be helpful in classification.

Life in Transition

Although all life on earth originated in the seas, and today's terrestrial species exhibit the culmination of eons of evolutionary adaptation to land, many of today's marine species have come about through a reversal of this movement. The marine flowering plants—of which there are actually very few species—have evolved from freshwater species that themselves were derived from terrestrial forms. Eelgrass *(Zostera marina)* is closely related to the freshwater pondweeds *(Potamogeton* spp.). And the cetaceans (such as whales and dolphins) evolved from land mammals whose own remote ancestors were sea creatures. Fossil whales have been found in late Eocene deposits, so their return to the sea must have occurred many millions of years ago.

A number of invertebrate forms apparently are in passage from land to sea, and vice versa. Some of these, such as the ghost crab *(Ocypode quadrata),* are described in later chapters. Further, there are many freshwater and terrestrial invertebrates that, while probably not on the way to a totally marine existence, have adapted to the semiaquatic environment of the marshes and intertidal zones. The phylum Mollusca and the phylum Arthropoda (which includes the crustaceans) contain many of the species occupying such transitional or amphibious ecological niches.

9. A ghost crab sits in the entrance of its burrow near the toe of the foredune (Bodie Island).

The Water Environment

Sea Water

The ecology of marine habitats is greatly influenced by variables in the water medium, including temperature, rate and degree of temperature changes, turbidity, and turbulence. But the overriding factor in the marine and estuarine water environment is salinity—particularly the variations in salinity over space and time. The degree of salinity and the changes that take place are a function of the mixing of sea water and fresh water. The proportions range from almost pure sea water along the open coast, where salinity is more than 30 parts per thousand (30 o/oo), to the upper zone of estuaries, where salinity is as low as 0.5 o/oo. In the middle of the Atlantic Ocean it is 36 o/oo. (Parts per thousand is the equivalent of grams per kilogram.)

The variations in salinity that occur with the changing proportions have a major influence in determining

INTRODUCTION

the makeup of marine and particularly estuarine communities, directly affecting both plants and animals.

Salinity is defined as the mass of dissolved solids per unit mass of sea water; suspended particles do not operate as a factor in salinity. It is an all-important fact that most properties of sea water are a function of its salinity. For example, the *freezing point* and the *temperature of maximum density* both decrease with increased salinity. (At a salinity of 24.7 o/oo both points are reached at −1.33° C, or 29.61° F.) At normal oceanic salinities, vertical convection occurs as the surface water cools and the denser particles of water sink. Eventually—given enough time—an entire water body can be cooled to the freezing point. Because of this phenomenon, the ocean does not freeze as readily or as rapidly as freshwater bodies.

Although the salinity range is great from midocean to upper estuary, and is variable within a given zone of an estuary or lagoon, the relative proportions of the dissolved substances are quite constant. Thus one can get a fair index of salinity by measuring any one constituent. The proportions of the major constituents of sea water are given in Table 1.

Sea water also has very small concentrations of virtually all other natural elements. The elements and compounds associated with living plants and animals, such

Table 1: Proportions of the Major Constituents of Sea Water

Ion	Grams per Kg of water with a salinity of 35 o/oo
Chloride	19.353
Sodium	10.762
Sulphate	2.709
Magnesium	1.293
Calcium	0.411
Potassium	0.399
Bicarbonate	0.142
Bromide	0.0773
Strontium	0.0079
Boron	0.00445
Fluoride	0.00128

as carbon, oxygen, nitrates, and phosphates, are present in variable degree.

Tides

Until Sir Isaac Newton published the law of gravitation, the true nature of tidal forces was not understood, although for some 16 centuries it had been known that tidal cycles were tied in some way to the sun and the moon. Gravitation can be described simply: it is the mutual attraction of any two masses. The sun, the moon, and earth are subject to Newton's law, which states that two objects attract each other with a force proportional to the product of their masses and inversely proportional to the square of the distance between them. The law applies to the sun and the earth, the sun and the moon, and the earth and the moon. With this in mind, the tides can be explained in basic terms.

The mass of the sun is much greater than that of the moon; but because the moon is much closer to earth, it exerts a tide-producing force about 2 1/4 times greater than the sun's. The sun, in effect, merely decreases or increases the strength of the lunar tides, depending on its relative position. In accordance with Newton's law, the solid mass of earth responds to gravitational pull

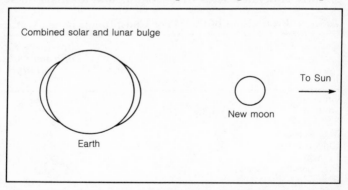

Combined solar and lunar bulge

Earth

New moon

To Sun

10. Spring tides (sun and moon in phase). Spring tides also occur at the full moon (when the sun and moon are on opposite sides of the earth).

INTRODUCTION

toward the moon in inverse proportion to the square of the distance between its center and that of the moon. On the earth's surface the water, being fluid, responds as individual particles. Each particle has a mass that is infinitesimal as compared with the moon, and so is pulled strongly. And because the moon attracts the water mass, there is always a high tide on the side of the earth facing the moon. At the same time, there is also a high tide on the opposite side of the earth. This is because the solid mass of the earth, whose center of attraction is 4,000 mi. closer to the moon than is the water on the earth's far side, is pulled toward the moon with a greater force.

When the earth, sun, and moon are in line—at the time of full moon and new moon—the greatest range between high tide and low tide occurs. This is called *spring tide.* The tide with the minimum range, called *neap tide,* occurs when the sun and the moon are at right angles, in the first and third quarters of the moon's phases, and thus are not exerting their gravitational force on the earth in concert (from the same direction

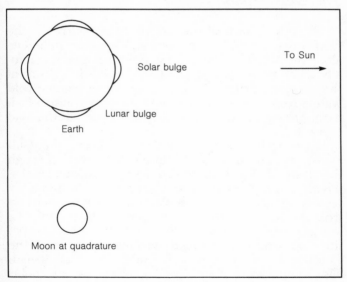

11. Neap tides (sun and moon out of phase).

or from opposite sides). Locally and regionally, tidal range and times depend also on coastal configurations and barometric pressure. Tidal ranges vary over the earth's surface—from less than 2 ft. (0.6m) off oceanic islands to as much as 50 ft. in parts of the Bay of Fundy.

Figures 10 and 11 illustrate the forces producing the spring tides that occur during the new moon. More detailed explanations of the tidal forces and regimes, which have been greatly simplified here, can be found in some of the references in the Bibliography under Coastal Geomorphology. (See, particularly, Willard Bascom's *Waves and Beaches* and Arthur N. Strahler's *Physical Geography*.)

For studies of intertidal and shallow subtidal life, the seashore explorer can take advantage of the extra exposure at low tides, checking an almanac or calendar for the phases of the moon, and tide tables for local tide times. Spring tides, of course, provide the greatest opportunities to study the organisms of the lower intertidal and sublittoral zones.

The Gulf Stream

The best known of the world's ocean currents, the Gulf Stream, or Florida Current, has some influence along the Middle Atlantic coast, though it does not actually touch those shores. The Gulf Stream is a result of the general vertical circulation of ocean waters: cold waters from the north sink, and warmer waters originating in equatorial regions flow north above the cold current.

Discovered in 1513 by Ponce de León, the Gulf Stream rises in the Gulf of Mexico. As it passes through the Straits of Florida (between the peninsula and Cuba) it is about 50 miles wide. Flowing northeast, it is roughly parallel to the coast and is separated from it by a narrow strip of cold water. Its average speed is about 4 mi. (6.4 km) per hour. Gradually it slows and spreads out. Opposite Cape Hatteras it begins to move away from the continental land mass. At its beginning the Gulf Stream has a temperature of 80° F (27° C), but it becomes cooler as it moves northward.

INTRODUCTION

By the time it has reached a point 700 mi. northeast of New York City, the Gulf Stream has merged with the rest of the ocean drift and lost its identity. The common belief that it continues northeast as a warm current, producing the mild winters of the British Isles and Scandinavia, is incorrect; that condition is an effect of a different set of currents.

In addition to giving the East coast of the United States somewhat higher temperatures than are the average for these latitudes, the Gulf Stream affects distribution of animal life. It is responsible for occasional appearances of warm-water species along the Long Island and New England shores.

The Human Factor

The human presence on the Middle Atlantic coast, much increased in recent decades, has had growing significance for the ecological health of the seashore environments—and for our economic welfare. On any summer day and on spring and fall weekends, long lines of automobiles crawl like processions of ants between the population centers and the outer beaches and estuaries. Most of the flow of humanity to and from the seacoast is of vacationers and day-trippers drawn from their homes by the opportunity to swim and sun and fish, to exploit the rich resource of the intertidal flats, to boat in sheltered waters, or just to get away from the heat of the city. Increasingly, the pressure thus applied to the natural environment is intensified by amusement parks, marinas, and other resort and recreational developments.

The vast majority of visitors who go beyond the resort attractions confine their activities to a narrow zone: sunbathers and swimmers to the ocean beach; clammers to the intertidal flats and shoals; boaters to the navigable waters. Few are aware of the complex life communities that exist throughout the broad belt that separates the deep offshore waters from uplands beyond the influence of tides and salt-laden winds. Few are aware of the interplay of the physical processes that have created the barrier beaches and estuaries and that are constantly changing and adjusting the contours of the land-sea interface. The allure the seashore holds for us and our lack of understanding of the physical and natural forces at work create serious conflicts that are compounded by pollution and other unintended stresses. Even as our understanding of the problems grows, the tension between man and nature at the seashore is increasing. New bridges, causeways, and roads open up new areas for dense development. More homes, hotels, and resorts are built on or near the shore, and the accessibility of the water's edge diminishes. Those who visit the seashore in search of solitude and quiet are frustrated as dunelands, marshlands, and the beach itself are taken over by vehicular traffic and private and commercial structures. The greatest impact is on the complex natural systems, which are disrupted and destroyed despite sometimes heroic efforts to minimize the harm. The effects of human activities on nature and the search for measures to alleviate the degradation and destruction are the objects of many research and management studies. The nature of some of the conflicts between us and preservation of the seashore is explored in the following chapters.

CHAPTER ONE

Geomorphology of the Middle Atlantic Coast

The Atlantic Plain

Geomorphologists—geologists who study the configuration and evolution of landforms—have their own ways of looking at the Atlantic coast. These ways may bear only indirect relationship to a biologist's viewpoint. For example, a malacologist—one who studies mollusks—would designate the region encompassed by this book as the *Virginian Subprovince* of the *Boreal Province,* based on distribution patterns of native mollusks.* As it happens, this Virginian Molluscan Subprovince corresponds quite neatly to the *Embayed Section* of the geomorphologist's *Atlantic Coastal Plain Province*—a designation that has nothing to do with animal distribution. Still another term, the *Atlantic Bight,* is used to designate the broad, curving coastline of the Embayed Section.

The Coastal Plain Province is one of two physiographic provinces that make up the Atlantic Plain (see the accompanying map, Fig. 12). The Coastal Plain Province is the part of the Atlantic Plain lying above sea level. Rising gradually from high-tide line, it meets the *Piedmont Plateau Province* (which is part of the *Appalachian Division*) at elevations ranging from sea

*For an explanation of marine faunal provinces and a map of molluscan faunal provinces of North America, see R. Tucker Abbott's *Seashells of North America: A Guide to Field Identification.*

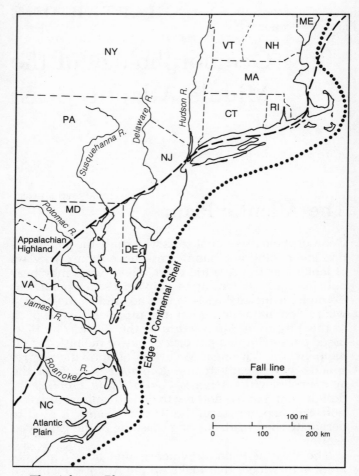

12. The Atlantic Plain.

level at the mouth of the Hudson River to 500 ft. (150 m) in the south.

The *Continental Shelf Province* is the submerged part of the Atlantic Plain. It is a broad belt (up to 200 mi. or 320 km wide), sloping away from the land's edge to a depth of 600 ft. (180 m).

This book describes the ecosystems along the inter-

GEOMORPHOLOGY

face between the Continental Shelf and the Coastal Plain—in other words, where land and sea meet. Within the latitude range of the Middle Atlantic region, the Coastal Plain is approximately equal in area to the Continental Shelf; the Coastal Plain, however, narrows from south to north, owing to movements of the earth's crust that tilted this part of the Atlantic Plain downward to the northeast. Included in the Coastal Plain are Long Island, Martha's Vineyard, Nantucket, and Cape Cod; about two-thirds of New Jersey; all of Delaware; and the eastern parts of Maryland, Virginia, and North Carolina. Because the Piedmont Province meets the Continental Shelf along the Connecticut and Rhode Island mainland coast, the only parts of these two states included in the Coastal Plain are offshore islands. The salt ponds and estuaries of the Connecticut and Rhode Island shore are not part of the Atlantic Plain.

The Continental Shelf gives way at its outer edge to a sharply descending Continental Slope, which marks the limit of the North American continental land mass. The Shelf is a deep layer of sedimentary materials eroded from the uplands, carried seaward by streams, and distributed by ocean currents. The Coastal Plain itself is former sea bottom, having been built up in the same way and later brought to above sea level by upwarping of the earth's crust in the region. In recent times much of it was again inundated in a process called *submergence,* as the sea rose with continued melting of the continental ice sheet. That part of the Atlantic Plain thus became part of the Continental Shelf (as that physiographic province is herein defined). North of Cape Cod none of the Atlantic Plain remains above sea level. The great fishing banks of the western North Atlantic —from Georges Bank off Cape Cod to the Grand Banks off Newfoundland—are higher parts of the submerged Atlantic Plain.

Erosion of the uplands and deposition of sediments on the Continental Shelf still occur, of course, and this is a factor in the continuous process of change in coastal topography. The process of submergence, too, is ongoing, and is particularly significant along the shore of the Embayed Section of the coast (which is coincident with

13. Erosion of the rocky shoreline is proceeding slowly on Sachuest Point, Rhode Island.

the region covered by this book). Besides the continued melting of the polar ice caps, which is reflected in a worldwide rise in sea level, crustal movements may be contributing to the process of submergence in the Embayed Section.

Many shoreline features on this coast have developed as a direct result of submergence. An example that has occurred in recent times is Sandy Hook, New Jersey (Fig. 14). As the sea rose, waves cut into cliffs along the shore at what is now Long Branch. A barrier beach developed, and the predominantly north-flowing currents produced a spit extending into the large bay into which flow the waters of the Hudson, Raritan, Passaic, and Hackensack rivers. When the spit had extended about 2 mi. (3.2 km) north of the Navesink Highlands, a hook recurving to the west developed. (It was perhaps then that the spit got its name; today it only slightly suggests a hook.) Later, the spit began to grow northward again, and at a length of about 3.5 mi. (5.6 km) another hook formed. Subsequent further growth extended the spit by 1840 to a length of about 5.5 mi. (9 km). In the meantime, it had been breached by storms at two points in the spit's slender base. The breaches

GEOMORPHOLOGY

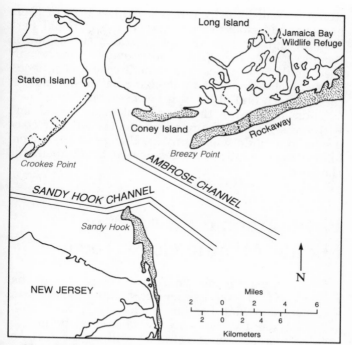

14. New York Harbor spits.

were closed by natural forces in 1877, and the spit has not been breached since. Topographic maps show that between 1954 and 1970 the point of the spit was built out about 0.1 mi (0.16 km). But Sandy Hook spit cannot be expected to extend farther across the bay toward New York, because it has now reached to the very edge of the ship channel from Raritan Bay, which is kept open by dredging. Although a hook formed at the point of the spit about a century ago, it is no longer in evidence. In the early decades of this century, a lagoon, Spermaceti Cove, was formed when spits on the bay side lengthened from the north and the southeast. These spits were later breached and are now islands.

Present trends indicate net attrition of Sandy Hook spit, and reshaping is continual. Some shores are eroding while others are accreting. The slender base, breached in the past, is reinforced by a riprap (loose stone) seawall built by the U.S. Army Corps of Engineers. Sandy Hook is now part of the National Park System, and the seawall will be retained. Erosion in recent years has been particularly severe on the heavily used southern beaches, and some areas have of necessity been closed. About a mile-and-a-half of shoreline at the northern end of the spit has been accreting.

Thus, both over the long geological period and within the span of a human lifetime, the Atlantic coast is seen to be undergoing constant change. Much of what follows deals with the processes that bring about the changes.

Physiographic Features of the Middle Atlantic Coast Today

A look at a map of the U.S. Atlantic coast reveals that from Cape Cod south barrier beaches and the estuaries and lagoons behind barrier beaches—which are often called bays and sounds—are the characteristic physiographic features. Since estuaries will be the focus of much of this book's content, it will be well to explain what they are.

Like many other names of physical features, *estuary* has various meanings, depending upon the user and the context. In the sense that is applied here and that is most commonly used by scientists, an estuary is a semienclosed coastal body of water that has a free connection with the open sea and that is affected by a measurable mixing of sea water with fresh water from land drainage. It is possible—when evaporation exceeds the input of fresh water from inflow and precipitation —for an estuary to have a higher salinity than the adjacent ocean; but such *negative estuaries,* as they are called, are not found on this stretch of Atlantic coast. The salinity range in estuaries here is from salt water of 35 parts per thousand (35 o/oo) to fresh water.

Other notable features of the Coastal Plain physiography, often part of or associated with the barrier beaches and estuaries, are the extensive salt marshes,

GEOMORPHOLOGY

fresh marshes, and swamps. There are bogs, too, but they are not as prevalent as in the glaciated part of North America. (Except for Long Island, Martha's Vineyard, Nantucket Island, and Cape Cod, the ice sheet did not extend into any of the Atlantic Plain that remains above the sea today.)

Although freshwater wetlands and fresh ponds are important in the ecology of some barrier islands, and of some mainland coastal areas such as Cape Cod, this book is mainly concerned with ecosystems under the direct influence of waves, tidal and *littoral* (shore) currents, oceanic winds, salt spray, and the mixing of saline and fresh waters, along with the inshore oceanic waters. In the case of large estuaries, where tidal influence reaches many miles from the open coast, we will be venturing far from what is normally considered the seashore. Thus, the ecosystems included in this spectrum are subtidal and intertidal beaches of spits and barrier islands and of mainland coasts; intertidal sand and mud flats; subtidal lagoonal and estuarine waters; salt and brackish marshes; seagrass beds; dunelands; maritime

15. Mallard pair on a baldcypress pond in Seashore State Park, Virginia. Freshwater ponds, on barrier islands as well as among old mainland dunes, support waterfowl and other wildlife.

Physiographic Features 33

forest and thicket communities; and the above-mentioned freshwater habitats where they occur on barrier islands.

The Glaciated Coast

The northern and southern parts of the Embayed Section are different in two respects: the coast from Cape Cod to Staten Island lies within the region of North America that was covered by the Pleistocene ice sheets; and this Glaciated Coast lacks the large estuaries so evident from New Jersey south, where the Atlantic Plain has not been entirely submerged. These differences, along with the effects of climate and ocean currents, are directly related to the difference in the biophysical interfaces of the two regions. Both the glaciated and the nonglaciated parts of the Embayed Section, however, are characterized by barrier islands and spits; on the Nonglaciated Coast, they are almost continuous.

To explain the Glaciated Coast, we must go back thousands of years to the time of the Late Wisconsinan

16. The beach at Brewster, Massachusetts, on the somewhat protected Cape Cod Bay shore, has patches of marsh grass and is studded with glacial erratics.

GEOMORPHOLOGY

phase of the continental ice sheet, the last of the glaciers to move far down into the continent. There is reason to believe that it advanced to just short of the outer fringe of present-day barrier beaches from the western end of Long Island to Nantucket Island. Even so, great masses of rock material borne in and on the glacier were left in the region. Much of it, carried by glacial streams far beyond the terminus of the ice sheet, was deposited in the form of overlapping fan-shaped masses of rock, silt, and sand. One long, overlapping row of these *outwash fans* was the foundation of Long Island.

About 11,000 years ago, after a long period during which the glacial front lingered in this region, a warming trend began, and the melting of the ice front exceeded advance movement of the still flowing glacial mass, resulting in a new retreat. This final retreat of the Wisconsinan Stage of the ice sheet did not proceed at a steady pace. At two points it paused long enough for large amounts of glacial debris to be deposited along its front. During these pauses, when melting of the front was in balance with the forward movement of the glacial mass, the double backbone of Long Island was

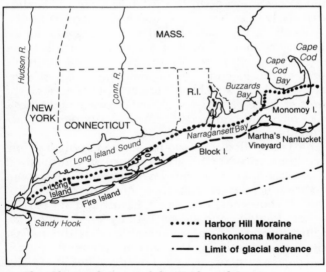

17. The Glaciated Coast of the Embayed Section.

Physiographic Features

formed. Ronkonkoma Moraine may actually represent the farthest advance of the glacial front.

With the melting of the ice sheet, sea level rose. In time the waters inundated the depressions between the higher areas of glacial drift, forming the sounds of the region—Long Island, Block Island, Vineyard, Nantucket, and Rhode Island sounds—and Narragansett and Buzzards bays. From Staten Island north, the offshore islands and Cape Cod are all that remain of the Atlantic Plain above the sea. Beyond Cape Cod the Plain is entirely submerged; the islands off the northern New England coast are the tops of hills and mountains that existed long before the continental ice sheet covered this land.

The Nonglaciated Coast

The part of the Atlantic Coast where the Coastal Plain remains above water coincides with the nonglaciated region—everything south of Staten Island. The typical development along the Atlantic coast, with its gently sloping sea floor (as contrasted with that of the Pacific coast), has been the establishment of barriers. Particularly from New Jersey south, the barriers tend to lie well off the mainland. Broad, shallow lagoons behind the barriers have enabled extensive marshlands to develop. These often border the barrier and mainland shores of the lagoon, and in some cases almost completely fill them. Marshlands are also prominent on the shores of large estuaries such as Delaware and Chesapeake bays and hundreds of smaller estuaries and embayments.

The Outer Banks, a 250-mi.-long system that embraces the entire North Carolina coast, exhibit the most striking example of barrier development. The lagoons here are much larger than those of southern New England or those between Long Island and its barrier beaches. Pamlico Sound—an estuary or a lagoon according to one's choice of definitions—is the largest body of water inside any U.S. barrier. Albemarle Sound, classified as an estuary, is in its lower reaches essentially a lagoon. By the definition of *estuary* that requires an

GEOMORPHOLOGY

18. The Outer Banks of North Carolina (NASA satellite photograph).

open access to the ocean, it does not qualify—as a look at the map of North Carolina shows. Bogue, Core, Roanoke, and Currituck sounds, along with Back Bay (the last two situated behind the Currituck Banks), are best classified as lagoons.

From New York Harbor to Cape Henry, Virginia, during the period since the pace of the rise in sea level slowed drastically, there has been a seaward extension of the coast. Bottom sediments here are so plentiful that, up to recently, longshore currents could not transport all of it, and enough has been piled onto the beach to more than offset the submergence that has occurred during the past few thousand years. Presently this eastward extension is in abeyance; submergence and deposition are in somewhat of a dynamic balance. And south of Virginia there appears to be a net retrogradation in many sections. Cape Hatteras has been eroding on its

19. On parts of the Outer Banks, erosion of the ocean beach is occurring at a rapid rate.

ocean side at an accelerated rate—as much as 21 ft. in a year. In other places, as at Oregon Inlet on Bodie Island, 43 mi. (69 km) to the north, accretion is occurring. On the Bodie Island side of Oregon Inlet, deposition of a sand plain has created a 1/3-mi.-wide beach.

The Formation of Estuaries

In the Embayed Section, the large estuaries have been created as the rising sea filled in the lower valleys of eastward- and southeastward-flowing rivers. South of New York Harbor—in Delaware and Chesapeake bays and in Currituck, Albemarle, and Pamlico sounds—where the interface between the marine and terrestrial provinces is broad, it is difficult to draw a sharp line delineating the Coastal Plain and the Continental Shelf. Mean high tide-line is the theoretical boundary; and that is easier to define on the barrier beaches than on the coastal marshes.

The boundary between the low-relief, low-elevation

GEOMORPHOLOGY

Coastal Plain and the Piedmont Plateau is the *fall line*. The bedrock of the Atlantic Plain is relatively soft and easily eroded; that of the Appalachian Division where it meets the Atlantic Plain is composed of more resistant Paleozoic formations. Because of this disparity, headward erosion by the rivers has been retarded at the line of separation. Waterfalls develop as the rivers drop from the hard Piedmont to the soft Plain rocks. The fall line marks the upper limit of tidewater in the region from Staten Island southwestward to southern Virginia. Below Virginia the fall line is less distinct; but it roughly defines the Coastal Plain to the south and west, around the Gulf of Mexico. Northward, beyond Staten Island where the Atlantic Plain is largely submerged, the fall line is offshore, except where it crosses the shoulder of Cape Cod from Buzzards Bay to Plymouth; there it disappears to emerge no more.

For several reasons, most of the older Middle Atlantic seaboard cities not built directly on the coast were situated along the fall line: because of the water-power potential of the falls; because navigation stops there; and because the rivers below the fall line broaden out on the relatively flat terrain and could be crossed only by ferry. Even today, when bridges span many wide tidewater rivers, some major north-south highways of the Atlantic coast states approximate the trend of the fall line.

The differences in resistance to erosion of the various bedrock types are also reflected in the amount of suspended materials carried in the rivers flowing into the Atlantic. Although northern rivers such as the Delaware and the Susquehanna, which flow mostly through the Appalachian Highlands on very resistant bedrock, have greater rates of discharge than do southern rivers such as the James, Potomac, and Roanoke, they carry less suspended sediment. This contrast between northern and southern rivers is stronger yet in the case of the Hudson and Connecticut rivers, whose valleys were scoured by glacial erosion and glacial meltwater; their loads of sediment are miniscule compared to those of the James and Roanoke rivers.

Along with the deeper scouring and lesser supply of

sediment of northern rivers, the greater net rise in sea level in the north is reflected in the drowned river valleys. The ecology as well as the morphology of the coastal interface is affected by these differences. The principal sources of the surficial (occurring on the surface) sediments on the bedrock of the Continental Shelf are materials derived from the bedrock itself, river sediments, biogenic contributors, and, in the north, glacial till and outwash deposits. Because the river sediments today are largely trapped in the estuaries and coastal marshes, they do not contribute greatly to the sediments overlying the Shelf. Studies have indicated that the amounts of suspended materials carried by the rivers are about equal to those that would be required to keep the eastern coastal marshes in balance with the rising sea level.

The estuaries of the Middle Atlantic region are highly productive biological systems; Chesapeake Bay has been called the most productive estuary in the world. That picture is somewhat flawed, however, by growing problems of pollution and habitat destruction and by competition with human needs for recreation, industry, navigation, and living space, as well as by efforts to maximize fish harvests in order to satisfy demands for protein and fertilizer. There is not an estuary between Cape Cod and Cape Hatteras that has not been the focus of a struggle between conflicting interests that affect the health and integrity of these fragile ecosystems.

The Dynamic Interface— Beaches, Waves, and Currents

The nature of a seashore area is determined by the physical interfaces that waves, tides, winds, currents, crustal movements, and other natural forces generate. These interfaces are not fixed but are everywhere to some degree dynamic; that is, all shorelines are undergoing continuous realignment and adjustment. On

GEOMORPHOLOGY

20. The boardwalk at Atlantic City, N.J., after an April 1984 storm. Both the physiographic and biologic interfaces have been severely altered by human activities on much of the Atlantic coast.

Maine's rockbound ramparts, the process is slow; there, a person during a lifetime of observation may observe no perceptible change in the land-sea interface. But to the south, in the Embayed Section, any part of the exposed seashore—with a few minor exceptions where there are rocky shores, as in southeastern Rhode Island —can undergo conspicuous reshaping during a single day or night.

Of all major physiographic interfaces, the land-sea interfaces formed by barrier beaches are the most dynamic; and this is reflected in equally dynamic *biological* interfaces. That a substrate consisting of highly mobile materials such as sand is subject to constant shifting by waves, currents, and winds is not surprising. The biological component, as well, must adjust to these stresses and changes. Unfortunately, the human tendency to equate change with instability leads to attempted "corrections" of the very elastic dynamism that is the barrier beach's natural, healthful state. If constant change and long-term stability seem mutually exclusive, consider that the barrier-beach systems along this coast have survived and thrived for thousands of years, and that human efforts to thwart the natural pro-

cesses have resulted in serious damage to and sometimes loss of barrier beach, marsh, and adjacent aquatic
systems. Paradoxically, natural systems that cope successfully with the stress of storm winds, tides, and currents prove dangerously vulnerable to measures that
are designed to stabilize and protect. The discussion of
barrier-beach dynamics later in this chapter will help to
explain why this is so.

Beaches

Throughout the region covered by this book,
beaches occupy almost all of the interface between the
open seas and the land. The term *beach* as used here
encompasses all of the shore substrate composed of rock
fragments subject to being moved, shifted, rolled, or
disturbed by wave action. Some of the beaches have a
significant proportion of nonrock materials, such as
shell fragments, sea urchin spines, and other remnants
of marine animal life.

The upper, or landward, limit of the beach zone is
the highest level at which "ordinary" storm surges—
reaching 2 to 3 ft. higher than the normal tide range—
move and reshape the deposits. The upper limit is

21. Close examination reveals that the sand of Assateague
Island consists of a mixture of rock and shell fragments.

marked generally by the highest line of beach wrack (not including debris thrown up by unusually severe storm waves). Because the size of the waves varies greatly from day to day, so do the shape and the width of the beach. The change is continual, and seasonal changes are drastic, with the typical winter beach differing greatly from the summer beach. Hurricanes and major winter storms often move ocean waters inland beyond the beach zone, or carry back to the sea large amounts of beach materials.

Determining the lower, or seaward, limit of the beach zone may be difficult, and is subject to varied interpretations. A common criterion is the greatest depth to which waves affect the bottom. Ocean waves move sediment on the sea floor at depths as great as 33 ft. (10 m). As will be seen, there is a direct relationship between the size of a wave and the depth to which there is water movement related to the wave. As one standing on the beach might visualize it, disturbance of particles on the bottom is occurring well beyond the outermost line of breakers.

Beach profiles along the Middle Atlantic coast are usually steep at higher levels and more gently sloping below the upper intertidal zone, owing to the differences between the action of waves bringing sand to the upper beach and that of currents carrying sand away. The beach-profile zones have been given names, as follows:

1. The *back beach* is the zone of the berm, or berms; these are sand ridges landward of the foreshore. This zone is more variable in width than the foreshore. The back beach is not always present on coasts in other regions. It tends to be widest on low coasts attacked by large waves. It may be absent or very narrow at the base of sea cliffs, as at Gay Head, Martha's Vineyard, and Newport.
2. The *foreshore,* or *beach face,* is the area between high- and low-tide shorelines.
3. The *shore face* is the seaward zone, between the foreshore and the limit of wave action on the bottom sediments.

When the term *offshore* is used in this book, it refers to waters and bottoms beyond the shore face.

The Dynamic Interface—Beaches, Waves, and Currents 43

22. The beach is virtually nonexistent on much of the Rhode Island shore, as at the Newport Cliffs.

COMPOSITION OF BEACHES

Waves not only move rocks and rock particles around but break them down into smaller fragments and sort the fragments according to size and density. In time the rocks are broken down into sand grains. The source of much of the rock material is granite, the main components of which are quartz and feldspar. Feldspar disintegrates into fine particles of silt that form clay deposits in estuaries and on offshore bottoms. Quartz, however, is too hard for the waves to break down into particles smaller than sand size. So quartz grains, with minor amounts of other hard minerals, make up most of the sands of the Atlantic coast.

Sand beaches, by definition, are those composed of rock particles from 0.07 mm to 2 mm (about 1/300 in. to about 2/25 in.) in size (see Table 2). Such beaches predominate on the Middle Atlantic coast. Pebble, cobble, and boulder beaches are found on many coasts but are rare or unknown between Cape Cod and Cape Hatteras. Small, flat stones from sedimentary rocks, called *shingle,* make up many beaches in Great Britain, but do not concern us here. The term *shingle* is sometimes applied to pebble beaches, but it is more properly used in reference to stones of flattened shape, which do not roll but are readily moved about by the waves.

GEOMORPHOLOGY

23. A pebble-cobble beach at Sakonnet Point, Rhode Island. (A ballpen is shown for scale.)

Gravel is sometimes used to designate rounded pebbles. However, it is also applied to the uneven, non-water-rounded rock fragments too coarse to be called sand and too small to be cobbles. Gravel is typical of the mixed glacial moraines and outwash plains of the Gla-

24. A boulder beach at Sachuest Point, Rhode Island.

The Dynamic Interface—Beaches, Waves, and Currents 45

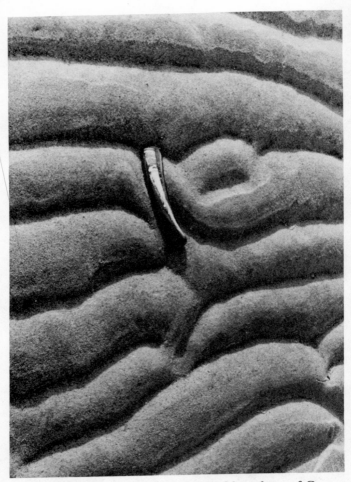

25. A fine-sand beach on the protected bay shore of Cape Cod, at Rock Harbor. (Note pencil-length razor clam.)

ciated Coast. Some of the headlands along the southern New England shore are made up of such deposits, and they provide material for beach building. Gravel makes up part of the deposits that have built bay-mouth bars in southeastern Rhode Island. And the north shore of Long Island is made up of glacial materials from Ronkonkoma Moraine.

GEOMORPHOLOGY

Table 2: Sizes of Beach Materials

Grade Name	Size Range	
	Millimeters	*Inches*
Boulders	More than 200	8
Cobbles	76 to 200	3 to 8
Pebbles	5 to 76	0.2 to 3
Sand		
Coarse	2 to 5	0.08 to 0.2
Medium	0.4 to 2	0.016 to 0.08
Fine	0.07 to 0.4	0.0028 to 0.016
Silt or clay	Less than 0.074	Less than 0.0029

Source: U.S. Army Corps of Engineers standard

On quieter shores, as where offshore islands or peninsulas protect the beaches from ocean waves (Cape Cod Bay, Long Island Sound, Delaware Bay, etc.), materials finer than sand are found. The sands on barrier-island lagoonal beaches also tend to be smaller than those on the ocean beaches. An observant visitor to beaches will discover that there is a relationship between the slope of a beach and the size of the sand grains. Steeper beaches tend to be made up of coarse sand or pebbles.

Grade sizes of rocks and rock particles, both on the open coast and in estuaries and sounds, are of great

26. Wave action on unprotected ocean beaches prevents deposition of materials finer than sand.

The Dynamic Interface—Beaches, Waves, and Currents 47

importance in determining the distribution of the thousands of species of aquatic organisms that live in the water-saturated deposits of beaches, marshes, and flats, as well as in seagrass beds and shoal deposits. Particle size also affects sediment transport by waves, currents, and winds, and passability by vehicular and foot traffic on beaches and intertidal flats.

WHERE DOES THE SAND COME FROM?

The source of most of the beach sands in the northern sector of the Middle Atlantic region—the Glaciated Coast—is the material that was carried south and southeastward and deposited on the Coastal Plain by the great ice sheet more than 10,000 years ago. Barrier beaches along the south shore of Long Island, and those of the southern New England shore, are all derived from such sources. Long Island itself is a great low ridge of such glacial debris; Cape Cod and the islands of the region have a similar origin.

South of Long Island, the main source of sand is the rivers that flow down from the eastern highlands of the Appalachian Provinces. Enormous quantities of rock particles are carried by these rivers. In some cases it is more accurate to say they "were" carried; for dams on some of the streams have now drastically reduced the amount of sediment that reaches the coast.

The sediment in the streams consists mostly of quartz grains and clay particles, with other minerals, such as magnetite and garnet, in varying amounts according to source. The origin of the materials making up a beach can be determined by analyzing the kinds and proportions of minerals present. In the Embayed Section, the other minerals carried are mainly those characteristic of metamorphic rocks. The nature and amount of materials of animal origin—for example, bits of crustacean shell, sea urchin spines, and tiny mollusk shells—also contribute to the differences in the beaches, even in adjacent ones that receive identical mineral components. Beaches with relatively less direct exposure to ocean waves and strong currents may have high proportions of fine materials and organic fragments, and they often have a muddy consistency. However, most of

GEOMORPHOLOGY

the fine, light particles (silt and clay) that have not been deposited in estuaries are carried out to sea, where they eventually settle and form the soft bottom deposits of the Continental Shelf and beyond. The larger particles (primarily quartz), being heavier, are no longer held in suspension when the rivers, slowing down upon reaching the sea, lose their carrying power. These sands, deposited, are subject to movement by the waves and longshore currents. This is the derivation of most of the sand making up the spits and barrier islands between Staten Island and Cape Hatteras. Today, however, little sand makes it to the sea from the southern highlands, since most of it is trapped in the estuaries and lagoons.

THE MOBILE INTERFACE

The predominant coastal interface of this region, that of a highly mobile sand beach, is controlled by two fundamental processes: transport of sands along and across the interface; and stabilization by plant growth of sands transported inland. A healthy coastal ecosystem depends on a natural balance between these two processes. Virtually all human actions along the shore—

27. When off-road vehicles and human foot traffic were unrestricted in Cape Cod's Barnstable Dunes, destruction of vegetation resulted in *blowouts*—removal of the sand by wind action.

The Dynamic Interface—Beaches, Waves, and Currents 49

construction of homes and recreational facilities; leveling of dunes; clearing or trampling of vegetation; removal of fresh water from the natural underground reservoirs; building of sea walls and groins; dredging of inlet channels; use of over-sand vehicles; and even the repairing of storm damage and the building of "protective" foredunes—interfere with the natural processes and are therefore damaging to the integrity of the ecosystem.

The root of the problem is ignorance of or disregard for the natural forces that govern erosion and transport of shoreline materials. Easiest to observe of these forces is *ocean waves*. We will next examine their physical properties and effects.

The Mechanics of Wave Motion and Beach Dynamics

HOW ARE WAVES GENERATED?

Tie one end of a long rope to the branch of a tree or to an object on the ground. Jerk the other end with a sharp up-and-down movement. Watch the wave of energy that passes along the rope and exerts a violent force against the object to which the rope is tied. The rope itself has not moved in the direction of the wave of energy. In much the same way, a wave set in motion by winds hundreds or even thousands of miles at sea travels toward the continent as a rolling swell at high rates of speed, with little loss of energy and with no landward movement of the water mass. (Note: wave motion in a tidal current may be in a direction opposite that of the flow of water.) One ocean wave was calculated to have traveled at a velocity of 78 m.p.h. (125 kph).

Not all ocean waves are generated by the wind. In the category of ocean waves are the wake of a passing ship, earthquake waves (called *tsunamis*), waves generated by landslides or glaciers, and the tides themselves. Most significant in shaping the barrier beaches, however, are wind waves.

Wind waves are produced by the drag force of the

wind on the sea surface. It doesn't take much wind to set very small waves in motion—as one can demonstrate by blowing across a basin of water. One sometimes becomes aware of a breeze only when ripples or wavelets are seen. If you should be in a position to watch how waves are generated when a breeze springs up in a part of the sea where the surface was previously glassy calm, you would notice that at first a ruffling of the surface creates ripples that move in the direction the breeze is blowing. With their sloping surfaces for the wind to push against, the ripples are quickly built into wavelets. The bigger they get, the more resistance they offer to the wind, and thus they continue to increase in height. The maximum size of the waves that a wind can produce is determined by three factors:

1. Wind velocity
2. *Fetch,* or the distance the wind blows across the water
3. *Duration,* or the length of time the wind blows

When the waves have become large, new ripples and wavelets are generated on their crests and troughs. These small waves quickly reach the limit of *steepness* (the ratio of height to length). The ratio that expresses this limit is 1:7. When this point is passed, the wavelets collapse, and much of their energy is absorbed by the longer, more stable waves, called *seas,* which can thereby rise higher.

As the short waves continue to rise and collapse, the longer ones continue to grow. The accumulated energy may build to the point that the seas can move thousands of miles across the ocean, travelling well beyond the area where they were generated, to break eventually upon a distant shore. Such waves are called *swells.* Because swells, unlike seas, are not directly under the influence of winds, they have a smoother, rounder contour. And because they have long wave lengths and greater velocities, swells have much energy stored within them. They can be quite destructive as they break with great force upon the shore.

By the time an ocean swell reaches the land its shape has changed, as has its velocity. When the wave reaches

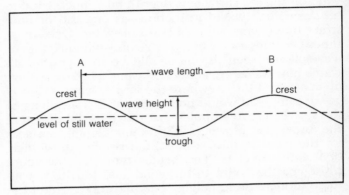

28. The parts of a wave.

shallow water it is slowed by friction with the bottom; it then steepens and breaks, and crashes with force great enough to roll boulders or displace large amounts of sand—though no wind may be ruffling the surface.

The parts and dimensions of waves have specific names, and the most important ones to know are the following:

Crest: the highest part of a wave
Trough: the lowest part between two adjacent crests
Height: the vertical distance from trough to crest
Length: the horizontal distance between two adjacent crests
Period: the time (in seconds) for a wave crest to travel a distance equal to one wave length–or, put another way, the time required for two wave crests to pass a given point

WAVE HEIGHT

There is a direct relationship between wave length and wave period; but wave height is independent of either of these factors—except that wave height cannot be greater than one-seventh wave length. Table 3 gives the typical range of height and period for a variety of wave types.

GEOMORPHOLOGY

Type of Wave	Height	Period in Seconds
Wind waves	0–120 ft.	0–15
a) Of severe hurricane in Gulf of Mexico	To 75 ft.	11
b) Of severe storm in North Atlantic	To 100 ft.	10–15
c) Of typhoon in Pacific	To 120 ft.	10–15
d) Typical wave on U.S. Atlantic coast	A few feet	5–10 (usually 6–8)
Swells (wind waves in origin)	0 to 20 ft.	10–20
Tides (caused by moon and sun)	0 to 40 ft.	12–24 hours
Tsunamis (earthquake- or landslide-generated)	0 to 100 ft.	Several hours

Fig. 29 shows a wave that has reached a point where the depth is less than one-half the wave length—a point where friction, slowing the movement of water particles close to the bottom, causes the wave to steepen. An ocean swell has a smoother, more rounded contour but may have small disturbances—ripples and wavelets—superimposed upon it by local winds.

And ocean swells do not reach the heights of wind

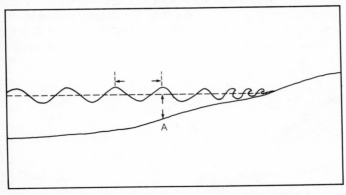

29. Waves in shallow water. At point A, where depth is one-half of wave length, wave velocity and length decrease, and steepness increases; at a depth equal to 1.3 times wave height, the wave becomes unstable and breaks.

The Dynamic Interface—Beaches, Waves, and Currents 53

waves. In Fig. 28, the wave period is the time in seconds for Wave Crest A to reach Point B. Periods range from a fraction of a second for a ripple to 12 or 24 hours for the tides, which are generated by the gravitational pull of the moon and the sun. There is a great range in wave height; the height of one wave was measured at 112 ft. (34 m). But for tides, despite their long periods and wave lengths, the height ranges only from zero to a maximum of about 60 ft. (18 m).

OSCILLATORY WAVES

Even though a wave is moving energy rather than moving mass, there is, obviously, movement within the wave structure, since the shape of the water surface is changing as the wave passes. To illustrate the motion of the particles of water within the wave form, Fig. 30 shows the movement of a small chip of wood that is floating on the surface as a nonbreaking wave passes. Keep in mind that the wood chip is making the same motion as the water it replaces would.

The diameter of the circular orbit is equal to the wave height. This orbit represents the motion of a particle floating on the surface; underwater, the orbit of, say, a plankton organism—which displaces its own weight of water and thus has no tendency to rise or sink—assumes an elliptical shape. The greater the depth, the smaller and more elliptical the orbit; a particle of water at the

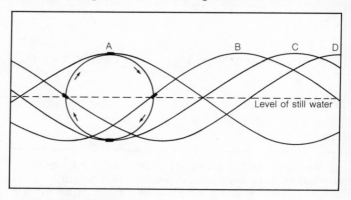

30. An oscillating wave.

GEOMORPHOLOGY

bottom of the wave (one-half the wave length below the surface) moves in an almost flat ellipse. Below that depth there is no movement related to the wave.

It takes one wave period for the floating chip to move around its circular orbit. By the time the second wave crest reaches Point A in Fig. 30, the particle is back in its original location; but it is now riding a different crest. Since the deeper orbits are much smaller, it is apparent that the velocity of the water particles decreases with depth (each particle describing its orbit in the same length of time). This principle relates to waves in deep water—that is, where the water depth exceeds one-half the wave length and particle movement is not affected by bottom friction.

SHALLOW-WATER WAVES

A wave travelling in water of a depth that is less than half the wave length is defined as a *shallow-water wave*. Thus, a wave with a length of 1,000 ft. (305 m) would become a shallow-water wave at a depth of 500 ft. (252 m). We are concerned here primarily with the behavior of waves over the shore face and the beach face, since the velocity of the wave is a major factor in beach dynamics. One immediate effect of a wave's reaching shallow water is a decrease in velocity, or, to use another term, *phase speed*—the speed with which the wave form advances. The formula for calculating phase speed in shallow water is too complicated to go into here; but when the wave reaches very shallow water—one-tenth of wave length—its phase speed in relation to the depth can be determined more simply. Table 4 shows how the velocity of a 10-second wave approaching the shore diminishes with decreasing depth. Note that in moving from a depth of about 50 ft. (15 m) to a depth of about 3 ft. (0.9 m) the speed of the wave diminishes from 40 ft. per second to 10 ft. per second (12 m per second to 3 m per second).

It was stated earlier that wave height, which is essentially independent of wave length and period, nevertheless cannot exceed one-seventh the wave length. Another limiting factor is the depth of the water; a wave cannot be higher than 0.8 times the water depth.

Water Depth	Phase Speed for 10-second wave
49.2 ft. (15 m)	39.7 ft./sec. (12.1 m/sec.)
32.8 ft. (10 m)	32.5 ft./sec. (9.9 m/sec.)
16.4 ft. (5 m)	23.0 ft./sec. (7.0 m/sec.)
3.3 ft. (1 m)	10.2 ft./sec. (3.1 m/sec.)

This is of no consequence in waves of the open sea, since the limit of wave height is about 120 ft. in practical terms. But in the shallow water of the beach the limitation does come into play. A person swimming where the still-water level is 7 ft., for example, will not encounter waves more than 5.6 ft. high.

When waves slow down on reaching shallow water, their crests move closer together. In the direction of wave advance, therefore, the energy per unit distance increases, and the height of the waves increases. This is called *shoaling*. When the height of a wave is at 0.8 times the water depth, it breaks (as a wave in deep water breaks when it reaches a height equal to one-seventh the wave length). At this time, the wave crest spills forward, and the orbital movement of water parti-

31. Waves may break over an offshore bar and then reform to break again near the beach.

32. Waves approaching the beach obliquely break progressively as they reach shallow water.

cles is disrupted as the wave rushes up the beach slope in tumbling confusion. Sand is stirred up by this near-shore turbulence, as any surf bather knows. And as anyone who has tossed a stick into the surf for a dog to fetch knows, it traces no neat, vertical circular orbits as it floats on the surface. Beyond the breakers, the stick would do just that; any progress toward the beach

Beach line

Wave crests

33. Waves reaching shallow water. As waves approach the beach on a gradually sloping shore, they slow down because of friction with the bottom.

The Dynamic Interface—Beaches, Waves, and Currents 57

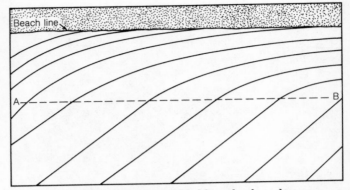

34. Waves approaching a beach obliquely slow down as they pass the contour representing a depth equal to one-half the wave length (line A–B). The bending of the wave front enables the outer parts of the wave to partially catch up with the parts of the wave closer to the beach line.

would be due mostly to wind on the surface and would be almost imperceptible.

Coastal engineers, using information on wave height and period, bottom topography, and direction of the wave advance, can calculate how waves will behave upon reaching shallow water. The distribution of the energy in the waves is important in determining potential damage to shoreline structures and the effects on movement of sand to and from the beach face. The point at which there is shoreward movement of the water mass is a factor in potential damage. Engineers choose to build breakwaters in deep water for a practical reason: if they are placed beyond the point at which waves break, they are less subject to damage.

For a more complete discussion of waves in shallow water, as well as other aspects of beach dynamics, read Willard Bascom's fascinating and well-illustrated book, *Waves and Beaches.*

WAVE REFRACTION

You have undoubtedly stood on an ocean beach and noticed that, while the waves offshore were approaching obliquely (the usual case), the breakers near you seemed to be almost parallel to the beach. This change

GEOMORPHOLOGY

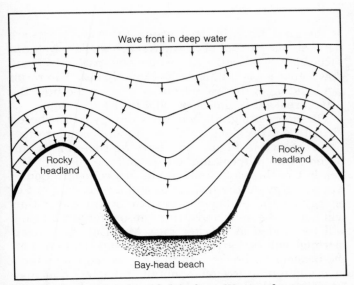

Wave front in deep water

Rocky headland

Rocky headland

Bay-head beach

35. Waves on an embayed shoreline. Wave refraction concentrates wave energy on the headlands of an embayed shoreline; materials eroded from the headlands are deposited on the bayhead shores, forming beaches.

of alignment of the wave front is known as *wave refraction.* It is determined by the configuration of the underwater topography, and it can either concentrate or spread out the energy in a wave.

Fig. 33 shows how the decreasing depth of the water affects waves approaching, at right angles, a straight shoreline with an evenly sloping beach. As the ocean swells reach a point where the depth is one-half the wave length, the wave begins to slow down because of friction with the bottom. The slowing shortens the wave length, or the distance from crest to crest, much as the distance between automobiles in line will decrease as they approach a stoplight, with each one decelerating in turn.

Most often, ocean waves approach the beach not at right angles but obliquely. Line A–B in Fig. 34 represents the contour of the bottom at a depth of one-half the wave length. The oblique waves, too, slow down at this point; but not all parts of the wave reach the line at the same time. In deep water, the wave fronts are parallel, but parts of each wave reach shallow water in succession. Consequently, while one part is slowing down another is still moving relatively fast. The result is a bending of the wave front, so that by the time the wave breaks it is almost parallel to the shoreline.

On such a straight beach, wave energy is distributed virtually equally along the shore. A more complex situation is shown in Figure 35. Here the shoreline is embayed, with alternating coves and headlands. The bending of the wave front results in a concentration of wave energy on the headlands and a spreading out of energy on the embayment shores. Storm waves thus will batter the headlands with unusual force, and they will be eroded at a faster rate. Much of the eroded material will be carried shoreward and deposited on the beaches of the cove; in this way ocean waves tend to straighten an irregular shoreline. Factors that may interfere with this straightening process include offshore islands and manmade structures. The most stable shoreline is a broadly curving beach with no such barriers, where the waves break everywhere at nearly the same time; this idealized condition, however, is more the exception than the rule.

LITTORAL DRIFT

Because on most beaches the wave front almost always strikes at an oblique angle—even with the refrac-

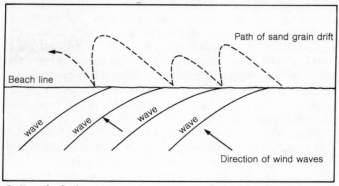

36. Beach drift.

tive effect—disturbance of the beach materials results in a gradual movement of sand and pebbles along the shoreline. Fig. 36 shows how individual sand grains and pebbles are moved by each wave that catches them. When a wave reaches the point where its height is 0.8 times the water depth, it breaks and rushes shoreward. A sheet of foaming water slides obliquely up the beach slope; this is called the *swash*, or *uprush*.

The distance the uprush travels is determined by two factors: the slope of the beach and the height of the waves. The slope, depending partly on the coarseness of the sediment, may range from less than 3° for fine sand to 20° for large pebbles. The greatest vertical distance a wave's uprush can reach is about three times the wave's height.

The uprush carries sand and pebbles with it, in an oblique direction. When the energy of the swash is spent, some of the water sinks into the sand; the rest—the *backwash*—flows down the beach slope. But the backwash flow is direct, rather than oblique, since only the force of gravity and the contour of the beach determine its direction.

Through this process of swash and backwash a sand

37. On shores with a gentle slope, like this one on Assateague Island, the swash, or uprush, moves far up the beach.

The Dynamic Interface—Beaches, Waves, and Currents 61

38. In addition to carrying food for sanderlings and other shorebirds, the swash moves sand along the beach in the process called beach drift.

grain is gradually carried along the beach interface. Repeated many times, and affecting myriad particles, the process transports a great mass of material in a direction governed by the prevailing direction of wave action. This form of littoral transport is called *beach drift*.

Another kind of littoral drift occurs when strong on-shore winds raise the level of the water near the beach. The piled-up water tends to flow up-beach (along the shore in the direction of wave-front movement). The resulting longshore currents, which can be easily detected by waders and swimmers, are the immediate cause of the sand movement, which is called *longshore drift*. One easily feels the moving sand on one's legs when standing in the surf zone. The velocity of such a longshore current can be quite high—on the order of about 3 ft. (1 m) per second.

EROSION AND DEPOSITING SHORES

Water action on the land-sea interface creates two fundamentally different types of shore. *Erosion shores* are created by wave action. An example is the ocean shores at the eastern end of Long Island, where uncon-

GEOMORPHOLOGY

39. The sediments on the beach in Ninigret Pond, a lagoon on the Rhode Island shore, where wave action is minimal, are a mixture of mud and sand. (The birds are herring and great black-backed gulls.)

solidated glaciofluvial deposits are attacked directly by ocean waves. Much of the material removed from these deposits by waves is carried westward by longshore currents and incorporated into the chain of barrier beaches extending from Shinnecock Inlet (near Southampton) to New York Harbor. These barriers, including Fire Island, are *depositing shores.* On depositing shores both waves and currents (along with offshore winds) are moving about sediments that have come from elsewhere. Depositing shores are predominant on the Middle Atlantic coast.

Not all the material contributing to a depositing shore comes from eroding shores. Much of it is sand, silt, and mud carried to the sea by rivers. Glacial materials are not available to the depositing shores on the southern part of the coast.

The types of material available and the degree of wave action determine the composition of a beach on a depositing shore. Where wave action is too great for deposition of finer particles, a beach may be composed of pebbles or cobbles. Muddy shores occur only where water movement is gentle, as in estuaries and the upper reaches of deep embayments. Because water action is greatest on the upper part of the intertidal zone of such water bodies, the upper shore is often sandy, while mud content increases as the low-water mark is approached.

Despite the name, a depositing shore is not necessarily accreting, or even stable. Because of the vagaries of current velocity and direction, periods of calm and storm, and varying supplies of sediment, most depositing shores are dynamic, with material being removed by backwash and currents as it is deposited by other water action. Thus, at any given time, movement of sand and pebbles to and from a beach is likely to be unequal. If more sand is being carried to a beach than from it (by waves, currents, and—from the landward side—wind), the beach will be built outward; this process is called *progradation.* And if more sand is being removed than deposited, attrition, or narrowing, of the beach is the result; this is called *retrogradation.* When wind and waves are strong, with resulting strong littoral currents, visible changes can occur in the span of a single day. The most dramatic alterations to the back beach and foreshore occur during unusually severe storms or at the changes of seasons. Winter beaches are often drastically narrowed; the contrast is striking to an observer returning in the winter following summer visits.

SPIT FORMATION

Spits are formed when littoral drift along a relatively straight shoreline carries sand into the open water of an embayment and gradually builds out a beach from the shoreline. The underwater building and lengthening of the spit is aided by the transportation of material from the shore toward the end of the structure by the swash and backwash of obliquely breaking waves. If it were not for the tides, building by water action would proceed only underwater; if the water surface were at a constant elevation the submerged ridge would not be raised above the surface by the action of waves and currents. Lengthening of spits and bars occurs when the waves are moving in a direction that results in movement of material toward the end. Wave action

GEOMORPHOLOGY

40. Sandy Neck, at Barnstable, Mass., is a large (6 mi. long and almost a mile wide) spit with a well-developed system of high dunes.

perpendicular to the axis of a submerged ridge will widen it. In the case of spits, which owe their existence to wave action, if wave action is neither perpendicular to a spit nor angled toward its end, the spit may be shortened.

Typically, a growing spit tends to curve inward at its extremity. As refracted waves transport material across the end of the spit toward the main shore, a hook may eventually be formed. This process may be enhanced by changes of wind direction or by tidal or hydraulic currents. A vivid example of hook building in progress may be seen at Assateague Island. The barrier island's trend of southward growth, parallel to and several miles from the mainland shore, has been modified by the formation of a large hook called Fishing Point.

In the same way that hooks are built, refracted waves can build *looped bars*. But the process operates more uniformly here, and eventually the bar rejoins the shore. A looped bar, unlike a bay bar, starts from a relatively straight shoreline (to which it returns). The location of the beginning, or windward, end of a looped bar, which originates in shallow water on a gently sloping bottom, is determined by the relative water depth,

The Dynamic Interface—Beaches, Waves, and Currents 65

the energy of the waves, and the amount of sediment being carried by beach drifting.

One supplementary source of sand for longshore drift and spit building is sand picked up and carried seaward from the back beach and dunes by winds blowing from the land. Given the westerly winds prevailing in the region, this may be of some significance for the Atlantic coast barrier system.

CONTROL OF LITTORAL DRIFT

Residents and managers of barrier islands and spits (as well as of mainland beaches) have long sought methods for eliminating or controlling the effects of longshore transport of beach deposits. Fig. 41 shows a barrier beach formed over many years by northward longshore currents. Homes built too close to the beach are being threatened by erosion. The natural state of affairs is for a barrier beach to erode on the seaward edge and accrete on the lagoon side, with the result that the barrier migrates slowly toward the mainland. But to impede the attrition of their beach front, owners of the homes at Point A build a *groin*—a low, small jetty, extending in most cases perpendicularly from the shore about 100 ft. (30 m) into the water. The result is an interruption of the longshore current, which in slowing drops part of its load of sand, building up the beach just south (down-current) of the groin.

All well and good—so far. But what happens north of the groin? Deprived of much of its normal sand supply, and suffering removal of sand by the waves and the new longshore current they generate, the beach here is rapidly eroded back. New groins are built, each creating the need for the next. The expensive groins are usually short-term solutions at best; and the net loss of sand eventually demands other methods of beach protection or replenishment. Though there are voices saying that we should let nature take its course, allowing the barrier beaches to grow, migrate, and change as they have for thousands of years, these voices are almost invariably overruled by private landowner and commercial interests—despite the fact that the cautionary voices are often those of the persons most knowledgeable

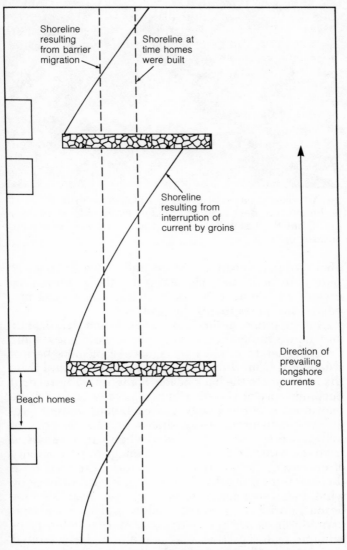

Shoreline resulting from barrier migration

Shoreline at time homes were built

Shoreline resulting from interruption of current by groins

Direction of prevailing longshore currents

A

Beach homes

41. A barrier beach with predominantly northward longshore currents, showing the effects on the shoreline of groin-building.

The Dynamic Interface—Beaches, Waves, and Currents 67

42. A typical groin built to control longshore drift. Sediments are deposited on the up-current side of the groin, but the beach below the groin is deprived of sand and retrogrades.

about beach dynamics. More and more homes and hotels are built, and this aggravates the condition, increases the demand for protection from natural processes, and perpetuates the problem.

Among other methods of barrier-beach stabilization and nourishment being tried are building sea walls, pumping sand from nearby lagoons or offshore bars or trucking it from dunelands, and bulldozing sand from the foreshore to the back beach. Sometimes littoral drift becomes part of the distribution process. Beyond the enormous expense involved, beach-nourishment programs create problems of their own. The ecology of sounds and estuaries is disrupted when sand is removed from the natural deposits; great damage to productivity often ensues. In addition, the material dredged from these systems is usually too fine, so it is carried away by wind and water action or is otherwise unsuitable for beach nourishment. Coastal inlets and offshore sand bars and shoals are alternative sources of beach-replenishment materials that may sometimes be exploited with minimal damage to ecological integrity.

Jetties—barriers built to protect harbor entrances from littoral drift—function like groins. When a jetty is

GEOMORPHOLOGY

43. Old and new dunelines are prominent features of the landscape at Cape Henry, Virginia.

in place, sand is deposited on the up-drift side of the harbor and erosion occurs (usually) on the down-drift side. One of the measures adopted to resolve this problem has been *sand bypassing*—transporting sand from one side of a harbor to another. Such a bypass is a sort of artificial link in the littoral-drift regime, and may minimize the disruption of natural processes.

COASTAL PROCESSES AT
CAPE HENRY, VIRGINIA

Cape Henry, the southern side of the Chesapeake strait, illustrates a number of coastal processes that have played a major role in shaping the sea-land interface of the Nonglaciated Coast. Studies of its present landforms have produced a probable history of the changes that have occurred here during recent geological time. Some centuries ago, a cape existed to the west of the present straight Atlantic shoreline. Over the years, tidal currents and storms carried sand into Chesapeake Bay, providing sediments for dune-building. Winter winds from the northeast formed low dune ridges in back of the beach. The process of beach drift carried sand around the point and westward along the shore beyond

Lynnhaven Inlet. Some of this sand went into the building of longshore bars, and because a tidal delta had been built outside Lynnhaven Inlet these longshore bars curve out around the inlet. (A delta has also been built inside the inlet.)

The sand of some of the longshore bars washed ashore and built up the beaches, and in time it was blown into dune ridges. The old shoreline trended from west of Lynnhaven Inlet east-southeast along the present southern shoreline of Broad Bay toward the ocean. Lynnhaven Bay is a drowned stream-valley estuary; Broad Bay is a coastal lagoon formed when barrier beaches developed off this shore. Continuing accretion of the barrier beaches built out the cape as a series of roughly parallel dune ridges separated by wet swales.

During periods of static shore position, and while the barriers accreted to the northeast, dune ridges reaching from 5 ft. (1.5 m) to 50 ft. (15 m) in height were built. These dune ridges probably extended farther southeast than they do today, as they have apparently been truncated by the present shoreline at North Virginia Beach.

The present cape is about 3 mi. (4.8 km) north and

44. Baldcypress pond in Seashore State Park, Cape Henry, Virginia.

GEOMORPHOLOGY

2 mi. (3.2 km) east of the old shoreline. Between the dune ridges are low, wet swales and a few small lakes. A cluster of small ponds exists southeast of the Seashore State Park Campground; these have developed baldcypress communities that are one of the prime attractions of the region.

All of Cape Henry is forested today, except where land has been cleared for residential and commercial development. The highest dune ridge, with irregular contours and many points exceeding 50 ft. (15 m) in elevation, arches around the cape about a half-mile from the shoreline. Between this ridge and Broad Bay, several of the park's hiking trails follow the crests of other dune ridges. To find barrier beaches in this area today, one must go south from Cape Henry some 15 mi. (24 km) to Back Bay National Wildlife Refuge, or cross the Chesapeake strait to the islands off Cape Charles.

Barrier Beaches

Theories of Barrier-Beach Formation

There is a consensus that the East coast barrier-beach system is less than 5,000 years old. At different times various explanations of its origin have been accepted. Today there is general agreement that no one process can account for the existence of all barrier beaches. But apparently most of the Middle Atlantic Glaciated Coast barrier islands have been created by the breaching of spits. The formation and growth of spits and barrier islands, as well as their attrition in many cases, are readily observable.

A theory widely accepted for a time held that barrier islands grew from offshore bars, or sand ridges, that pushed above the surface and were nourished by Continental Shelf sediments transported across the land-sea interface by wind and waves. First promulgated in 1845, this theory has been downgraded in significance by evidence accumulated in this century.

The *drowned-beach-ridge* theory, applied to much

of the Nonglaciated Coast, relates barrier-beach formation to the rise in sea level that occurred with the melting of the ice sheets. For several thousand years, the melting and the resulting rise proceeded at a rapid rate. Then about 5,000 years ago the rise in sea level slowed for a period; this allowed dune ridges to develop along the mainland shore of the Coastal Plain. Because more of the Plain was then exposed, this dune-ridge shoreline was well to the east of today's land-sea interface.

Though sea level continued to rise at a slow pace—with some temporary halts or reversals—the sea did eventually flood the lowlands behind the beach ridges, forming broad lagoons. Progradation of the beaches occurred during the periods when sea level remained static or dropped, and new dunes would then form behind the beaches. When the sea was rising, on the other hand, the barrier beaches retreated toward the mainland. The net result was that they were gradually pushed back to their present alignment. They are still slowly retreating.

Supporting evidence for the drowned-beach-ridge theory includes the discovery that mainland sediments deposited before the last glaciation (which affected sea level throughout the world) extend under the lagoons to the barrier beaches of the Southeast coast; and stumps of trees have been found in the lagoons. Sediments behind spits that had grown across open water would be marine rather than mainland in origin. Also, salt-marsh peat and remains of old forests can sometimes be seen at low tide on the outer beach. And deep in the sediments in the lagoons and marshes behind barrier beaches are found the buried shells of mollusks typical of estuarine communities; if the lagoons had been sea bottom, as explained in the older theory, only marine shells would be found at those depths.

Unlike the barrier beaches of the Glaciated Coast, which are nourished by eroding glacial headlands, these more southern barrier islands do not have sources of new material, since little of the abundant sediments reaches the outer beaches. They develop and are reshaped through the reworking of old Coastal Plain deposits.

45. Tree stumps exposed at Seashore State Park, Del., attest to the landward migration of the barrier beach.

Another theory explains barrier beaches as the product of reworking, by waves, currents, and winds, of sediments brought down to the sea by rivers. This is of more significance in the case of barriers of the Gulf and West coasts, where rivers reach the ocean with heavier sediment loads. Dams on many West coast rivers, however, now trap so much of the sediment that some beaches are suffering serious attrition.

The barrier beaches within this book's range, from Cape Cod to Cape Hatteras, appear to accommodate each of the theories—breached spits, emergent offshore bars, engulfed beach ridges, and perhaps to a limited extent river-borne sediments—as well as combinations of these processes. On the Glaciated Coast, spit formation and breach by storm surges offer the best explanation for the existence of barrier beaches.

ORIGINS OF FIRE ISLAND

The barriers off the south shore of Long Island are a good demonstration of how physical forces and natural processes have created many dynamic barrier-beach systems, with their constantly changing shapes and

Barrier Beaches   73

their unique biotic communities. The creation of Long Island itself was touched upon previously in the discussion of the last advance and beginning retreat of the Wisconsinan ice sheet. Fire Island is the child of Long Island; and its story begins with the melting of the ice front.

By about 4,000 years ago, the rising sea had almost reached its level of today. (Actually, it is rising slowly at this time). The south shore of Long Island between Montauk Point and Southampton was at that time about 1.25 mi. (2 km) seaward of its present location. Thus the stage was set for the long process that culminated in today's Fire Island.

Barrier islands develop only where the land slopes gently beneath the sea. Off what is now southern New England, the Atlantic Plain, overlaid with glacial deposits, extended well beyond the shoreline as the sea rose and advanced landward. As the predominantly southwestward-flowing littoral currents carried wave-eroded materials from the Montauk-Southampton headlands, a spit grew from Southampton, at an average rate of about 80 ft. (25 m) per year. Wind and waves built the spit higher and wider, forming the dunes and the sand apron behind them.

In 30 or more centuries, the sand spit grew to a length of about 50 mi. (80 km). Its average width has never exceeded 1,000 ft. (300 m). Sometime in recent centuries storms breached the spit at two points; the section farthest west, now more than 30 mi. (50 km) long, is Fire Island.

Dune Formation and Migration

Although one who knows barrier beaches only from experience with highly developed seashore resorts may not realize it, dunes are as characteristic of the Atlantic shore as is the beach itself. Dunes begin to form as soon as a spit has been built up enough that a part of it is beyond the reach of most ocean waves. When the sand has dried at the surface sufficiently that winds blowing onshore can move it, it begins to drift. Any object in its path—a shell, a piece of driftwood, a dead horseshoe-

GEOMORPHOLOGY

46. At Fire Island National Seashore, a vertical section of a foredune, exposed by erosion, reveals its sedimentary, or layered, structure.

crab, a windrow of eelgrass and cordgrass fragments—will serve as a trap for the blowing sand, creating a miniature dune. The higher a dune grows the more resistance it offers to the wind and the more sand will be caught on its face or dropped over the crest. The steepness of the lee slope of an active dune is deter-

47. Marram and dusty miller, by trapping sand, begin the dune-stabilizing process.

mined by the angle of repose—the steepest incline on which the particular size and shape of sand particles can come to rest. Thus, as more sand spills over the crest, the dune tends to advance steadily in the prevailing direction of the winds.

Along with the sand being washed and blown over the beach interface, however, seeds and parts of dune plants are carried by the wind to the dune face and rear slope. Some of the seeds and plant fragments, having survived their period in the ocean, germinate or regenerate and take root.

The establishment of plants is encouraged by the organic material added to the otherwise sterile sand. Algae washed ashore from the sea are broken down by bacteria and other decomposers, increasing the moisture-retention capability of the sand as well as making the substrate more fertile. The new growing plants offer additional resistance to the wind, trapping more sand and helping build the young dunelet into a full-sized dune. Some of these plants are so well adapted to growth on a continually rising and shifting substrate that they can emerge alive even after complete burial. The increasing plant cover begins to stabilize the dune, making it hospitable to such nitrogen-fixing species as

GEOMORPHOLOGY

48. On Sandy Neck, marram has been planted and off-road vehicles have been banned in an effort to stabilize the Barnstable Dunes.

bayberry and beach-pea, which add further to the nutritive quality of the soil.

Sand not deposited on the face or dropped over the crest may blow farther inland, to create secondary dunes, or may be transported across the spit, widening it by encroaching on the shallow water beyond.

Old dunes that have been stabilized by a good cover of herbaceous and woody plants may begin to move when the vegetation is destroyed by human traffic or by natural causes. The onshore winds pick up sand from the denuded or partly denuded windward face, and the migration process is under way. This wind-induced dune travel is not necessarily harmful but is a part of the barrier-beach turnover cycle, which is discussed below.

Barrier-Beach Retreat

The rise in sea level that has been occurring since the Wisconsinan ice sheet began to melt is a worldwide phenomenon. An apparent exception is the Arctic region, where isostatic rebounding of the earth's crust resulting from the decreasing weight of the ice cap is manifested in a rise of the land mass that more than offsets the rising water. The net effect is an observed lowering of sea level. But in the Middle Atlantic coastal region the sea is rising approximately 1 ft. (0.3 m) per century. This is of special significance in the South, where the broad tidewater belt, with much land that is barely above sea level, is likely to undergo considerable submergence during the next few centuries. Part of the city of New Orleans, in fact, is already 1 ft. below sea level.

Even without shoreline erosion, then, the East coast interface would be retreating. But in the case of barrier beaches—those, at any rate, whose natural dynamics have not been unduly inhibited by human activities—landward retreat does not mean a shrinking of the above-water terrain. There is a tendency to regard any retrogradation of the shoreline as a purely destructive event that must at all costs be reversed. In reality, the natural dynamic process is a landward migration of an entire ecological system. In their book on the ecology of Cape Lookout National Seashore (see Bibliography), Paul J. and Melinda M. Godfrey refer to this retreat as a "rolling over" of the barrier beach. It can result in a complete landward displacement of the system in one century—in geological terms, a mere moment in time.

The chief agent of the barrier-beach rollover cycle is a process called *overwash*, the importance of which has barely begun to be appreciated. It is vital to the dynamic stability of a barrier-beach system, yet until very recently it has been widely regarded as a menace to be dealt with through drastic remedial action. For the barrier beaches, the real threat, however, is not overwash but ignorance of the process and its long-term effects. Knowledge of the mechanics and ecological implications of overwash is a major key to understanding how our low, fragile barriers can survive the continuing rise in sea level and the intermittent impact of ocean storms.

Overwash occurs when high winds push the ocean tides up against the beach berm and foredunes, creating a buildup of water that invades the barrier island

GEOMORPHOLOGY

49. This overwash channel developed on Assateague Island during a 1982 storm.

through dips in the dune system (*overwash channels*). The surging waters pick up large quantities of sand from the seaward side of the island and move it toward the lagoon side. As the masses of water spread out on the flatter land beyond the dunes, the sand load is deposited in large *overwash fans*. Especially strong surges may carry the sand all the way across the barrier island (or spit), depositing it in the marshes and shallow lagoon waters—smothering the former while creating new intertidal flats in the latter.

In time, the new surfaces that have been built up by this deposition process to a level above the highest tides become vegetated with dune grasses and other plants that grew on the island before the overwash occurred. Those areas of the new surface that are reached by only the highest tides become high marsh, typically a salt-meadow cordgrass (*Spartina patens*) community. In the zones where new deposits are subject to inundation by daily tides, the highly productive low marsh, or salt-marsh cordgrass (*Spartina alterniflora*) community, commonly develops. If water movement prevents the establishment of rooted vegetation, the new deposits

Barrier Beaches

may remain as sand flats. These salt-marsh communities, particularly the valuable *S. alterniflora* habitat, have been the focus of a vital struggle between the environmentalists on one hand and the developers and exploiters on the other along the entire Atlantic coast. The dynamics of coastal geomorphology make this contest inseparable from that involving the manipulation of the outer beach–sea interface.

In the manner described above, as sand is removed from the seaward edge and added to the landward side of the barrier beach by wind and by overwash, the barrier migrates toward the mainland. In some sections of the barrier beach coast, this movement is as much as 30 ft. (9 m) per year. Left to nature, a barrier beach undergoing this rollover process will in a few years— barring major storm surges—develop an ecological profile corresponding closely to what existed before the overwash occurred.

Beyond a critical width limit, which varies according to the island in question, overwash is not an effective transport mechanism for moving sand from the ocean to the lagoon. In his *Barrier Island Handbook*, Stephen Leatherman sets this limitation for Assateague Island at 400 to 700 ft. (122 to 213 m). In the wider parts of barrier islands lateral growth is controlled primarily by inlet dynamics—breaching of the island and subsequent formation of flood deltas on the lagoon side. As the landward side is built up through this process, erosion of the ocean side occurs, and the barrier migrates. Vertical accumulation of sand on the island is still achieved through the agents of overwash and wind transport, with plants providing the anchoring mechanism.

Inlet breaching occurs frequently on the Atlantic barrier systems. When certain factors, such as erosion on the lagoon side coinciding with retrogradation of the outer beach, result in a narrowing of a part of the barrier, a major storm can cut an inlet. During and following the storm large quantities of sand may be carried through the new inlet and deposited in the lagoon. The higher parts of this new substrate soon develop marsh vegetation, just as when overwash builds new intertidal flats. Deposits closest to the inlet, where currents are

50. Erosion of bayside shores occurs on some barrier beaches, like this one at Delaware's Seashore State Park.

strong, may remain as sand flats or shoals.

Longshore drift, by building a spit on the updrift side of the inlet and removing sand from the downdrift side, results in a migration of the inlet. As the inlet moves in the direction of littoral drift, the marshes on the lagoon side are progressively eroded. Unless they are kept open by dredging operations, barrier-beach inlets tend to close with time, with new marshes forming in broad expanses of sand flats deposited behind the inlet. A barrier island with a migrating inlet at each end migrates not only landward but in the direction of the longshore currents.

Not to be overlooked in barrier-beach retreat is the significance of dune migration. Sometimes a severe storm damages formerly stable dunes, or their vegetative cover is removed by human activities—and they migrate by the normal drifting process, invading and passing the marshes and encroaching on the lagoon. There waves and currents redistribute the sand, providing for new marsh development.

All of these processes that operate to roll the barrier

Barrier Beaches 81

beach toward the mainland also have the effect of keeping it ahead of the rise in sea level. The sand blown, washed, and carried by inlet and lagoon currents is constantly raising both the barrier-island topography and the bottom of the lagoon. So, ultimately, as long as the natural landward migration and building-up process proceeds at a normal pace, the ecosystems remain intact and dynamically healthy. But man seems obsessively intent not to let well enough alone. And therein lies the greatest threat to our coastal system.

Not surprisingly, with all the differences in climate, ocean-wave action, sources of beach sands, and topography of the substrate on both sides of the land-sea interface, there are differences in the physiographic and biotic profiles of the barrier beaches of the region. On the Glaciated Coast, barrier beaches are rather narrow, have dune ridges close to the beach, and are vegetated by dune grasses, shrubs, and maritime forest species. Which plant types occur reflects to a large extent the degree of protection from salt spray, winds, and storm surge. The dunes of the Glaciated Coast lie atop earlier overwash deposits.

On the coast south of New Jersey, where overwash is

51. Shrub thickets behind the low frontal dunes on Ocracoke Island are heavily pruned by salt spray.

a fairly regular occurrence, a gradually sloping barrier made up primarily of overwash strata and terraces develops. These rather flat barriers are largely grassland, with scattered thickets toward the mainland side and with extensive salt marshes on the lagoon interface. An accreting or relatively stable barrier beach may have forested uplands and, in the interdune hollows, ponds, marshes, or swamps. The Outer Banks barriers are generally wide, with low, scattered dunes occurring some distance from the beach.

The study of barrier-beach dynamics is a rather new science, and the relative importance of the various processes operating in the retreat of barriers toward the mainland is the focus of much of this study. For the most up-to-date information on this complex subject, consult the above mentioned *Barrier Island Handbook*, which is profusely illustrated with helpful photographs and diagrams.

Despite all these variations on the barrier-beach biophysical profile, the problems generated by man's often misguided development-and-protection activities are much the same along the length of the coast. Some of the ways in which the natural processes have been disrupted have already been discussed. A few require more extensive treatment.

Man Versus the Barrier Beaches

Too frequently, the efforts of coastal geomorphologists and ecologists to educate the public and to promote restraint in dealing with the natural processes of barrier-beach dynamics meet with widespread indifference or determined resistance. The massive disruption of barrier islands and their adjacent marshes, with economic and ecologic consequences that reach far beyond the coast, continues unabated on most of the shoreline that remains under private and corporate ownership. Many of the barrier beaches retained as public recreation areas and preserves are in as precarious a state.

The vast system of barrier beaches of the Atlantic and Gulf coasts, the most extensive in the world, was

52. Because of groins and channel dredging of the inlet between Ocean City, Maryland, and Assateague Island, the north end of the island is undergoing accelerated retrogradation and rapid migration toward the mainland.

created by oceanic forces—and responded to those forces for 50 centuries, in a vigorous cycle of migration and adaptation. But modern development sometimes makes these natural forces, which cannot be nullified, into destructive agents. The problem has become acute only during the second half of the 20th century, when in a relatively hurricane-free period a spurt of building, dredging, and control measures has occurred.

Chief among the perpetrators in this story of degradation have been the builders of second homes and resorts on the very interface of land and sea; the building generally has proceeded with little regard for the inevitable landward retreat of the barrier. Most of the structures have been built with the aim of enhancing vacation recreation opportunities, but ironically, the very charms of the barrier-beach coast that first attracted visitors are rapidly giving way to urbanlike concentrations of humanity with concomitant destruction

GEOMORPHOLOGY

53. A February 1983 storm ripped out the street and left homes isolated at South Bethany Beach, Delaware.

of the beach itself. The ensuing massive efforts to restore the beach result in further interference with natural processes and even greater threats to life and property as well as to the barrier-beach ecosystem. The taxpayer bears the brunt of the enormous cost of control measures and, through the Federal Flood Insurance Program, even the cost of rebuilding storm-destroyed property. This arrangement makes more difficult the task of prevailing upon developers and owners to give heed to the natural processes that dictate against unlimited construction on and alteration of the barrier beaches. In the meantime, the natural attractions of the seashore environment are yielding priority to developments unrelated to the seashore, such as water slides and shopping malls.

It is often federal or state agencies that build the sea walls, jetties, groins, and artificial dunes; that dredge the inlets and boat channels; and that persist in fighting nature with measures foredoomed by rising seas and inevitable storm cycles. The U.S. Army Corps of Engineers, for example, once proposed to "stabilize" the whole of Fire Island with a 20-ft.-high, 30-mi.-long dike. Even the National Park Service, contrary to the advice of its own scientists, must occasionally yield to pressure

54. An October 1982 storm caused extensive damage to the primary dune on Assateague Island—in some places removing both the dune and the paved road behind it.

and retreat from announced restrictions that would protect the shores and dunelands. In general, though, responsible resource agencies endeavor to let the natural cycles of drift, deposition, overwash, breaching, migration, delta-building, and revegetation govern their management programs as much as possible given the realities of conflicting demands and pressures.

Most of the building of vacation homes and hotels, and of business communities developed to serve and profit from them, has taken place since the early 1960s, during a period when the normal pattern of East-coast hurricane activity has been in abeyance. What will happen when another giant storm hits the region? Many of the built-up areas, no longer mere summer resorts, have sizable year-round populations; and many of the homes and hotels are considerable distances from the bridges and causeways that offer escape routes to the mainland. The loss of human life that might accompany a fall hurricane or unusually severe spring northeaster is staggering to contemplate. Will it take such a catastrophe to bring about the reversal of the abuse and well-intentioned protective measures that is necessary to restore to health our coastal barrier systems?

55. Bulldozers built a new, unnaturally high foredune to protect this heavily used southern sector of Assateague.

ARTIFICIAL BARRIER DUNES AND OTHER DELUSIONS

It seems logical enough: if ocean waves and storm surges are eating away at our barrier beaches, building a high dune just behind the normal high-tide line should be effective protection for structures located close to the sea's edge. This commonly held conviction, despite repeated and expensive lessons to the contrary, dies hard among beachfront owners. The history of dune construction along the Outer Banks illustrates the pitfalls—if not the utter futility—of this approach to barrier-beach conservation.

Although during historic time grazing cattle, sheep, and horses, and rooting and grubbing hogs, have affected the vegetation of the Outer Banks, it is doubtful that, except for certain wide sectors such as Buxton Woods, this barrier-island system was ever under dense cover. Storm surges and the resulting overwash have always resulted in landward migration and ecological turnover. Photographs and maps, as well as the memory of persons still living, attest to the fact that the barrier

Barrier Beaches   87

islands here were characterized earlier in the century by broad beaches, with low natural dunes that offered no real obstruction to the storm surges. The storm waves spent much of their energy in rolling over the broad, gradually sloping beaches; when the waters crossed the beach berm they found easy passage through overwash channels in the dune fields. During surge-free periods the revegetation cycles described above restored the pattern of grassland, grass-shrub, and marsh zones. The broad beaches prevailed through long centuries of this ecological and physiographic dynamism. But the frequency of major storms off Cape Hatteras made these barrier islands less stable than some to the north. It was not until the 1930s that a permanent road network was established on the Outer Banks. To protect the roads and other "improvements," an ocean-front artificial dune system was proposed. In the late 1930s, the federal government erected along the Banks about 550 mi. (880 km) of fencing to trap blowing sand and build a continuous barrier dune close to the sea. Most of the construction was done in the low-dune zone, but extant photographs of the operation show some fence building on the broad, flat beach itself.

With the help of plantings of grass, trees, and shrubs,

56. Dense shrub growth on the lee side of the narrow frontal dune system on Ocracoke Island.

GEOMORPHOLOGY

by the middle of the century the barrier islands of the Outer Banks were almost completely vegetated. As part of this process, because of the protection from overwash and salt spray afforded by the 30-ft.-high stabilized dune, the shrub zone spread seaward across the islands. This shrub community, forming in places an impenetrable thicket reaching almost to the beach, required control measures—including fire—to reduce it.

More serious developments came about because of the apparently increased security from the effects of storms. In ignorance of the geological realities, or despite knowledge of them, a rash of building followed the stabilization program. Summer cottages, resort facilities, park recreational structures, and even a U.S. Naval base were built immediately behind the artificial barrier dune. Nature, however, was not to be denied. No longer was there a gradual beach slope and low dune system on which the storm waves could spend most of their energy before spreading out on the flatlands. The beach itself had become narrowed in the inevitable process of retreat. Unable in most places to breach the barrier dune, the storm surges attacked its base and further eroded the beach. Eventually the beach retro-

57. On the northern New Jersey coast, where massive sea walls have been built to control shoreline erosion, even at low tide there is virtually no beach. This is particularly the case during the winter months. The sea walls themselves are doomed to eventual destruction.

Barrier Beaches

graded to the barrier dune, which then eroded under even normal wave regimes; soon, the manmade structures were exposed to the force of storms.

This dramatic demonstration of the ocean's irresistible power to reshape the coastal interface might have been a valuable lesson. But instead of recognizing the inevitable, most sought new methods of fighting it. Following the great storm of the spring of 1962, which opened a new inlet between Buxton and Avon, the government replaced the lost roadway, filled in the inlet, and rebuilt miles of barrier dunes. This was accomplished, of course, at great expense; but it provided no permanent solution. In the ensuing years, groin-field and beach nourishment programs added millions more to the accumulating price of human obstinacy.

The efforts to draw a permanent line between land and sea, to control the location of inlets, and to stabilize the land forms have persisted, in lieu of adapting to nature as many scientists have urged. From Ocracoke, the southernmost community on the Outer Banks, to Kitty Hawk, near the northern access route to the Banks, development proceeds unabated except where the barriers are in public ownership; and environmental problems escalate. Increasing summer residence, growing year-round communities, and expanding recreational and service facilities result in heavier demands on the limited barrier-beach underground freshwater reservoir, further leveling of the terrain and removal of vegetation, greater destruction of wildlife habitat, and ever more pressure on government to protect the owners' and developers' investments.

Just north of Cape Hatteras, on Hatteras Island, where a costly beach replenishment and dune stabilization program had been carried out, a moderate February northeaster in the mid-1970s wiped out 2 mi. of the dunes, buried the highway under 3 ft. of sand, and partially destroyed three motels. (Because of the last, the National Park Service was forced to resume its discredited sand-pumping program.) Visitors to the Outer Banks in the mid-1980s have been witness to relocation of washed-out roads and construction of new frontal dunes on Ocracoke Island, ongoing costly efforts to save

historic Hatteras Lighthouse from the encroaching sea
—a project that many believed doomed—and still other
attempts to thwart nature's dynamic barrier-beach processes.

Clearly, human efforts can never respond effectively
to the rise in sea level. Only the natural agents—overwash, inlet formation and migration, and wind-induced
dune migration—can, through gradual landward retreat and upward deposition, enable the barrier-beach
system to survive the assault by the same oceanic forces
that created it.

CHAPTER TWO

The Ecology
of Barrier Islands

The Physical Environment

On barrier islands, the oceanic climate greatly influences the makeup of biotic communities. The waters surrounding barrier islands moderate air temperatures, so that Fire Island and Monomoy Island, for example, have mean daily January temperatures between 24° and 28° F(-5° and -2° C). Their mean daily maximum July temperature is approximately 78° F (26° C), the same as that in the northern tip of Maine. The mean length of the freeze-free period of Fire and Monomoy islands is 210 days. Hatteras Island, about 400 mi. (675 km) to the south, boasts a freeze-free period with a mean length of 270-plus days, about the same as Gainesville, Florida.

While air and water temperatures are moderated by the oceanic situation of barrier islands, plant and animal organisms are subjected to physical stresses that add up to a severe, even hostile environment. Only a species that can contend with salt spray, occasional overwash by sea water, storm winds, shifting sands, and lack of protection from summer midday sunlight can maintain a foothold on the typical barrier island. For this and other reasons, the islands' species diversity is low compared with that of most inland environments. Particularly in the beach and dune zones, the vegetation is dominated by annuals—better adapted to an unstable

58. Three species of trees—American holly, sassafras, and shadbush, or thicket serviceberry—dominate the canopy layer of the Sunken Forest almost to the exclusion of other species.

environment—rather than perennials. It is not unusual on the barrier islands for a community to be dominated by a single species, or two or three, almost to the exclusion of competitors. For example, nearly 100% of the trees in the Sunken Forest of Fire Island belong to just three species—an unusual situation for a deciduous woodland. Understory species here are also very limited. And because of the dynamic nature of the landform and the currently rising sea level, a plant-and-animal climax community may never develop, or may develop and be eradicated within the span of a century. Stumps of former forests seen rising from marshes or studding an ocean beach, not only on Fire Island but on Assateague and other barrier islands, attest to this.

Winds and Salt Spray

The effects of winds on barrier islands are governed by wind direction and intensity, seasonal variations, and the orientation of the islands. While Fire Island has a roughly east-west alignment, Monomoy is oriented in a north-south direction; so they are most strongly affected by different winds. Along the Atlantic coast winter winds, the most intense, are predominantly northerly; summer winds are predominantly from the south and west. At Fire Island, onshore winds occur mostly in spring and summer. Bodie Island, in the Outer Banks, has a northwest-southeast orientation; there, onshore winds predominate in winter and offshore winds in summer. Onshore winds, particularly if they are the stronger winter winds, are the most important in carrying salt spray onto the barrier islands.

What is meant by salt spray is not the drops of water knocked off the tops of breakers—the airborne wetness you can feel when wading in the surf or standing at the water's edge. Few winds carry these drops inland to splash onto the dunes and vegetation. The term *salt spray* is somewhat misleading; it actually refers to an invisible vapor formed when droplets are ejected from the sea surface by the bursting of air bubbles. One is not aware of this vapor in the beach air, though it can wreak havoc with the unprotected parts of cars or the intricate circuits in an automatic camera.

The amount of salt spray carried over the beach onto the dunes and beyond is determined by the intensity and direction of the winds. Its effect on the vegetation, however, is qualified—particularly in the north—by the season of the year. Because the predominant vegetation in the more northern barrier islands is not evergreen, it would be advantageous for the plants to experience the salt-bearing winds in winter—despite the winter winds' greater intensity—rather than in summer when leaves are on the branches. The process by which salt spray affects tree growth will be explained below in the discussion of the maritime forest.

Storms

The severe northeasters and occasional hurricanes that strike the Atlantic coast have a dramatic effect on barrier islands. In fact, many such islands have been created when one of these intense storms cut a gap through a spit; sometimes an existing island is divided into two when a new inlet is formed.

This is the case with Assateague Island, which was part of a 48-mi. (76 km) barrier beach attached at its northern end to the Delaware mainland. In 1933 a hurricane cut a gap through this spit south of Ocean City, Maryland. In the normal course of events, the inlet would likely have been closed in time by longshore drift, but by means of jetty-building and periodic dredging, the storm-built inlet has been kept open to allow passage of boats into and out of Assawoman and Sinepuxent bays; so Assateague will remain a separate island for the foreseeable future. Low spots near the northern end of the island and at least one location near the southern end are potential sites of new inlets in the event of a powerful northeaster; overwash occurs quite frequently at some of these points. At Assateague such severe storms occur most often in winter and early spring.

Precipitation

The oceanic situation of barrier islands, which moderates the temperature patterns, also tempers the atmospheric disturbances that bring about precipitation. For this reason annual totals of rainfall and snowfall tend to be lower than on nearby inland areas. But higher humidity and lower evaporation rates, as well as more frequent fog, offset this difference somewhat. Annual precipitation along the barrier-island chain from Cape Cod to Cape Hatteras is upwards of 40 in. (100 cm).

Hydrology

The presence of freshwater ponds and bogs on barrier islands—which are, after all, narrow strips of land composed of highly permeable sands and surrounded by the sea—may seem strange. Likewise, one might expect the soils, too, to be salty; but actually they often have a lower concentration of chlorides (less than 0.03%) than many mainland soils. This is because the very porous nature of barrier-island sands permits the rapid percolation of rainwater downward through the substrate.

Fresh water, with a lower specific gravity, tends to float on sea water, and beneath the surface of the barrier island the fresh water forms a lens separated on its underside from the water of the ocean. Laterally, the freshwater lens is separated from the salt water by a narrow zone of transition. Theoretically, the depth of this freshwater lens is said to be about 40 times the height of the island water table above sea level. On developed barrier islands, however, withdrawals of fresh water from these natural reservoirs have exceeded the capacity of the rains to replenish them, with the result that the water tables are dropping and the lenses are shrinking. Salt now intrudes into many of the wells upon which island residents and visitors have depended.

For a more detailed discussion of the hydrology of barrier islands and for bibliographic references, see *Ecological Studies of the Sunken Forest,* by Henry W. Art. For our purposes, however, the essential point is that, unless overexploited, most barrier islands have supplies of fresh water sufficient to sustain nonmarine plant-and-animal communities.

Topography

Most of the ocean beaches along the Atlantic coast are backed by a ridge of sand thrown up by the onshore winds—except where development of one sort or another has removed it. This frontal ridge is known as the primary dune, or foredune; and this is the only part of the dune system with which the average beachgoer is at all familiar. In areas that are under protection, such as national wildlife refuges and state parks, a belt of duneland ranging from a few yards to a few hundred yards wide exists. This topography is most conspicuous on barrier islands and spits, but extensive dunes have sometimes developed on mainland shores, as at Cape Henlopen and Cape Cod.

The profile of a typical barrier island reveals, from ocean to lagoon, a rather clearly defined series of biophysical zones:

1. A relatively flat *beach* sloping gradually to the toe of a primary dune
2. The *primary dune,* which has slopes, both seaward and landward, that are often maximally steep—that is, at the sand grains' maximum angle of repose
3. An *interdune swale,* or hollow
4. A *secondary dune ridge*
5. A *bayshore* (lagoon shore)

In the south, wide, flat grassland zones often occupy most of the island's width between the primary dune and the bayshore.

The characteristic dune-and-swale topography of barrier islands comes about largely through the action of the winds and through the wind-resistant and sand-anchoring properties of plants. Winds of speeds greater than 14 ft. (4 m) per second at the ground surface will move sand grains of the size typical of barrier islands. Wherever a plant or piece of driftwood slows the wind below that velocity, sand grains will be deposited. The sand tends to build up around the bases of plants and in the lee of obstructions, thereby contributing to the building up of the dune. At some point—determined by the characteristics of the sand, the intensity and direction of the winds, and the vegetation's capacity to respond to the burying effect—a *maximum* or *equilibrium height* will be reached. There is also a *maximum slope,* which on a dune that is sparsely vegetated or barren is determined by the sand's maximum angle of repose.

The Subtidal Zone of the Outer Beach

This is the ecological zone that extends from the low-tide mark to the lower limit of wave action; thus, it corresponds to the geomorphological seaward zone, the shore face, and varies in width as the wave height changes. It is much wider on more gently sloping beaches, of course, and tends to be more regular in its contours on sandy than on rocky shores. But it is also much more unstable on sandy shores, since the sediments are subject to being moved about by tides, currents, and storm waves.

Plants of the Inshore Waters

Ecologically, the subtidal zone of the outer beach is characterized, on most of the Middle Atlantic coast, by a dearth of macroflora. On the southeastern coast of Rhode Island and on the Massachusetts coast from the Rhode Island border to Buzzards Bay, rocky shores support a heavy growth of macroalgae, notably *Fucus,* a genus of algae with strong holdfasts that enable these plants to withstand the force of severe wave action. And on such protected sandy-beach shores as the mainland on Nantucket Sound, rooted plants may maintain themselves in the inshore waters. For example, off Red Beach, in the town of South Harwich, Massachusetts, the growth of eelgrass *(Zostera marina)* is so dense that the bottom is visible only in spots. Generally, though, on the Middle Atlantic coast—except for the algae attached to shells, driftwood, and other objects moved about by wave and current action—the only plants found in inshore waters are the drifting phytoplankton.

When the tide is high, the waters of the intertidal zone become for all practical purposes part of the subtidal zone, for the swimming animals move in with the tide, and the plankton organisms, having little control over their movements, are carried with the waters. The *benthic* (bottom-dwelling) organisms of the outer-beach intertidal zone are discussed later in this chapter under Life Between the Tides. The macroalgae and the so-called seagrasses (notably *Zostera marina*) are discussed in other chapters (see Index).

Though it may lack diversity and is often next to invisible, the plant life of the subtidal zone, along with the zooplankton, forms the base of an animal community comprised of invertebrates and vertebrates. This community, while also lacking in diversity, is at times extremely populous, and the resident and visiting animals of these waters attract predators—especially birds —from other habitats. This habitat zone consequently is one of the most rewarding for the wildlife watcher as well as for the angler.

Animals of the Inshore Waters

Among human visitors to the ocean beach, it is the surf fishermen who are most familiar with the animals that inhabit the close-inshore waters—the surf zone and the shallows immediately beyond. In their year-round quest for game fish, surf fishermen may become acquainted with many nongame species, including animals that are cast up dead and dying on the beach. Bathers and surfers, on the other hand, may hardly be aware that they are using the habitat of a diverse animal community. Beachcombers, at least, are familiar with such oddities as mermaid's purses, mermaid's necklaces, and the more easily recognized of the many kinds of mollusk shells; all these are remnants of animals that have lived in the subtidal waters.

In the turbulent *surf zone,* conditions are particularly harsh. Relatively few species occupy the substrate in this zone of breaking waves and churning sands. Beyond it, where conditions are more favorable, a number of invertebrates and vertebrates burrow in and crawl over the bottom, or feed close to it. A number of cartilaginous and bony fishes swim in these inshore waters, often in the breakers. And a few animals are adapted to the highly unstable *swash-and-backwash zone*—that

59. The quahog (discussed in Chapter Three under Benthic Macroinfauna) inhabits ocean-beach subtidal bottoms as well as bays, to about 60 ft. (18 m) depth.

part of the beach that at a given time is being washed by the waves. These are treated in upcoming sections.

Some burrowing forms that live in the middle and lower intertidal zone are found in much greater numbers below the low-tide mark. For example, the mole-crab, which feeds in the swash-and-backwash zone in summer, retreats during the colder months to the subtidal bottom.

The animals of the subtidal zone can be grouped into four categories: the *zooplankton,* which drift into these waters from the ocean and estuaries; the *nekton* (active swimmers); the *benthic animals,* which may spend one part or all of their life cycle in and on the bottom; and the piscivorous and invertebrate-eating *birds* that fish and forage here. The nekton includes such animals as sea turtles and horseshoe-crabs that come through the surf to lay eggs at the tide line or on the upper beach and that otherwise lead a pelagic or near-offshore life.

INVERTEBRATES

Evidence of subtidal vertebrate and invertebrate life

60. The egg capsules of the channeled whelk, shown here, are sharp-edged, unlike those of the knobbed whelk, which are square-edged. This genus of marine snails has lived in the earth's oceans for 60 million years.

is frequently found in the *beach wrack* (the seaweeds, shells, driftwood, and other materials cast up on the beach, often in windrows). What beachcomber hasn't happened upon the curious skate egg cases and chains of whelk egg cases—the mermaid's purses and necklaces mentioned above? The parchmentlike chains belong to the **knobbed whelk** *(Busycon carica)* and **channeled whelk** *(B. canaliculatum),* which stay well out of the middle and upper intertidal zones but are known by their abundant large shells on the beach. Both species are found from Cape Cod to Cape Hatteras but are principally inhabitants of bays and estuaries. The skates are discussed below under Cartilaginous Fishes.

The **wavy,** or **waved, whelk** *(Buccinium undatum),* a true whelk of the family Buccinidae, is the producer of another curiosity often discovered by beachcombers. This gastropod is a scavenger, reaching a height of 4 in. (10 cm), half the size of a channeled whelk. While it does not inhabit the intertidal or upper subtidal zone, its "egg case" is sometimes found on the shore. As strange as the chains of the knobbed and channeled whelks, it

The Subtidal Zone of the Outer Beach

61. The lady crab prefers subtidal sandy bottoms, and is common along the Middle Atlantic coast in summer. In the north it retreats to deeper water in winter.

is much different in appearance, being a baseball-sized, loosely packed cluster of small, transparent sacs of a tough, membranous material. When the ball is washed up intact, each sac contains unborn shells. These clusters were formerly called sea-wash balls by seamen, who used them as substitutes for soap.

A number of larger crustaceans also occur in the subtidal zone. The **lady crab** *(Ovalipes ocellatus)*, which has a penchant for nipping the legs of surf bathers, is one such shallow-water species. A predator, the lady crab moves in with the tide and does not discriminate against humans in sampling the available fare. Since it often digs into the sand, leaving only its eyestalks exposed, keeping watch for it is no cinch. Bad manners aside, the lady crab is a pretty creature, with a pattern of clustered purplish speckles on its carapace, colorfully marked claws, and yellow paddles on the last pair of legs. Like the similarly paddle-footed **blue crab** *(Callinectes sapidus)*, it is a good swimmer. Members of the family Portunidae, these two species are easily distinguished by their shape (the blue crab being much wider than long) and their coloration. The blue crab, while sometimes found in the subtidal zone of the ocean beach, is not averse to muddy bottoms and is common in estuaries and tidal creeks, even into fresh water. Its habits and economic and ecologic status are discussed under The Eelgrass Community.

The lady crab does not range as far into brackish waters as the blue crab, but it does reach about halfway up Chesapeake Bay, to a point where surface salinity in late spring is around 10 o/oo. It is a predator as well as scavenger, and it has been observed to use a unique method for capturing one of the surf-zone animals upon which it preys. It shoves its large claw down into a bed of mole-crabs, and if it chances to grab one of the smaller crustaceans the lady crab begins to run in a circle, all the time holding onto its victim. With this twisting motion it eventually pulls the mole-crab out of its pocket in the tightly packed sand, much as one removes a cork from a wine bottle.

Much of the food available to fishes and crabs in the subtidal zone is not sedentary but is brought to it by the tides and currents. The abundant phytoplankton and zooplankton are fed upon by the smaller fishes, which in turn furnish food for larger animals. In the surf zone there is little opportunity for small animals to settle or burrow into the sand, and they are kept in motion until eventually devoured. Exceptions to this are certain species of mollusks and crustaceans adapted for life in the turbulent swash zone. Two of these are described under The Intertidal Zone of the Outer Beach.

CARTILAGINOUS FISHES

Although they are called fishes, the animals in this primitive class of vertebrates are only very remotely related to the true, or bony, fishes. In fact, man is much more closely related to the bony fishes than are the so-called cartilaginous fishes, which lack bones and many other features of the five higher classes of vertebrates (fish, amphibians, reptiles, birds, and mammals). The most familiar members of the class of cartilaginous fishes (Chondrichthyes) are the sharks, of which ten families are represented in our Atlantic waters.

62. Spiny dogfish *(Squalus acanthias)* consume great numbers of small fish in Atlantic coastal waters.

The **spiny dogfish** *(Squalus acanthias),* surely the best known of sharks, is very abundant and is often hauled in on the lines of sport fishermen. It is generally considered a nuisance. It swims in great swarms, and unquestionably it has a big impact on the populations of the fishes upon which it feeds. It is a small shark, usually 2 to 3 ft. (0.6 to 1 m), with the female, typically for shark species, being the larger. Its common name derives from the sharp spine before each dorsal fin. (Greek *akantha* means thorn.) The eggs develop within the female's body, and the 2 to 11 young are born alive.

Spiny dogfish live from the surf zone down to a depth of more than 680 ft. (200 m). North Carolina is the southern limit of their Atlantic coast range. The dogfish is not without its redeeming qualities; oil from its liver is rich in vitamin A.

The **little skate** *(Raja erinacea)* lives over sandy bottoms down to a depth of 300 or 400 ft. (about 100 m). It swims close inshore and is frequently taken on the surf fisherman's tackle. When caught, it is usually either thrown back into the water or left to die on the beach; yet this species is quite good to eat. Like other skates, it is a bottom feeder. Its main foods are crustaceans and mollusks, which it crushes with its pavementlike teeth.

A cool-water animal, the little skate moves offshore in spring and reappears in the shallows in fall. Because

63. Skate egg cases are common objects along Atlantic beaches.

of its habit of coming in with the tide it is frequently stranded when the tide ebbs. It sometimes enters estuaries and sounds.

Like the much larger **barndoor skate** *(R. laevis)*, the little skate is found along the entire coast from Cape Cod to Cape Hatteras. In New England waters it is the commonest skate. The barndoor skate lives as deep as 1,400 ft. (425 m) and is seen less often than the little skate on the beaches.

Measuring up to 20 in. (50 cm) in length, *R. erinacea* can be distinguished from small individuals of the barndoor skate by its rounded nose and lack of spines on the median line of the tail. Its egg case is a tough, rectangular pouch of a black, horny substance, about as long as one's little finger. When produced (at any time of the year) it contains a single egg with a large yolk, and it is attached by tendrils borne on each corner to a stone, or to a seaweed anchored by its *holdfast* (basal attachment structure) to the bottom. This takes place in less than 80 ft. (24 m) of water. In a few months the egg hatches. Sooner or later the empty case drifts away or is cast upon the beach. When dried it is quite light and is easily blown about by the wind. These "mermaid's purses" are often found well back in the interdune area.

The Subtidal Zone of the Outer Beach

The rays and skates are sometimes grouped together in the family Rajidae, sometimes given separate status as the families Rajidae (skates) and Dasyatidae (stingrays), along with the Myliobatidae (eagle rays) and the Torpedinidae (electric rays). (Note: *raja* is from Latin *raia*, ray.) The second system is followed in this book. Several members of the Dasyatidae occur along the Middle Atlantic coast, and one species shares with the little skate and the barndoor skate the subtidal zone of the outer beach. It is a smallish species: the **bluntnose stingray** *(Dasyatis sayi)*, known along this entire stretch of coast but particularly abundant in the shallow waters off the Outer Banks. It bears a long, poisonous spine near the end of its tail.

The **Atlantic torpedo** *(Torpedo nobiliana)* is believed to be most common in water 60 to 250 ft. (18 to 75 m) deep and so is not primarily an animal of the seashore; but it is often taken from shallow waters. It is found throughout the Middle Atlantic range but is more abundant in the cooler waters to the north. It measures to 6 ft. (1.8 m) and 100 lbs. (45 kg), with rare specimens attaining double that weight.

The torpedo can deliver an electric shock of up to 220 volts. It uses this power to stun its prey, which includes flounders, eels, and, it is believed, spiny dogfish. It feeds principally on the bottom, like most of the skate-ray tribe.

Rays that venture into estuarine waters are treated in Chapter Three. Included there is the **smooth butterfly ray** *(Gymnura micrura)*, which is found in the offshore waters to a depth of 150 ft. (46 m) but is of special interest in the estuarine community because of its feeding habits. Most selachians (sharks, rays, and allies) are carnivores; some are scavengers; some are both.

BONY, OR TRUE FISHES

Waders and swimmers on ocean and bay beaches are often aware of schools of minnow-sized fishes swimming about among their legs as if curious to investigate the strange intruders. Sometimes these fish seem to be nibbling at the bathers' legs—perhaps attracted to the air bubbles that adhere to the leg hairs.

The presence of small fishes in the subtidal zone is largely due to the abundance of plankton available here, and may be explained in part by the efforts of the fish to escape large predators in the deeper waters. In these shallow waters the small fishes are of course more vulnerable to predation by terns and other diving birds. These fishes can be credited by the surf angler for attracting many of the game fishes he seeks in this zone. While some of the latter feed on mollusks and crustaceans, many pursue the schools of small bony fishes—often the young of the game fish species themselves.

Cynoscion regalis is one of the most familiar inshore fishes. Its common name, **weakfish**, refers not to a lack of vigor in this species but to the fact that fishermen's hooks easily tear loose from the soft mouth tissues. It is found in the surf zone along the coast from Cape Cod to Cape Hatteras. It also occurs in inlets, sounds, and estuarine channels and salt creeks; but it does not venture into fresh water. It is a popular game species and an excellent food fish. The weakfish prefers shallow water with sandy bottoms, where it feeds upon anchovies and other small members of the herring family, silversides, croakers, mullets, gobies, and spot, as well as the young of its own species. To a lesser extent it preys upon crabs, mollusks, clam worms, and small crustaceans.

Sold in the fish markets and restaurants as sea trout, the weakfish actually belongs to the drum family (Sciaenidae). This is part of a large order, the Acanthopteri, that includes the barracudas, swordfishes, tuna, mackerels, perches, and sea basses, as well as the sunfish-bass family. True trout (Salmonidae) belong to the order Isopondyli, which also includes the herrings and smelts. Such confusion reigns throughout the world of fish nomenclature. The only rational system is binomial nomenclature—and that undergoes constant revision in most invertebrate phyla and in the classification of bony fishes.

There is nothing weak about the mouth of the large, voracious **bluefish** *(Pomatomus saltatrix)*, which is armed with fierce teeth. This species commits mass slaughter on the weakfish. From the human viewpoint

The Subtidal Zone of the Outer Beach

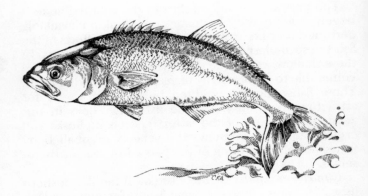

64. Bluefish *(Pomatomus saltatrix)*.

this destruction is not without extenuating circumstances: the bluefish itself is excellent eating. It is normally a deep-water fish, but it is found near the shore often enough to be of interest to the surf fisherman. It feeds on squids as well as on many other fishes, and it runs to 10 or 12 lb. (2.5 to 5.5 kg). A specimen of 50 lb. (23 kg) is the astonishing record for this fish.

The widely distributed bluefish is common from Cape Cod to Cape Hatteras, but its presence varies with the season and weather conditions. Smaller bluefish, travelling in schools, venture into the estuaries, sometimes well up tidal rivers. They have the same wicked teeth and rapacious habits as do larger individuals of this species. Given their cannibalistic tendencies, it is not surprising that all the fish within a school are of approximately the same size.

The most sought after game fish of the surf zone is the **striped bass**, *Morone saxatilis.* Here, too, the common name is somewhat ambiguous, since several families of fishes include species called bass. South of Delaware Bay this species is called rockfish, and one might have made a good case for the universal application of that name when it was classified as *Roccus saxatilis,* which means "rock of the rocks." *Roccus* was designated a genus of sea basses of the family Serranidae. But rockfish is also applied to more than 40 species of the family Scorpaenidae. *Morone saxatilis* is now placed in the Percicthyidae, a family that includes both freshwater and marine species. The striped bass is sometimes called rock bass—but that applies as well to a member of the sunfish family. All this is further evidence that in studying fishes one needs a reliable taxonomic guide.

The striped bass is abundant from Cape Cod to Cape Hatteras. It reaches weights of as much as 125 lb. (57 kg) by feeding upon other fishes and upon crustaceans and other invertebrates, including insects. In spring it moves into bays and up streams to spawn; the female may lay more than 2.2 million 1/8-in. (3 mm) nonsticky eggs. The eggs sink slowly in fresh water, and may drift in tidewater during the incubation period. They will hatch in three days at 58° F (11° C).

This species, known as a game fish of the ocean beaches, illlustrates the importance of estuarine environments to some marine species. The health of our estuaries is now recognized as vital to the future of many commercial and sport fishes. A major item in the ongoing issue of Chesapeake Bay restoration is the recent serious decline of *Morone saxatilis.*

The order Tetraodontiformes embraces a curious assortment of fish families, with most members exhibiting bizarre form and strange behavior. Some strange creatures of the puffer family, Tetraodontidae, and the porcupinefish family, Diodontidae, live in the shallow inshore waters of the outer beaches. They go by an array of colorful popular names, including puffer, swelltoad, swellfish, blowfish, and globefish; but all these are applied at one time or another to different species in these and related families. Here the Latin binomials are indispensible.

Few if any of these tetraodonts are widely sought for food; but despite the danger they present because of toxic qualities (see below), some are highly prized and highly priced gourmet items. They are at any rate a source of amusement and sometimes of annoyance for their outlandish appearance and wonderful ways. Some of them, using a distensible ventral extension of the stomach, can inflate themselves by swallowing water or air. This defensive maneuver is effective in discouraging attempts to seize or swallow them. Most species have spines that become erect when the body is distended, making them even less ingestible.

The **northern puffer** *(Sphaeroides maculatus)*, found throughout the Middle Atlantic coast, is very much an animal of the shallow subtidal zone. Slight disturbance is enough to cause it to blow itself up like a balloon. Sometimes described as having chisel-like teeth, it in fact does not have teeth. Its mouth, at the tip of the snout, is very small. The bones of the upper and lower jaws, with sharp cutting edges, are split in the middle, giving them the appearance of paired incisors. These are used in cracking clams and other mollusks. A bottom feeder, the puffer also eats crustaceans, including shrimps, amphipods, and isopods; worms; echinoderms, including sea urchins; and other invertebrates. A group of puffers may gang up on a solitary blue crab, vanquishing it by cutting through its hard shell with their own harder bony jaws. To the annoyance of anglers, puffers also eat fishing bait, which they deftly strip from the hooks.

The northern puffer also has the ability to bury itself partly in the sand by means of specialized clavicles, which because of the looseness of the skin on the fish's ventral surface can be used like shovels to move the sand.

The puffer spawns on this coast from mid-May through June, laying tiny eggs that sink and adhere to the first object they touch. The eggs hatch in four and a half days into active larvae that look like their parents when they reach a length of only 0.25 in. (6 mm). The larvae are brilliantly colored with orange, red, yellow, and black pigments. When the puffers are 0.5 in. (13 mm) long, they can inflate themselves—so much that the anal and dorsal fins are hidden—into a pea-sized ball. They grow to 10 inches (25 cm).

With the help of currents, this fish sometimes reaches Cape Cod. Some northern puffers are caught by surf fishermen; but the wise angler discards this species and its close relatives, for the skin, entrails, and roe are poisonous.

The **porcupinefish** *(Diodon hystrix)* is particularly

bristly. It bears numerous spines, some of which are two-rooted and movable. It is one of the larger fish of this primarily tropical group, reaching 3 ft. (0.9 m). A southern fish, it sometimes straggles north to Woods Hole, Massachusetts.

The **striped burrfish** (the preferred name), or **spiny boxfish** *(Chilomycterus schoepfi)*, is another member of the Diodontidae with a wider distribution, reaching the Gulf of Maine in the north. Smaller and with much shorter spines than the porcupinefish, it sometimes attains a length of 10 in. (25 cm). It does not have as great an ability to inflate itself as do some members of the family. And it is so slow moving that skin divers can catch it easily.

The young of the striped burrfish are hatched from eggs laid in summer. They do not resemble the adult fish until they have reached a length of at least 0.25 in. (6 mm). The food of this species is invertebrates such as oysters, barnacles, and hermit-crabs.

Another oddball of the nearshore waters is the **common trunkfish** *(Lactophrys trigonis)*. It belongs to the Ostraciidae, a family of fishes each of which has plate-like, six-sided body scales fused to form a solid, triangular shell, like a bony exoskeleton, from which the movable fins and tail protrude. The eyes and mouth also are movable. The protection the plates provide the trunkfish is at the cost of mobility. These fish are almost a part of the zooplankton, because the Gulf Stream carries the weak swimmers north from their home waters off Florida, and many smaller individuals drift in to the coast as far as Cape Cod. This species reaches a maximum of 10 in. (25 cm).

BIRDS

Most conspicuous of the animals of the subtidal zone are the birds that float, fly, and dive in search of the small fish that abound there. The ever-present gulls seldom dive but swim about beyond the line of breakers or forage in the swash zone, to snatch up chance morsels, including garbage as well as dead and living fish. It is the terns that are most adept at utilizing the major food resource of this zone, the schools of small fish. Less common are larger diving birds such as pelicans.

TERNS. The **common tern** *(Sterna hirundo)* is surely one of our most valuable esthetic resources. Who can resist its beauty, its graceful flight, and its headlong plunge into the water followed by its emergence with a tiny fish held crosswise in its bill? Unfortunately, this sight is now less frequent than the less satisfying one of a herring gull pecking away at a dead fish or horseshoe-crab. Owing to the increasing populations of the latter bird—brought about primarily by the proliferation of garbage dumps—the elegant common tern is on the decline. At present, in summer one can see this graceful flyer—whose apt specific name, *hirundo,* means swallow—along the Middle Atlantic coast. The common tern breeds from Cape Hatteras north. For the surf watcher, the actions of the tern can be as fascinating as the crashing waves. But unless the too readily available sources of food that humans have provided for the scavenging gulls are curtailed, the future for *Sterna hirundo* looks bleak.

That gulls feed on garbage may seem at first thought to bear no obvious implications for the terns. But herring gulls are primarily foragers, and under normal conditions the supply of food in the environment is limited and exerts a considerable measure of control over the gull populations. Proximity of large populations of gulls to tern colonies makes life more precarious for the smaller birds. Nesting survival is affected, for the gulls often destroy the eggs and young of small ground-nesting colonial birds. The terns have other enemies, too—among them the domestic cats kept by summer and year-round residents; feral cats (for visitors to the seashore too often abandon their pets when returning home); the egg-loving striped skunk, which has been known nearly to exterminate entire colonies of terns; short-eared owls; red foxes; and, probably, raccoons.

The common tern's own diet is almost entirely small fish, up to about 4 in. (10 cm) long. In inlets and bays it feeds on the **American sand lance** *(Ammodytes americanus),* a small, silvery fish that swims in schools and is able to bury itself in the sand with a quick movement. These slender so-called sand eels are often abundant

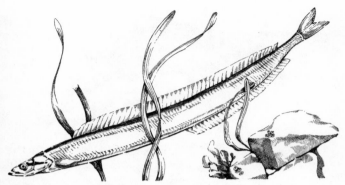

65. The American sand lance *(Ammodytes americanus)* is an abundant coastal fish; it favors sandy bottoms, burying itself when pursued by predators.

along protected sandy shores. The tern also eats the fry of larger species of fish and, in the estuaries, takes many **pipefish** *(Syngnathus fuscus)*.

Commercial fishermen sometimes locate bluefish by the presence of screaming terns, which feed upon the schools of fry that come to the surface in an attempt to escape the slashing jaws of the bluefish. Observing such a scene helps one understand why the production of thousands of eggs by mature fish does not result in over-populations of the species. The common tern's fishing behavior is a show well worth watching, particularly when a flock of the birds is dive-bombing a large school of sand lances or fry. Often a tern will go completely under the surface and then, screaming madly, reappear with a fish in its bill.

The only other tern regularly found along the Middle Atlantic coast is the **least tern,** *Sterna antillarum.* In size and flight behavior it is more like a swallow, and indeed it has been dubbed sea swallow by some. The least tern's beauty and delicacy at one time were almost its undoing. It was brought to the edge of extinction, being killed in large numbers, skinned, and stuffed for use as a decoration on women's hats. Its approachability and its habit of nesting in easily accessible colonies made it easy prey for the suppliers of the millinery trade. As many as 100,000 least terns were said to have

66. Least tern *(Sterna antillarum)*.

been killed on Cobb's Island, Virginia, in a single season. By 1903 none remained on this historic breeding ground. The colony on Bull's Island (now a part of Cape Romain National Wildlife Refuge) was wiped out in a season.*

In recent years, the threat to the least tern has been primarily from loss of habitat and from disturbance by recreationists and their pets and vehicles. The protection afforded these birds on the publicly owned seashore preserves is of vital importance to their survival as a species.

The least tern tends to choose nesting sites away from other tern species, probably because its small size and less aggressive behavior put it at a disadvantage in encounters with the larger common tern. Least terns lay their eggs—generally only two—in a shallow depression scooped out of the sand, usually above the reach of the highest tides. In the national seashores, wildlife refuges, and other protected areas, the breed-

*In his monumental *Life Histories of North American Birds* (republished by Dover Books), of which one volume is *Gulls and Terns,* Arthur Cleveland Bent cited many eyewitness accounts of the ruthless slaughter of various victims of the sport, food, and feather-trade industries.

ing colonies are off limits to human visitors and dogs. Merely approaching such a colony will bring upon the intruder a raucous, excited, dive-bombing assault. But though they may make one duck or shield one's head, the terns do not strike. It is an effective tactic, albeit pure bluff.

Considering the many hazards working against the least tern—over-sand vehicles, foot traffic, developments on barrier beaches, and other forms of human pressure, as well as the great increase in herring gull populations—it is not surprising that this species has suffered many reverses. Hunting of terns by humans ended with the diminishing demand for the birds for the millinery industry; but the terns still experience ups and downs in response to other influences. Accurate assessments of the species' status are difficult, partly because of its nonsynchronous nesting habits and small colonies. But apparently it is in the long run holding its own along much of the coast. In some of the states, notably Massachusetts, Connecticut, and New York, it may be increasing. One factor working in its favor is the establishment of dredge-deposition sites, which the tern is now quite frequently using for nesting. The vulnerability of these sites is potentially as high as that of barrier beaches, so management of these artificial island habitats may assume increasing importance.

GULLS. The gulls of the Atlantic coast are hard to categorize as to habitat, since they are found everywhere. When they are at the ocean front they may be resting on sandbars, flying up and down the interface, foraging in the swash zone, or floating beyond the breakers picking up dead fish or whatever else they can from the surface. Unlike the terns, gulls infrequently dive for their food.

In the northern sector of this stretch of coast, from Cape Cod to Sandy Hook, *Larus marinus,* the great black-backed gull, the largest member of the gull-and-tern family, reigns supreme in its habitat. This tyrant over the smaller gulls and raider of the nests of other birds has been increasing in recent years. Even so, it is still far from being as abundant as the herring gulls, with which it is often seen. Adult great black-backed

67. The great black-backed gull is almost entirely restricted to coastal waters. It has been extending its range southward.

gulls are easily distinguished even when size comparisons are not possible. The bird's black back and upper wings—which are actually dark slate, with only the wing tips truly black—contrast with its snow-white head, tail, and underparts, all of which make it unmistakable. Immatures of this species are less contrastingly marked and somewhat resemble immature herring gulls. The black-backed is larger, with a length of 31 in. (0.8 m) and a 5.5 ft. (1.7 m) wingspread. It is a splendid sight as it soars and wheels over the waves.

At the turn of the century the great black-backed gull was not known to breed south of Nova Scotia; today it not only is found wintering to South Carolina but breeds here and there along the Middle Atlantic coast. In recent years this species has been known to nest on islands in Oregon Inlet in Cape Hatteras National Seashore.

Like its smaller cousin, the herring gull, the great black-backed is a voracious, undiscriminating glutton. Besides destroying the eggs and young of other birds, it feeds on fish—mostly obtained when already dead—and on the carcasses of birds and marine animals, as well as floating garbage.

The **herring gull** *(Larus argentatus)* is surely one of the best known of all American birds, though as often as not it is referred to simply as the seagull. No one who has visited the Atlantic shore has failed to see this bird, which is most abundant near population centers. Formerly it did not nest south of Cape Cod; today breeding colonies are found to Cape Hatteras.

The herring gulls' nests, which in construction range from extremely crude to well woven and carefully shaped, are located in a great variety of sites. They may be on sand or gravel, in grassy fields, among the rocks, and even in trees.

This gull is one of the least fastidious feeders in the bird world. Its presence in garbage dumps is noisily conspicuous, but it feeds on the scraps of humanity's table wherever it can find them. The writer has had his lunch snatched from under his nose on more than one occasion when he failed to heed the gull's presence.

The list of the herring gull's "natural" foods is endless. As a scavenger, it plays a major role in keeping harbors, beaches, and estuaries clear of decaying carcasses. It eats many fish that have been stranded by the outgoing tide, cast up on the beach, or discarded by surf and commercial fishermen. As a predator its habits are wide ranging. Occasionally it plunges ternlike to catch small and medium-sized fish. It destroys the young of other birds. It spends much time foraging for clams, scallops, urchins, crabs, and other good-sized invertebrates. It commonly drops hard-shelled mollusks, crustaceans, and urchins from aloft onto hard surfaces—repeatedly, if necessary—until the shell breaks sufficiently to enable the gull to get at the contents.

This does not exhaust the herring gull's roster of edibles. It eats many insects, and it often follows the plow in spring to pick up exposed earthworms and grubs. A more surprising item in its diet is blueberries; of course the gull does not discriminate against the commercial, managed blueberry fields, so it is not popular with the berry growers.

The herring gull's depredations on other birds and its

undiscriminating diet notwithstanding, it is a splendid part of the coastal scene. Few birds can match its mastery of the air, and it is one of the most watchable of wild animals.

The Intertidal Zone of the Outer Beach

Life Between the Tides

Like the communities on pilings, sea walls, and rock faces that are alternately exposed and inundated, the life of the sand beach's intertidal zone is adapted to the rise and fall of the tide. But in the life community of the outer beach, exposed to ocean waves and currents, the most influential physical factors are not the alternating submersion and exposure but the turbulence of the water and the shifting nature of the substrate. This unstable habitat imposes severe demands on any organism, and it supports virtually no resident plants and animals. Except when exposed by the falling tide, the sand is in almost constant motion. Where sand has been deposited at the upper edge of the intertidal beach by the highest tides and by storm waves, it is subject as well to wind transport. Accordingly, this transition zone between the intertidal zone and the upper beach is probably the most sterile of all seashore habitats—except where windrows of beach wrack provide food and cover for amphipods and certain insects. Even lacking this resource, however, the transition zone may have burrowing amphipods and temporary burrows of young ghost crabs.

Between the high- and low-tide marks there may be an abundance of living things, some of them seasonal or transitory and some of them occupying only the narrow swash-and-backwash zone as it moves up and down the beach slope. But this is not a community characterized by diversity, though countless individuals of some species may at times occur in this unstable habitat. All the

forms are small, and most are minute. A single invertebrate species, found all along the Middle Atlantic coast,
is the dominant form of animal life in the intertidal
sands in much of its range.

THE MOLE-CRAB COMMUNITY

Typically, a natural community is named for the
dominant plant form or forms, or sometimes for both a
plant and an animal species. Thus, we have the salt-
marsh cordgrass community and the *Zostera* community. In the intertidal zone of the outer beach, no higher
plants can exist. The turbulent swash-and-backwash interface, constantly moving up and down the beach
slope as the tides ebb and flow, is a special habitat—and,
with its continually shifting substrate, a particularly severe one. It is a community (albeit a moving one) with
very little diversity, characterized by one or two dominant animal forms that move with it and that utilize its
unstable nature to their advantage.

Throughout the Middle Atlantic coast, the species
most identified with this sub-zone of the outer-beach
habitat, which we can call the swash zone, is the **mole-
crab** *(Emerita talpoida)*. It is well known to beachgoers,

68. The mole-crab *(Emerita talpoida)* is ubiquitous in the
outer-beach zone. *(M. Graham)*

The Intertidal Zone of the Outer Beach

sought by fishermen for bait, dug up by children for amusement, and preyed upon by blue crabs, lady crabs, shorebirds, and fishes. As any inhabitant of this shifting and turbulent zone must be, the mole-crab is built for rapid burrowing. It also must be able not only to cope with the churning water and sand but to migrate up- and down-slope, remaining, for feeding purposes, within the area of most active water movement. Its ability to burrow rapidly is necessary first to avoid being carried out by the surf or cast upon the beach and second to keep its period of exposure to predatory birds and invertebrates—of which there are many—as brief as possible. It is largely owing to the presence of these odd crustaceans that the outer beach zone with the greatest visible activity is the water's edge. But all of the mole-crab's food is brought to it by the surf, so while remaining essentially hidden it nevertheless must be adapted to secure this food.

Emerita is admirably designed for its life of constant rapid burrowing and shuttling up and down the beach slope. It is ovoid in shape, almost as smooth as an egg, and close to an egg in color. Thus, when its appendages are folded under it—as they are when one holds the mole-crab in one's hands—it very much resembles an egg. The female is 0.94 in. (24 mm), sometimes more, in length; the male measures less than 0.5 in. (12 mm). The abdomen, bent under the body, extends at least halfway to the anterior end of the animal. The last segment, called (as in shrimps and lobsters) a *telson*, is elongated and triangular; it is used in swimming (backward). As in hermit-crabs and fiddler crabs, the eyes are on the ends of movable stalks.

The mole-crab belongs to an infraorder of crustaceans, the Anomura, that includes the hermit-crabs and bears little resemblance to true crabs (Brachyura). Mole-crabs are sometimes called sand-bugs or sand crabs. "Mole" is not far off the mark as a reference to its mode of life, since this crustacean is highly specialized for burrowing. The short, stout, and hairy second, third, and fourth thoracic legs and the appendages of the sixth abdominal segment are used in digging and pushing. Examine a female mole-crab with a hand lens;

study its antennae, digging and swimming legs, and other structural adaptations. Note that it has no *chelate* (pincerlike) appendages, and that all its legs are flat, wide, and hairy.

The mole-crab faces up-slope and feeds only in the backwash. As the sheet of water flows down over its spot, the antennae trap minute animals or bits of organic matter. The mouth parts, which are not adapted for chewing, remove the food from the antennae.

To watch this feeding process you must crouch or kneel in the swash zone, ignoring the wetting you will get with each incoming wave. When conditions permit a smooth film of water to flow down on the backwash you may be able to see the antennae in the act of collecting food (the particles being invisible to you, of course).

Observation of this sand-colored animal in its natural habitat calls for sharp eyes, even where *Emerita* is abundant. Familiarity with its structure and behavior will help. Being there at the right time and the right place is largely a matter of luck. You may search in vain on one occasion, while at another time you'll catch a mole-crab on the first try. Generally these animals are present either in great numbers or not at all. Several methods are effective in capturing *Emerita*. An entrenching tool like those sold in camping supply stores serves well for digging into the wet sand just behind the backwash; or a pair of hands will suffice. Probe the scoop of sand quickly, before the mole-crabs have a chance to do their disappearing act. When they are on the move it's possible to catch them by just holding an ordinary kitchen sieve so that the backwash carries the animals into it.

To observe the great rapidity with which the mole-crab digs in, put one into a glass jar of sea water with a couple of inches of sand in the bottom. But don't try to keep these animals that are so well adapted to the demanding swash-zone environment. They will not live long away from it.

How to account for the often great abundance of these crustaceans? A host of predators and the hazards of storm waves operate to diminish their numbers.

The Intertidal Zone of the Outer Beach

Nevertheless, owing to the virtually unlimited food supply brought by the ocean waves, and to their reproductive capacity, populations sometimes reach amazing levels.

Mole-crabs constitute an important though not always available food resource for shorebirds and for inshore-dwelling larger crustaceans and fish. Sometimes the ebbing tide strands a mole-crab that missed the last backwash. If it isn't instantly snapped up by a predator, it burrows down into the sand to a depth where it can remain moist and secure from all but the most deeply probing bills.

That the up- and down-slope migrations of *Emerita* are in phase with the tides is not mystifying. Nor is such behavior unusual in animals of the intertidal zone in estuaries. What is remarkable is that individual mole-crabs do not make their moves independently; they advance and retreat in the aggregate, with an entire swarm going up on the same swash or down on the same backwash. How this activity is coordinated is a puzzle indeed. It is a more startling feat than the swooping of a flock of tree swallows in unison to drink from a pool; it is hard to imagine how the mole-crabs can communicate visually in their habitat.

The mole-crabs do not follow the tide all the way down the beach slope. Just before the water reaches the lowest level, they burrow into the sand. There they remain until the incoming tide overtakes them, when they again resume the upward migration.

The life history of these little decapods is comparable to that of most of the other higher crustaceans—shrimps, lobsters, and true crabs. Many of the female mole-crabs seen in summer bear masses of orange eggs under the carapace. In time these eggs hatch into a larval form that bears no similarity to the adult mole-crab. The larva is a *zoea* with a very long, curving *rostrum* (a beaklike projection). When carapace length reaches 3 mm, however, the young mole-crab's form resembles the adult's. In one respect *Emerita* is a degenerate form—that is, it has lost normative biological characteristics of its ancestors: during the mating season the male is semiparasitic on the female, remaining attached to her for long periods.

69. Coquinas, Bodie Island, Outer Banks.

COQUINA

In the Outer Banks, well within the range of *Emerita,* a small clam, **coquina** *(Donax variabilis)* largely replaces the decapod as the dominant organism of the intertidal zone. (A beach on Bodie Island is named for this little bivalve.) The coquina also lives in the shifting swash zone, but it is more conspicuous than the mole-crab, for it is constantly on the move and can more easily be seen before it digs in.

Donax variabilis is chiefly a species of the southeastern coast, and is found only spottily north of Cape Hatteras. Its larvae are occasionally carried by ocean currents to beaches as far as Fire Island, where it may occur temporarily in great numbers. It shares with *Emerita* the habit of moving up and down the beach slope with the tide, riding the swash and backwash, and digging in to feed. Though it is not a swimmer like the mole-crab, this mollusk is able to anchor itself quickly, upend, and dig into the sand at will. A filter feeder, *Donax* lives on food brought to it by the waves and thus may be a partial competitor with the mole-crab. It too must contend with predators, and not the least of these is man, by whom it is prized for chowder. It is also

The Intertidal Zone of the Outer Beach

important as the ultimate source of coquina stone, a natural building material formed chiefly from the shells of this animal—a fact that testifies to its enormous abundance in past eras.

The specific name, *variabilis*, refers to the colorful markings of the shells. They reach 0.8 in. (20 mm) in the Outer Banks; but in the northern part of their range, where conditions are less favorable, they are smaller and less colorful. Despite their diminutive proportions and fragile appearance, the shells are quite strong. They are wedge-shaped, with the *umbone* (the knob-like protuberance near the hinge) close to the posterior end.

But for a description of these tiny clams we can hardly do better than to turn to the engaging imagery of Augusta Foote Arnold and quote directly from her classic turn-of-the-century work *The Sea-Beach at Ebb Tide*:

D. variabilis. This little shell, the common Floridian form, exhibits every imaginable scheme of color combination, and defies general or comprehensive description. Probably the most usual pattern developed is a bluish-white background with purplish radiating lines. Another is a pure-white foundation with red lines. The surface is striated longitudinally with excessively fine riblets. Length one half of an inch or slightly more. In March and April these shells are thrown alive in millions upon the Florida beaches. Each wave seems to be laden with them, and when the foaming waters of each spent breaker recede, the little shells lie still on the sand for a moment, glittering like jewels in the sunlight; then, with a sudden protrusion of the foot and a quick turn, they all disappear like a flash, buried in the sand before the next breaker strikes them. One must be very quick to catch these active little mollusks.

BIRDS

The **sanderling**, *Calidris alba*, is sometimes seen on the upper beach, where it feeds on beach-fleas, flies, and other small arthropods associated with the drift line, and it is common on intertidal flats. But this little shorebird is so closely identified in the experience of beachgoers with the swash zone that it might be said to be a member of the mole-crab and coquina communi-

70. Sanderlings play tag with the waves as they feed in the swash zone.

ties. Its antics as it dashes up the beach slope with the swash at its heels, and back down with the backwash to feed on the food brought in by the waves, make it the liveliest actor on the scene. If one tries to approach sanderlings, which may be in a group of two or three or

71. The sanderling gets much of its food by probing the sand with slightly opened bill.

The Intertidal Zone of the Outer Beach

a flock of dozens, they skitter down the beach on twinkling black legs, then resume their feeding, probing the sand with their slender, slightly opened bills for small crustaceans and other minute animals. Undoubtedly adult male and young mole-crabs are an important component of this fare, but the adult females are much too large for them to handle.

A persistent effort to catch up with these lively birds as they feed in the swash zone results in their sudden departure. Launching instantaneously into the air, they swoop out over the surf in a close formation and then turn to fly parallel with the water's edge, alighting either farther down the beach or back in the direction from which the intruder had approached.

The sanderling is a great traveler, wintering not only along the Middle Atlantic coast but as far south as Argentina. It breeds in arctic and subarctic regions. Nevertheless it is often seen on our summer beaches; it is abundant most of the year, for example, on Assateague Island.

The **willet** (*Catoptrophorus semipalmatus*), much larger than the sanderling, is also familiar along the

72. Willets, as commonly seen in the swash zone as the little sanderlings, are rather drab in appearance.

edge of the outer beach surf. With its big bill it easily extracts and eats the adult female mole-crabs. It is as common on the marshes and tideflats, and is discussed in Chapter Four under Birds of the Salt Marsh.

LIFE BETWEEN THE SAND GRAINS

With the crustacean *Emerita,* the spottily abundant mollusk *Donax,* and a few birds we have exhausted the roster of readily observable residents of the outer-beach intertidal habitat. There are, however, minute organisms, mostly invisible to the unaided eye, living in the spaces between the sand grains. On the turbulent outer beach this *interstitial life,* as it is called, consists mostly of microscopic animals adapted to crawling about in the film of water that covers each sand grain. Some forms move between the sand grains without disturbing the sand itself. By definition they are extremely small; most are wormlike in form.

The importance of interstitial organisms in the ocean-beach ecosystem is apparently minimal. The sandpipers that probe the wet sand at the water's edge are seeking larger prey, such as young mole-crabs and smaller mollusks, along with small organisms carried in on the swash. Bigger shorebirds such as the willet are able to feed on female adult mole-crabs and larger animals cast upon the beach by the surf. The gulls, in addition to scavenging, feed on spider crabs, lady crabs, and stranded fish. It is doubtful that even the smaller ghost crabs feed upon the minute interstitial forms.

The interstitial community is much richer both in diversity and in abundance in the estuaries and protected bays, where the substrate is less disturbed and mud content is higher. Belonging to a variety of taxonomic groups, this assemblage of organisms is discussed in Chapter Three under The Benthic Meiofauna.

TIDEPOOL LIFE

A special condition of a number of sandy ocean beaches is the more or less temporary nature of tidepools where fish and other marine organisms are trapped between the tides. Gulls and shorebirds are attracted in great numbers to these accessible food supplies. These pools, which may be acres in extent, are unlike the tidepools of rocky shores in New England, where organisms such as anemones, barnacles, and rockweed find permanent places for attachment, and where mobile animals such as urchins wait out the tide. You can return to such a pool time and again to find essentially the same species. In contrast, the occupants of a sand-beach tidepool change with each flooding, and the pool itself may exist for only one tide cycle. The significant difference is that the rocky-shore tidepool is often an integral plant-and-animal community, with a base of green algae and a food web only partly dependent upon what the tide brings in, while the exposed sand-beach tidepool is no more than a temporary trap occupied by stranded animals. Determining the food chains in such transitory communities would be an unprofitable exercise.

The Upper Beach Zone

Along all of the barrier islands and most of the exposed mainland coast from Cape Cod to Cape Hatteras, the

73. Seaside goldenrod growing at the foot of the foredune, Cape Henlopen State Park.

oceanfront beach is sandy. The upper beach—the zone above the high-tide line—ranges from a few feet to as much as one-third mile (as at Oregon Inlet on Bodie Island). Its upper margin is the toe of the primary dune, or foredune. But some define it as including the seaward face of the foredune, with the upper margin at the dune crest; in such cases the zone may be referred to as the *backshore*. In places where erosion has brought the tides to the toe of the dune, the upper beach is nonexistent. This eroded state is more likely to occur during winter than in summer, when the tendency is for beaches to accrete. The upper beach life community described here coincides with the *back beach* as defined in Chapter One (Geomorphology) under Beaches.

Life on the Upper Beach

Though it occurs above the high-tide mark, the upper beach zone supports an association of salt-tolerant plants and of invertebrate animals that in most cases belong to marine rather than terrestrial groups. The vertebrates—birds and mammals for the most part—are present as predators upon the resident species and as foragers upon food cast up by the waves. Sometimes nesting colonies of terns and shorebirds occur on spits and barrier islands in what can be considered the upper beach zone. While the resident species are few, the numbers of individuals within populations sometimes reach thousands. The sanderlings that enliven the ocean beach with their antics in the swash-and-back-wash zone also feed at times on the upper beach. Other shorebirds, sparrows, grackles, red-winged blackbirds, fish crows, raccoons, and red foxes hunt and forage here for a variety of items ranging from seeds and sand-fleas to crabs and carrion.

The characteristic crustacean of the upper beach zone is *Ocypode quadrata,* the **ghost crab.** From Cape May south, in fact, the life in this zone can be called the ghost crab community. Within its range this crab is generally the commonest invertebrate of the zone—excluding *Orchestia* and other amphipods upon which

74. Sea-rocket is highly adapted for, and restricted to, life on sandy shores. Note rocket-shaped seed pods. It is one of the few plants that thrive on the upper beach on exposed coasts; look for it within a few yards of the water's edge.

it feeds; and these are either very small or are burrowing forms not conspicuously evident. The ghost crab is less a scavenger than some of its cousins, and spends much time seeking live prey. (Its habits are described later in this section.)

Plants of the Upper Beach

The base of the food web here is not green vegetation. Only a few vascular plants grow on the upper beach. *Artemisia Stelleriana,* one of several species of plants going by the name of **dusty miller,** and **sea-rocket** *(Cakile edentula)* venture from the dunes down to the high-tide mark. The latter species, incidentally, is one of the few organisms of the barrier beach that might be said to benefit from vehicular traffic. The seeds of this highly salt-tolerant species are cast upon the upper beach or blown there by the wind but will germinate only when buried. Thus the sprouting of the plant is facilitated by the passage of over-sand vehicles. It is not unusual to see lines of sea-rocket plants in the tire ruts below the toe of the foredune. (But let this not be considered as making a case for the beach buggies!)

A few other vascular plants grow on the narrow upper beach strip: **beach pea** *(Lathyrus japonicus)*, **seaside spurge** *(Euphorbia polygonifolia)* and **common saltwort** *(Salsola kali)*. The two grasses that dominate the foredune vegetation are **beachgrass** *(Ammophila breviligulata)* and, in the southern part of the Middle Atlantic coast, **sea oats** *(Uniola paniculata);* these are also seen on the upper beach as stragglers or pioneers.

Salsola kali is a bushy annual that grows on sandy lagoonal and estuarine shores as well as on the upper beach of the open coast. A relative of the *Salicornia* glassworts, it is sometimes aptly called **prickly glasswort;** but it does not resemble these plants in appearance. It is also known as **Russian thistle,** but unlike the thistles it is not a composite (the daisy family). The prickles are extensions of the leaf midveins and make identification of the plant easy. Most likely it is edible like other members of the goosefoot, or spinach, family (Chenopodiaceae), but this writer has not seen reference to its use as human food. Many wild animals, from mice to hoofed browsers, feed upon it, and in the west it is harvested before its "spines" have hardened and is fed to livestock. On the Atlantic coast its seeds are probably eaten by the whitefooted mouse and by sparrows.

Saltbush, or **seabeach orache** *(Atriplex arenaria)* looks a bit like saltwort but lacks its spines. This member of the spinach, or goosefoot, family (Chenopodiaceae) grows on the upper beach from Cape Cod south. It can be and is eaten cooked or raw, like spinach—but don't add salt to this choice wild food. It is utilized also by wild animals, including the seaside sparrow, which eats the seeds. *Lepidium virginicum* (**peppergrass,** or **poor man's pepper**), a member of the mustard family (Brassicaceae), can also be eaten like spinach; and the seed pods are a suitable substitute for pepper. It grows on the upper beaches of somewhat sheltered coasts, as does *Xanthium echinatum* (**beach clotbur**), a member of the ragweed family (Ambrosiaceae).

Despite the occurrence of these vascular plants in

The Upper Beach Zone

the upper beach zone, the food pyramid of this community on barrier beaches rests primarily upon beach wrack. Here, the role that living green plants play in most communities is sustained by an accumulation of various seaweeds; by *Phragmites* and *Spartina* fragments carried by currents from bay mouths and inlets; by sometimes large amounts of eelgrass leaves where this marine flowering plant grows in relatively protected coastal waters; by the remains of horseshoe-crabs (which often litter the beaches after the breeding period) and of fish and other marine animals; and by an assortment of other organic matter. Driftwood and such curiosities as whelk and skate egg cases are also part of the beach wrack. This cast-up debris may form windrows as much as a meter high and several meters wide where eelgrass constitutes a major component of the beach wrack. (Such sizable accumulations are not likely, however, on the most exposed ocean beaches.) The beach wrack not only provides a food resource but furnishes shelter from drying winds and prying predators, and even breeding places for some terrestrial invertebrates.

Animals of the Upper Beach

CRUSTACEANS

BEACH-FLEAS. When one turns over the beach wrack, it may explode into life with myriad tiny creatures that pepper one's legs as they hop about in confusion. Known variously as sandhoppers, sand-fleas, beach-hoppers, and beach-fleas, these active little invertebrates belong to a large group of Malacostracans called *amphipods* ("having feet on both sides"). This order of crustaceans includes swimmers, burrowers, and tube makers. Amphipods are found not only in, under, and near the beach wrack of sandy beaches but also in salt marshes, in the oceanic plankton, in tidepools of sandy, rocky, and muddy shores, in *Zostera* beds, under *Fucus* on rocky shores, among fouling organisms on pilings and buoys, under stones in the intertidal zone, and even hiding under the umbrellas of large jellyfish.

Beach-fleas are scavengers, feeding upon decaying plant and animal matter. They are eaten by many shorebirds, including sanderlings, black-bellied plovers, and ruddy turnstones; and by the ghost crab.

None of the several species of beach-flea found on the upper beaches of the Middle Atlantic coast has been dignified with its own exclusive common name; so the Latin names will have to suffice in this discussion. The layman could hardly be expected to distinguish them, at any rate, since with but few exceptions the members of the order Amphipoda require microscopic examination for positive identification.

The most familiar amphipod is *Orchestia agilis*—an aptly named creature, as many beachgoers know. It is most in evidence when the beach wrack under which it hides is disturbed. *O. agilis* exhibits the characteristics of a typical amphipod. It has an elongated, laterally compressed body, an abdomen of six segments and a telson, and a head that is not fused with the first segment of the thorax. It is large enough that these features can be seen with a hand lens. Close examination shows that the second of two pairs of *gnathopods* (the thoracic appendages, modified for grasping, just posterior to the *maxillipeds*, which are the first pair of legs, modified for feeding) are larger than the other thoracic legs. The three anterior abdominal legs are modified for swimming, the posterior ones for jumping.

Orchestia species are quite dark in color, from olive to reddish brown. In this range there are four species, measuring about 0.75 in. (19 mm); they are different from each other in such details as form of the telson, proportions of the antennae, and shape of the male's gnathopods.

The *Talorchestia* species of beach-fleas (family Talitridae) are a bit larger than those of the genus *Orchestia*. They are true emigrants from the sea to land, and they remain above the high-tide line though staying within the upper beach, where they burrow deep into the sand. Inactive by day, they come out at night to feed on the organic debris—and are fed upon by the ghost crab. Like moths, they are attracted to light; they can be captured in numbers by spreading a plastic sheet on the beach and placing a lantern in the middle. This is much easier than excavating these sand-colored amphipods one by one.

The most common *Talorchestia* species on the Middle Atlantic coast is *T. longicornis,* which measures to 1.2 in. (30 mm). *T. megalopthalma,* as its name suggests, has larger eyes; but it has shorter second antennae than *T. longicornis.* It is also the smaller of the two species. Both species are found throughout this range.

A few species of beach-fleas live in the salt marsh, preferring wet habitat to the zone in which *Orchestia* and *Talorchestia* live. They are a major part of the diet of the sharp-tailed sparrow as well as marsh-foraging shorebirds.

GHOST CRAB. The crab clan is indeed an ill-natured bunch—whence the term crabby, applied to persons of the same ilk. Nor is their behavior always defensive, as one who has been painfully nipped by a blue or lady crab can testify. But some crabs are less crabby than others, and many are a source of much amusement. In this category one might fit the members of the Ocypodidae—represented on the Middle Atlantic coast by the fiddlers and the ghost crab. The latter provides some of the best wildlife watching on the ocean beach.

Belonging to a warm-water family (the Ocypodidae), the ghost crab normally thrives only to the shores of Delaware Bay. (It can be seen at Cape May Point State Park in southern New Jersey.) One might ask how a crab that lives on the upper beach and is not a swimmer can stray so far—even to Rhode Island—beyond its normal range. The answer lies in the fact that the larvae of ghost crabs, like those of most other crustaceans, are aquatic forms that become part of the plankton and are thus subject to being carried afar by currents. Some of these larvae of the ghost crab make it ashore on Long Island and the southern New England coast, and they may survive long enough to reach maturity.

Ghost crabs do not have the thick shells and powerful

pinching legs possessed by some of their more formidable relatives. They are blessed, however, with protective coloration, swiftness of locomotion, and unmatched ability in burrowing. They are next to invisible against the beach sand, except when moving. This square-bodied crab often looks bigger than it is, for its legs are long in relation to the size of the shell, which measures to 2 in. (51 mm) in width, slightly less in length. It is sand-colored above, white below, with pincers often having a lavender tint; the young crabs are mottled with gray or brown. The four pairs of *pleopods* (abdominal appendages) of the female ghost crab are modified for the attachment of eggs.

The earlier scientific name of the ghost crab, *Ocypoda arenaria* (now *Ocypode quadrata*) meant swift-footed, of the sand. Nothing could have been more apt. Preferring purely sand beaches on the ocean or on the bayside of spits, it is much harder to catch than its little cousins, the fiddlers, which inhabit generally quieter estuarine shores. The ghost crab digs deeper and faster, and thus requires more effort on our part (or a predator's) to excavate. And trying to capture a ghost crab alive or on film can prove a humbling experience. Your efforts to overtake this small creature—the original Artful Dodger—will most likely be an exercise in futility. To get a close-up camera shot, one must adopt a strategy—and a long-focal-length lens with extension tubes will help. Patience and persistence are other tools needed.

Its nimbleness also helps the ghost crab in catching the acrobatic little beach-fleas upon which it feeds. These amphipods, bouncing about like true fleas, would appear to be safe from predation even by the ghost crab. But "swift-foot" doesn't attempt to run them down; it stalks and springs upon the beach-fleas like a cat catching a mouse.

Sometimes this crustacean builds its burrow on the backside of the primary dune, but more commonly it is on the upper beach near the toe of the foredune, or on the lower face. Young ghost crabs, however, generally burrow just above the high-tide line. Both the ghost crab and the beach-flea can remain for long periods out of water. Indeed, this species would drown if trapped by the tide; yet it has not completely lost its dependence on the salt water, even in the adult stage. It apparently goes into the surf to wet its gills from time to time. This may be why the young crabs' burrows are dug closer to the sea than are those of the large crabs, which can travel faster, farther, and more safely. These forays to the salt water probably are always made nocturnally.

Evidently the ghost crab, like the beach-fleas, is on the evolutionary march from the sea to a dry-land existence. But unlike the beach-fleas, it still has an aquatic larval stage, as mentioned above. Adults have a breathing slit on each side of the ventral surface between the basal joints of the third and fourth legs.

Being largely nocturnal in its habits, the ghost crab can minimize exposure to the searing sun. Yet it is often up, and sometimes active, in the daytime; as you walk along the upper beach you may see it standing watch in the entrance of its burrow. At night, it may wander far from home. (The writer was once startled to see a big specimen out for a midnight stroll in the campground at Oregon Inlet—one-third mile from the ocean's edge.) But no matter how far it may have strayed from its haven, this crab will not be easy to intercept. The fact that it must run sideways appears to be no handicap.

Using a spade, one can dig a ghost crab out of its burrow, which may be 3 ft. (1 m) deep and almost straight down; but with its protectively colored shell, often closely matching the sand, it is easily overlooked even when turned up by the spade. Care should be taken in digging so as not to harm the crab. And removing one from its habitat is inadvisable—in some areas, illegal.

The ghost crab's enemies as well as its prey are mostly nocturnal animals. The raccoon, which also roams the beach and dunes after nightfall, may be quick and clever enough to constitute a peril to the crab. During the day its habitat-matching coloration provides it with a measure of protection from most predators, including even sharp-eyed birds.

BIRDS

The upper beach, a transition zone from the intertidal zone to the dunes, has no birds that both feed and breed on it. A few colonial nesting birds do nest there. And it is visited by many that also are seen in the intertidal zone and many that belong to the more landward habitats. Sanderlings and other small shorebirds, gulls, fish crows, and songbirds come here to feed on resident crustaceans and flotsam of the beach wrack.

The **fish crow** *(Corvus ossifragus)*, which is discussed in Chapter Three under The Role of Birds in the Estuarine Community, is commonly seen on the upper beach, where it scavenges for anything edible.

A sort of slimmer version of the fish crow (but not of the same family) is the **boat-tailed grackle** *(Quiscalus major)*. The male is all black, almost as long as the fish crow but with a tail that accounts for much of its overall length (16.5 in., or 41 cm). The female is brown, is much smaller, and has a less prominent tail. It is the largest of the blackbirds (Icteridae) in the eastern United States. (It is exceeded in size by the **great-tailed grackle,** found as far east as Louisiana). Its habitat is the marshes and other intertidal and upland communities of the coast from New Jersey south. Any grackle seen on the upper beach in this range is likely to be the boattail. When in the intertidal zone—flats, marshes, or beach—it is most often poking about on the upper edge, searching out small invertebrates and organic matter.

The boattail's chief animal food is insects, particularly beetles and grasshoppers; crabs, shrimp, and other crustaceans; and small mammals (in the shrub-thicket and marsh habitats). It is one of the few birds that eat toads. In the dune-and-swale and shrub-thicket zones it feeds on bayberry, and it is known to eat wild grapes *(Vitis* spp,), which grow in maritime forest communities. In the marshes, these blackbirds are commonly seen the midst of snow geese, egrets, and other large water birds, probably foraging for small invertebrates, and looking somewhat out of place in that company and setting. But the boattail's most characteristic habitat is the upper beach zone. It is easily recognized, on the ground or in the air, by its long tail.

The **American oystercatcher,** treated in Chapter Three under The Role of Birds in the Estuarine Community, can as easily be considered a bird of the ocean beaches. It is often seen there, and it prefers to nest on barrier beaches and offshore islands relatively free of disturbance by humans. It is among the largest of shorebirds, and although it is not abundant it is so noisy and so spectacular in appearance that it does not go unnoticed when present. A strictly coastal bird, it shares with the black skimmer a bold black-and-white pattern; and, also like the skimmer, it has a highly specialized bill, reflecting its rather restricted diet. Larger and more heavily built than the skimmer, but not so long winged, the oystercatcher has a black head, nearly black back, white belly, and white wing and tail patches above. Its bill is a big, chisel-shaped, all-red implement well designed for use in opening bivalves. Its distribution on the Atlantic coast is similar to the skimmer's, but it winters to New Jersey.

The nest of the oystercatcher is typically a mere hollow scooped in the top of a small elevation of the upper beach. Under the right conditions, the two or three eggs laid in this nest may be left uncovered much of the time. They are inconspicuous, particularly on stony beaches. The young are also protectively colored; though they are able to run quite fast soon after hatching, they may, when warned by the parent birds, squat in the sand, where they remain next to invisible.

Many species of shorebirds are seen during spring and fall migration on the coastal beaches. (Most are even more likely to be seen on the sand and mud flats and in the tidal marshes.) Among these is the **semi-palmated sandpiper** *(Calidris pusilla),* smaller than the sanderling and not likely to be seen in winter along this coast. It frequents the intertidal sand and mud flats, where it feeds on worms and other small invertebrates. On the sand beaches it feeds in the swash zone like the sanderling; with its smaller bill it does not probe as deeply but dashes here and there, head held down, picking up what small items the waves bring in.

The **dunlin** *(Calidris alpina)* and the **western sandpiper** *(Calidris mauri)* are seen on the ocean beaches

75. Semipalmated sandpipers, seen here feeding in the beach wrack, are common on the outer beaches (and intertidal flats) during spring and fall migration.

(and intertidal flats) during migration and also through the winter. The dunlin is discussed in Chapter Three.

The Dune-and-Swale Zone

Life in the Dunes

In the barrier-island dunelands the physical conditions are, if anything, more severe than they are in the intertidal beach zone. Temperature extremes are greater. The midday summer sun, unobstructed by a forest canopy, beats down on the surface of the dunes; this can raise the temperature of the surface to 150° F (82° C). Because of the phenomenon known as *lens effect,* or *condensing effect,* the surface and the air next to it can be particularly hot in a hollow (see Fig. 76).

Aridity of the surface soil contributes further to the hostility of the dune environment. The porous sand, containing very little organic matter, may be virtually devoid of moisture to a depth not reached by ordinary plant roots.

Add to heat and aridity the salt carried into the dunelands by onshore winds and storm surges, and the inherent instability of the substrate, and it is apparent that

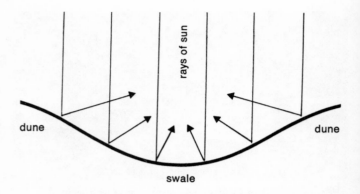

76. Lens effect: in hollows (including the swale itself, which is a large hollow), the sloping sides reflect sunlight and radiate heat toward the center, raising temperatures to levels as high as 50° C (122° F).

only special adaptations will enable an organism to survive here. A plant, particularly, must have a certain degree of physiological tolerance to both salt spray and substrate salinity. The latter condition, however, is not as serious here as it would be in a desert-coast duneland; the substantial year-round precipitation along the Atlantic shore prevents excessive accumulation of salt in the permeable surface stratum.

Survival in the dune-and-swale zone also requires that a plant have the capacity to withstand high winds and sandblasting, to resist drought, and to tolerate low levels of some nutrients, such as nitrogen.

This all adds up to what is possibly the harshest set of physiological demands of any environment in the eastern United States (excepting the peak of New Hampshire's Mount Washington). The adaptations for coping with these conditions are many and varied. Some function to conserve moisture; some minimize exposure to the direct rays of the sun; some enable a plant to respond to the undermining or burying action of moving sands; and some allow an animal to minimize the time it must spend on or in the hottest stratum—the surface, the immediately adjacent air, and the upper few centimeters of soil—during the day. The adaptations take the form of modifications in body structure, of specialized metabolism, of changes in life history patterns, of behavioral modifications, of devices to excrete excess salt, and even of variations from the characteristic coloration of the species. Many of the dune plants and animals possess several types of adaptations to the peculiar conditions.

Vegetation Patterns

Not surprisingly, in view of the uniqueness of the barrier islands' topography and their oceanic situation, they have a vegetational complex unlike that of any other environment. While the species associations (plant components of the communities) vary widely between different parts of the coast, and even between neighboring islands, they have developed in response to factors common to all of the islands: the characteristic topography and the direct influence of the adjacent waters and winds. Degree and duration of isolation from the mainland have also played a role.

Because a number of dune-and-swale plant species have wide distribution along the coast between Cape Cod and Cape Hatteras, a familiarity with these will be a good start in the study of barrier-island ecology. Among such plants are perennial grasses, including *Ammophila breviligulata* and *Andropogon* and *Panicum* spp.; the annual grass *Cenchrus tribuloides* (from New Jersey south); perennial forbs such as *Euphorbia polygonifolia* and *Solidago sempervirens;* and the annual forbs *Cakile edentula* and *Strophostyles helvola.* Shrubs, which are more diverse with increasing distance from the beach, include these species found from Cape Cod to Cape Hatteras: *Parthenocissus quinquefolia, Rhus toxicodendron, Myrica pensylvanica,* and *Hudsonia tomentosa.* A number of tree species successfully compete with dune conditions, but *Sassafras albidum* is the only tree of this habitat that is found on both Cape Cod and Cape Hatteras.

Various communities, ranging from grassland with a few intermixed forbs to shrub-dominated associations with the grasses almost entirely excluded, are found in this zone. There are areas of almost bare sand, and areas where creeping and bushy woody plants cover the ground completely.

Any two duneland communities along the Atlantic coast differ in their specific makeup, and a comparison of that on Monomoy Island with that of Hatteras Island will reveal few species in common. But in each case the distribution pattern would prove to be determined largely by distance from the ocean and the degree of protection from salt-laden winds.

Typically, the primary dune supports a grassland community that gradually gives way to a mixed grass-shrub community (and is eventually replaced by a shrub-thicket zone forming a narrow barrier just seaward of the bayside marsh zone). This mixed grass-shrub community could be regarded as a wide transition zone, or *ecotone*, between the grass-dominated community on the face of the foredune and the shrub-dominated thicket community. But often it occupies by far the greater part of the island's width, even counting the salt-marsh zone of the bayside shore (which itself can be considered a transition zone between island and lagoon). This is the case in the Wilderness Area of Fire Island National Seashore and on much of Assateague Island. On some of the Outer Banks islands a quite different condition prevails, with no significant development of shrubs and with the grassland community extending from the upper limits of the tides on the outer beach to the salt marsh. At the opposite extreme, in the Talisman area of Fire Island, a dense shrub thicket covers the island from the crest of the primary dune to the very edge of Great South Bay (with no salt-marsh zone but with the shrub thicket approaching maritime-forest dimensions on the bay shore).

Another common vegetation pattern is seen where the grass-shrub community merges rather sharply into a maritime forest. Some maritime forests are dominated by species seen in the dune-and-swale and the shrub thicket; but here they attain enough height to provide a canopy that permits the development of a layered forest community. The understory consists of shrub species, along with saplings of canopy-tree species and vines; the herb layer consists largely of shade-tolerant forbs and seedlings of canopy trees. A classic example of such a maritime forest is discussed later in this chapter under The Sunken Forest of Fire Island.

Somewhat unexpectedly, freshwater ponds are often present in the dune-and-swale zone, and they may occur even at the landward foot of the primary dune. These may be ephemeral, seasonal, or permanent. In spring and early summer, this writer has stood on a boardwalk crossing at the crest of a primary dune and heard the rhythmic roar of the surf blending with the trills and calls of frogs and toads (the first of these groups of vertebrates particularly is known to have a very low tolerance for salt.) Cattail marshes sometimes occur only a few hundred feet from the surf zone, but on barrier islands they are seldom of great extent. Possibly they have been largely replaced by *Phragmites,* the tall reedgrass that has taken over so many wetland habitats —fresh as well as brackish.

It would be difficult to single out a barrier island having a "typical" duneland vegetation complex. The following is a very generalized picture of the kind of plant life that represents this ecosystem on the Middle Atlantic coast. It is safe to say that a close observer can find different zonation patterns and species associations on every island, and often wide variations on a single island.

Some Plants of the Primary Dune

Because dunes tend to migrate in the direction prevailing winds blow, plants living on the windward side of a dune are subject to having the ground cut out from under them, and those on the lee side are susceptible to periodic burial. One plant especially well adapted to the seaward zone of the duneland, and which grows throughout the range covered by this book, is *Ammophila breviligulata.* Arguably the most important of all coastal plants except for saltmarsh cordgrass, it is known variously by such common names as American beachgrass, marram, sea sand-reed, psamma, and dune-grass. The most commonly used name is **beachgrass;** but since it is not primarily a beach dweller, here it will be called **marram** or by its scientific name.

Marram grows to about 3 ft. (1 m) high, and it spreads over the dunes by means of horizontal rhizomes that run a few inches under the surface. From these rhizomes fibrous roots descend, sometimes several feet, to moisture. Short stems grow up from some of the nodes along the rhizomes, and from these grow long leaves. Marram grows from the lowest spots in the swale to the crests of the highest dunes. It is often the first plant to take hold on newly formed dunes or on the shifting surface of a migrating dune. Once the grass has taken root, the parts of the plant above the surface begin to trap the blowing sand, and stabilization of the dune has begun. The stems continue to grow upward as sand builds up around them, and the rhizomes spread rapidly in all directions.

With its great tolerance of salt spray, marram is one of the few plants that thrive on the face of the foredune, the surface most exposed to winds from the ocean. Sometimes it is the only plant growing there, but often others are able to get a foothold after marram has anchored the sands. Among these are **seaside goldenrod** *(Solidago sempervirens)*, occurring from Cape Cod to Cape Hatteras; **dusty miller** *(Artemisia Stelleriana)*, from Cape Cod to New Jersey; **cocklebur** *(Xanthium echinatum)*, Cape Cod to Cape Hatteras; **sea-rocket** *(Cakile edentula)*, Cape Cod to Cape Hatteras; **beach pea** *(Lathyrus japonicus)*, Cape Cod to Sandy Hook; **beach plum** *(Prunus maritima)*, Cape Cod to Cape Henlopen; and **sea oats** *(Uniola paniculata)*, Cape Henry to Cape Hatteras.

Identifying *Ammophila breviligulata* is easy, for it is the only grass that has parallel ridges (10 or 12) running the length of the grass blade on its upper surface. (Use a lens to see this.) Each of these ridges encloses a vein. The ridged structure is associated with the plant's ability to curl its leaves inward—to roll up more or less like a tube—when conditions are dry. This adaptation, not present in any other coastal grass, helps the plant to survive in the desertlike conditions that sometimes prevail in the dunes.

Not only is *A. breviligulata* extremely tolerant of the instability of the soil in frontal-dune habitats, but there is reason to believe that such conditions are actually favorable to it, and that conversely its vigor decreases as the substrate becomes more stable. One researcher has proposed that burial by sand is a requirement for stimulation of new root production by this plant. Each part of the marram plant is short-lived; new growth is achieved primarily by budding from the rhizomes, sprouting from seeds being infrequent. Stability of the site may be a major factor in decline of vigor in this true pioneer species.

Marram's superlative adaptability to the unstable conditions in active dunes, along with its capacity to decelerate sand movement and create conditions in which other plants can gain a foothold, have made it an invaluable tool in barrier-beach management programs. This in turn has contributed to its increasing prevalence along our Atlantic coast, even in areas it did not naturally inhabit.

77. Dusty miller is not usually a dominant, but here (at Watch Hill, Fire Island) it occupies the crest of the foredune with marram.

The Dune-and-Swale Zone

Dusty miller, engagingly named for its curious appearance, is of interest for its special adaptations to life in a habitat subject to extreme exposure to salt and sunlight. It is one of the very few species able to grow on the upper beach zone reached by the highest tides —surely a reflection of its great tolerance for salty conditions.

Artemisia is the genus of wormwoods in the vast family of composites; so this plant might logically be called by the more indicative name **beach wormwood,** particularly since several other plants have been given the name dusty miller. Moreover, the one we are concerned with here is an alien. Like **saltspray rose** *(Rosa rugosa),* also identified with Middle Atlantic ocean beaches, beach wormwood was introduced from Asia and has spread widely. Immigrants such as these, which thrive in hostile environments where few native plants can prosper and which are so attractive to the eye, are welcome indeed. Dusty miller certainly plays a role, albeit a small one, in stabilizing the upper beach and foredune; and saltspray rose adds color to the scene as well as furnishing cover and food for wildlife.

78. Saltspray rose, or rugosa rose, with very spiny stems and deeply wrinkled leaves, is common on the coast from New Jersey north.

Like marram, dusty miller has horizontal rhizomes; but they are at the surface rather than underground. It is less tolerant of burial by blowing sands, is far less abundant, and is never a dominant in the interdune zone.

Examining a leaf of *Artemisia* with a hand lens, one sees that its "dusty" look is due to a dense coat of woolly white hairs, a feature that undoubtedly serves to protect the plant from both strong sunlight and heavy spray and that probably minimizes moisture loss from the leaves. Although dusty miller is often described as a matted and creeping plant, it sometimes develops a rather shapely bushlike form, as on the sound shore of Long Island, which is a less stressful environment than the ocean beach. Dusty miller grows on this coast from Cape Cod to Cape Henry; it is less easily found in the southern part of its range.

Once over the crest of the primary dune one discovers new species of plant life. Some of those found on the upper beach and the face of the foredune, such as dusty miller and sea-rocket, may be hard to locate here, as they must compete with plants that, while unable to tolerate conditions at the very edge of the ocean, are well adapted to the less exposed interdune zone. Marram, however, often persists (with decreasing density) all the way to the shrub-thicket zone.

One plant that often appears on the lee side of the foredune and that is frequently dominant in much of the interdune zone is **woolly hudsonia** *(Hudsonia tomentosa)*. This plant, despite its preference for the interdune habitat, is sometimes called beach-heath or beachheather. An evergreen, ground-hugging shrub, it is, like *Artemisia*, protected by a thick coat of whitish hairs, in which are enmeshed its tiny, needlelike leaves. Neither a conifer nor a heath, but related to St. Johns-wort, this plant forms a year-round carpet of green in large areas of duneland. (It actually takes on a grayish color during rainless periods.) It is apparently very well adapted to the aridity of the substrate and the unrelieved heat of the sun. Its growth form provides shelter for animal life from both direct sunlight and enemies.

The Dune-and-Swale Zone

Hudsonia sends out threadlike roots for some distance around it, and secures for itself most of the available moisture. Thus other plants are at a disadvantage, and hudsonia tends to grow in patches isolated from other plants. In winter and after a dry period it becomes a dull gray in color; but with a new supply of moisture it springs forth in sage green. When hudsonia is in bloom, one should kneel on the sand to get close enough to examine the tiny but beautiful yellow star-shaped flowers. Collectively, they add a dash of color to the dunes in May and June; and they are an intriguing subject for close-up photography.

Plants of the Interdune Swale

The protection the primary dune provides from the wind and from the salt it carries is advantageous for plant life; consequently many more varieties grow in the interdune zone than on the face of the foredune. Typically, the diversity and density of plant cover increase with distance from the ocean beach, as new plants with decreasing tolerance for salt are able to contend.

Evergreen bearberry *(Arctostaphylos uva-ursi)* is a

79. A shrub growing on the lee side of the foredune on Ocracoke Island is pruned by salt spray to the level of the dune crest.

THE ECOLOGY OF BARRIER ISLANDS

trailing shrub that appears at the crest of the primary dune in much of our range. Look for it from Cape Cod to Cape Henry. Recognize it by its wedge-shaped-to-elliptic, inch-long leaves, green on both upper and lower surfaces; small white or pink flowers in early and mid-summer; and red, globular fruits that often persist through winter. Bearberry, as its name suggests, is food for bears where it occurs in their range. In the dune-lands it is sometimes browsed by deer, and birds eat the fruits. Its dominance in the dune-and-swale zone is sometimes so great that it covers acres to the virtual exclusion of other plants.

Pitch pine *(Pinus rigida)* makes its first appearance farther from the beach than does bearberry. It may become quite common a hundred yards (90 m) or so into the swale. But where the frontal barrier dune is especially high, in its shelter pitch pine may grow much closer to the sea—and in an upright form rather than in the sprawling, ground-hugging, untreelike aspect it assumes where it is subject to salt spray and constant winds.

In zones well away from the beach pitch pine may reach a height of 65 ft. (20 m). But generally in most of the dune-and-swale communities the tree is shrubby, dense, and matlike, lacking a trunk and perhaps reaching a height of no more than 3 ft. (1 m). This growth form provides excellent cover for small wildlife and is undoubtedly an effective stabilizer of the sandy substrate. It's a good guess, too, that the ground under these low pines is the moistest in the interdune zone. Consequently, for purposes of wildlife observation and photography, one might well pay attention to these sites. They have, for example, proven to to be a likely place to find the **northern fence lizard** *(Sceloporus undulatus hyacinthinus)* wherever the ranges of the pitch pine and the lizard coincide—from Sandy Hook to Cape Henry. (Not surprisingly, this reptile is often called the **pine lizard.**) It's also a good place to look for the **hognose snake** *(Heterodon platyrhinos).*

From Cape Henry south to Cape Hatteras, **sea oat** (or sea oats) is a more conspicuous duneland plant than marram, though the range of the latter extends to

North Carolina. The range of sea oat extends from Northampton County, Virginia, to Texas. This tall, picturesque grass, like marram, grows from the toe of the foredune back through the swale. Where there is no secondary dune, as on Ocracoke Island in the Outer Banks, it may grow right across the island. Its sand-stabilizing capacity is considerable, though it does not grow from horizontal rhizomes as does marram. Sea oat sometimes performs a rearguard action in the struggle of the land against the encroaching sea. As the dune line retreats, a clump of the tall grass may stand isolated on the berm, its roots holding back a pedestal of sand above the general level of the beach.

There are a few nonflowering plants in the dune-and-swale zone. The lichen *Cladonia cristatella,* **British soldiers,** adds a bit of color to the dune surface where it grows on decaying wood. But the casual observer will probably miss these minute, red-capped plants that adapt to the physical conditions through a symbiotic partnership of fungus and alga. A few other species of *Cladonia* also occur in the community. Compared to them, *Usnea barbata,* **old man's beard,** is conspicuous; it grows on dead branches of beach plum and other shrubs, where it can't be missed.

Among the most interesting plants of the dunelands are the **earthstars.** Related to the edible puffballs, these mushrooms are common on the coastal dunes. Their thick, segmented outer layer, which encloses a ball-like inner spore sac, remains closed during dry conditions. But when rain brings moisture, this layer splits open and the pointed segments curl downward, sometimes raising the whole plant above the sand. The inner sac, thus exposed, releases the abundant, minute spores through the mouth opening on the top. Earthstars grow on both open and wooded areas of the dunes. A common earthstar is *Geaster triplex,* which when closed has a diameter of 1 to 2 in. (25 to 50 mm).

Fire Island's Dune-and-Swale Zone

A classic example of a dune-and-swale community is the belt of duneland on Fire Island, between the

Sunken Forest and the ocean beach. From a boardwalk trail one can easily observe the vegetation pattern described below.

On the narrow strip of beach adjacent to the toe of the foredune, only a few plants have taken root. Here the decaying vegetation and other flotsam that have been cast up by storm waves provide a favorable site for some plants with a high tolerance for salt. While this strip is not a part of the duneland habitat, rather a transition zone between beach and dunes, it is here that the plants of the primary dune appear closest to the sea. Along this drift line and just above it are scattered sea-rocket, seaside spurge, and seaside goldenrod. Runners of *Ammophila*, which is dominant on the foredune, extend onto this upper-beach subzone.

Sea-rocket *(Cakile edentula)* is a succulent coastal plant of the mustard family (Brassicaceae). Its name derives from the distinctive rocket-shaped, 0.5 to 0.8 in. (13 to 20 mm) pods that follow the summer's small, light purple flowers. It is distributed along our entire Atlantic coast, and is typically found on the toe and face of the primary dune; where the dune is low and offers little protection to competing plants, it may be seen on the back side. In the Sunken Forest area, it is found within the first 8 meters measured from mean high tide mark.

Seaside spurge *(Euphorbia polygonifolia)*, also found on our entire Atlantic coast, is a wiry, prostrate plant that hugs the sand surface, with very small leaves and minute flowers, and seed capsules 0.13 in. (3 mm) long.

Seaside goldenrod *(Solidago sempervirens)* must be considered one of the most successful of all coastal flowering plants. Not only is it tolerant enough of salt that it can grow on the upper edge of the beach and thrive on the face of the foredune, but it is vigorous and adaptable enough to compete with other plants in the broad dune-and-swale zone, and in salt marshes and along tidal streams as well. A showy form of the plant is found on the coast south to New Jersey, where its range overlaps that of a less showy form (with a range from New York to Florida). Both are distinguishable from other

The Dune-and-Swale Zone 151

goldenrods by the smooth, toothless, often fleshy leaves, with lower leaves clasping the stout stem. Seaside goldenrod and sea-rocket are probably the only two plant species found on both the ocean's edge and the edge of open water of the lagoon (Great South Bay) on Fire Island.

Much drier than the drift line at the upper edge of the beach, and nearly devoid of organic soil components, the seaward face of the primary dune is the unquestioned domain of *Ammophila breviligulata;* but living space is given up for scattered individuals of some aforementioned species, particularly the hardy dusty miller, beach pea, and seaside goldenrod. Also encountered here are **Virginia creeper** *(Parthenocissus quinquefolia);* **beach plum** *(Lathyrus japonicus),* south to New Jersey; **bayberry** *(Myrica pensylvanica);* and **poison-ivy** *(Rhus radicans).* Three of these—goldenrod, beach plum, and Virginia creeper—persist as part of the vegetation to the beginning of the maritime forest, nearly 200 yds. (175 m) from the ocean. One, poison-ivy, hangs on through the maritime forest into the upper marsh on the bay side of the island.

At the crest of the foredune marram grass begins to surrender its sovereignty. This is possibly owing as much to the greater stability of the substrate as to competition from other species. Also, in the wind-salt shadow on the lee side of the foredune dusty miller and beach pea become scarce, while beach plum and bayberry become more abundant, achieving dominance on some sites. **Bearberry** *(Arctostaphylos uva-ursi)* and **American holly** *(Ilex opaca)* make their appearance in some numbers. Bearberry becomes the dominant species in some interdune sites, as marram was on the face of the foredune. In the maritime forest community, holly will be seen to be a co-dominant with two other tree species.

Some of these woody plants, though less tolerant than marram of heavy doses of salt spray, do have in common with that grass a high capacity to withstand burial by the shifting sands. Bearberry, however, is found in relatively undisturbed sites. In the most stabilized areas of the dune-and-swale community it achieves dominance, forming dense mats of considerable extent. Woolly hudsonia, which fills a similar niche in the Henlopen Dunes of Delaware, is associated here in the Fire Island community with the disturbed sites, as is the similarly adaptable seaside goldenrod. In these sites, called *blowouts,* the finer sand has been removed by the wind, and the pebbly substrate is inhospitable to most plants.

Except on blowouts and disturbed roadside sites, both diversity and density of cover tend to become greater with increasing distance from the ocean. On the northern, landward side of the swale, woody shrubs and trees gain greater dominance. Among these are **pitch pine** *(Pinus rigida),* mostly procumbent in growth form; **black cherry** *(Prunus serotina);* **Virginia juniper** *(Juniperus virginiana);* **dwarf sumac** *(Rhus copallina);* and **highbush blueberry** *(Vaccinium corymbosum).* In the transition to the forest community most of these are gradually replaced by American holly, **sassafras** *(Sassafras albidum),* and **oblongleaf juneberry** *(Amelanchier canadensis).* Highbush blueberry remains a prominent species here and into the maritime forest understory; and Virginia creeper, poison-ivy, and beach plum, all of which appeared on the primary dune, retain a place in the vegetation of the secondary dunecrest.

Water-seeking and Water-conserving Adaptations

One of the biggest problems for dune-dwelling plants is the need for water. Where the water table is several or many feet below the surface and the soil is extremely porous, a deep root system is essential, or the plant must have a means of taking up and storing precipitation directly and special adaptations for water retention.

Some plants that ordinarily do not have deep roots develop a tap root in the dune environment. Among these is **wild lupine** *(Lupinus perennis),* which grows in much of the Middle Atlantic coastal region. Dusty miller and woolly hudsonia have dense coats of whitish

80. Prickly-pear cactus, Ocracoke Island.

hairs or down that minimize water loss through evaporation. The leaves of hudsonia, moreover, are very small, scalelike, and pressed close to the stem. **Prickly-pear cacti** *(Opuntia* spp.) belong to a group of mainly desert plants and are adapted in several ways to the heat and aridity of the dunes. Although able to survive internal temperatures approaching 145° F (63° C), they are also adapted to minimize the effects of heat from the sun's rays. For example, their external surface area is small in proportion to the volume of the plant. There are no green leaves; photosynthesis is carried on in the stem joints, which tend to grow with their flat surfaces facing east and west, in this way avoiding much of the effect of the midday sun. Their roots are shallow, and so able to take advantage of light rainfall; and the stems have tissues with great water-storage capacity. The *stomates,* or pores, are sunk below the general surface of the stem and can close during the heat of midday. One penalty the prickly-pear and other cacti pay for extreme specialization is a slow rate of growth, which under ordinary conditions puts them at a competitive disadvantage. But in the poor soils and harsh environment of the dunes, where competition is principally for moisture, not for growing space, cacti fare well. Some members of the Cactaceae can be found on barrier

81. Woolly hudsonia not only thrives in actively migrating dunes, but with its great sand-trapping capacity tends to slow the movement of the sand.

islands and mainland dunes from Cape Cod to Cape Hatteras. There also are quite dense stands of them on Sandy Hook, New Jersey (where a virulent and abundant strain of poison-ivy discourages foot traffic off the trails and provides some protection for the cactus).

Woolly hudsonia, well equipped to cope with the intense heat of summer on the dunes, is an evergreen flowering plant. It retains its scalelike leaves in winter, but during that season the plant is somewhat dormant. The winter foliage—brittle, dry, and dull grayish olive —contrasts with the bright green of the pitch pines with which which it is sometimes associated. A spring rain, however, can revive the hudsonia with surprising suddenness. Several dune plants share this phenomenon with many plants that grow in desert regions.

Woolly hudsonia's survival adaptations combined with its habit of dense growth make it a most important plant. No other species has its sand-trapping capacity— a fact easily confirmed by anyone traversing the dunes in its range (from Cape Cod south, almost to Cape Hatteras), where a related species, *Lechea villosa*, grows.

The Dune-and-Swale Zone   155

This effective dune builder and stabilizer is significant in minimizing erosion by storm overwash and is a controlling factor in the landward migration of barrier islands.

Some dune plants, belonging to genera that normally have dry, fibrous stems, in this environment possess succulent, fleshy stems in which they can store water. Seaside goldenrod, with a stout, succulent stem and often fleshy leaves as well, grows along the Atlantic coast; its inland relatives lack these adaptations.

Dune Migration and Plants

Where vegetation, artificial barriers, or both are insufficient to slow the transport of barrier-beach or mainland sands, dunes migrate in the direction of the prevailing winds. The great Henlopen dune, which not many years ago was advancing rapidly inland, has now been largely immobilized by grasses, shrubs, and trees. But in some areas, such as the tip of Cape Cod, dunes are moving rapidly enough to create control problems. On Cape Cod the Provinceland dunes were formerly well vegetated and stabilized. But removal of the conifers in the last century began a destabilization process, and so far efforts to reverse the trend have had limited success. An *Ammophila*-planting program has been part of the restoration program, along with attempts to limit or ban the use of over-sand vehicles by commercial and private operators in the dunelands.

A migrating dune can overwhelm trees in its path; many trees are killed when they are partially or completely buried. But some, with enough of their crowns remaining above the sand, continue to grow, and they may hang on to life until the dune has passed them.

One might be puzzled to see mushrooms growing near the crest of the dune, where conditions could be expected to be too dry. Their occurrence is sometimes the result of the burial of a tree whose rotting trunk reaches almost to the surface. Capillary action enables water to move up through the wood from the roots many feet below, even though the tree is dead. The mycelium of the fungus (its vegetative body of fine threads), growing in the wet, decaying wood near the surface, produces fruiting bodies (the mushrooms) where the dryness and shifting sands preclude the growth of most plants. Termite colonies may dwell in the buried tree trunks, as well.

Animals of the Dune-and-Swale Zone

ARACHNIDS AND INSECTS

Animals, being mobile, have a greater variety of means than plants for coping with the harsh physical conditions prevailing in the dunelands. Many of them simply stay underground or under vegetative cover during the day, foraging or hunting only at night, or perhaps being most active near daybreak and sunset. Burrowing **wolf spiders** *(Geolycosa* spp.) can dig as deep as 3 ft. (1 m) to relatively cool sand. Like most of their relatives (Lycosidae) they are nocturnal; they spend the day at the bottom of the burrow.

To find the entrance of a wolf spider's home, look for a pencil-sized hole with the sand grains cemented together with silk. In good weather the spider may bring its egg sac to the entrance to be incubated in the sun.

82. Wolf spider *(Geolycosa missouriensis)* at its burrow.

But your best chance to see the spider is to go into the dunes at night, when it ventures forth in search of insect prey. Take a flashlight; the spider is the color of sand, but its four larger eyes (of a total of eight) will shine brightly as green points in your flashlight beam.

Wolf spiders, menacing enough to insects upon which they prey, are harmless to humans and, in fact, make interesting pets. But they are terrorized by large wasps of the family Pompilidae, which seek out the spiders, deliver paralyzing stings, and lay their eggs upon the arachnids' bodies. When the pompilid larvae hatch, they feed on the immobilized spiders. The warfare is not entirely one-sided, however; sometimes the spider puts up enough of a fight to make a well matched contest of the encounter.

From Fire Island south, the ambiguously named **velvet ants** (family Mutilidae) inhabit the dunelands, ranging over the sands during all but the hottest hours of the day. These insects actually are not ants but were so named because the females lack wings and appear somewhat antlike. (They are more stout-bodied than ants.) Velvet ants, like the true ants (Formicidae), are but one of many families, including bees, hornets, ichneumons, various "wasp" families, sawflies, and others that make up the order Hymenoptera. The order includes more than 100,000 species of four-winged insects.

The "velvet" part of the name derives from the dense coat of hairs that covers these insects, which are often brightly colored. This protective coat, like that of dusty miller, enables the velvet ant to withstand the hot summer sun as it goes about the business of feeding and the task of laying its eggs in the burrows of other insects —including wasps. When the temperature at the surface of the dune nears 120° F (50° C) the velvet ant seeks the shade of plants. This horizontal migration is the means by which many dune animals excape extreme temperatures.

The larva of the **tiger beetle** *(Cicindela lepida),* like that of the wolf spider, lives in a vertical burrow. Adult tiger beetles avoid the extremes of summer heat by evasion; they are highly mobile animals. But the larva is a different case; its burrow is shallow, barely beneath

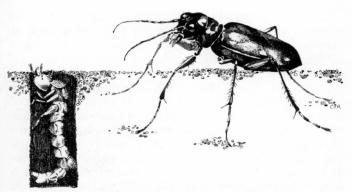

83. Adult tiger beetle (*Cicindela* sp.) and larva in burrow.

the surface, and it obtains its food by waiting for insects to pass the entrance. Its very large, sand-colored head, bent at right angles to its body, neatly plugs the entrance of the burrow, with the powerful mandibles extending upward and spread open. In this position, it readily catches unwary passersby. On a hump of its fifth abdominal segment the larva has two sharp, forward-directed hooks that it thrusts into the wall of the burrow as an anchor, aiding in the capture of insects much larger than itself. With its head thus exposed, the *Cicindela* larva needs insulation. What it has is minimal—a sparse coat of white hairs that help to reflect the sun's rays. But it is apparently tolerant of or resistant to overheating, since it dwells successfully in the uppermost, hottest layer of sand.

When the tiger beetle larva is mature, it closes the burrow and pupates. Emerging in spring, the adult is an active, diurnal beetle—a long-legged runner and a strong flier. Capturing this alert, nimble-footed, swift-winged creature is no cinch. With large, bulbous eyes it has keen sight; it can travel fast over the ground; and if it takes to the air it will land facing its pursuer. If you manage to get one despite these difficulties, be careful! The enormous mandibles are sharp-pointed and armed with teeth, and the beetle can deliver a painful bite. *Cicindela,* as both larva and adult, is a formidable member of the dune community.

The Dune-and-Swale Zone

In most terrestrial environments, the base of the food pyramid is quite evidently green vegetation such as grasses, forbs, and trees. In the duneland habitat, almost all the animals seem to be either preying upon or parasitizing each other. Nevertheless, there are those here, too, that eat plants. The box turtle is a case in point; an omnivore, this reptile feeds on green plants, fungi, and insects and other invertebrates. And there are a number of strictly vegetarian animals. Among these are grasshoppers. The **sand locust** *(Trimerotropis maritima),* a member of the short-horned grasshopper family (Acrididae), is so close to the sand in color that it is unlikely to be noticed until it flies. When not feeding on the plants it often rests on the sand, rising high on its legs to avoid the hot surface. It can also cool off by taking short flights.

Ants (Formicidae), the most ubiquitous of dune animals, are less directly but just as surely dependent upon plants. They are primarily feeders on other animals—which they take dead or alive—that are themselves herbivores. Some ants also herd aphids, much as humans herd cows, for the "honeydew" they secrete. The aphids feed upon the juices of green plants and are given tender loving care by the ants. Because the ants make tunnels and underground chambers, they can avoid the physical stresses of the dune environment.

The abundant ants are an important part of the diet of many species of larger animals. Among the ant-eating birds to be found in or along the edges of the dunes are the savannah sparrow, song sparrow, northern flicker, gray catbird, northern mockingbird, red-winged blackbird, and rufous-sided towhee. The most interesting duneland ant predator is a little-known insect with a well known name, the **doodlebug.** It is actually not a bug, but the larva of the **antlion** *(Myrmeleon immaculatus).* The careful observer will notice many curious little tracks winding erratically about, up hill and down dale, looking much as though someone had aimlessly dragged a pointed stick over the surface. These tracings, at times very abundant, are made by the larva as it travels molelike and seemingly without a sense of direction just under the surface. At one end of the trail will be found a small mound, under which one can discover the larva; or, if it has chosen its hunting station, there will be a small, conical pit, its sides at the maximum angle of repose, so that at the least disturbance sand grains slide down to the bottom. This pit is the ingenious trap in which the antlion larva captures its prey.

Waiting just under the sand at the bottom of the pit is the doodlebug, a harmless-looking insect except for the pair of pincerlike jaws with which it is armed. To see the larva one must lie down on the sand, for it is protectively colored, and all that remains in view are the sharp tips of the jaws. To see it in action, one can drop an ant (or other small insect) into the pit. As it scrambles to escape, sand grains slide down the slope, hampering the ant's attempts to get a foothold. The doodlebug further hinders the ant by throwing up sand grains with its head —creating a miniature volcanic crater. Sooner or later —in the usual scenario—the ant falls into the waiting jaws of the larva. Once within the doodlebug's grasp it is not likely to escape; the antlion, which moves backward more readily than forward, tugs hard to hold its victim. The ant is then injected with a paralyzing fluid that liquifies its tissues, and it is soon sucked dry. The doodlebug is not selective in its diet, but ants are the most abundant insects walking over the dunes, and are therefore the most likely to tumble into the pit.

After a year or two the antlion larva, which has grown gradually on its insect-juice diet, undergoes metamorphosis. The adult antlion, unlike its voracious offspring (or former self), is a fragile-looking, graceful insect resembling a damselfly. (It belongs to the same order as the delicately beautiful lacewings.) The adult antlion does not feed at all, and lives only long enough to lay its eggs in the sand for a new generation of doodlebugs.

There are many predatory flying insects in the dune community. Among the commonest are the **sand wasps,** members of the subfamily Nyssoninae of the order Hymenoptera. The subfamily alone contains nearly a thousand known species. The best known genus is *Bembix.* All bembicids nest in soil, and generally in soil that is sandy. One species with a wide distribution in eastern

84. Sand wasp *(Bembix spinolae)*.

North America is *B. spinolae,* which despite the study that has been devoted to it has not been honored with a common name of its own. It is generally referred to as "sand wasp" or "digger wasp"—names equally applicable to hundreds of its cousins.

The female *Bembix* digs a burrow in the dune sand in which to lay her egg (single, not plural—for *Bembix* has nature's smallest brood). Because she performs her labors by day, not even taking a siesta during the midday heat, one can watch the part of the process that takes place above ground. Except for a brief respite after laying her egg in the completed burrow, *Bembix* occupies herself with digging, hunting, and provisioning her fast-growing young. All the work must be carried out by sight. Few creatures raising multiple offspring work harder to raise a family. The male *Bembix* plays no role in nesting; the female must perform all the household duties, as well as doing the hunting to feed the larva.

Bembix does not maintain more than one brood nest at a time. A new nest is dug only after she finally closes a burrow that has been fully provisioned for the larva. In the initial stages of digging a burrow the wasp is exposed to the high temperatures at the surface of the sand. Lacking the insulating hairs of the velvet ant, *Bembix* must utilize other means to avoid overheating. When she is starting the burrow she hovers in the air over the sand, then drops vertically and digs furiously for a moment. Then she rises above the superheated layer of air adjacent to the surface for a quick cooling off, before dropping again to make another pass at excavation. Eventually the burrow reaches a cooler layer of sand, and the wasp can remain there to finish the job.

But the wasp's domestic preparations do not end with the completion of digging. Like hunting wasps everywhere, she must provide for the young that will hatch from the egg; wasp larvae do not forage on growing plants as do most caterpillars, nor do they embark immediately upon a predatory career as do young mantids. So immediately upon completing the burrow the sand wasp courses over the dune in search of a fly. Any fly will do. A most efficient fly hunter, the wasp returns in a few minutes with the first victim, which is taken into the burrow. After laying an egg on the dead fly, *Bembix* temporarily closes the burrow and begins a three-day holiday. When the egg hatches, the wasp larva will quickly consume the fly, and it is time for the parent to reprovision the nursery. As the larva grows, the tasks of providing it with food and keeping the burrow and entranceway clean become more time consuming. She may bring in a fly every 5 to 15 minutes during the day. Between trips she keeps the burrow closed; while she is occupied with reopening it, she must also remain alert for hijackers. In a few days the larva pupates. The grub spins an intricate cocoon, suspended like a hammock, lined with a masonry of sand and coated outside with a thick varnish. In this the adult wasp plays no role, for her job as a parent is finished.

More often than not there are hitches in these proceedings. While one female *Bembix* is opening the burrow to feed her grub, another female of the species may steal her fly. Furthermore, living on the dunes is a red-eyed fly that, unwilling or unable to dig and provision its own burrow, foists its young upon the sand wasp. One or more of these flies may be waiting near the entrance of the burrow when the wasp returns with a dead fly. This great fly hunter does her best to outmaneuver them, but before she can get safely into the burrow with her burden they often manage to lay an egg or eggs upon the fly intended for the wasp larva.

The Dune-and-Swale Zone

The fly larvae that hatch from these eggs compete with the wasp grub for food, endangering its survival; to add injury to insult, they sometimes devour the wasp grub itself. Through these agents the sand wasp, dependent upon flies for its existence, is in peril of extinction by flies. Why this skilled fly killer does not attack the flies that victimize it is one of the mysteries of nature.

Bembix spinolae has still another formidable foe—the velvet ant, which also lays its egg in the wasp's burrow. The velvet ant's larva will feed upon the sand wasp's larva. Perhaps the greatest mystery is how *B. spinolae* can survive as a species, given its habit of laying only one egg at a time and the fact that it must suffer such enemies as velvet ants and red-eyed flies.

COLD-BLOODED VERTEBRATES

Reptiles are easily enough pictured as inhabitants of the shifting duneland sands, since they are an important part of the desert fauna. Amphibians, usually associated with moist environments, are less expected here. With a coastal distribution (from Massachusetts to North Carolina) corresponding neatly to the range covered by this book, **Fowler's toad** *(Bufo woodhousei*

85. Fowler's toad, Fire Island.

fowleri) is the characteristic amphibian in the dune-lands. As a cold-blooded animal, with a body temperature responding to its immediate surroundings, the toad must avoid overexposure to direct sunlight and to the surface of the dune during the heat of midday. And like most amphibians it must seek bodies of fresh water at breeding time. This has eliminated some of the barrier beaches from its habitat. Along most of this coast, however, there are temporary pools, ponds, and fresh marshes enough for its breeding needs, and it either finds shade or buries itself deep in the sand during the hottest hours. The female Fowler's toad lays some 8,000 eggs at a time, so even a low survival rate will ensure the continuation of the species. It also benefits from some degree of protection offered by its coloration, which blends with the sandy environment. Its chief enemy in the dunelands is the hognose snake, for which this amphibian is the staple diet. The primary food of Fowler's toad is insects. These are secured by a sticky tongue, attached to the floor of the toad's mouth at the front end and free at the rear, which it flicks forward to snap up its living prey.

As the Fowler's toad is for its class of vertebrates, the **eastern hognose snake** *(Heterodon platyrhinos)* is the characteristic species of reptile in the coastal dunelands. Its range begins, like that of the toad, in northeastern Massachusetts and continues past Cape Hatteras. (It's a good bet that the **southern toad** *(Bufo terrestris)*, which is abundant in sandy areas, replaces Fowler's toad in the hognose's diet south of Cape Hatteras all the way to the tip of Florida, where both of their ranges end.) In the Middle Atlantic range, Fowler's toad and the hognose snake share the same habitats, a fact that is probably no mere coincidence. The hognose is often easier to find, for it can be tracked over the sand, to be discovered sometimes in the open and sometimes hiding under a clump of hudsonia or bearberry. It is primarily diurnal. Besides toads, its diet includes frogs and tadpoles. Young hognoses eat insects.

One's first encounter with the hognose snake is likely to be a startling experience, for its response to the approach of a human is an apparently belligerent—but actually totally defensive—set of maneuvers. Spreading

86. Hognose snake in defensive posture, with head
flattened cobralike, poised to "strike."

its neck cobra fashion, the hognose opens its mouth
wide, hisses menacingly, and strikes repeatedly. The
strikes, however, invariably fall short of the mark; but
even if the hognose did make contact, its bite would be
harmless, for it is nonpoisonous. The entire performance, in any event, is a bluff. If one stands one's ground

87. The same hognose snake a few moments later, "playing
dead."

THE ECOLOGY OF BARRIER ISLANDS

the snake resorts to another ruse: it suddenly rolls over onto its back with its mouth gaping wide, in a most realistic imitation of death. But turn the snake right side up, and it immediately flops over onto its back again. The snake may repeat this many times before it abandons its routine. This performance undoubtedly has survival value; but one wonders how such a defensive behavior pattern evolved, and why it is not observed elsewhere in nature.

Also making corkscrewlike tracks across the dune sands in this range is the **milk snake** *(Lampropeltis doliata).* (The subspecies occurring in North Carolina is called **scarlet king snake.**) This is a medium-sized constrictor, feeding on rodents and any other small animals it can capture—probably including small hognose snakes. Snakes of this genus vibrate their tails rapidly when disturbed, and if they are in dry leaves this makes a sound resembling that of a rattler. This behavior may have survival value; but it is surely unconscious and not mimicry; snakes cannot hear.

The **black racer** *(Coluber constrictor),* common on Cape Cod and Cape Hatteras and in many areas between, also cruises over the dunes and grasslands. Like the hognose and milk snakes, it is diurnal, and it must therefore seek shade at times. The black racer is not a constrictor; it has a wide-ranging diet that includes insects, rodents, birds, and other reptiles. Found in other coastal habitats as well, it is a good climber that may take to the trees when pursued.

A few other species of snakes, while not as characteristic of the dunes as are the hognose and milk snakes, are often found there. Among these are the **garter snake**

88. Garter snake *(Thamnophis sirtalis).*

The Dune-and-Swale Zone 167

89. Six-lined racerunner *(Cnemiodophorus sexlineatus)*.

(Thamnophis sirtalis), which ranges from Cape Cod to North Carolina, though it is not known on the Outer Banks; and the **ribbon snake** *(T. sauritus),* which shares the same general range but is found on Bodie and Hatteras Islands.

Most lizards tend to restrict their wanderings, sticking close to shade in which they can cool off; but some do inhabit the dunes. The **six-lined racerunner** *(Cnemidophorus sexlineatus),* in fact, prefers open areas. It is found on the Outer Banks, and on the Currituck Banks just to the north, as well as in Back Bay National Wildlife Refuge in southeastern Virginia, in the scrub zone of the dune habitat and even sometimes on the foredune. *Cnemidophorus* does not climb trees and shrubs; it escapes by running fast, either outstripping its pursuer or taking refuge under vegetation or other cover. Like most lizards, it is an insectivore. Belonging to the family of whiptails—the Teiidae—the racerunner is somewhat skinklike in form, but it is easily distinguished by its dull appearance. (The shiny skinks prefer moist habitats and are likely to occur in the eastern coastal dunes only in forest zones.)

Another reptile sharing the racerunner's affinity for dunes—preferring tall and thick grass—is the **glass lizard** *(Ophisaurus ventralis).* It is found only from the Currituck Banks south. Commonly called the "glass snake," this legless lizard has movable eyelids and external ear openings, which snakes never have. Because its brittle tail, which is very long—a 36-in. (0.9 m) specimen having a tail of about 25 in. (0.6 m)—breaks off easily, this lizard seems to be as fragile as if made of glass. It is easy to imagine the survival value of such a characteristic; a hawk that seized a glass lizard by its middle would end up with only the tail or a portion of it. The head and body part would grow a short new sharply pointed tail. But the tail-shedding adaptation, found in many lizards, in this case is fully effective only once, since the regenerated part is a mere suggestion of the original long tail.

Besides insects, glass lizards prey upon other lizards and small snakes. The record eastern glass lizard is 37.5 in. (0.95 m); this makes it, next to the more southerly **slender glass lizard** *(Ophisaurus attenuatus)*, which grows as long as 42 in. (1.1 m), the longest lizard in the United States.

The most familiar reptile of the dunes is everybody's favorite, the **box turtle** *(Terrapene carolina)*, found throughout the Middle Atlantic region. The only turtle one can expect to encounter in the dune-and-swale environment, it is also found in thickets and forested areas. Its varied diet, including fungi, insects, and berries, and its ability to burrow beneath the surface to avoid extreme heat enable it to function well in this stressful habitat.

The box turtle lays only two to seven eggs. But this slow-moving reptile may live through several dozen breeding seasons. It has a few enemies, but is highly vulnerable only in the early stages of life. The thin-shelled eggs, which are buried in a shallow cavity in the ground, are dug up by raccoons and skunks. Hatching out after three months, the 1.2-in. (30 mm) young turtles are subject to predation by snakes, snapping turtles, and carnivorous mammals and birds. As they approach maturity, however, they are increasingly well protected by their hard, strong shells, which they can close tightly so that no fleshy parts are exposed.

The wide-ranging diet of the box turtle enables it to find food in a variety of habitats and at all seasons, but, being a cold-blooded animal, it must hibernate in the northern part of its range. This it does by digging well down into the ground—a relatively easy task in the duneland sands. Before hibernating it may become so fat that it can't close its shell tightly, making it at that time somewhat more vulnerable.

Terrapene carolina is a familiar sight on the Middle Atlantic coast. Its lack of wariness makes it easy to discover; it is one of the few wild vertebrates that with little effort one can observe going about its normal business. Generally the turtle withdraws into its shell upon the close approach of a human, but if one stands back and waits a moment it will soon emerge and resume its leisurely foraging for food. The photographer needs no stalking skills to catch this animal on film.

BIRDS

Warm-blooded animals, because they have temperature-regulating mechanisms and are generally highly mobile, abound in the dune-and-swale zone; but they may not be conspicuous to the casual observer. The birds of this environment are diurnal in their habits. Mostly they are visitors from nearby habitats or are species that rest and feed here during migration. A few find nesting sites in the dunes; very few are year-round residents.

An unexpected nester in the dunes is the **American black duck** *(Anas rubripes)*. As lacking in discrimination as the mallard, the black duck will raise its young in almost any site on the ground that offers concealment, as well as in holes and crotches of trees and snags —or even in abandoned crow or hawk nests. But despite this casual choice of breeding sites, the nests are not always easy to find. For example, where procumbent pitch pines and other shrubby growth provide ideal cover, one might search in vain for the nest of ducks seen in the vicinity. During the breeding season pairs of blacks are indeed sometimes seen in the dunes. Other than berries and seeds of some of the plants, which are not a major item of diet for black ducks, there is little to attract them to this habitat other than potential nesting sites.

90. Savannah sparrow *(Passerculus sandwichensis)*.

Some shorebirds, gulls, and terns nest in transition zones between the beach and the dunes. Bird species that both feed and nest in the dunes are rather few. Perhaps the most typical is the **savannah sparrow,** *Passerculus sandwichensis.* Also inhabiting the upper edges of the salt marsh, the savannah sparrow is seen year round north of Delaware Bay but is primarily a wintering bird on the southern coast. It nests on the ground, in a hollow under vegetation. The nest is made of fine grasses with a lining of hair or rootlets. Like most members of the finch family, the savannah sparrow is primarily a seed eater. It also consumes many insects. *Ammophila* seeds make up about a third of its diet, with panicgrass *(Panicum* spp.) being of lesser importance. The flight of this bird helps in identification; undulating and zigzagging for a short distance, the savannah sparrow ends its flight with a sudden drop into the grass. Occasionally it does alight briefly on a shrub or tree, but it spends most of its time on the ground. It is often possible to approach this sparrow quite closely to confirm its identity.

Similar in appearance to the savannah sparrow is the **song sparrow,** whose habitat overlaps that of the savannah. The song sparrow, however, favors thickets and brushy dunes rather than the grassy areas chosen by the other. It is seen throughout the year on this stretch of coast, but is more common in winter, when northern birds of this species are present. Its food habits, similar to those of the savannah sparrow, are discussed in detail later in this chapter under The Thicket Zone.

The **mourning dove** *(Zenaida macroura),* another seed eater, is found the year around along this entire coast. In the dunes it eats seeds of panicgrass and other herbaceous plants. It is perhaps the most strictly vegetarian of any of the region's birds; the rare traces of insects that turn up in studies of its diet are probably ingested accidentally. The mourning dove usually builds a very crude nest of sticks in a tree, but sometimes it nests on the ground.

A number of insectivorous species that are generally associated with shrub-thicket or forest communities are more easily seen when they occur in the dune-and-swale zone, where they are less shielded by cover. Thus, on Fire Island, the **gray catbird,** which is never found far from dense shrubbery or forest undergrowth and normally is more often heard than seen, is perhaps the most conspicuous bird of the dune-and-swale zone. And here the **yellow warbler,** whose breeding range embraces all of this coastal area but the Outer Banks, ventures into the open from the shrubbier zones where it nests. **Brown thrashers** and **northern mockingbirds** (year-round residents of this coast) are not restricted to thickets, and they are seen commonly in the more open zones. The **rufous-sided towhee,** another bird of the bushy thickets, also inhabits the forest community, and it is often seen in the transition zone between dune-and-swale and shrub-thicket communities.

In this edge habitat, or ecotone, indeed, the greatest variety of plant species combines with good visibility to provide the best birdwatching. Ants are very abundant here, and the thrasher, mockingbird, catbird, towhee, and savannah and song sparrows all feed on these insects. The black cherry and other wild cherries, which grow along the entire coast and are often part of the edge habitat, are eaten by catbirds, mockingbirds, thrashers, and towhees.

The visitor to the barrier islands who wants to see the birds should take note: they are most active, and most likely to sing, in early morning hours.

MAMMALS

Most of the mammals that hunt and forage for food in the dunes are nocturnal; thus, their presence in this habitat is most often revealed by their tracks in the sand. Some of them spend the day in nearby thickets or forest; some remain underground until dark. The best time to observe their tracks, which crisscross the dunes in bewildering profusion, is in early morning before the wind obscures them. Most abundant are those of deer, cottontails, foxes, and small rodents.

There are the tiny, erratic tracks of voles. Those of the white-tailed deer are unmistakable, and not quickly obliterated by wind-blown sands. The dainty tracks of the red fox, notable for the fact that, running or walking, it places one foot directly in line with the other and thus makes a trail only about 3 in. (8 cm) wide, wander unendingly over the dunes. Cottontails themselves, as well as their distinctive tracks, are frequently seen, particularly in early morning. Easily recognized are the five-toed, handlike prints of the raccoon. This is perhaps the only mammal besides the white-footed mouse that frequents all land habitats of the barrier islands and mainland seashores, and it is the only one of these two species that ventures into the waters of the estuaries and marshes. (The white-footed mouse does occupy the marsh, but it prefers to keep out of the water.)

If one follows the trail of the **raccoon** *(Procyon lotor)* long enough it will generally lead back into the thickets or forest where its den is located. Or the trail may disappear on the beach where incoming tide has erased the signs of its beachcombing activities. Raccoons are catholic in their tastes; everything from insects to fruits, as well as the leavings of picnickers and campers, is devoured; but they are especially partial to aquatic animals—frogs, mollusks, crustaceans, and fish. With few enemies but man, and of late becoming overabundant in some of the protected areas along the coast, the raccoon now constitutes an ecological and management problem. It is particularly a threat to the survival of endangered sea turtles, whose eggs it may dig up and devour on the very night they are laid. It probably spends little time in the open dunes and grasslands but

91. An adult red fox on an early morning hunt in the dunes of Fire Island.

forages on the way across them when going to and returning from the beach.

The **red fox** *(Vulpes fulva)*, which not only hunts in the dunes but lives and raises its family there, is also primarily nocturnal in its habits. But the early bird can often get a glimpse of a fox as it roams over the dunes around daybreak. If a den is located, the springtime visitor can observe the fox family sunning and playing at the entrance. Intrusion into the foxes' domain may cause them to move to another site. This calls for discretion and a pair of binoculars, along with respect for the foxes' right to be left alone in their natural habitat.

Red foxes are no less promiscuous in their eating habits than raccoons, except for the penchant of the latter for eating our leftovers. They are less adept than raccoons at capturing aquatic animals, but they can and do run down cottontails in the dunes and manage to find food in a variety of habitats. Besides any small animals they can capture, they eat acorns and other fruits of dune plants, including bayberry, waxmyrtle, wild cherry, and Virginia creeper. They can be quite destructive of ground-nesting birds, and in some wildlife refuges and other managed preserves along the coast foxes are controlled for waterfowl protection. Trapping and poisoning are used for this. On the other side of the score sheet, the red fox is a major control on rabbit and rodent populations. A far greater threat to ducks, geese, and shorebirds is the continuing attrition of suitable habitat through human activities. Shrinking wetlands and lowering water tables make nesting sites both scarcer and more accessible to other species that compete with or prey upon aquatic birds. All in all, loss of habitat and increasing disturbance by hordes of people and their vehicles affect the waterfowl populations more than does predation. In a healthy, undisturbed natural environment carnivores such as foxes are important links in the food web—balancing in their influence rather than destructive.

An abundance of small mammal footprints on the dunes attests to the presence of rodents, but identifying the authors of these markings is not easy. Nothing short of a live-trapping program can establish the makeup of this component of the community. The **white-footed mouse** *(Peromyscus leucopus)*, America's most widely distributed mammal, makes tracks too delicate to imprint clearly on the sand; but they can often be identified where the animal has run across the muddy edge of a duneland puddle. An omnivore, this rodent eats seeds of many herbaceous plants, the kernels in wild black cherry pits, acorns, blueberries, holly fruits, grasshoppers, beetles, and centipedes. Although itself the prey of many birds, raccoons, foxes, snakes, and weasels, it is a most prolific animal, bearing several litters each year. This adaptable little animal will nest in any nook or hole it can locate, and sometimes even roofs over an abandoned bird nest as a home for its offspring.

The **meadow vole** *(Microtus pensylvanicus)*, commonly called "field mouse," differs greatly in appearance from the white-footed mouse. *Peromyscus,* as befits its nocturnal way of life, has great black eyes and big ears; and its tail is long. It is altogether an endearing little mammal. In contrast, *Microtus* is active both day and night, although it favors the early morning and late afternoon hours. It is much larger than the white-footed mouse, but its beady eyes, its small ears almost hidden in the dense fur, and its short tail add up to a less prepossessing creature. More of a vegetarian than the mouse, it lives almost entirely on herbivorous plants, tender

The Dune-and-Swale Zone

bark, grass shoots, rootstocks, and various seeds. Some of its close relatives are known to consume snails, caterpillars, centipedes, and other invertebrate life; but the degree to which *M. pensylvanicus* utilizes this food resource is not known for certain. Because these voles chew their food well, stomach analyses are difficult. Goldenrod is on their known list of foods and, along with grass seeds, can be presumed a part of the meadow vole's diet in the dunes.

One of the conditions the meadow vole has in common with the white-footed mouse is a long list of enemies. In the dunes this includes hawks, owls, red foxes, weasels, raccoons, and snakes. More vulnerable than *Peromyscus,* owing in part to its diurnal habits, the meadow vole has an effective survival mechanism; it is very prolific—in fact, among American mammals it is the champion for reproductive capacity. One (captive) female produced 17 litters in a single year, and one of her offspring had 13 litters before her first birthday. Even in the wild, *Microtus* sometimes breeds throughout the winter. Its role in the natural community—turning vegetable matter into flesh for carnivores—can hardly be overassessed.

The **white-tailed deer** *(Odocoileus virginianus)* ranges freely over the barrier islands, from the salt

92. Three white-tailed deer feeding at dawn in the beach-plum thicket on the crest of the foredune at daybreak (Watch Hill, Fire Island).

marsh to the ocean beach. Its tracks are often seen in dunes where the grasses are mixed with woody shrubs; but the deer are less likely to be spotted in predominantly grassy dunes, for this animal is a browser (a feeder on woody plants) rather than a grazer (eater of grass and other herbaceous plants). It is abundant on some of the barrier islands, such as Assateague and Hatteras, and on Cape Cod; and there is a substantial population on Fire Island, where it is most readily seen during seasons when fewer humans are present.

Among the plants favored by whitetails in the dune-and-swale and the ecotone between it and the shrub zone are wild black cherry, American holly, bearberry, and huckleberry. The deer eats acorns of the scrubby oaks that grow in this zone, and has been known to eat bayberry, waxmyrtle, goldenrod, and sandbur. Another barrier island plant on its diet is *Phragmites*, which is found in the dune-and-swale only in some wet sites. This very mobile animal finds food in many habitats, and its food habits in the shrub thickets and maritime forests are discussed in the sections on those communities. The whitetail often uses the ecotone between open duneland and thicket as a travel route to avoid the dense vegetation of the shrubland and forest understory. This is a good place to look for the deer. At night it travels in the dune-and-swale or along the beach on the ocean or bayside for even easier movement.

Like the whitetail, the **cottontail** *(Sylvilagus floridanus)* finds a greater variety of food plants in the brushy edges where grassland and thicket habitats merge. But this herbivorous animal is often seen in the open dunelands. Both a browser and a grazer, it feeds on herbaceous plants and on the twigs and bark of woody plants. Dune plants eaten include panicgrass and other grasses, seaside goldenrod, wild black cherry, Virginia creeper, and acorns where scattered oaks grow, as at Cape Henlopen.

The cottontail is common on barrier islands and in mainland seashore habitats. It is active chiefly at night, but is often observed feeding during the hours after dawn and before dusk. In the dunes it may wait out the hot hours of the day in its *form* (resting place) under a

93. The eastern cottontail inhabits a wide range of habitats from marshland to forest.

clump of vegetation, sleeping but ready to dash from its hiding place if discovered by a predator. And its enemies are many: red foxes, raccoons, and other carnivores; and birds of prey such as the great horned owl. Young rabbits are preyed upon by crows, large snakes, and weasels. The cottontail's defense is a fast getaway and enough speed to outpace its pursuer. This animal requires good cover in any habitat; the dense thickets of greenbrier found on barrier islands such as Assateague are undoubtedly a boon to the cottontail.

Dunes of the Mainland Shore

On coastal mainland dunes, physical conditions are similar to those on barrier islands, but oceanic influences are not as marked. Because of greater human impact, a lesser degree of biological isolation, and a longer history of development, the mainland dunes are not as extensive and have a less distinctive biological component. With the exception of a few locations, such as Cape Henlopen, Delaware; Sandy Hook, New Jersey; and Cape Cod, where some of the dunes have been

protected by public agencies as parkland, the opportunities to study a natural coastal-dune ecosystem are
limited to barrier islands. But most of the phenomena
discussed in the foregoing sections apply equally to life
on dunes of the mainland shore. Both plant and animal
species tend to be more diverse on the mainland, since
isolation is not complete there and physical conditions
are somewhat moderated. (Temperature extremes, on
the other hand, are greater than on the ocean-
moderated islands.) Appendix I lists a number of these
accessible and rewarding mainland dune areas remaining in relatively unspoiled condition, as well as the barrier islands accessible to the public by auto or boat.

The Thicket Zone

The thicket zone is a band of dense shrub growth between the grassland and the maritime forest or, in the
absence of a forest community, sometimes extending
from the lee side of the foredune all the way to the
bayside high marsh. Sometimes it is a mere ecotone a
few yards wide between the dune-and-swale community and the maritime forest or the bay. Where it is
clearly distinguishable from adjacent zones it can be
treated as a separate life community with an array of
animal and plant species unequalled elsewhere on the
barrier island. Because it contains plants and animals
characteristic of both the forest and the dune-and-
swale, as well as species whose normal habitat is shrubland, it is a densely populated community.

The distribution of shrub thicket and the form of its
growth are influenced by the wind and salt spray, and
this influence is reflected in the profile of the shrub
thicket along a transect at right angles to the trend of
the beach. For example, if the thicket community begins fairly close to the ocean, the first shrubs are likely
to be prostrate, and the thicket becomes progressively
taller toward the bayshore. The tops of these shrubs
tend to be closely sheared by windborne salt spray,
forming a smooth, compact canopy sloping upward

away from the ocean. When a single shrub or a clump of shrubs occurs in the dune-and-swale zone, it also tends to exhibit this characteristic form. An exception occurs where a pocket of shrub thicket grows in the lee of a high foredune; here, protected from the ocean winds, it may attain normal height and show no signs of salt-spray pruning.

Where a thicket association exists, physical conditions are more favorable for plants than they are in the dune-and-swale habitat. The thicket-zone soil is noticeably darker than the grassland's because of increased organic content derived from the cycle of death and decay. This improves the soil's water-retention capacity and makes available more mineral nutrients.

Among the woody plants closely identified with this zone are **northern bayberry** *(Myrica pensylvanica),* south to Virginia; and **southern bayberry,** or **waxmyrtle** *(M. cerifera),* from Cape May south. Other woody plants prominent in this zone include **black cherry** *(Prunus serotina);* several species of oaks, no one species of which is found along the entire coast; the ubiquitous **poison-ivy** *(Rhus radicans);* that eminently successful Asian invader **Japanese honeysuckle** *(Lonicera japonica);* **pitch pine** *(Pinus rigida),* from Cape

94. Northern bayberry *(Myrica pensylvanica).*

THE ECOLOGY OF BARRIER ISLANDS

95. Wild black cherry bears profuse blossoms in May on Ocracoke Island. This species of the shrub thickets throughout the Middle Atlantic coast is a tree in inland environments.

Henlopen north; **American holly** *(Ilex opaca);* and **yaupon holly** *(I. vomitoria),* on Currituck Banks and the Outer Banks.

A number of nonflowering and herbaceous flowering plants also are found in the thicket zone. Among these are **crowned earthstar** *(Geaster coronatus),* a fungus; **British soldiers,** or **red crest lichen** *(Cladonia cristatella);* **old man's beard** *(Usnea* spp.), a lichen; **sheep sorrel** *(Rumex acetosella);* and **wild sarsaparilla** *(Aralia nudicaulis).* A thicket may have only a few of the above species, and no thicket will have all of them; but this list is a starting point for examining any thicket in the range covered by this book.

For the wildlife watcher, the thicket community and the adjacent transition zone with the dune-and-swale offer rich rewards. Many of the above plants provide food for a number of birds and mammals, as well as insects. *Dendroica coronata,* the **yellow-rumped warbler** (formerly known as the **myrtle warbler**) is so adapted to a diet of waxmyrtle berries that, although this is normally a migratory species, many individuals

The Thicket Zone 181

96. The yellow-rumped warbler winters in southern bayberry (waxmyrtle) and northern bayberry thickets, feeding on the plentiful berries, on barrier islands and mainland coasts.

live year round on some of the barrier islands of the Middle Atlantic coast. The **song, field, and white-throated sparrows, northern cardinal, gray catbird, yellow warbler, brown thrasher, northern mockingbird, rufous-sided towhee, American robin, white-eyed vireo,** and **Carolina wren** are just a few of the other songbirds to be found in the thicket habitat. Also, some birds that do most of their feeding in more open areas, such as the **mourning dove** and **red-winged blackbird,** build their nests in the cover of the thicket.

Not only is the bird component of the barrier-island ecosystem most diverse in the thicket community; many of the species reach their greatest abundance in this zone. This reflects in part the great variety and abundance of plants that bear edible seeds and fruits. These and other plants valuable to bird life also support a large insect population, which is an important food resource for many birds. (Even seed eaters often feed insects to their nestlings.)

Table 5 shows the usefulness to a number of songbird species of some of the thicket plants' seeds and fruits. Box turtles eat them, too, as do white-footed mice and other small mammals; red foxes and raccoons eat the seeds and fruit and prey on the mice. Additionally, the buds, twigs, inner bark, and foliage of thicket trees, shrubs, and herbaceous plants provide sustenance for a host of animals, from caterpillars through the abundant cottontails to white-tailed deer. The whitetails often develop a network of trails through the thicket as a safe means of getting about during the day; at night they are likely to travel in more open zones. Generally, these trails are accessible to humans only if they are willing to go on hands and knees and put up with the thorny greenbriers so abundant in this habitat—to say nothing of the poison-ivy. The armored greenbrier vines that make the thicket impassable for us and that also create formidable barriers in the maritime forest are actually an item in the deer's diet. How the deer manage to eat them is not clear, but signs of browsing on these plants are commonplace (especially noticeable on Assateague Island, where more than one deer species occurs).

As well as providing cover for native mammals, the thickets also shelter feral cats—animals descended from pets abandoned by vacationers. These cats, which prey on native songbirds and small mammals, are considered undesirable aliens in this natural ecosystem and when abundant they can have a deleterious effect on wildlife

97. The sika, an alien deer from Japan, finds cover and food in the greenbrier thickets of Assateague Island.

The Thicket Zone

Thicket Fruits	Northern cardinal	Rufous-sided towhee	White-throated sparrow	Black-capped chickadee	Carolina wren
Waxmyrtle	X	X	X	X	
Bayberry	X	X	X	X	
Redcedar					
Poison-ivy	X	X	X	X	X
American holly		X	X	X	X
Greenbrier		X	X	X	X
Virginia creeper		X	X	X	X
Wild cherry		X	X	X	X
Blackberry		X	X	X	X
Serviceberry			X	X	X
Sassafras		X	X	X	
Black huckleberry			X		X
Highbush blueberry			X	X	X
Pitch & loblolly pine	X			X	
Sarsaparilla					
Honeysuckle					X
Oaks				X	
Wild grape		X	X	X	X
Blackgum		X		X	X

Shrubs Eaten by 15 Species of Birds

Cedar waxwing	Wood thrush	Red-eyed vireo	Purple finch	Fish crow	Yellow-rumped warbler	Northern mockingbird	Gray catbird	Brown thrasher	American robin
	X			X					
	X			X					X
X	X	X	X					X	
		X			X	X			
X		X			X	X			X
						X	X		
X	X	X			X	X		X	
X	X	X			X	X	X		X
X	X				X	X			
	X					X	X		
	X		X						
	X	X				X	X		X
	X		X	X					
		X				X			
		X						X	
	X								
X	X				X	X	X	X	X
					X	X	X	X	

populations. Feral cats have been known to exterminate populations of birds on islands—in some cases,
varieties found nowhere else in the world and consequently made extinct by this predation. On Assateague
the thicket zone and shrub thickets within the forest
shelter another alien, the introduced **sika** *(Cervus nip-
pon),* a Japanese deer, which seems particularly at
home in the greenbrier jungle.

Reptiles of the thicket include the **box turtle, hognose snake, black racer,** and **garter snake.** The Cape
Cod-to-Cape Hatteras coast lies within the range of
each of these species, and thus each is a potential inhabitant of the thickets of barrier islands and mainland
shores. The **milk snake** also occurs throughout most of
this coast, although it has not been recorded on the
Outer Banks. In food habits these species differ. The
diets of the box turtle and hognose snakes were discussed earlier in this chapter. The **northern black racer**
(Coluber c. constrictor) eats both vertebrates and invertebrates, and includes many rodents and birds in its
diet. The garter snake is as wide-ranging in its food
habits as in its choice of habitat; it devours invertebrates
and vertebrates alike, but it seems to favor amphibians
and even goes into the water to catch fish. In captivity,
it can be induced to eat dead fish or pieces of raw meat
—and thus makes a fairly easily kept pet—but whether
it scavenges in nature is doubtful. The milk snake is a
prime destroyer of small rodents, and except in the case
of young snakes unable to handle vertebrate prey, other
food is of minor importance for it.

Snakes, one of the few major groups of totally carnivorous vertebrates, prey upon (and are prey for) other
carnivores, as well as upon such herbivores as the
meadow vole. They thus occupy niches in the tertiary
and higher levels of the food pyramid. But none of the
snakes is a primary consumer—on the level occupied by
a wide array of insects, rodents, birds, and even some
reptiles (such as turtles).

The only animal among those mentioned above that
is strictly dependent on the thicket habitat is the **gray
catbird** *(Dumetella carolinensis).* This species is virtually never seen far from shrubby vegetation—the

denser and thornier the better. It does venture into the open duneland, but only within easy reach of its favored shrubby cover. It also occurs in the maritime forest, in pockets of understory thicket.

The Maritime Forest

By definition, a maritime forest is a community dominated by trees and under the influence of oceanic, salt-laden winds. It may be deciduous or evergreen, coniferous or broad-leaved, or a mixed forest. Frequently, it is characterized by thick-leaved evergreen species, somewhat dwarfed and flat-crowned owing to the effects of salt deposition, and marked on its seaward margins by strikingly pruned contours.

Many barrier islands are devoid of maritime-forest communities, though most have shrub thickets that exhibit to some degree the pruned appearance caused by wind-borne salt. Forests of tall loblolly pines growing less than a half-mile from the ocean beach on Assateague Island betray no visual effects of the maritime environment. These influences are, however, evident in varying degrees in Buxton Woods, a 3,000-acre (1,200-hectare) forest community on Hatteras Island. This forest, it should be noted, is in the middle of the widest section of barrier beach on the Atlantic coast; Hatteras Island at the town of Buxton is 3.2 mi. (5.2 km) across, measured from Cape Point to Pamlico Sound.

The Maritime Forest in Buxton Woods

Buxton Woods exhibits a diverse forest canopy, dominated by **live oak** *(Quercus virginiana)*, with subdominants **laurel oak** *(Q. laurifolia)*, **loblolly pine** *(Pinus taeda)*, **American holly** *(Ilex opaca)*, **flowering dogwood** *(Cornus florida)*, **redbay** *(Persea borbonia)*, and **ironwood** *(Carpinus caroliniana)*. This forest canopy is much richer in species than that of Fire Island's maritime forest, which is described in the section that fol-

98. This loblolly pine forest, the home of sikas and native wildlife, grows only 300 yards from the Assateague Island ocean beach, but exhibits few of the characteristics of the true maritime forest.

lows. In the normal course of events, however, Buxton Woods might be expected, through the process of natural selection, to become a live oak forest.

In Buxton Woods, only the trees on the seaward edge

and those growing on higher sites—that is, those most exposed to airborne salt—are pruned and distorted. Others, growing in sheltered spots in the old dunes (some of which exceed 55 ft., or 17 m, in elevation) have growth forms that are more typical for the species. The live oak, for example, in exposed sites is salt-pruned to a stunted, shrublike form; but within the forest it assumes a fair size. Also worth mentioning is an individual flowering dogwood in Buxton Woods with a trunk diameter of more than 1 ft. (31 cm).

Low spots in the forest contain swamps and small stagnant ponds. Shrubby areas are made into jungles by tangles of woody vines, including **greenbrier** *(Smilax* spp.) and **Virginia creeper** *(Parthenocissus quinquefolia)*. **Southern bayberry** *(Myrica cerifera)*, which is a common shrub on the open areas of the Outer Banks, here in the protection of the forest grows into a small tree.

Other prominent plants of the Buxton Woods understory are **yaupon holly** *(Ilex vomitoria)*; **beautyberry** *(Callicarpa americana)*, which grows north to Maryland; **Hercules-club** *(Aralia spinosa)*, which grows as either a shrub or a small tree and has been known to reach a height of 35 ft. (11 m)—though it doesn't find the conditions for such growth on the Outer Banks; and **southern prickly-ash** *(Xanthoxylum clava-herculis)*, related neither to the ashes nor to Hercules-club, though it has spiny stems like that plant.

Of special interest in Buxton Woods is a colony of **dwarf palmetto** *(Sabal minor)*. Thirty miles from the mainland, the colony enjoys a moderate climate (other than the notorious Cape Hatteras winds) and may be the northernmost stand of any palm in the eastern United States. This picturesque shrub produces a fruit, ripening in fall, that is eaten by a number of animals living in this forest, including the **American robin, yellow-rumped warbler** (occurring there fall through spring), **northern mockingbird, raccoon,** and probably the **fish crow** (which likely visits the forest, if it doesn't nest there).

The dense and diverse canopy and understory in much of Buxton Woods provides ample food and cover for wildlife. Because about 1,000 acres (405 hectares) are included in Cape Hatteras National Seashore, much of this prime habitat should endure. Unfortunately, a large part of the original forest has been destroyed or exploited by man, and cut-over areas show no signs of recovery even when abandoned to nature.

Some of the adaptations of the forest plants to the conditions of salt spray are mixed blessings. For example, waxy leaves or fruit (southern bayberry, for example) supply hot-burning fuel that intensifies the effect of wildfire. In periods of drought, fire invades even the marshes. Not all plants are destroyed by the fires; after the fire passes, having burned small plants to the ground, many resprout from their roots. Most of the larger trees survive, even though Cape Hatteras's winds tend to support fast-burning fires.

The Sunken Forest of Fire Island

Many miles north of Buxton Woods, beyond the direct influence of the Gulf Stream but still with a climate moderated by its situation between a wide lagoon and the sea, lies a barrier island with a much studied and heavily visited maritime forest. In the western sector of Fire Island National Seashore is the unique Sunken Forest, a prime attraction for vacationers and students. It is described here as a striking example of the influence of the ocean environment on the establishment and maturation of a forest community.

Transit of Fire Island from the ocean to the bayshore in the Sunken Forest area is facilitated by a boardwalk that serves a double purpose—protection of the environment and, for the visitor, avoidance of such hazards to health and comfort as greenbrier and poison-ivy. When, in traversing the dune-and-swale zone, one arrives at the top of the secondary dune, a striking contrast between the habitat just left and the one being met is revealed. In the swale behind, much of the ground surface is bare sand. Vegetation is generally scattered, except where a solid patch of bearberry provides a dense, ground-hugging cover. Up the seaward slope of the secondary dune the shrubby growth becomes denser and more diverse. At the crest it appears trimmed by a giant hedge clipper, as if in an attempt to make it conform to the contour of the dune. As one looks north toward Great South Bay, the intervening forest looks as though the hedge clipper, by shearing off all the trees at the same level, had been used to make a flat-topped canopy at the elevation of the secondary dune crest. One could almost imagine walking across the roof of this forest. No clue as to the nature of the terrain beneath it is visible; but when one walks down the back slope of the secondary dune into the forest, one discovers that the topography is uneven and hummocky. The bases of the trees are at widely varying elevations, though their tops are on the same level. Most of the trees are less than 20 ft. (6 m) in height.

Standing on the dunecrest on a day when there is a good onshore breeze, one notices that the wind is stronger here than it is in the swale. Down in the forest, the air is relatively still—ideal for mosquitos, if not for midsummer human visitors.

That salt-laden ocean breeze sweeping over the top of the secondary dune is responsible for the flatness of the forest roof. It has deposited minute particles of its salt burden on the topmost leaves and twigs. These trees are less tolerant of salt than are the species growing close to the beach, and only in the lee of the dune are they protected from the wind-borne salt. So the growth that projects above the level of the dunecrest is killed. The trees, thus inhibited in their upward growth, can only spread out sideways, creating a dense woodland with an almost unbroken canopy. The understory plants, which in the Sunken Forest are scattered and limited to a relatively few shade-tolerant species, are not handicapped by excessive salt; the rains that wash the salt accumulation down from the canopy quickly permeate the sandy soil, carrying the dissolved salt with them to the subsoil and the water table.

Three species of trees are dominant in the Sunken Forest almost to the exclusion of other trees. In numbers of individuals **sassafras** *(Sassafras albidum)* predominates; but **American holly** *(Ilex opaca)* accounts for a greater biomass. The other dominant species is **oblongleaf juneberry** *(Amelanchier canadensis).* Where conditions are atypical, one finds a few other tree species. In boggy places **sour-gum** *(Nyssa sylvatica)* grows; but in this environment it never approaches the great heights (up to 125 ft., or 38 m) it achieves elsewhere. These four tree species also make up part of the understory in the Sunken Forest.

Tree species other than the above appear to be relics of the Sunken Forest's past. **Pitch pine, redcedar,** and **black oak** *(Quercus velutina)* are in evidence, but except for a very few black oaks they are represented in the interior of the forest by dead specimens only. The present forest is apparently a climax community, destined to survive here until landward migration of the barrier island overtakes it or some unusually violent storm wipes it out. Fortunately, it is under strict protection from human depredations. Visitors must use the boardwalk trail to explore it, and, as part of the National Park System, it is in no danger of being leveled for construction of cottages or resort facilities.

Returning to the understory of the Sunken Forest: here are found species that grow in the dune-and-swale, as well as some that would not be found in situations so exposed. Three of the holdovers—**Virginia creeper, poison-ivy,** and **wild sarsaparilla** *(Aralia nudicaulis)*—are, along with **black huckleberry** *(Gaylussacia baccata)* and **highbush blueberry** *(Vaccinium corymbosum),* the dominant nontree species in the understory. Poison-ivy, in fact, is not only found in almost every terrestrial habitat of Fire Island but is a dominant species in many sites. Unfortunately this is much the case for the entire range covered by this book. (An extenuating circumstance: poison-ivy discourages users of the barrier islands from straying off the trail in areas where it is abundant, and this is advantageous ecologically.)

Of the four major canopy species, sassafras is most abundant in the understory. In low spots, **swamp azalea** *(Rhododendron viscosum)* is common. Other species that figure prominently in the shrub layer of the Sunken Forest are the saplings of juneberry, black gum, and American holly; **low gallberry holly** *(Ilex glabra),* a shrub that doesn't much resemble its overstory cousin; *Rosa rugosa*, the **saltspray rose** (U.S.D.A. name, **hedgerow rose**), a plant often found much closer to the sea elsewhere in its range along the Atlantic coast south to New Jersey; and **starry false solomon's-seal** *(Smilacina stellata)*, which has a similar range.

Most of the above woody plants also appear in the canopy layer. But it should be noted that in such a low-profile forest, in which a dense growth of *lianas*—poison-ivy, common and glaucous greenbrier, Virginia creeper, and wild grape *(Vitis* spp.)—occupy the entire vertical strata, there is no sharp division into forest layers. Although these woody vines are all rooted in the soil, it is difficult to assign any of them to a particular layer of the forest.

Two of the lianas—poison-ivy and Virginia creeper—can be said to be dominants on the forest floor, or "herb layer." In this forest that layer is almost entirely an association of woody plants, with a paltry few herbaceous species. Other than **starry false Solomon's-seal** *(Smilacina stellata)*, **Canada mayflower** *(Maianthemum canadense)*, **bracken**, or **brakefern** *(Pteridium aquilinum)*, and **starflower** *(Trientalis borealis)*, along with wild sarsaparilla, which has a slightly woody stem and could be classified as a shrub, no herbaceous plant accounts for more than 0.1% of the ground cover, according to a 1976 study of this forest by Henry W. Art. Apparently, the environment is not favorable to herbaceous plants.

The dominant species of the dune-and-swale—bearberry, marram, beach plum, and woolly hudsonia—are absent from the Sunken Forest. **Shining sumac** *(Rhus copalina)*, also called dwarf, or winged, sumac, grows along the forest margins, as does pitch pine. Both of these are fairly common in the dune-and-swale.

Succession in Maritime Forests

It is an almost universal phenomenon in both wetland and upland habitats that one community replaces another through the long, orderly process of change that ecologists call succession. Succession is not brought about by outside forces so much as by the normal life functions of the community itself. Changes the plants and animals in a community make in the physical habitat make it less hospitable for the existing species while creating conditions favorable to establishment of a new complex of species. An animal or plant may occur in only one stage of the succession sequence, or it may persist through several. It is unusual for a complete change of species to occur from one stage, or *sere,* to the next; but the *dominants*—the species that are most prominent in the community and that exert the most influence in control of the habitat—typically are distinct from those in earlier or later seres.

In the normal state of affairs, the process of succession continues until it culminates in a community that does *not* create conditions unfavorable to its own survival. Such a community will then maintain itself indefinitely until external forces, such as storms, fire, or human alteration of the environment—or an outbreak of disease affecting one or more dominants—set it back to an earlier stage or wipe it out completely. After such a setback, there may be a resumption of the original pattern of change toward the same *climax community,* as it is called. Or, conditions may favor a different succession pattern resulting in a new climax community. The history of man's abuses of natural systems is replete with examples of setbacks so severe that once productive regions have become barely capable of supporting life—even barren deserts. The ruthless exploitation of tropical rain forests and mountain-slope redwood climax communities are current instances of actions that make almost certain the permanent loss of these priceless life systems.

Setbacks may occur, of course, at any stage in the succession process. In fact, in some environments these conditions may be the rule rather than the exception. For example, in some western regions of the United States lightning-induced fires occur so frequently that a climax community never develops. Or, in another sort of interference with the normal state, the human hand may, through protection from wildfire, permit an orderly progression toward a climax community in a situation where the normal pattern would be stabilization of a sub-climax community dominated by fire-resistant species. This is apparently the case in the giant sequoia community in some areas of the Sierra Nevada, where these fire-resistant bigtrees (alternative common name) have been found to be in danger of replacement by other conifers that under natural conditions had been held back by wildfire. Reproduction of these conifers, enhanced by suppression of wildfire by the National Park Service and U.S. Forest Service, was crowding out the seedlings of the bigtrees. To prevent ultimate loss of the forest to these species, suppression of wildfires as a management tool has been discontinued, with controlled burning programs instituted to restore something approximating the original natural conditions. Visitors to some forests on the Eastern seaboard witness similar controlled burning operations that are being carried out for the same reasons. This type of management tool is also utilized in other seashore habitats, including marshlands. It is sometimes a means of reducing or eliminating undesirable plant species (usually aliens), such as *Phragmites*.

The orderliness of community succession on barrier islands is severely affected by the instability of the environment and the stresses placed on the vegetation by frequent and intense storm activity. Yet a fairly complete history of the natural succession that led to the present Sunken Forest community has been put together from investigative data and educated guesses.

Sometime between 200 and 300 years ago the site of the Sunken Forest was an area of bare, windblown sand, as are all newly formed barrier beaches and spits and all parts of barrier islands overlain with sand deposits from storm-induced washover. In time this barren area was invaded by the seeds of pioneering dune plants—much the same species as grow now on the back shore and the face of the primary dune. Marram probably came first, while sand was still being deposited on the dunes. In spots where the wind was removing sand, woolly hudsonia and seaside goldenrod may have gained the first footholds. Once established, these plants helped stabilize the site by trapping the windblown sand, thus building up the substrate. In the relatively sterile soil of the new sand deposits, the pioneering plants had to get most of their nutrients from the air—or, more accurately, from the wind-borne salt spray off the ocean, with some help from dust and plant fragments from the mainland.

As the vegetation became denser and the plants passed through the cycles of life and decay, organic material was added to the sand. Gradually an environment was created that enabled increasingly diverse plant associations to develop. The dunes that grew with the help of the pioneer plants contributed to the improvement of the habitat by providing barriers to wind and salt spray. The new soil and microclimate were favorable to such plants as bearberry, bayberry, poison-ivy, Virginia creeper, and beach plum. In the more stable sites, pitch pine and redcedar took root. The woody plants—shrubs, vines, and trees—came to dominate the vegetation on the crest of the secondary dune and beyond, at the expense of the herbaceous plants.

The secondary dune became stabilized at a height of perhaps 30 ft. (8 m), and in its wind shadow, conditions were now much less influenced by the maritime environment. The existing dominant plants were gradually replaced by an association of less tolerant species that had been unable to grow where salt deposition was heavy. The dominants in this new community were black cherry, post oak and other oaks, and highbush blueberry, along with pitch pines and redcedars persisting from the shrub community. The pioneer plants, such as marram, seaside goldenrod, and woolly hudsonia, had by this time disappeared from the zone beyond the secondary dune, either because conditions were no longer favorable for them or because they could not successfully compete with the new plants for the available nutrients, moisture, living space, and sunlight.

This black cherry-oak-highbush blueberry-redcedar-pitch pine forest community thrived on the newly stabilized terrain. But this association, made up of species well adapted to the somewhat modified maritime environment, created conditions unfavorable to some of its constituents. Redcedar and pitch pine seedlings, for example, require a sunlit site. Consequently, these trees could not reproduce successfully in their own shadow.

Seedlings of American holly, sassafras, and juneberry, however, are tolerant of shade, and, in the lee of the secondary dune where they are shielded from the salt-laden winds, these species gradually began to take over from the former dominants. Here and there, low, wet sites created microhabitats where black gum grew as a dominant.

The wind shadow created by the secondary dune extended to an elevation of about 30 ft. (8 m), and this is the effective height limit of the forest canopy. Above that height deposition of salt by the winds inhibits growth. The few, scattered redcedars that grow today near the margins of the Sunken Forest may sometimes project above the general level of the canopy; this suggests that they are less vulnerable to salt deposition than the other tree species present. Their need for sunlight inhibits their occurrence in the forest interior.

In this new community, today's Sunken Forest, only a few pitch pines, oaks, black cherries, and the above mentioned redcedars remain; and these appear to be stragglers in a last-ditch struggle for survival in the unfavorable environment. But these dominants of the earlier forest community persist on the crest of the secondary dune as well as along the forest margins.

Note in Table 6, listing common and dominant plants of the Sunken Forest and the adjacent dune-and-swale, that although glaucous greenbrier is common in both zones, no species that is dominant in the dune-and-swale occurs at all in the Sunken Forest. The species now living in the Sunken Forest will probably be able to persist, under the conditions prevailing, with roughly the same hierarchy of dominance and lesser status. Today's maritime forest, then, is a true climax community, and the succession process has reached its natural culmination. Major changes could come about through erosion of the bayshore, where in places the forest is separated from the lagoon by only a narrow strip of marsh; by encroachment of the secondary dune on the ocean side of the forest; or by loss of the primary dune, which would bring oceanic influences closer to the forest. But at present there are no signs of changing boundaries between the plant communities in this area, other than some dead trees in the transition zone be-

Table 6: Dominant and Common Plants of the
Dune-and-swale and Maritime Forest
Zones in Fire Island's Sunken Forest

Species	Common Name	Dune-and-Swale	Maritime Forest
Amelanchier canadensis	Thicket serviceberry, juneberry		D
Ammophila breviligulata	Marram, American beachgrass	D	
Aralia nudicaula	Wild sarsaparilla	x	D
Arctostaphylos uva-ursi	Bearberry	D	
Artemisia stelleriana	Dusty miller	x	
Baccharis halimifolia	Groundsel-tree		x
Cakile edentula	Sea-rocket	x	
Cirsium horridulum	Yellow thistle	x	
Gaylusaccia baccata	Black huckleberry		D
Hudsonia tomentosa	Woolly hudsonia	D	
Ilex glabra	Low gallberry holly, inkberry		x
Ilex opaca	American holly	x	D
Juniperus virginiana	Eastern redcedar		x
Lathyrus japonicus	Beach pea	x	
Lechea maritima	Inkberry		x
Maianthemum canadense	Wild lily-of-the-valley, Canada mayflower		D
Myrica pensylvanica	Northern bayberry	D	
Nyssa sylvatica	Swamp tupelo, sour-gum, blackgum		D
Panicum spp.	Panicum	x	
Parthenocissus quinquefolia	Virginia creeper	x	D
Pinus rigida	Pitch pine	x	x
Prunus maritima	Beach plum	D	
Prunus serotina	Black cherry		x
Pyrus arbutifolia	Red chokeberry		x
Rhododendron viscosum	Swamp honeysuckle, swamp azalea		D
Quercus stellata	Post oak	x	D
Quercus velutina	Black oak	x	D
Rosa rugosa	Saltspray rose		x
Rhus copalina	Dwarf sumac, shining sumac	x	x
Rhus radicans	Poison-ivy	x	D
Sassafras albidum	Sassafras	x	D
Smilacina stellata	False solomon's-seal	x	D

The symbol D indicates that the plant is a dominant species in the zone.

Table 6 (continued)

Species	Common Name	Dune-and-Swale	Maritime Forest
Smilax glauca	Sawbrier, glaucous greenbrier	x	x
Solidago sempervirens	Seaside goldenrod	x	x
Vaccinium corymbosum	Highbush blueberry		D

tween the salt marsh and the forest. (In places on Fire Island's bayshore the salt-marsh buffer has disappeared entirely and trees are actually falling into the water.)

There does not appear to be active natural succession occurring in the dune-and-swale zone, where the effects of wind and salt spray seem to have achieved a dynamic balance in the vegetation pattern. This state of affairs is somewhat akin to the situation, described earlier, in the sequoia forest, where frequent lightning-caused fires historically held back species that had the capability of replacing the bigtrees.

In a transit of Fire Island from the beach to the Sunken Forest, the changes in vegetation one encounters are probably a fair approximation of the changes that occurred over time, through natural succession, in the broad zone beyond the secondary dune. The swale today may closely resemble the corresponding zone as it appeared two centuries ago. And the seaward face of the foredune illustrates the earliest stage in the development of a plant community on a newly born barrier beach.

Animals of the Maritime Forest

A natural community is an association of plants and animals in a particular habitat; the changes of plant cover occurring through the process of natural succession are paralleled by changes in the makeup of the animal component. This reflects the fact that animals are either directly or indirectly dependent on the plant life in their habitat. Generally, increasing diversity of the plant life brings increasing diversity of animal spe-

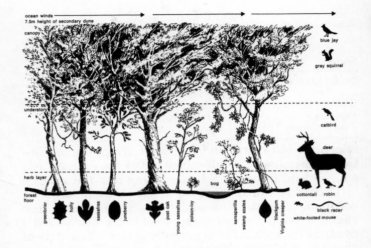

99. The Sunken Forest of Fire Island is a classic example of a salt-pruned maritime forest. It is dominated by three tree species—sassafras, American holly, and thicket serviceberry (also called juneberry or shadbush); and in low boggy areas by blackgum. About 11 species of mammals and twice as many birds breed in the forest; other bird species visit it during spring and fall migrations. It supports many species of cold-blooded vertebrates and invertebrates as well. *(M. Graham)*

cies. This trend probably continued, in the case of Fire Island, through the early forest community dominated by oaks, redcedar, and black cherry, with diversity leveling off and probably declining with the attainment of a climax community. The greatest diversity of both plants and animals in the Sunken Forest area of Fire Island today is in the ecotone between dune-and-swale and the maritime forest—where conditions are more like those in the early forest community than those in the present forest's holly-juneberry-sassafras association. There may be comparable diversity in the ecotone between forest and marsh on the lagoon side.

Today there are about a dozen species of mammals and about two dozen species of birds breeding in the Sunken Forest. Many others forage in it or, in the case of birds, pass through it on migration. The diversity of mammals is undoubtedly less today than it was before human activities made the environment less hospitable. Unquestionably, some species were extirpated by hunting and trapping on the barrier island. Two centuries ago it probably sheltered otter, gray fox, bobcats, and even black bear.

Despite human influences, the Sunken Forest is a good habitat for wildlife. One of the major factors in making it hospitable is the abundance of fruit-bearing trees and shrubs. Not surprisingly, a number of the resident species of birds—**robins, catbirds, mockingbirds, towhees,** and **brown thrashers**—are feeders upon fruits, including those of holly, greenbrier, sassafras, Virginia creeper, juneberry, grape, chokeberry, viburnum, and poison-ivy. Many of the migrants stopping over on their fall journey to the south also feed on these fruits, as do the resident red foxes and raccoons.

Assateague Island, with many small forest communities and some sizeable ones on its south end, also is rich in animal life. Along with the alien sikas and the semidomesticated, formerly feral ponies, there are many ter-

100. The black rat snake, one of the commonest reptiles in coastal thickets and forests, preys on smaller animals and is in turn preyed upon by larger species.

101. The red-shouldered hawk is a year-round resident of the coast south of Cape Cod.

restrial birds, mammals, and reptiles. In the loblolly pine forest growing among old dunes (to 40 ft., or 12 m) on the bay side of the southern part of Assateague, the sikas feed on greenbrier and other plants. The **great horned owl** *(Bubo virginianus)* hunts at night for cottontails, opossums, white-footed mice, and other small mammals; and for **black rat snakes** *(Elaphe o. obsoleta)*, **eastern hognose snakes** *(Heterodon platyrhinos)*, and **eastern garter snakes** *(Thamnophis sirtalis)*. Its daytime counterpart is the **red-shouldered hawk** *(Buteo lineatus)*, a woodland species that has an even broader diet. In addition to mammals (rodents are favored) it eats birds, reptiles, frogs, snails, grasshoppers, and beetles, and has even been known to eat earthworms. This species inhabits coastal forests from Rhode Island south.

Not common on Assateague Island, but known to occur, is the **northern fence lizard,** or **pine lizard** *(Sceloporus undulatus hyacinthinus),* an insectivorous reptile that is much easier to find in the Henlopen dunes some miles to the north. The forest amphibians here are **Fowler's toad** (described earlier under Cold-blooded Vertebrates of the Dune-and-swale Zone) and the **green treefrog** *(Hyla cinerea),* found only near fresh water or in damp spots in the woods.

Two species of deer are found on Assateague Island. The **white-tailed deer** *(Odocoileus virginiana)* occurs in most of the island's habitats. But a species introduced from Asia, the **sika,** or Japanese deer, is more abundant, with a large population on the southern end of the island (Chincoteague National Wildlife Refuge). Most of the sika's time is spent in the forest, but it is also often seen feeding in the open marshes. Unlike the browsing whitetail, the sika is both grazer and browser, and finds food in great variety and abundance on Assateague.

The surest way to see Assateague's forest animals is to go on one of the ranger-guided nighttime "safari" trips in a special passenger vehicle that makes a circuit of the wildlife trail—a route that passes through woodland habitats. Early morning walks will bring glimpses of the sikas and whitetails. An alert visitor may see the rare **Delmarva Peninsula fox squirrel** *(Sciurus niger),* which is much larger than its cousin, the gray squirrel, and spends more time on the ground. For a description of this rodent, see Appendix II, Endangered Species.

The Outer Banks, the southernmost barrier islands in the range covered by this book, have a surprisingly rich forest fauna, considering their isolation from the mainland and the wide separation of the forest communities from each other. The birds, of course, are not handicapped by these distances, and each forest has much the same resident species. But in the case of mammals, reptiles, and amphibians, there are great differences between the species on each island. For example, within the boundaries of Cape Hatteras National Seashore the **Virginia opossum** *(Didelphis marsupialis)* and the **gray**

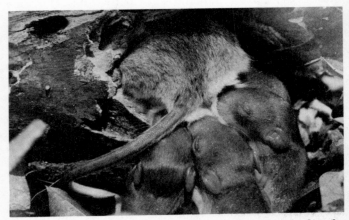

102. Young of the white-footed mouse are born naked and grow rapidly, reaching a fairly large size before their eyes open; they can breed at an age of two months.

fox *(Urocyon cinereoargenteus)* are found only on Bodie Island, while the **southeastern shrew** *(Sorex longirostris)*, the **white-footed mouse,** the **gray squirrel** *(Sciurus carolinensis)*, the tree-climbing **cotton mouse** *(Peromyscus gossypinus)*, and the **white-tailed deer** are found only on Hatteras Island. A look at the map suggests that at least some of the species must have arrived on Hatteras with the help of humans. Some years ago **bullfrogs** *(Rana catesbeiana)* were introduced into Buxton Woods; but they soon disappeared.

Several forest animals are found on both islands—the **least shrew** *(Cryptotis parva)*, the raccoon, the **amphiuma,** a salamander *(Amphiuma means)*, **Fowler's toad,** the **green treefrog** *(Hyla cinerea)*, the **squirrel treefrog** *(Hyla squirella)*, and the **eastern narrow-mouthed toad** *(Gastrophryne carolinensis)*. The ubiquitous eastern cottontail is found on all islands of the national seashore, and is of course not limited to the forest habitat.

Of the species noted above as occurring on Hatteras Island, only the following have definitely been reported in Buxton Woods: gray squirrel, white-footed mouse, cotton mouse, cottontail, white-tailed deer, amphiuma, the treefrogs, Fowler's toad, and the narrow-mouthed toad.

The distribution of snakes on the Outer Banks is not completely known, but the following species have been reported in Buxton Woods or are presumed to occur there: the big **brown water snake** *(Natrix taxispilota),* which has been known to reach a length of 69 in. (1.75 m), the **northern black racer,** the **hognose snake,** the tree-climbing **yellow rat snake** *(Elaphe obsoleta quad-rivittata),* and the **corn snake** *(Elaphe g. guttata).*

CHAPTER THREE

Estuarine Communities

Estuaries, Sounds, and Lagoons

On published maps, there is little consistency and less logic in the designations of the main types of coastal embayments and semienclosed bodies of water. Even less reliable are the names applied locally to the various types of coastal water areas. The term *bay*, for example, is applied to a wide range of shoreline indentations. Here we will reserve that term for a broad, deep recess in the coastline that is not closed off by a barrier or peninsula, and that may or may not be the mouth of a large river (as is the lower part of the Delaware estuary but not Cape Cod Bay). Because according to this usage a bay is widely open to the ocean, it has, at least at its mouth, a salinity of 30 o/oo or greater. Most bays are deeper than the bodies referred to herein as sounds; but depth is not a definitive factor. Much of Cape Cod Bay, incidentally, is very shallow and exposed at extreme low tides. No large rivers flow into Cape Cod Bay.

Among the accepted but misleading geographic names for coastal bodies of water is Great South Bay. This large, very shallow stretch of water between Fire Island and Long Island is actually a *lagoon*. Chesapeake Bay is actually an *estuary* or *estuarine complex*, fed by some 150 rivers and tributaries. Long Island Sound, however, is a classic example of a *sound* according to our definition: a relatively large body of water, generally elongate, open at both ends to the ocean or ocean embayments.

From 80% to 90% of the Atlantic coastline consists

ESTUARINE COMMUNITIES

of estuarine and lagoonal shores. The lagoons between Cape Hatteras and New York Harbor are mostly compounded by much larger estuaries. The estuaries above New York Harbor are smaller and are less filled with sediment. The more conspicuous lagoons, often called *salt ponds* in Rhode Island and Massachusetts and usually designated as bays farther south, tend to be elongate to the coastline and frequently lie athwart the mouths of streams.

Sounds—and most estuaries and lagoons—have direct connections with the ocean. The degree of protection from ocean waves they enjoy depends partly on the breadth of their ocean connections, partly on their orientation. Most of Chesapeake Bay is much too distant from the Atlantic to be affected by ocean waves and currents, but its length and breadth are such that it can develop its own storm waves of a magnitude that may be limited only by the shallowness of the water. Long Island Sound, open wide to the Atlantic at its eastern end (and connected to New York Harbor at its western end), is vulnerable to destructive northeasterly storms. Cape Cod Bay is protected on the south, east, and northeast by the embracing arm of the cape and on the west by the mainland; it is open to the sea only on the north, and thus it is exposed to direct oceanic winds only from that direction. Many large bays are partly blocked by islands; Narragansett Bay's broad mouth, opening onto Rhode Island Sound, is largely closed off by islands, making it virtually a big salt lake under the influence of oceanic tides. Unlike Cape Cod Bay, it has a number of rivers entering its upper reaches, giving it something of the character of an estuary.

The Nature and Types of Estuaries

Estuaries differ from sounds and bays in that the estuary's salt water from the ocean is significantly diluted by fresh water from runoff. Salinity ranges from that of sea water at or near the mouth to that of near-fresh water at some point upstream; that point is called the head of the estuary. Specifically, the head is the point where with maximum salt-penetration (during seasons of minimal contribution of fresh water) salinity is 0.5 o/oo. But it should be kept in mind that during heavy spring runoff periods, the 0.5 o/oo salinity point may be much farther down the estuary than at other times.

Water enters an estuary from three sources: land runoff, tidal exchange, and precipitation. The first two are the most important. The volume of river water that is replaced by ocean water during a tidal cycle is called the *tidal prism*. Estuaries are classified into hydrologic types by the ratio of the freshwater discharge during the tidal cycle to the tidal prism; this is referred to as the *flow ratio*. Circulation within the estuary depends on the tidal range and the amount of vertical mixing between the fresh water and the salt ocean water. There are three circulation (hydrologic) types, and each merits some discussion.

Hydrologic Classifications

I. TWO-LAYERED ESTUARY

The two-layered estuarine system occurs when there

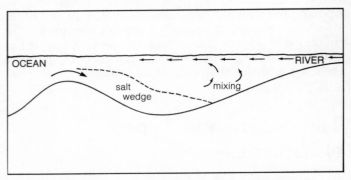

103. Two-layered estuary. Large flow ratio (freshwater discharge much greater than the tidal prism); moderate mixing; salt wedge present.

ESTUARINE COMMUNITIES

is a lot of freshwater runoff and a small tidal range. It is characterized by a high flow ratio: when freshwater discharge is much greater than the tidal prism (see Fig. 103). There is little vertical mixing in this type of estuary. The less dense river water floats on top of the salt. At the interface, some of the sea water is entrained by the outflowing fresh water and carried back to sea; it is replaced by slow bottom inflow, creating a small tidal prism. There is a sharp salinity boundary between the two layers.

II. PARTLY MIXED ESTUARIES

In the partly mixed estuary the flow ratio is medium; runoff is moderate, and the tidal range is larger than in the two-layered estuary. Though the tidal exchange is moderate, the larger tidal prism and stronger tidal currents cause more vertical mixing during a tide cycle. There is no well-defined wedge of salt water penetrating the estuary, and because of the smaller ratio of fresh to salt (as compared to that in a Type I estuary), the vertical salinity gradient is less steep. More sea water has to flow into the Type II estuary to replace the salt water that has been entrained by fresh water and carried out by the surface current. As Fig. 104 shows, there are three layers in the vertical salinity structure.

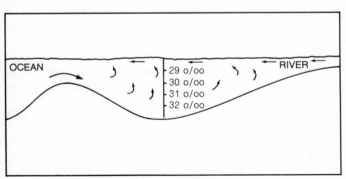

104. Partly mixed estuary. Medium flow ratio—runoff is moderate and the tidal range larger than in Type I. There is more mixing, less variation in the vertical salinity gradient, and no salt wedge.

The Nature and Types of Estuaries

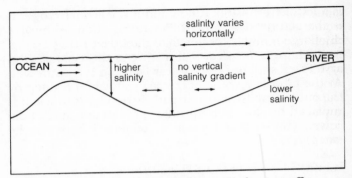

105. Well-mixed estuary. Small flow ratio (low runoff compared to large tidal prism); currents produce much mixing and uniform vertical salinity; no salt wedge.

III. WELL-MIXED ESTUARIES

The well-mixed estuary occurs where there is significant tidal flow—that is, where there is a small flow ratio, with low runoff in relation to a large tidal prism. As the water level rises and falls with the tide, a volume of water (the tidal prism) is exchanged between the estuary and the ocean. Thus in Type III estuaries the tidal current is added to the river outflow and the inflow of bottom water. The large tidal prism and strong currents produce much mixing, and the salinity is uniform top to bottom. The dominant variation in the well-mixed estuary, then, is in the horizontal plane, ranging from fresh water above the reach of the tide to the salinity of the open ocean off the mouth of the estuary.

If freshwater runoff is so small as compared to the tidal exchange that salinity in the embayment is not significantly diluted, the system is a bay rather than an estuary. Thus, by this criterion, Buzzards Bay is a bay, while Chesapeake Bay is an estuary.

The circulation type of an estuary is a major factor in determining what life forms can exist there. Circulation determines salinity variation, and plants and animals in a given estuary must be able to tolerate the salinity changes that occur. An enormous range of tolerance is exhibited by estuarine organisms. Some can survive only slight dilution of sea water; some can exist from the

ESTUARINE COMMUNITIES

mouth of the estuary to its head. A wide tolerance would be valuable, for instance, to an organism whose chief predator is limited in its distribution by a relatively narrow tolerance. A good example is the Atlantic oyster, which exists in waters ranging from 5 o/oo to 30 o/oo; the oyster drill *(Urosalpinx cinerea)*, a small gastropod that destroys most of the oyster seed crop in lower Chesapeake Bay, tolerates brackish water only down to a salinity of about 15 o/oo, and thus cannot reach the less salty upper bay.

Knowing the circulation type of an estuary is also helpful in determining how pollutants will be dispersed in it. In a two-layered estuary (Type I), pollutants are carried out to sea in the top layer. In a well-mixed estuary (Type III), a pollutant introduced during flood tide will be moved upstream and will be discharged only gradually.

Third, circulation determines sediment transport. In a two-layered system, one type of sediment (such as mud) may be carried out near the surface, while another (shells, for example) is coming in below. In a well-mixed estuary, river sediment is carried out only gradually because there is no strongly flowing top layer.

Geomorphological Classifications

In addition to being defined according to their hydrologic cycles, estuaries also are classified by the earth-shaping forces that created them. Most of the estuaries of the Atlantic coast were formed when lower valleys of rivers were drowned by a post-Ice Age increase in sea level. Those of the Glaciated Coast differ in some respects from those farther south.

Drowned river valley estuaries. The drowned-river-valley type of estuary is characteristic of the coast south of New Jersey, where the Coastal Plain widens. Chesapeake Bay is the prime example, being the drowned lower valley of the Susquehanna River and the lower valleys of its tributaries. These are also sometimes called *coastal-plain estuaries.*

Fjords. A second geomorphological type of estuary is

one that has been gouged out by glaciers. There is frequently a sill formed by glacial deposits at the mouth of such an estuary, with a deep basin inside. Some fjords do not have a river entering at the head, and without significant inflow of fresh water these fjords do not classify as estuaries. Somes Sound in Mount Desert Island, Maine, is such a nonestuarine fjord. Within the Middle Atlantic range, the lower Hudson River estuary is considered a fjord.

Bar-built estuaries. Bar-built estuaries form when sand spits and barrier islands develop between headlands, with one or more inlets allowing tidal exchange. In this kind of estuary the enclosed area is generally elongate parallel to the coastline—as with lagoons. The volume of fresh water contributed by runoff usually is not great, though several rivers may enter the estuary. The lower valleys of these tributary rivers may have been drowned by rising sea levels; in such cases the water body may be considered a composite system— part bar-built estuary and part drowned-river-valley estuary. Typically, the inlets connecting a bar-built estuary to the sea are small in relation to the dimensions of the embayed area, with relatively little tidal action consequently occurring. Like a lagoon, the embayment is usually shallow, and the wind provides the important mixing mechanism.

Pamlico Sound, North Carolina, is an example of a bar-built estuary. It is separated from the ocean by a long segment of the Outer Banks barrier chain. Because its free connection with the open sea is very narrow relative to its horizontal dimension, it is a borderline case; an argument can be made that it is a lagoon rather than a true estuary. It is not, at any rate, a sound; and its waters are diluted significantly by several rivers. Albemarle Sound, just to the north, is another bar-built estuary. Back Bay and Currituck Sound, behind the northern section of the banks, with no direct outlet to the sea, are best classified as lagoons.

Estuaries produced by tectonic processes. This is a catch-all classification, including coastal indentations caused by faulting or by local subsidence. San Francisco Bay is an example of such an estuary. This type does not occur on the Middle Atlantic coast.

There are three basic forces that produce motion and mixing of the water in estuaries. Wind is the dominant factor in bar-built estuaries, as a rule. In a river-dominated estuary, like that of the Mississippi, mixing is caused mostly by the breaking of unstable interfacial waves at the upper boundary of the saltwater wedge. In most other estuaries tides are the dominant force. The turbulence associated with the tidal currents results in mixing of the salt- and freshwater components, producing density gradients.

Estuaries Versus Lagoons

It is evident from the variations noted in the estuarine types and related bodies of water that lagoons and estuaries are not easily distinguished. Some researchers say that the two classifications can be differentiated by analyzing the instability of salinity. When the inflow of fresh water in a separated basin develops a stable body of brackish water, it may be considered a lagoon. On the other hand, if the mixing of fresh and sea water is not stable but shows periodic changes, the basin is considered an estuary.

A lagoon may be *hypersaline,* like a kind of "negative estuary." (Laguna Madre, Texas, is a prime example.) This is not a common situation on the Middle Atlantic coast, but can occur when there is no substantial input of fresh water from streams, as in Sengekontacket Pond, on Martha's Vineyard. Brackish-water lagoons are more typical. They may exhibit a richer spectrum of benthic species adapted to the reduced salinity than do estuaries.

Estuarine Mud and Sand Flats

The Nature of Intertidal Flats

The term *flats* applies to unvegetated parts of the littoral zone in sounds and lagoons as well as in true estuaries. Their upper and lower boundaries are defined by the limits of the spring tides. Intertidal flats exist also in some areas that are not classified as estuaries, sounds, or lagoons. For example, broad flats are seen in Cape Cod Bay and in other similarly protected coastal indentations where there is little or no mixing of fresh water with the salt. These flats, however, are not populated with true estuarine species.

Often lifeless in appearance except for the visiting gulls, waders, and shorebirds, the unvegetated intertidal flats are, to the casual eye, the least attractive and least promising of all the estuarine communities. A closer look at this habitat, however, reveals mollusks and crustaceans of varying sizes, and even some signs of plant life. A little digging may turn up a surprising diversity of invertebrates under the surface. Because of the interactions and interchanges between the flats and other estuarine habitats, the life in this zone is often rich and varied despite the absence or sparsity of *macrophytes* (plants large enough to be easily visible to the naked eye). The waters that move on and off the flats with the tidal rhythms bring nutrients, microscopic and macroscopic plants and animals, and animals of the nekton that invade the zone under their own power when the tide rises. Predatory birds visit it during periods of both inundation and exposure. Many species of invertebrates spend their entire lives here except for the earliest planktonic stages; but an understanding of intertidal-flat ecology can be achieved only in the context of the estuarine environment as a whole.

An "unvegetated bottom" is one that lacks, in significant quantity, rooted plants, such as grasses, shrubs, and *seagrasses (Zostera, Ruppia,* and other marine flowering plants), or macroscopic algae. Diatoms, microalgae, and blue-green algae may abound on the surface of the flats and in the upper few centimeters of mud or sand. Attached or free-floating sea lettuce *(Ulva lactuca)* may be quite common. Flats that at low tide are covered with water up to a few feet in depth are called *shoals.*

While these habitats are usually referred to as either mud flats or sand flats, the majority of the deposits are a mixture. Even the apparently pure mud of some flats has some grains of sand intermixed. The nature of the

ESTUARINE COMMUNITIES

106. Intertidal flats are generally a mixture of sand and mud.

sediments is determined by the prevailing physical conditions as well as by the types of suspended materials carried by the tides and currents. In high-energy environments, such as inlets where strong tidal currents run, and broad lagoons where wave action is high, the flats consist mostly of coarse sediments—sand, pebbles, and shell fragments. The finer material remains suspended until the action of currents and wind waves is diminished. Silts and clays are deposited only where water movement has been almost completely stilled.

The sediments in high-energy environments are relatively unstable. Continual erosion and deposition vary the level of sediment, with the result that an area of bottom may be alternately intertidal and subtidal. The instability of the sediments is a major factor in determining which species and which life stages of animals dwell in and on the substrate, and, by extension, which species visit it to feed; it also limits the growth of microflora on the surface and in the upper centimeters of the deposits. Despite the instability of such bottoms and the relatively low organic content of the sediments, they may support a flora and a fauna of considerable variety and density.

Estuarine Mud and Sand Flats

The chemistry of the sediments, the availability of nutrients, and the degree of salinity (and range of variation in salinity) are all important factors in determining the composition of intertidal flora and fauna. Extremes of temperature related to the seasons, to tidal flow, and to alternating inundation and exposure are also factors. Turbidity of the water, which can significantly limit photosynthetic activity—particularly of phytoplankton—is greatly variable; in true estuaries, it tends to be a larger factor in determining species composition than it is in sounds and lagoons. Benthic (bottom) algal production in the intertidal zone is less affected than phytoplankton by turbidity because at low tide the benthic algae are exposed to direct sunlight.

Because variations and extremes in salinity, turbidity, and temperature tend to be greatest in estuaries, these are the most severe coastal basin environments for intertidal-flat plants and animals. All intertidal organisms, even those living within the upper centimeters of the sediments, are affected by exposure to the sun's heat, wintry winds, and desiccating air. Most marine animals in this habitat feed only when it is submerged. Those that live in the deposits—the *infauna*—are relatively well protected at low tide, though for many feeding must be curtailed at this time. The *epifauna*—animals living on the surface of the sediments—are mostly limited to the lower intertidal zone, where exposure is less prolonged. The same limitation applies to the seagrasses; *Zostera* is almost entirely subtidal, with only sparse growth, if any, in the lower intertidal zone—despite the greater availability there of sunlight.

Plants of the Intertidal Flats

Though too small to be seen individually by the unaided eye, the *benthic microflora*—green microalgae, diatoms, blue-green algae, and other microscopic plants—are often conspicuous because of their abundance and their frequently vivid coloring. In the high intertidal zone blue-green algae often form dense mats; at low tide they may become hard, blackish crusts.

These tiny but numerous plants are major components of the basic trophic level of the intertidal food pyramid. There are two main groups, in terms of environmental niches: the attached and the mobile microalgae. The attached forms, usually very small organisms, adhere to the surfaces of the particles of sediment; the mobile forms move up and down in the sediments. Though the microalgae often descend to depths of 4 in. (10 cm), they are generally found within the top 3/4 in. (2 cm). Intertidal flats, by definition, are essentially lacking in macrophytes. But attached to shells and other hard substrates one can often find sea lettuce and other green and brown algae. Floating mats of green filamentous algae sometimes occur in this zone. (Mats of microalgae are also found floating after being detached from the surface of the deposits by water motion when the tide rises.)

Bacteria and fungi are of great ecological importance in the intertidal flats. Bacteria are especially abundant in muddy sediments, where the finer particles provide more surface area for the colonies and where organic content is greater. Both bacteria and fungi function as decomposers, converting dead plant and animal matter

107. Looking north across the broad intertidal flats of Cape Cod Bay at Brewster, Mass. Note the stand of *Spartina alterniflora* (see Chapter Four) on the upper part of the intertidal zone.

to inorganic nutrients. As described in the discussion of detritus (in Chapter Four, under Cordgrass Communities), the protein-rich bacteria are themselves important links in the food chain, being consumed in enormous numbers by small invertebrates.

The intertidal flats are far from being a closed ecosystem. The detritus upon which the bacteria and fungi feed comes primarily from other estuarine communities. The tidal waters also bring organisms of other trophic levels. The supply of detrital material is generally greater on the low-energy mud flats than on sand flats, where water movement is greater. Since it is more concentrated in the higher levels of the deposits, the detritivorous animals are most abundant in the upper few centimeters. In addition to the small invertebrates that depend heavily on detritus (chiefly for its bacterial burden), many fishes, such as herring, silversides, mullet, and the young of larger species, feed on this material when in the intertidal-flat zone. At times when other food resources are in short supply detritus may become a very important part of the diet of both adults and young of species not normally detritivorous. Among those invertebrates of the flats that are highly dependent upon this resource are small crabs, *isopods* (a group of freshwater and marine crustaceans, mostly less than 1 in. and mostly of flattened body shape), many mollusks, and a vast array of *vermiform* (wormlike) animals.

Phytoplankton often attain high concentrations in the intertidal flats. When the tides cover these areas, temperature and light conditions induce rapid growth and reproduction of the minute, drifting plants. In turn, zooplankton thrive and the entire food web prospers. Winter in the intertidal zone is a period of relatively low phytoplankton production, and higher trophic levels are accordingly depressed; many larger invertebrates and fishes are absent from the zone during this period.

Phytoplankton on the whole represent a minor part of the total primary production of the estuarine system, being greatly outranked in this respect by the seagrasses and marsh grasses, particularly *Zostera, Spar-*

tina, Ruppia, and *Juncus.* Though these are produced in the marshes and subtidal areas, they provide most of the detrital material that makes its way into the intertidal-flat community.

Food Chains of the Intertidal Flats

The plant component described above—phytoplankton, benthic microflora and macroflora, the bacteria-bearing detritus derived from the macroflora, and floating filamentous algae and sea lettuce—is the base of the food pyramid in the intertidal-flat system. The relative importance of these constituents has not been determined, but much research is underway in this field. Those estuaries, lagoons, and sounds with large expanses of open water, such as Albemarle Sound, Chesapeake Bay, and Great South Bay, can be presumed to owe a larger share of their total productivity to phytoplankton than do marsh- and seagrass-dominated systems such as Back Bay and Brigantine national wildlife refuges.

In any estuarine system, the base of the food web is composed of a very few plant species, while the organisms feeding directly on this base may be very diverse, representing myriad invertebrate species and many juvenile and adult vertebrates. The bulk of the phytoplankton and benthic microalgal production of the intertidal flats is consumed by invertebrates, among which are both suspension feeders and deposit feeders.

SUSPENSION FEEDERS

The suspension-feeding tribe includes some of the marine animals most familiar to us: clams, oysters, and scallops. Their food is suspended particles, typically obtained when the animal passes a current of water through the body cavity and out past the gills; the gills act as a filter to trap the particles, which include not only plankton but also resuspended benthic microalgae and smaller detrital particles. Other suspension feeders utilize a variety of filters, sieves, and tentacles to separate their food from the water. Among these filter feeders are vermiform dwellers of the benthic deposits, benthic epifauna, and zooplankters such as comb jellies, along with many larval fishes. The best known suspension feeders are clams and oysters.

The filter-feeding process, by which most suspension feeders obtain their food, is not totally selective, and along with the microflora a filter feeder ingests living and dead microfauna. In an area where deposit feeders are abundant, the sediments are likely to be stirred up, and this can be detrimental to suspension feeders, whose filters may become clogged by the particles of sediment. Thus filter feeders and deposit feeders tend to occupy different sites in the flats.

DEPOSIT FEEDERS

Deposit feeders ingest the sedimentary deposits and, in the process of passing the mass of material through the gut, remove the bacteria and fungi on the surface of the detrital particles and the microalgae living in the spaces between the particles. Among the deposit feeders, some are quite nonselective in their feeding, and some are selective only in terms of the sizes of particles retained. The sediments at and near the surface, being the richest in these sources of food, are utilized to the greatest extent. Included among the deposit feeders are the lugworm, *Arenicola;* a vermiform echinoderm, *Leptosynapta tenuis;* and, on sand flats, the golden acorn worm, *Balanoglossus aurantiacus* (some acorn worms are suspension feeders). Inhabitants of the intertidal flats that one can watch apparently feeding on deposits are fiddler crabs (*Uca* spp.); but rather than ingesting the mud or sand, the fiddlers remove the algae, detritus, and other organic matter and cast aside the remainder.

PREDATORS

Animals that actively feed upon the living invertebrates of the intertidal flats are numerous. Many live within the sediments: some of these swim about when the flats are inundated. *Nereis* (described in detail later in this chapter under Clam Worms), *Glycera,* and other

108. Bloodworm *(Glycera dibranchiata)* with proboscis extended; the four black fangs are not visible in this photograph.

errant *polychaetes* (bristle worms); and *Cerebratulus* and other *nemerteans* (a group of leechlike worms) are among the vermiform animals that prey upon their neighbors. Some of the more voracious of these invertebrates even take young fish.

SCAVENGERS

The sanitary workers of the intertidal flats include most crabs, many species of gastropods (molluscs with a single spiral shell, and related forms), and a number of flatworms. Sometimes the only conspicuous living things on a mud flat are hordes of inch-long mud dog whelks *(Nassarius obsoletus),* common gastropods that gravitate to dead fish and other carrion. (These snails are discussed later in this chapter under Mobile Epibenthos of the Intertidal Flats.)

Amphipods are such efficient scavengers that they have been utilized as skeleton cleaners in preparing biological specimens for use in laboratories and classrooms. *Gammarus mucronatus* and other *scuds* (a large genus of amphipods with a characteristic habit of swimming or moving over the bottom on their sides), while associated generally with seaweeds and seagrasses and with tidepools, feed also on mud flats, on a variety of organic material. Scuds are generally larger (to nearly 2 in., or 50 mm) than the related beach-fleas (*Orchestia* and *Talorchestia* spp.), which abound on ocean and bay-side beaches near high-tide mark, where they scavenge on fish and other organisms, including seaweeds and seagrasses, that have been cast ashore. Some of the isopods, too, are scavengers; *Cirolana concharum,* or **greedy isopod,** scavenges over the bottom when the tide covers it for dead fish, crabs, and other animal matter.

Visiting vertebrate and invertebrate scavengers include the ubiquitous, omnivorous herring gull, which forages here as well as in every other seashore habitat; and beetles and other insects that range into this zone when the tide is low, feeding on any dead animals they can find.

PARASITES

Nowhere is the couplet that begins "Big fleas have little fleas" more applicable than in the estuarine intertidal communities. The parasitic way of life is represented here in an array of invertebrates from protozoans to crustaceans. Some isopods of the family Bopyridae are parasites permanently attached to crabs or hermit-crabs. The oyster crab, *Pinnotheres ostreum,* generally considered a commensal, lives in the mantle cavity of oysters, scallops, and mussels, and sometimes in the tube of the parchment worm. (Commensalism is a relationship in which two organisms live in close association with neither being a parasite on the other.) Because the oyster crab sometimes nibbles on the gills of its molluscan host and does purloin some of the mollusk's food, it can justifiably be called parasitical. *Pinnixa cylindrica,* a related crab, lives as a commensal with lugworms.

The young of the **opal worm** (*Arabella iricolor*) are parasites in the body of the **plumed worm** (*Diopatra cuprea*). Vermiform and *protozoan* parasites are no less common here than in any other habitat; the invertebrates that at an early stage of life parasitize other ani-

ESTUARINE COMMUNITIES

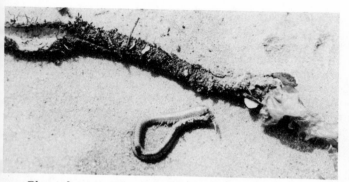

109. Plumed worm *(Diopatra cuprea)*; the soft but very tough tube has been slit with a sharp blade so the worm could be extracted. Note the sea lettuce *(Ulva lactuca)* attached to the end of the tube.

mals are themselves as adults invariably hosts to parasites. One phylum, the Mesozoa, is made up essentially of tiny parasites on marine invertebrates including flatworms, nemerteans, annelids, and mollusks. A nemertean worm, *Carcinonemertes carcinophila*, which itself may carry internal Mesozoan parasites, is found on the gills of female blue crabs. (It is pinkish when parasitizing virgin crabs, red on breeding crabs.) The blue crab is also victimized by *Loxothylacus panopaei* (a member of a parasitic order of barnacles, Rhizocephala), which takes up residence under its abdomen; and it may carry in its gill chamber *Octolasmus lowei*, a small goose barnacle. Striped and turtle barnacles often travel attached to its carapace.

Benthic Epifauna of the Intertidal Flats

The benthic epifauna of the intertidal flats consists of the animals—invertebrates all—that live in more or less fixed positions on top of the substrate, as opposed to those that move about freely on and in the sediments, which are called the *mobile epibenthos*, and those that live buried in the deposits, which are called the *infauna*. On the Middle Atlantic coast, the reef-building

Atlantic oyster and blue, or edible, mussel are the most conspicuous members of the epifauna. These mollusks form shoals or bars of considerable extent. The oyster bed is often a distinct community, with the oyster shells providing a substrate for attachment of bryozoans, sponges, barnacles, and hydroids, as well as algae. Oysters, like mussels, are suspension feeders; phytoplankton, including diatoms and other algae, constitute a major part of the diet of both mollusks.

MOLLUSKS

Atlantic Oyster. Extremely valuable commercially, a favorite of gourmands, and the subject of much biological and management research, this bivalve, *Crassostrea virginica,* has undoubtedly been given more attention by humans than any other marine invertebrate. Its welfare is a major objective in estuarine pollution studies, and its artificial propagation and cultivation are an important enterprise.

A female oyster lays around 50 million eggs in a spawning period. In light of the vast array of parasitic and predatory enemies, diseases, and environmental hazards, such fertility is hardly excessive. Perhaps only an average of a dozen of the eggs laid will ultimately produce mature individuals. The larvae, which drift with the tidal currents, are fed upon by myriad planktivores.

The oyster is an estuarine animal that thrives in brackish water rather than sea water, and since, because of the added outflow of the rivers, the ebbing tide flows more strongly than the rising-tide currents, the larval oysters must have an adaptation that prevents their being carried out to sea. This is achieved by their settling to the bottom on the outgoing tide, then rising to let the incoming tide carry them up the estuary. For those larvae carried to the more brackish upper part of the estuary, this behavioral adaptation has further survival value, as will be seen.

Eventually the developing oyster larvae settle down and cement themselves to a hard substrate—often old oyster shells—to begin the sedentary period of their growth to maturity. The youngest *spat* oysters are vul-

110. Atlantic oyster *(Crassostrea virginica)*.

nerable to a host of predators, including killifish, flounders, anchovies, grunts, spot, and young lookdowns *(Selene vover)*. Larger oysters are prey to sea stars *(Asterias* spp.), flatworms, the oyster drill *(Urosalpinx cinerea)*, scoters, the cownose ray, and the oystercatcher. Then, if they are not harvested first by humans, parasitized by the fungus *Dermocystidium,* smothered in silt, or weakened by commensals such as sponges *(Cliona* spp.), boring clams, mud worms, and crabs (see *Pinnotheres,* in the next section under Blue Mussel), they may survive to lay eggs for another generation.

The larval oysters that are carried far up the estuaries and settle as spat in water of less than 15 o/oo salinity are spared one hazard as maturing oysters. Two of their worst enemies—the oyster drill and the sea star—cannot tolerate such low salinities, so are not found in the upper estuary.

Blue Mussel. *Mytilus edulis* ("mussel, edible") is treated here as part of the benthic epifauna, but it is not inalterably bound to the substrate to which it first attaches itself. This bivalve, like other mytilids, is able to cast off its anchoring byssal threads, extend its foot, and throw out new byssal threads to reanchor itself. By a succession of such laborious steps the mussel can move to a new location. Its mobility is of course not comparable to that of another bivalve, the scallop, which, by clapping its valves, can swim with jerky movements.

Unlike other mollusks, mytilids have a single adductor muscle rather than a pair—or, in some cases, have a greatly reduced second adductor. This evolutionary development is related to the changing of shell shape that resulted in the mussel's valves' opening lengthwise rather than sideways.

The blue mussel is widely distributed in the northern hemisphere, and lives from slightly brackish water in the lower reaches of estuaries to deep offshore waters, so it is by no means identified solely with the intertidal flats. It thrives best where solid substrates such as pilings, rocks, and shelly bottoms occur; but it sometimes forms extensive, densely crowded beds on sandy or even muddy bottoms. The carapace and other parts of the horseshoe-crab's exoskeleton are sometimes heavily festooned with growing mussels.

The blue mussel attaches itself beak-downward to the substrate, with its ventral margin extending above the sand or mud. It is a filter feeder, and pollutants tend to become concentrated in its system, making possible contamination a source of concern for humans. Until recent years this was not a major problem, since this country did not share the European taste for these bivalves. But their increasing acceptance, particularly in restaurants featuring Old World cuisines, has made mussels at the same time a more sought-after resource and a subject of management concern.

Mussels are eaten by the same array of invertebrate and vertebrate predators as other mollusks, are infested with parasites and disease, and are imposed upon by such uninvited guests as the **mussel crab** *(Pinnotheres maculatus)*, which lives within the mantle cavity of the mussel and other bivalves. For any one of a number of reasons, perhaps most importantly stresses of the physical environment, the beds of mussels are somewhat transitory. Where a colony of full-grown mussels exists one year, the next may reveal bare mud or a bed of seed mussels. With the growing appreciation of its culinary qualities and commercial potential, the mussel is likely to be the subject of a great deal of research in population dynamics, biology, and ecology during the coming years.

Mobile Epibenthos of the Intertidal Flats

Included in the mobile epibenthos are the marine animals, mostly predators and scavengers, that move freely about the bottom in search of food, which they obtain from the surface of the deposits or by probing beneath the surface. Not included are the shorebirds, fish crows, grackles, and other birds that forage in the intertidal zone but are not confined to the marine environment. Also eliminated from this group are the fishes that come in with the tide to feed over the flats. (But see the oyster toadfish, in Chapter Five under Bony Fishes.) Most prominent of the mobile epibenthic animals are arthropods, and of these far and away the most important are crabs and their relatives.

ARTHROPODS

CRUSTACEANS. When the sandy and muddy intertidal bottoms are exposed by falling tides, three species of the small, nimble, semi-aquatic **fiddler crabs** can be seen feeding actively. When the tidal waters cover the flats, the **lady crab** (on sandy bottoms), the **green crab,** the **blue crab,** the **spider crab,** and the **mud crabs** (Xanthidae) forage for food. Mud crabs, small as they are, destroy many young clams and oysters; they are more strictly predatory than the others.

Fiddlers, which are discussed in Chapter Four under Animals of the Salt Marsh, are almost exclusively herbivorous; they can be observed in daylight, scraping microalgae from the surface or nibbling on sea lettuce and other macroalgae. The green crab, a scavenger, is most active at night, and is easily found by flashlight. Not known from Delaware south, it is most typical of New England shores, where rocks provide more hiding places. Like the fiddlers, the green crab is characteristic of intertidal estuarine habitats, and it tolerates quite low salinities. The lady crab and the blue crab are found subtidally and in the littoral zone when it is inundated. During most of the year the adult blue crabs prefer deeper water, but in moderate weather they forage over the intertidal zone, digging out shallow-burrowing polychaetes, thin-shelled bivalves such as *Macoma balthica,* and young **hard clams** *(Mercenaria mercenaria).* Able to tolerate salinities down to zero, *Callinectes sapidus,* the blue crab, is abundant and has a major impact on estuarine ecology as well as being of great importance economically.

Walking about in the habitat of the blue crab or lady crab carries the risk of a nasty pinch on the feet from one of these ill-tempered crustaceans. They often lie half-buried in the sediments, and are then difficult to see. Despite their aggressive behavior, both species are primarily scavengers. The blue crab is found on a wide variety of bottoms; the lady crab prefers sand, and often occurs on subtidal ocean beaches.

Some crustaceans and other arthropods that live in the marshes or on the upper shore venture onto the flats at low tide to feed. Several amphipods, including *Orchestia* spp. (discussed in Chapter Two under Animals of the Upper Beach), are also found on the higher levels of the intertidal flats, where they feed on the blue-green algal mats, or near the high-tide mark, where they feed on decaying windrows of *Zostera* and other debris. Both the blue-green algae and the wrack are also grazed by larval dipterans, mites, and nematodes (the last-named belonging to a phylum different from that of the arthropods).

Common Spider Crab. *Libinia emarginata* is found throughout the Middle Atlantic coast in estuaries and in offshore waters to a depth of at least 160 ft. (48 m). It occurs on sandy, muddy, or shelly bottoms, and is often seen at the very edge of the water in shallow estuaries and lagoons. Invariably the spider crab is draped with living plants and debris. Placed there by the crab itself, this miniature garden evidently serves a concealment function, though it is a mystery how the crab developed this adaptive behavior.

The spider crab's shell is covered with short, hooked hairs that make the task of self-adornment easy. Among the items it "plants" are algae, including sea lettuce; eelgrass; and hydroids, bryozoans, and sponges—all animals with plantlike growth forms. One also finds barnacles on the carapace, but these probably attach themselves during their early life stages. A nonstreamlined, naturally slow-moving animal anyway, *Libinia* probably suffers no great inconvenience from carrying its living burden.

The spider crab selects its masking objects seemingly with care rather than haphazardly. It is able to transplant both hydroids and sponges without damaging them. For this task it uses its long, flexible *chelipeds* (legs with pincerlike claws). The object is first held to the crab's mouth, where a dab of some kind of cement is applied, then placed on the carapace in the chosen spot. If it doesn't hold at the first location, the process is repeated. Like a housewife making changes in the furniture arrangement, the crab may at times even switch the locations of two kinds of organisms—perhaps a sponge and an alga.

This sluggish animal's diet is not well known, but it is probably a scavenger. Spider crabs are eaten by cod and other bottom feeders. Young crabs have been known to hitchhike in the bell of the mushroom cap, a jellyfish. Given its normal manner of locomotion, this may be the fastest mode of travel for the species.

Green Crab. One who explores the seashore communities north of Delaware Bay will probably encounter the green crab *(Carcinus maenas)* more than any other crab species. It is hard to miss this crustacean on the southern New England coast, where young green crabs are particularly abundant in intertidal areas; look for them under stones and in hiding places. Because it will tolerate salinities as low as 6 o/oo, *Carcinus* is found well up-estuary; it is also found on protected, stony ocean beaches such as that at Hammonasett, Connecticut, which is partly shielded from ocean waves by Long Island.

How does this marine animal cope with the low salinities? In such conditions the green crab's blood is *hyperosmotic*—maintained as a more concentrated solution than the surrounding medium. This is achieved by an increase in urine production; it is about four times as great in estuarine water of 18 o/oo salinity as in sea water.

Though the green crab varies some in color, not all

individuals being conspicuously green, identifying it is easy. (With the tiny young crabs one needs a hand lens.) Just count the "teeth" on the anterior edge of the carapace; there are five on each side. Young green crabs might be mistaken for mud crabs, which also have 10 marginal teeth; but on the green crab the two pairs of teeth adjacent to the eyes are partially fused, and there is a notch in the margin between the eyes.

The green crab's specific name, *maenas*—pronounced "meanes"—is Latin for frenzy; and mean it is. Indeed, the French call it *crabe enragé*. But it's easier to handle than the even more pugnacious blue or lady crabs. Extracting the green crab from its hiding place under big rocks or in crevices in rock jetties is tricky; sometimes it can more easiily be captured by looking under seaweeds or by turning over small stones.

C. maenas is said to have been unknown north of Cape Cod in the nineteenth century; in 1931 William Crowder (in *Seashore Life Between the Tides*) gave its range as Cape Cod to New Jersey. But Augusta Foote Arnold, who wrote of it in *The Sea Beach at Ebb-tide* in 1899, at that time had no trouble finding it in tidepools at Bar Harbor, Maine. At any rate, as the end of the twentieth century approaches, the green crab ranges to Nova Scotia, being quite common in the Gulf of Maine. Its absence from the southern half of the Embayed Section might be due to water temperatures; yet it has been reported from various tropical and subtropical locations. Possibly it reached those areas by clinging to fouling organisms on ship's bottoms, and has not established stable populations in southern realms.

Horseshoe-crab. The only living member of the class Merostomata of the phylum Arthropoda, *Limulus polyphemus* is surely the most easily recognized member of the mobile epibenthos. Like the blue crab, it is a swimmer that forages on and in the deposits. It is able to breathe air, and ranges from the high-water mark to a depth of about 75 ft. (23 m). At times—during the spring and early-summer breeding season—it is the most conspicuous invertebrate on many estuarine shores. This living fossil, essentially unchanged for some 200 million years, appears, often in great numbers, to lay its eggs at

111. Horseshoe-crab *(Limulus polyphemus),* ventral surface.

the upper limits of the sandy flats. Like trains of coupled freight cars, the horseshoe-crabs come ashore, with the larger female in the place of the pulling locomotive and the males—four or five of them—each clinging to the tail of the individual in front, and all being dragged along by the female. In time, the female deposits her eggs in a depression in the sand, where they are fertil-

112. The eggs of *Limulus.*

Estuarine Mud and Sand Flats

ized by the male (or males) and left to be covered by the incoming tide. Small windrows of the greenish eggs are sometimes formed at the high-water mark on bayside beaches. Even those that are buried in the sand below that point are subject to predation by laughing gulls and glossy ibises; too greedy to wait until the horseshoe-crabs have finished their work, the birds congregate in the midst of the breeding arthropods to feed upon the minute but abundant eggs.

When the eggs hatch, the tiny, pale, tailless, free-swimming young horseshoe-crabs disperse into the shallow waters, where they remain until considerably grown and darkened in color. For some time after the breeding period begins, the shores may be littered with adults, mostly upside-down and struggling to right themselves, or mostly dead and dying. Gulls eat the edible parts of the stranded arthropods; the shells may remain for years as part of the upper-beach substrate.

The horseshoe-crab is a predator; it plows through the sandy or muddy sediments with the aid of its carapace, which has a beveled edge, in search of mollusks and worms. Despite its lack of jaws it can crush shelled prey—grinding the victim between its shoulders, so to speak. The first four pairs of its five pairs of walking legs bear on their bases spiny projections that function for this purpose. It can be quite destructive of young clams, but it plays a nonpredatory role in the estuarine community as well. The arthropod serves as a hard substrate for attachment and a means of transport for an array of plant and animal commensals. It is not unusual to find a large specimen of *Limulus*—past the exoskeleton-shedding stage of life (in other words, full grown)—carrying about on its carapace living specimens of sea lettuce, barnacles, slipper shells, hydroids, tube worms, and limpets. On its gill books, described below, it frequently carries the commensal flatworm *(Bdelloura candida)* or related limulus leeches.

The service *Limulus* provides hitchhiking plants and animals may have real significance in an environment where the substrate is too unstable for organisms that lead a sedentary lifestyle. This arthropod is also of some importance to humans; its blood (which is blue) is today used in certain kinds of medical diagnosis. In the past, abundant horseshoe-crabs have been utilized as fertilizer and even as chicken and hog food.

L. polyphemus was formerly placed in the class Arachnida. Its *gill books*—groups of thin plates in which the blood circulates—are similar enough in plan to the lung books of terrestrial arachnids (including spiders, harvestmen, mites, and pseudoscorpions) that the lung books were believed to have derived from some sort of gill book. *Limulus* does have a body plan basically like that of arachnids; it is divided into cephalothorax and abdomen, with six pairs of appendages, the first pair being pinching legs (chelicerae) and the other five pairs walking legs. Biologists believe that its closest living relatives are spiders.

MOLLUSKS

GASTROPODS.   This is a group of freshwater, marine, and terrestrial mollusks, some shell-less and some with a single spiral shell.

Northern Moon Shell. *Lunatia heros* is less conspicuous than the horseshoe-crab, but is common on estuarine and bay shores from Long Island north—and its

113. Northern moon shell *(Lunatia heros).*

Estuarine Mud and Sand Flats   233

occurrence is not limited to the breeding season. This medium-sized gastropod's presence is revealed by two visual clues. The curious "sand collars," found wherever the moon shell lives, were mistaken by early naturalists for some strange invertebrate form. In fact, they are the egg masses of the moon shell, held in a matrix of sand grains cemented by a gelatinous mucus. They tend to disintegrate when dry, though they seem quite substantial when you find them in the shallow water. And distinctive trails are left by *Lunatia* as it moves just under the surface in search of its bivalve prey—much as a mole pushing through moist soil leaves a telltale ridge of dirt or turf. At one end of the moon shell's trail is found a small mound of sand; digging into this reveals a globose shell as much as 4 in. (10 cm) in diameter, most often partly or entirely enveloped by the fleshy foot. The moon shell is able to retract this foot by expelling the water held in it.

The moon shell's name derives from its smooth, gray-to-tan, rather shiny, spherical shell. Small individuals of the northern moon shell are easily distinguished from the **lobed moon shell** *(Polinices duplicatus)* by the open umbilicus of the former. The umbilicus of the latter species is covered by a heavy callous deposit. Both species are found throughout the Middle Atlantic seashore, and both are highly predaceous; it is said that one lobed moon shell (also called double moon snail or shark eye) eats about 100 soft-shelled clams per year. South of Long Island *L. heros* lives in deeper water. But even in areas where it does not live on the intertidal flats, bivalve shells with the characteristic holes are often found on the beaches as evidence of its depredations.

Lunatia uses its *radula* (a tonguelike rasping organ) to bore a neat, beveled hole in the shell of a clam or other bivalve; it then sucks out the flesh of its victim. It sometimes feeds upon dead fish. This snail is most easily found in very shallow water or just above the water line where the sand is saturated and easily plowed. Sometimes it pushes through the sand only half buried. This animal illustrates the fuzziness of the division between infauna and epifauna; one could classify the moon shell as belonging to either.

ESTUARINE COMMUNITIES

Mud Dog Whelk *(Nassarius obsoletus)*. Also called **mud basket shell** and **eastern mud nassa,** this snail is the gastropod most closely identified with the mud flats and intertidal muddy creek and river banks. It is also found subtidally. As it moves across the mud flats, it leaves a characteristic groove as a trail. Basically dark reddish brown, this snail is usually so discolored with mud stain and algae that its true hue is not evident. The specific name *obsoletus,* meaning worn out, refers to the surface of the eroded shell, which reveals virtually no sculpturing. Its very nondescript nature, along with its extreme abundance, somewhat simplifies identification. *Whelk* is a misnomer, however, for this snail belongs to the basketshell family, Nassaridae. It is sometimes placed in a genus of its own and designated *Ilyanassa obsoleta.*

Because of its numbers, its wide distribution, and its scavenging habits, the mud dog whelk must be counted among the major constituents of the estuarine fauna. It is a good food source for puffers and other fishes, black ducks and other waterfowl, various wading and shore birds, and the muskrat. It lays transparent, angular egg capsules on eelgrass and cordgrass. Individuals may attain a height of up to 1 in. (25 mm), but most are smaller.

ECHINODERMS

SEA STARS. Oystermen of our coastal bays have sometimes made a practice of cutting up specimens of *Asterias forbesi* they caught, then throwing the pieces back into the water. This was intended as a control measure on a species known to be a major predator on oysters and other shellfish. But this method of combating **Forbes' asterias** was misguided, for sea stars have remarkable powers of regeneration; severed parts often develop into whole new individuals.

A. forbesi is the most familiar echinoderm of the Middle Atlantic coast. It is found in the intertidal zone and subtidally to depths of 150 ft. (45 m) at Cape Cod, and at increasing depths southward. (This sea star could as easily be treated as a member of the offshore benthic community of the open coast, but it is more commonly seen in the estuaries and protected bays.) *Asterias* dis-

114. Forbes' asterias *(Asterias forbesi)*.

plays a range of colors including brown, yellow, red, and purple, but is distinguished by a bright orange *madreporite*—the porous "sieve plate" through which the internal water-vascular system opens to the exterior —situated on its upper surface at the angle of two arms. It tolerates salinities down to 15 o/oo, but in waters with lower salinities oysters are safe from its depredations.

Sea stars move about the bottom with the help of numerous *tube feet,* which are borne in rows on the oral (under) side of each arm (of which there are five in *Asterias*). The sea star moves in a straight line, with one arm in advance, at a speed of only a few inches per minute. These members of the epibenthos can also float free and travel with the aid of currents.

The tube feet of sea stars function like sucking discs with a force of as much as 9 pounds per square inch pressure—much more than is needed for locomotion. But this capability serves two other needs: it enables the animal to resist the action of strong waves and currents, and it functions in predation. Anyone who has tried to open an oyster without tools can imagine the problem encountered by a soft-bodied predator with neither jaws nor teeth. The sea star overcomes the oyster or clam by attaching its arms to the two valves with its tube feet and exerting a steady pull. Since the muscles

ESTUARINE COMMUNITIES

the shellfish uses to keep its valves closed are as strong as those of the sea star, the contest becomes one of endurance. For the echinoderm to open the valves of the mollusk even a slight amount may take several hours. But an opening about 1/250 in. (0.1 mm) wide is enough. The sea star inserts its eversible stomach through this narrow crack and proceeds to digest the soft body inside the mollusk's shell.

Asterias reaches breeding age in about a year, when it has attained a size of perhaps 2.5 in. (64 mm). It reproduces by shedding eggs—in the case of Forbes' asterias as many as 2.5 million—into the sea, where they are fertilized. This process may begin suddenly in a whole population when a single female starts to shed her eggs, immediately stimulating other females to follow suit and males to shed their milt. The breeding behavior can even be set in motion by the accidental crushing of a female ripe with eggs. The eggs develop into transparent larvae that swim about at the surface for a few weeks, feeding on minute animals until they are about 1/3 in. (8 mm) long, then settle down and metamorphose. It must be during the larval period that they suffer the greatest predation, for sea stars otherwise do not appear to be eaten by larger animals as much as are the related sea urchins (which are human food as well). Sea stars are numerous enough to constitute a real economic threat to the shellfish industry; one individual may consume many small clams (swallowed whole) in a day.

ECHINOIDS. Sea urchins are more familiar to people who explore the tidepools of the northern New England coast than they are to visitors to the Middle Atlantic coast; but one species is found between Cape Cod and Cape Hatteras. *Arbacia punctulata,* the **purple sea urchin,** occurs near jetties or pilings in the lower intertidal zone as well as subtidally on sand bottoms or oyster beds. It is an omnivore, feeding on seaweeds and sedentary invertebrates, and is a scavenger on dead animals. Like sea stars, sea urchins have tube feet; and if you removed the spines from an intact exoskeleton (called a *test*) of a sea urchin, or found a test washed up on the shore, the same five-part radial pattern that characterizes sea stars would be revealed. Sea urchins move by pulling with their tube feet and levering with their spines. Many fish feed upon them, including the oyster toad, pigfish, sea bass, Atlantic needlefish, pinfish, bighead searobin, filefishes, and northern puffer. Crabs, gulls, and sea stars also prey upon them.

The **sand dollar** *(Echinarachnius parma)* belongs to the same class of invertebrates as the sea urchin, but it is flat rather than globular. The dead tests are familiar to many beachgoers. In life the sand dollar has a feltlike coating of fine spines instead of the bristly armor of the urchins. It feeds by plowing through the loose sand that is its habitat, eating diatoms and other microorganisms, and is fed upon by cod, flounders, and haddock, and by sea stars.

Benthic Infauna of the Intertidal Flats

The animals that live under the surface of the sand and mud flats are, except for a few fishes that are commensals in the burrows or tubes of worms, exclusively invertebrates. They range widely in size, and for convenience biologists divide them into three groups. *Microfauna* are those that will pass through a 0.062-mm mesh. *Meiofauna* are those that will pass through a 0.5-mm mesh but not a 0.062-mm mesh. *Macrofauna* are retained on a 0.5-mm mesh. Of course these distinctions do not parallel taxonomic categories; moreover, some species belong to one group in the larval stage and to another when fully grown.

THE PHYSICAL ENVIRONMENT

There is some correlation between the diversity and size of benthic faunal populations and the type of bottom. The makeup of the macrofauna component of the infauna, particularly the burrowers, is much affected by the physical qualities of the sediment. Because organic particles are light and subject to suspension and transport by the gentlest of water movements, they are more common in muddy sands and muds, which are deposited in quiet waters. Sand deposits, because they occur in places where currents and waves are of consequence, are relatively free of organic materials and are inhospitable to animals that require a stable substrate.

The water content of the deposit decreases when the tide goes out, but the degree of decrease depends on the rate of drainage. Sand deposits drain relatively rapidly when the tide goes out. Muddy deposits, with their smaller particles, higher organic content, and generally very gradual slope, tend not to drain between tides but to remain relatively wet until the tide again covers them. This minimizes the problem of desiccation for the inhabitants of mud flats. When water covers a flat, it can be observed that silt—very fine inorganic particles—is held in suspension at the surface of the mud and is very easily stirred up.

The organic content of mud is primarily detritus. Breaking down the detritus particles are bacterial films, a particularly significant element in the ecology of these flats because they provide most of the food of deposit feeders: nonselective feeders, such as *Arenicola,* which swallow muddy sand and digest the organic component; and selective feeders, such as *Nereis,* which ingest only those particles that have food value for them. Deposit feeders tend to be more numerous in the lower levels of the mud flats, where detritus is more abundant.

Although sand contains less organic material than mud, all sands contain some detritus from various sources—primarily decaying plant and animal matter. Because sand deposits are generally situated where there is a degree of turbulence, the amount of detritus is too slight to clog the interstices and bind the sand grains together. When the tide ebbs, the water-filled interstices drain relatively quickly. As the water moves downward in the deposits, its oxygen content is reduced by respiration of bacteria and of meiofauna and by oxidation of chemical substances. At some point below the surface of the sand, determined by its organic content, is a level at which no oxygen remains. This may be a small fraction of a centimeter or many centimeters below the surface. It is marked by a dark coloration called the sulfide layer. This black sand is the indirect result of the activity of bacteria on decaying organic matter.

The meiofauna species are essentially restricted to the sandy deposits, where oxygenation is deeper than in finer sediments. Burrowing and creeping anemones, creeping tunicates, amphipods, cumaceans, sand shrimps, long-eyed shrimps, opheliid worms, and other invertebrates occupy this oxygenated zone above the sulphide layer.

ANIMALS IN MUD AND SAND

When epifauna and infauna are both considered, muddy sands and sandy muds support many more animals than do nearly pure sands or slimy muds. Sand deposits, despite their instability and their relative lack of organic material, are habitable to a greater depth because of the availability of oxygen. Many of the organisms in these sandy bottoms are interstitial plants and animals. The plants are mostly diatoms and dinoflagellates. The latter have an animal-like ability to swim about in the film of water covering the sand grains, by means of whiplike flagellae. Among the interstitial animals are protozoans, tardigrades, copepods, archianellid worms, gastrotrichs, and roundworms. The two last-named groups are filter feeders and need to avoid areas where large amounts of fine material, which might clog their feeding devices, are in suspension. Thus gastrotrichs and roundworms are more likely to be found at higher levels of intertidal shores, and in sandy rather than muddy deposits.

Some of the sedentary polychaetes are successful in sandy deposits, where they make permanent burrows in which they live encased in sandy or mucous or membranous tubes. One of the most interesting of these tubes is the slender cone of the **trumpet worm** (*Pectinaria gouldii*), which under the magnification of a hand lens is revealed to be made of a single layer of uniform-sized quartz grains cemented together in a remarkably precise bit of mosaic engineering. The worm, growing to 2 in. (50 mm) in length, is itself a beautiful creation. It is pinkish in color, with deep red and blue mottling; and it bears a fan of long, golden bristles with which it digs in the sand and collects food particles. These bristles also serve, like the operculum of a snail, as a sort of lid for the tube.

ESTUARINE COMMUNITIES

The trumpet worm lies in the deposits with only the tip of its cone above the surface for breathing. It is found on both muddy and sandy shores throughout the Middle Atlantic range, intertidally and in shallow subtidal waters. It tolerates salinities as low as 15 o/oo.

As sandy deposits merge into bottoms with increasing amounts of fine materials, establishment of permanent burrows becomes easier, and many species utilizing suspended plankton or the organic material in the sediments are present. Stocky-bodied animals, for which sand deposits are not generally hospitable, are characteristic of sandy-mud and mud sediments. Such forms as the **stout tagelus** *(T. plebeius)* and the **common razor clam** *(Ensis directus)* burrow deeply into sandy mud flats throughout our coast. Deposit feeders such as *Arenicola* spp. and *Scoloplos acutus* (polychaetes); and *Macoma balthica, Cardium edule,* and *Phyllodoce maculata* (bivalves) are common in sand containing an appreciable amount of fine particles. Vermiform invertebrates are particularly evident in muds and sandy muds of the intertidal zone. Besides lugworms *(Arenicola)* there are other sedentary polychaetes such as the tubiculous parchment worm and many mud worms *(Ophelia, Travisia,* and *Ophelina* spp.). Also present are isopods, the mantis shrimp, and bivalve mollusks.

The parchment worm *(Chaetopterus variopedatus)*, which draws particles into its burrow and collects them on a mucus net, would be handicapped by the presence of too many net-clogging fine particles. Look for it, then, in waters where not too much fine particulate matter is in suspension, as in eelgrass beds.

Very fine muds, which tend to be slimy, are inhabited by some of the tube-making amphipods and by terebellid worms. The life in such sediments is concentrated in the upper few centimeters—even the top centimeter—because of the extreme shallowness of the oxygenated zone.

THE BENTHIC MEIOFAUNA

Although the organisms of the meiofaunal component of the benthic infauna are so minute as to be invisible or nearly so to the naked eye, and for this reason will not be described in detail here, some further explanation of their relationship to the deposits is in order. The variety and abundance of the interstitial animals increase as one moves from pure sand deposits into sediments with increasing mud content. (In this habitat the terms interstitial and meiofaunal are synonymous.) The chief factors accounting for this pattern are the increasing organic content (carbon) and the decreasing size of the particles making up the sediment. Coarser sediments provide a smaller total surface upon which bacteria and microalgae can grow, and thus furnish a lesser food resource. But the spaces between particles are smaller in mud, too, and interstitial fauna must necessarily be smaller. The size of many of the meiofaunal animals approaches the size of the particles amongst which they move, and this makes separating these animals from their surrounding medium difficult for the collector.

The variety and abundance of meiofauna do not continue to increase as one moves from sandy muds to nearly pure muds; instead, the trend reverses itself here. The point of diminishing returns is reached when the space between particles is too small for many of the interstitial organisms or when the bottom of the extremely shallow oxygenated zone characteristic of muddy deposits is approached.

The meiofauna play a limited role in the estuarine food chain, particularly on sand flats, for not many predators are adapted for feeding on them. It has been shown that meiofauna in muds are more available to consumers because they are concentrated in the top layer of deposits. Sand deposits are oxygenated to a much greater depth, but have a much poorer interstitial fauna; there the labor required for a consumer to obtain the thinly dispersed food makes feeding less efficient.

The meiofaunal animals of sands, adapted for a life among the sand grains, are mostly vermiform. Despite this similarity of form, almost every phylum of the animal kingdom is represented in the intertidal meiofauna: there are hydroids, archiannellids, mollusks, seacucumbers, and nematodes ranging in size from 150 microns to 3 mm (1/10 in.). Some are large enough to be

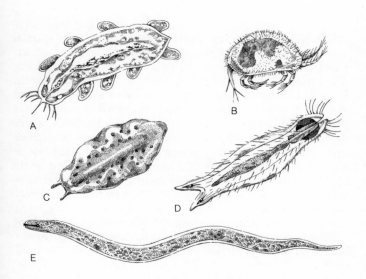

115. Benthic meiofauna: A. Tardigrade. B. Ostracod.
C. Flatworm. D. Gastrotrich. E. Nematode.

seen by the naked eye. It may be hard to imagine mollusks and echinoderms so small as to be able to move
about between the grains of sand, but they exist in this
habitat. Protozoan meiofauna, on the other hand, tend
to be larger than their relatives from other habitats.
One interstitial protozoan is 4 mm. long—very large
indeed for a single-celled animal. The reason for this is
not known, but apparently too small a size is as much
of a disadvantage in this habitat as is too large a size,
perhaps because of predator-prey relationships.

Among the other groups represented in the meiofauna of sand and mud flats are the polychaetes, copepods, and isopods, which include macrofauna species
discussed elsewhere in this book. A very small class of
minute creatures, the Gastrotricha, is represented by
marine meiofaunal species that, instead of moving
about among the sand grains, attach themselves to the
grains permanently and feed upon diatoms, protozoans,
detritus, and bacteria. A class of flatworms, the Turbel-
laria, also includes many interstitial forms.

TARDIGRADES.   One group of interstitial animals,

Estuarine Mud and Sand Flats

while of no known ecological importance, is of special interest. The **tardigrades**—sometimes classified as arthropods but sometimes placed in their own phylum, Tardigrada—are mostly less than a half-millimeter in length. Consequently, they are seldom seen. They are not limited to marine habitats; those tardigrades that are marine are mostly a part of the meiofauna of sandy deposits. They may be very numerous—*Batillipes mirus* has been found in concentrations of 300 individuals per 100 cubic cm in this habitat—but this is not its chief claim to distinction. The most remarkable characteristic of tardigrades is their ability to withstand desiccation of their environment. A tardigrade under such conditions shrivels into a minute anabiotic granule. Metabolism ceases until such time as the medium again becomes wet, perhaps years later. Then the animal swells and resumes feeding and reproducing. (Their feeding habits are not well known.)

Tardigrades are the animals sold by mail (in the anabiotic form—that is, in a deathlike state of suspended animation) to unsuspecting young readers of comic books and magazines as "water bears." The seductive advertisements, with drawings of bearlike creatures swimming about in a fish bowl, fail to include the information that the animals are too small to be seen by the unaided eye.

NEMATODES. When it comes to sheer numbers, the **nematodes,** constituting a class of Aschelminthean worms, are without rivals in the intertidal flats. Belonging to a phylum of minute, unsegmented, mostly vermiform animals, the nematodes are of great importance as parasites of humans, domestic animals, and wildlife; and also as pests of crops. Nematodes exist in incredible numbers. Ninety thousand have been found in a single decaying apple; their occurrence has been calculated at 4.5 million per square yard (per 0.9 square m) in a mud flat off the Netherlands coast. Though they are abundant on the Middle Atlantic coast, as elsewhere, most of the species are microscopic or near-microscopic. There are many kinds, with upwards of 10,000 species known but perhaps 500,000 more to be discovered.

Nematodes are subjects of study chiefly by parasitologists. Identification is made no easier by the fact that they exhibit little variation in form. The meter-long human parasite, *Dracunculus medinensis,* infests a copepod, *Cyclops,* in its alternate stage. Close examination of fishes, crabs, sea urchins, and other vertebrates and invertebrates will reveal their presence, for all fishes and most of the lower animals of the seashore harbor these worms.

THE BENTHIC MACROINFAUNA

Other than the edible mollusks, perhaps the best known inhabitants of the sediments in the intertidal flats are polychaetes, or bristle worms. One prominent group, called sedentary polychaetes because of their habit of living permanently in a burrow or tube, includes the lugworms (*Arenicola* spp.) and the parchment worm *(Chaetopterus variopedatus).* Another group, called errant polychaetes because they sometimes leave their burrows to go hunting (they are good swimmers), includes the familiar clam worms (*Nereis* spp.)

The mollusk component of the benthic macroinfauna consists mostly of bivalves, but some gastropods (snails and kin) are primarily or occasionally found in the deposits. (The status of the moon snail as both infaunal and epifaunal has already been mentioned.) Several of the better known of the mollusks of the infauna are discussed in this section.

SEDENTARY POLYCHAETES. This classification is as much a convenience as a strict taxonomic grouping, but these bristle worms do have certain things in common as a rule. Their bodies are divided into two regions, thorax and abdomen; the head is usually equipped with special food-gathering and respiratory devices; and the food is generally small particles such as detritus and plankton. Not all are as wormlike in form as the members of the genus of lugworms described below.

Lugworms. Like most sedentary polychaetes, the lugworm is a tube dweller. *Arenicola* species are found worldwide. The **common European lugworm,** *A. marina,* is found in this region only subtidally, on the south shore of Cape Cod. The **Brazilian lugworm,** *A. brasili-*

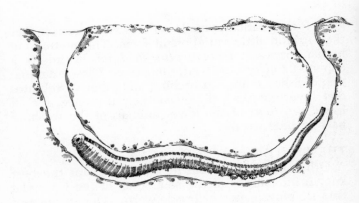

116. A lugworm *(Arenicola cristata)* in its burrow.

ensis, is also known on the south shore of Cape Cod, as well as in Brazil and parts of the Pacific Ocean. *A. cristata* (its only name) is the species most likely to be encountered on the Middle Atlantic coast; its northern limit is Cape Cod, and it ranges far south of Cape Hatteras. It is abundant in many relatively undisturbed sediments.

Arenicola is a sediment feeder, burrowing at a depth of 2 to 6 in. (5 to 15 cm), everting its proboscis and then inverting it to swallow the sand and mud sticking to the mucus-covered papillae of that organ. It functions as a funnel feeder when it constructs a semi-permanent, L-shaped burrow. With its head at the toe of the burrow, it pumps sediments in through the "tail shaft." Periodically it backs up to the opening at the surface to deposit its feces a few inches away from the burrow. As it feeds, the sand collapses around the opening of the tail shaft —above the toe of the burrow—forming a funnel-shaped depression.

In *A. marina* and *A. brasiliensis* the castings are coiled much like those of the terrestrial earthworm; *A. cristata* deposits a simple uncoiled mound of fecal material. Incoming tides, while bringing a new supply of food, erase traces of the lugworm's presence. When the tide is out, the characteristic funnels and castings make the lugworm easy to locate; but digging out an intact specimen is another matter, as the slender posterior

ESTUARINE COMMUNITIES

117. Lugworm castings and egg mass.

third of the worm's body usually breaks off. Keeping the worm in a suitable container where it can feed enables it to regenerate the lost part.

Lugworms bear gills on the segments of the middle third of the body. *A. cristata* grows to about 1 ft. (30 cm), and has 11 pairs of gills. It prefers intertidal flats where the mud content is high, and it is tolerant of brackish water to salinities as low as 6 o/oo. The eggs of *A. cristata* are laid in large blobs of mucus tapered to a point at one end, which are anchored in the sand. When the eggs hatch, the embryos feed upon the mucus; they leave when they have developed into segmented larvae. Soon after escaping they burrow into the sand near low-tide mark.

Fishermen use these polychaetes as bait, and they have long been objects of study in biology classes. Because they are abundant in places and process great quantities of sediment, and because they are food for many other species, lugworms are of some ecological importance. Although relatively secure from most cold-blooded vertebrate predators, they are nevertheless fed upon by certain cartilaginous and bony fishes that

Estuarine Mud and Sand Flats

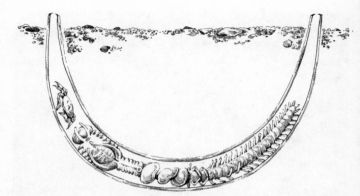

118. Parchment worm *(Chaetopterus variopedatus)* with the commensal crab *Polyonyx gibbesi* in its tube.

dig pits in the sediments. Among these are the cownose ray *(Rhinoptera bonasus)*, spot, and croakers. And a number of shorebirds possess long bills enabling them to probe the burrows.

Parchment Worm. Another sedentary polychaete, *Chaetopterus variopedatus,* was mentioned earlier in this chapter in connection with the distribution of fauna in sand and mud. Found all over the world, *C. variopedatus* has a highly differentiated body and a highly specialized feeding mechanism. It is primarily subtidal, and is found in *Zostera* beds as well as in mud flats; search for it only at the lowest intertidal level during spring tides.

This worm is able to survive in the mud and sand deposits because of its ability to draw water through its parchmentlike tube. The yellowish tube is roughly U-shaped, about a half-inch in diameter, with the openings at two small, chimneylike structures projecting above the sediment surface. The tube is made of very tough material; the worm itself is extremely delicate. Segments 14, 15, and 16 each bear a pair of fanlike structures whose movement draws water in through the anterior end of the tube and out the posterior end. The plankton suspended in the water are filtered out by means of a mucus net held by two winglike structures. When the net has collected a supply of food it is rolled

ESTUARINE COMMUNITIES

into a ball and passed forward to the mouth along a ciliated mid-dorsal gutter. The size range of particles that can be filtered out of the water by this device is not known; but the mucus net of another (unrelated) worm, *Urechis,* has openings about 4/25,000,000 in. (1/250,000 mm) in size. (Similar mechanisms are possessed by a variety of suspension feeders.) The water currents produced by the parchment worm's well-coordinated fans serve in respiration as well as in feeding.

Commensal crabs are often associated with the parchment worm. One of these, the **parchment worm polyonyx** *(Polyonyx gibbesi),* which measures up to 0.5 in. (12.5 mm) is seldom found anywhere except in the tubes of *Chaetopterus,* which itself measures up to 10 in. (25 cm), and occupies a tube not much bigger than itself. This habitat is also typical of *Pinnixa chaetopterana,* a pea crab. Other pea crabs *(Pinnotheres* spp.) that are often commensals with various bivalves inhabit the tube of *C. variopedatus,* where they feed upon the plankton brought into it by the worm.

The parchment worm is trapped inside its own tube, which is tapered at both ends. But it is not secure from predators; deep-probing birds such as the willet manage to extricate it. *Chaetopterus* also lives in eelgrass beds, where it is not so vulnerable to predation by birds. But other enemies feed on it in subtidal as well as intertidal deposits: the cownose ray can excavate it from its subterranean home, and crustaceans feed upon various parts of the worm's body. However, great powers of regeneration enable *Chaetopterus* to replace tentacles, fans, feeding cups, head, or tail, so it is not entirely vulnerable to the latter type of "predation."

Parchment worms reproduce by discharging eggs and sperm into the water, where fertilization takes place by chance. Various factors, such as the lunar cycle, tides, temperature, time of day, and weather, determine the timing of spawning.

ERRANT POLYCHAETES. Like the corresponding designation *sedentary polychaetes,* this is a largely practical classification. The term *errant* derives from the fact that most members of the group sometimes leave their homes to wander about; but not all do this. Most of them are long and slender, with no distinct body regions; most have eversible prosbosces with jaws; most are tube dwellers; and most are carnivorous.

Clam Worms. These polychaetes, *Nereis* spp., are known to the fishing fraternity as desirable bait; they are worth knowing also for their ecology and at least in some species for their beauty of form, color, and motion. The observer who thinks of worms as ugly creatures may have a change of heart when watching a 3-ft. *Nereis virens* as it swims with gracefully undulating movements, its body an iridescent blue green dappled with red or gold and glinting in the sunlight.

Authorities on polychaetes consider clam worms best qualified for the designation of "average" annelids (the phylum of segmented worms, which includes leeches and earthworms). They are relatively unspecialized in structure and food habits, as compared with earthworms and leeches. They are herbivores, predators, and omnivores living in bays and estuaries, in intertidal and subtidal sand and mud deposits, on algae, on eelgrass, and among fouling organisms. Some of the clam worms are tube dwellers.

Like other polychaetes, those of the genus *Nereis* (rhymes with "here he is") have bristle-bearing *parapods* (lateral footlike appendages) along each side. In the clam worms these are used both in swimming and in respiration; each parapod contains an intricate network of thin-walled capillaries that function in the exchange of gases with the surrounding medium. *Nereis* spp. are specialized chiefly in the segments of the anterior end. Within the pharynx are two horny jaws; when the pharynx is everted through the mouth, these jaws come into play as weapons; prey is seized and swallowed by withdrawal of the pharynx. Some species, including *N. virens,* browse on sea lettuce or diatoms. Others eat detritus, and some are cannibalistic on their own species. Some are able to function as filter feeders, using a funnel of mucus threads through which the worm draws water; the funnel is ingested along with the collected food particles.

One species, *N. diversicolor,* is very much an omnivore; it has been found to feed upon diatoms, turbellari-

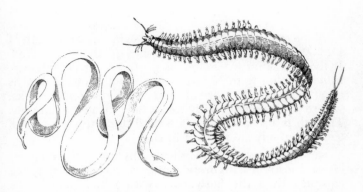

119. *Left:* milky ribbon worm *(Cerebratulus lacteus); right:* clam worm *(Nereis virens).*

ans, nematodes, polychaetes, copepods, ostracods, crustacean eggs, other arthropods, plants, dead animal matter, and detritus. Because of the nereids' abundance (a density as high as 1,000 per square meter), their wide-ranging food habits, and their role as a link in food chains ending with man, they are of great ecological importance. Often the dominant invertebrate forms in bay, lagoonal, and estuarine communities, they are a major food resource for commercially important fishes.

Nereis virens is the best known clam worm in the Embayed Section of the Middle Atlantic coast; it is found from Delaware Bay north (and has been reported in Virginia), from the upper intertidal zone to subtidal waters at considerable depths (500 ft., or 152 m). It inhabits a great variety of deposits from sand to clay, in coastal bays and brackish estuaries. It is common on eelgrass bottoms. Typically a foot or less in length, it sometimes reaches 3 ft. (0.9 m). It has 200 segments, and its head bears four pairs of tentacles of equal length.

N. virens lines its burrow with mucus, and moves frequently to new sites. This clam worm is a voracious predator, feeding on other worms, crustaceans, carrion, algae, and small fishes. It is in turn fed upon by fishes, particularly drums; by rays; and by shorebirds. It is dug for bait by and for sport fishermen. Look for this species under stones and in seaweed, as well as in its burrow. (Try attracting it with clam meat.)

Estuarine Mud and Sand Flats 251

N. succinea is the common estuarine species south of Delaware Bay, though it also ranges north to Cape Cod. It lives in salinities as low as 9 o/oo. This polychaete, much smaller than *N. virens,* has been found at depths of 3 ft. (0.9 m) and more in mud and marshy peat banks, where it has contact with the surface through channels. Though it also occurs in fine sand deposits, it burrows less effectively there than in silt.

NEMERTEANS. A primitive phylum (Rhynchocoela) of mostly carnivorous animals, structurally more complex than the flatworms (with which they were once classified) but taxonomically well below the more advanced annelid worms, these unsegmented worms lack appendages but do possess a gut. They are characterized by an eversible proboscis, used as a weapon, that is thrust out through a tiny opening anterior of the mouth to impale prey.

Milky Ribbon Worm. *Cerebratulus lacteus* is the best known nemertean. It is found intertidally along our entire coast, hiding under stones or burrowing in sandy mud. It is a good swimmer, but essentially it is a member of the infauna.

One of the most frustrating experiences one can have in exploring the seashore is attempting to capture intact one of the nemertean worms. Look for the milky ribbon worm near low-tide mark, where it is most common; but handle it with great care, for like its relatives it breaks easily into pieces (each of which may regenerate into a whole new individual). As its name suggests, this species is ribbonlike in form and creamy white, sometimes pinkish in color. Males turn bright red when breeding, females brownish.

The rapidity with which such soft-bodied, fragile worms burrow is surprising. Their ability to change shape is an advantage in this activity; and use of the proboscis, which can be thrust out and expanded as an anchor to pull the worm forward, is also helpful. A ribbon worm that is two feet long when contracted may extend to 12 feet or more. The very numerous young measure a few inches to a foot, but adults commonly reach 4 ft. (1.2 m) in length (contracted).

120. A fragment of the milky ribbon worm is the most one can usually capture.

The proboscis of the ribbon worm is not connected with the digestive system. This organ, which in some nemerteans is as long as the body, lies inside a muscular sheath just above the digestive tract, attached to its sheath near the anterior end. It is turned inside out when quickly protruded and as quickly withdrawn completely. When a potential victim approaches, the proboscis is ejected through the pore and wraps around the prey, entangling it with the aid of a sticky mucous secretion. In some nemerteans the proboscis is armed with a sharp stylet that pierces the victim and injects a poison from glands in the proboscis. Swallowing of the prey is accomplished by a part of the esophagus that is ejected through the dilatable mouth and retracted after enveloping the victim—which may be a polychaete worm, swallowed whole, bristles and all. The bristles and spines often perforate the intestine and work their way out through the ribbon worm's body wall, with no apparent injury to *Chaetopeterus*. The action of the proboscis and the feeding behavior can be observed easily in a captive specimen.

Estuarine Mud and Sand Flats

BIVALVES. Most bivalves are infaunal or benthic epifaunal animals, and most of these are filter feeders. Because this group includes many mollusks valuable to man as food and for other uses, they are familiar forms. As food for an enormous array of birds and mammals, as well as of aquatic animals, they are important ecologically. The health of an intertidal-flat ecsosystem can often be related to the production of bivalves.

Soft-shelled Clam. *Mya arenaria* is a medium-large bivalve (growing to 4 in., or 10 cm) known to millions as "the steamer," but it is also the "fried clam" of New England. This is the common clam of mud flats and muddy subtidal bottoms in estuaries and sounds with salinities as low as 5 o/oo. It is widely dug by clammers from burrows as deep as as 1 ft. (30 cm).

M. arenaria has a large siphon, surrounded by a leathery periostracum or epidermis—the "neck" of the clam to people who eat it. This siphon is completely retractile. The soft-shelled clam is one of the group of bivalves that are too big for their shells to close tightly. At high tide the clam lies just below the surface of the substrate, with its siphon projecting to take in water from which it extracts food particles. At low tide it remains out of sight, but when one walks on the flats it senses the tread and quickly retracts its siphon, expelling jets of water vertically from the burrow and revealing its presence.

The soft-shelled clam is valued as food by predators other than man. For example, at low tide it is dug up by the shellfish-loving raccoon. Diving ducks—ruddy ducks, scoters, goldeneyes, and buffleheads—feed upon it. The whistling swan can extract large specimens from their burrows with its big bill. The cownose ray, moon snails *(Lunatia heros* and *Polinices duplicatus)*, and the horseshoe-crab *(Limulus)* prey heavily on the clam.

Young soft-shelled clams, mussel-like, attach themselves before the burrowing stage by byssal threads, but adults do not. *M. arenaria* is found throughout the Middle Atlantic coast, and is the only member of its family (Myidae) in the region. Although *arenaria* means "of the sand," this species prefers bottoms with a high mud content. It is harvested from the sediments in Chesapeake Bay by hydraulic dredge. (This method, efficient but certainly disruptive to habitat stability, may on balance do more harm than good. It is not fully known what the long-term effects are.)

Quahog. It is no coincidence that the Latin name of this clam, *Mercenaria mercenaria,* conjures up images of monetary dealings. The name derives from the American Indians' use of this species' shell for making wampum. The common name, quahog, comes from the Narragansett Indian word, *poquaûhock.* This bivalve is found along the coast from Cape Cod south, in bays and on ocean beaches as well as in the lower reaches of estuaries. A most popular seafood today (served as "clams on the half shell"), it is still a commercially valuable bivalve, second only in importance to the oyster.

The quahog differs from the soft-shelled clam in being broadly ovate rather than elongate, in having a smaller siphon and a much harder shell, and in being able to close up tightly. It cannot tolerate waters of such low salinity as the soft-shelled clam; it is found in salinities from 15 o/oo upward and to depths of 60 ft. (18 m) as compared with the softshell's limit of about 30 ft. (9 m). It also prefers sandier bottoms.

M. mercenaria may live 25 years; the old clams, however, tend to be tough eating. Undoubtedly its hard shell gives this clam some defense from predators, but gulls have learned to drop bivalves and crustaceans onto hard pavements or rock ledges to break the shells for access to their flesh.

While *Mercenaria mercenaria* in New England is the quahog (pronounced as if spelled kohog), it is called round clam or hardshelled clam to the south. There are also size designations: littleneck (the smallest), cherrystones, and chowder clams.

Baltic Macoma. A small clam, *Macoma balthica* is very common throughout the Middle Atlantic range; it is both intertidal and subtidal in its distribution, and although its burrowing habits make it inconspicuous, its shells are washed up onto the shore in great numbers. The Baltic macoma belongs to a family of bivalves (Tellinidae) notable for the length of their siphons. It is a dweller on muddy and sandy-mud bottoms in the shallow water of quiet bays and inlets, and also in estuaries, where it lives in tributaries with salinities as low as

5 o/oo—approximately the limit for the soft-shelled clam. (In the Baltic Sea, where salinities are more stable and the clam does not have to tolerate great fluctuations, it extends its range into waters with 3 o/oo salinity.)

M. balthica is a deposit feeder, deriving its nutrition chiefly from the bacteria colonies on the surface of the detrital particles it ingests. It lies buried in the mud with its two long, slender siphons projecting above the surface of the sediments. Through its inhalant siphon, which sweeps the area around the burrow, it draws in deposit material as well as water. The gills extract oxygen from the water, and the *labial palps* (elongate sensory organs) remove planktonic and other food particles; the water is then ejected through the other siphon along with the waste materials it has taken up. (The siphons, which would be vulnerable to predators of the bottom fauna, are retractile.) The Baltic macoma can also function as a filter feeder.

This clam is fed upon by shorebirds and waterfowl capable of probing its burrow to extract it. Since *M. balthica* is a shallow burrower, it can be taken even by birds other than the deep-probing clan. Both waders and divers feed upon it. It is a preferred food of the oystercatcher. The greater scaup preys heavily on it, and the ubiquitous willet probably takes many. The whistling swan is primarily a plant eater; but it occasionally feeds on mollusks, and is certainly capable of digging the Baltic macoma from its burrow. The clam is also excavated from its muddy matrix by the southern stingray, cownose ray, and smooth butterfly ray, and by the blue crab.

The Baltic macoma does not live in sandy deposits where water movement makes for an unstable substrate, because there the clam cannot maintain the long, narrow burrows for its siphons. And this stout-bodied bivalve is unable to burrow quickly back into the deposits when exposed, as can the lively little coquina. It uses water jets from fast-closing movements of the valves, dilation and contraction of the foot, and a rocking motion to pull itself down into the mud. Because it is a deposit feeder and clears a circular area about 1.6 in. (4 cm) across with its inhalant siphon, this clam benefits from an occasional move to a new site for its burrow. This it accomplishes by using its foot to push itself over the surface, leaving a furrow about 0.2 in. (5 mm) wide, usually in a straight line. It has been observed to travel 2 in. in four minutes.

M. balthica measures just over an inch long—sometimes as long as 1.5 in. (38 mm). It has a dingy pink shell (sometimes yellowish, bluish, or rusty, depending upon the nature of the deposits in which it lives), with almost round valves that are approximately equal in size.

BURROWING GASTROPODS. Most marine snails are epibenthic organisms, but in the muddy and sandy-mud deposits of the intertidal flats live representatives of this group that burrow. *Hydrobia minuta* (now called *H. totteni* by some malacologists) is a tiny snail common in salt-marsh pools but also found on sea lettuce in the intertidal shallows; it ranges from New Jersey northward. It is able to burrow into the mud, and does so during part of the time in which its habitat is exposed by the ebb tide. Too small—1/8 in., or 3 mm, at most—to travel over the mud flats with enough speed to migrate with the tidal movements, this snail floats on the surface by means of a mucus raft that also functions to trap food. Extremely abundant, *Hydrobia* is preyed upon by a number of waterfowl and shorebirds. Like the northern moon shell, *H. minuta* must be considered a part of the mobile epibenthos despite the fact that it spends much of its time beneath the surface of the deposits.

CRUSTACEANS. Marine members of this class of arthropods are chiefly epibenthic and nektonic; some are on the evolutionary path from aquatic to terrestrial existence. But a few are burrowers in the deposits. (We exclude fiddler and mud crabs from the infauna because they spend so much time above the surface when the flats are exposed by low tide.)

Mantis Shrimp. *Squilla empusa* is a secretive crustacean—sizable but hard to find—belonging to the Stomatopodia, a group distinct from the commercial shrimps and the various other orders of shrimplike crustaceans. It is found on the lower intertidal flats as well as subtidally. It inhabits mud bottoms, where it hides in

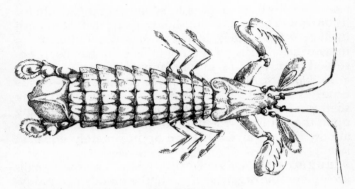

121. Mantis shrimp *(Squilla empusa)*.

burrows with multiple exits. It is flattened rather than compressed laterally like most so-called shrimps; the second pair of thoracic limbs are jointed so that the sharp points of the outer segments are directed forward, giving them the appearance of the raptorial claws of the praying mantis—hence its common name. This claw closes like a jackknife, with the outer segment fitting into a groove in the inner segment.

Members of this order have a feature unique among crustaceans: the eyes and *antennules* (small antennae characteristic of crustaceans) are on movable segments. The mantis shrimp, which reaches a length of 10 in. (25 cm), is large enough for easy examination of its body structure—but beware the claws! These are formidable weapons, with which the mantis shrimp captures its prey in slashing strikes that often snip the victim in two. It feeds on crustaceans and other invertebrates.

Animals of the Estuarine Waters

The Larger Zooplankton

Dictionaries usually define plankton as minute or microscopic plants and animals that float or drift at the mercy of currents. But some planktonic animals are far from being minute and some do have limited powers of locomotion. Most of these larger, motile plankton organisms belong to two phyla: the Cnidaria (hydroids, jellyfishes, and corals) and the Ctenophora (comb jellies). There are also a few mollusks; arrow worms (*Sagitta* spp.) of the phylum Chaetognatha; some polychaetes; *Oikopleura,* which is itself minute but drifts in a transparent house as large as a cherry; and salps such as *Thalia democratica,* a primitive, 1-in. (25-mm) *chordate* (the highest phylum, which includes vertebrates). Several species of the first-named two phyla, Cnidaria and Ctenophora, are of interest here.

CNIDARIANS

JELLYFISH. The class of jellyfish, Scyphozoa, is characterized by the dominance of the *medusoid* generation (generally bell-, umbrella-, or saucer-shaped) over the *polyp* generation (generally cylindrical and attached at the base to a firm support). Some scyphozoans skip the polyp generation entirely, but the three species described following are *polymorphic*—alternating the medusa with the polyp (hydroid) phase. In this region's estuaries, it is the dominant medusoid phase that is prominent and easily observable.

Jellyfish generally attain their full growth in one season. When mature they reproduce by developing a larva that becomes a sessile (attached) polyp, a tubular organism, generally less than 0.5 in. (13 mm) high, closed at one end and with its mouth and tentacles at the other. In winter the polyp sheds disclike *ephyrae* (larvae) a small fraction of an inch (1 to 2 mm) in diameter; these ephyrae swim in the plankton and eventually —if they survive—reach adult size and begin the cycle again. Strangely, the medusa, though the dominant stage, dies at the end of its single season, while the polyp phase may live for several years, producing ephyrae each winter.

Lion's Mane. Also called **red jelly,** *Cyanea capillata* swarms on the Middle Atlantic coast from spring through summer, depending on the latitude. It reaches 8 in. (20 cm) in the waters between Cape Hatteras and Cape Cod. Exceptional individuals north of that range have attained much larger size—8 ft. (2.4 m) in the Gulf

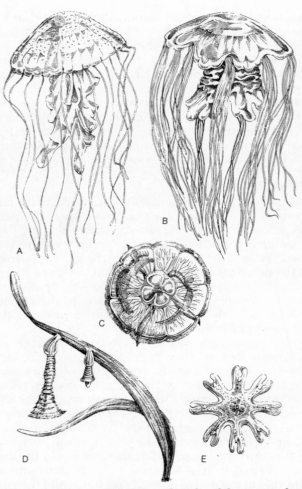

122. Medusae of three jellyfish and earlier life stages of one.
A. Sea nettle *(Chrysaora quinquecirrha)*. B. Lion's mane
(Cyanea capillata). C. Moon jelly *(Aurelia aurita)*.
D. Scyphistomae (polyp generation) of the moon jelly, on
blade of eelgrass. E. By contraction of its muscles, the
scyphistoma releases a large number of minute ephyra
larvae bearing eight sensory tentacles; the ephyrae
(enlarged for detail) live in the plankton and develop into
mature moon jellies.

123. Lion's mane jelly *(Cyanea capillata)*. Even when it is cast upon the beach, the tentacles of this venomous jellyfish can sting.

of Maine and even more in the Arctic. In fact, an argument can be made that *C. capillata* is the longest animal in the world, since its tentacles extend as much as 200 ft. (60 m).

The lion's mane has a broad, flattened bell with eight primary lobes and eight clusters of tentacles. In the Middle Atlantic range it is yellow or orange-brown. In the inshore waters and sounds of the Outer Banks, where it is called the winter jellyfish, it occurs from

October to May; toward Cape Cod it occurs in spring and summer. It is venomous; its sting, while not dangerous to humans, does produce a rash and a severe itching and burning sensation. This does not generally require medical attention.

Moon Jelly. *Aurelia aurita*, which like the lion's mane is a member of the class Scyphozoa, occurs from late spring through early fall in North Carolina waters and, and for a somewhat shorter span of time toward Cape Cod. It is found in estuaries to salinities as low as 16 o/oo. Its disc varies from clear to opaque white and is quite flat, with numerous, fringelike tentacles on the margin. The four-lobed stomach is outlined by four horseshoe-shaped gonads in gastric pouches, and from them ciliated radial canals extend to the bell margin. These canals are part of the digestive system.

The moon jelly may exceed 20 in. (51 cm) in diameter on this coast, but it usually reaches no more than half that size. It is essentially harmless, with a venom not potent enough to bother humans. It feeds on small planktonic organisms that are caught on sticky mucus bands on the umbrella and are licked off by the arms of the *manubrium* ("mouth-arms").

Sea Nettle. The dreaded invader of swimming beaches, *Chrysaora quinquecirrha* is primarily an estuarine species, tolerating salinities as low as 3 o/oo but preferring waters from 15 o/oo to 30 o/oo. It is most notorious in Chesapeake Bay, where enclosures are built around bathing beaches to protect swimmers from it. Somewhat smaller in this region than are the two aforementioned species, the sea nettle nevertheless has a more potent venom, which produces rash, swelling, itching, and respiratory difficulties; these symptoms often require medical attention. The estuarine form of *Chrysaora* is milky white or, sometimes, clear or striped; and the form of its bell is more domelike than the above species. Visible in the bell are the four horseshoe-shaped gonads characteristic of jellyfish of its class. Though it is largely at the mercy of currents, the sea nettle does have an easily observed movement, which is achieved by pulsations of the bell.

The sea nettle is more dangerous to comb jellies such

as *Mnemiopsis leidyi* (see below) than it is to humans, for it devours them by the millions. But it is a nonselective predator, feeding on zooplankton, small fish, crustaceans (crabs, amphipods, and copepods), and polychaetes. It has been estimated that one sea nettle may eat more than 20,000 copepods in a day. It is an enemy of other cnidarians, such as the medusae of *Aurelia aurata*, as well as of the comb jellies.

Despite its venom the sea nettle has its own enemies; it is eaten by sea turtles, notably the loggerhead, and by some fishes.

CTENOPHORES

COMB JELLIES. Gelatinous, fragile, and translucent organisms like the jellyfish, the comb jellies nevertheless belong to a different phylum, the Ctenophora. They, like the jellyfish, are often bioluminescent. But there are many differences between the two groups. The comb jellies are bilaterally rather than radially symmetrical; they have a more complex digestive cavity; they do not exhibit polymorphism; only one genus possesses *nematocysts*, or stinging cells (the others catch their prey by means of adhesive *colloblasts*, or lasso cells); most have only one pair of tentacles; and they swim not by contractions of a muscle band around the bell but by means of eight rows of fused cilia, or *combplates*, positioned meridionally.

Most comb jellies are small, measuring up to 6 in. (15 cm) or so. **Leidy's comb jelly** *(Mnemiopsis leidyi)* is the commonest ctenophore of the Middle Atlantic coast. It tolerates very low salinities, and thus penetrates well up into the estuaries. It can be found in winter, sometimes being quite abundant in Chincoteague Bay, for example, during that season. Unlike more primitive comb jellies such as the **sea gooseberry** *(Pleurobrachia pileus)*, Leidy's comb jelly does not have exceedingly long, contractile tentacles with which to sweep the water for prey. It feeds mostly on larvae and other small organisms, which are caught on ciliated grooves and swept toward the mouth. In form *Mnemiopsis* is a somewhat flattened oval with a pair of long lobes extending well below the body proper.

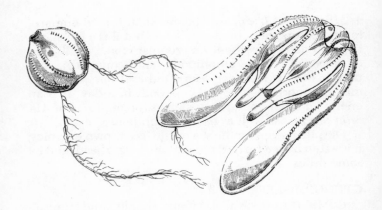

124. *Left:* sea gooseberry *(Pleurobrachia pileus); right:* Leidy's comb jelly *(Mnemiopsis leidyi).*

In swimming, *Mnemiopsis'* comb rows beat synchronously in each quadrant, with the animal normally moving mouth-forward but able to avoid objects encountered by reversing the wave of movement of the combplates. It is able to avoid rough water by descending well below the surface. Located in the body at the end opposite the mouth is a sense organ, the *statocyst,* that controls coordination and maintains vertical orientation.

Like other comb jellies *Mnemiopsis* develops directly, without a distinct larval or sessile phase. Comb jellies are hermaphroditic, shedding both female and male gametes into the sea where fertilization occurs. The larvae resemble adults of the more primitive species of comb jelly, and they are difficult to identify. The larvae of *Mnemiopsis* gradually attain the form of the genus, and reach a length of 4 in. (10 cm). The young of a burrowing anemone, *Edwardsia leidyi,* parasitize *Mnemiopsis,* living in its gut.

You can safely handle comb jellies, for they cannot sting. They must be handled gently; when you hold one in your hand it becomes a shapeless blob of gelatin. To get a close look at one, scoop it up carefully into a glass jar. When sunlight strikes the combplates at the right angle they refract the rays, producing prismatic coloring of great beauty.

Estuarine Chordates

The subphylum Vertebrata of the phylum Chordata is represented in the intertidal-flat habitat chiefly by the cartilaginous fishes—selachians and their allies—and by the true, or bony, fishes. Almost without exception they come into the flats only when they are inundated by the tides. Other than fish that remain in the tidal creeks and marsh pools, there are very few genuinely intertidal fishes. Some species are able to take refuge in water-filled depressions in the sand and mud flats when left behind by the falling tide. And a handful of fish species remain in the intertidal zone by burying themselves in the sand or remaining under rocks while the tide is out. The sand lance, described in Chapter Two under Animals of the Inshore Waters (in the section on terns), is sometimes dug up from estuarine sand flats by clam diggers. There are even species that live in the burrows of annelid worms, where they are safe from being stranded by the ebbing tide.

The greatest ecological impact on the intertidal community, however, is made by cartilaginous and bony fish that visit when the tide is in. Several species of these —mostly predators—are described below. Some of them come into the flats from tidal creeks, some from deeper estuarine waters or adjacent bays and sounds. Some are found in the intertidal zone throughout the year, some only seasonally; some are present only during coastwise migration periods, or on the way to fresh water from the sea or vice versa; and some are there during only one stage of their life history. All spend enough time in the intertidal zone to interact directly with the permanent inhabitants. This interaction takes several forms. Chief of these is predation by the fishes upon residents of the zone—members of the benthic epifauna, the mobile epibenthos, and the benthic infauna, as well as the plankton that also comes in with the tide. Some predatory estuarine species are not direct consumers of the intertidal community but prey subtidally on those that do feed there. In this group are the sandbar, dusky, scalloped hammerhead, and Atlantic sharpnose sharks, among the cartilaginous fishes; and the American eel, Atlantic needlefish, striped bass, bluefish, spotted seatrout, red drum, and butterfish among the true fishes. Because of their interaction with the fauna of the intertidal flats and their role in the larger estuarine ecosystem, some of these are included in the discussions and tables that follow.

Some intertidal fishes, notably mullets, feed upon the micro- and macroflora. The fishes also have an impact through their disturbance of the sediments—the digging of pits by rays, for example. The very fact of their presence in great numbers, affecting the ecosystem through their life functions—defecation, excretion, and respiration—is of great consequence. Lastly, the fishes themselves are sometimes food for permanent members of the littoral zone and for birds.

SELACHIANS

The orders Squaliformes and Rajiformes include most of the species in the class Chondrichthyes—variously called sharks, rays, skates, stingrays, sawfishes, mantas, electric rays, and so on. Only a few selachians enter the estuaries, and of these none is dependent on this environment for completion of its life cycle. The spiny dogfish and the barndoor and little skates, described in Chapter Two under Animals of the Inshore Waters, visit the estuary at times, but have minimal impact on its ecology. One ray and several species of stingray are of interest because of their predatory activities. Feeding on the bottom in the shallows and the submerged intertidal zone on both the invertebrate and vertebrate fauna, they leave physical evidence of their predation in the form of the pits dug in the sandy or muddy bottom. Both rays and skates can be extremely damaging to oyster and clam beds. The damage they do is not limited to their consumption of mollusks and other benthic animals; great numbers of smaller animals living in the deposits are destroyed by the disruption of their habitat.

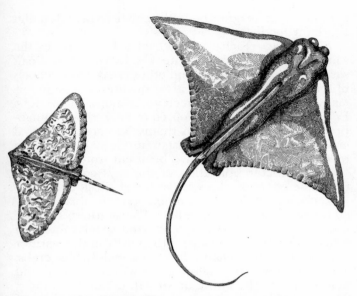

125. *Left:* smooth butterfly ray *(Gymnura micrura),* a member of the stingray family; *right:* cownose ray *(Rhinoptera bonasus),* a member of the eagle ray family.

Pinfish and other predatory bony fishes tag along with the rays and skates to take the leavings. In time, normal succession processes return the pits to their former state.

RAYS. The **cownose ray**, *Rhinopotera bonasus,* is a member of the eagle ray family (Myliobatidae), which is distinct from the skate and stingray families. It forages over the flats in search of clams, oysters, and scallops, and it is especially destructive of soft-shelled clams *(Mya arenaria).* It excavates mollusks by stirring up the deposits with its pectoral fins, or "wings," generating turbulence that causes the sand and mud to stream out behind it. The mollusks thus separated from the substrate are crushed by the ray's pavementlike teeth, and swallowed. Later the undigested shells are regurgitated. These rays have been accused of rooting up the estuarine bottoms as completely as a drove of hogs would do. Despite the handicap of the presence of root systems in the seagrass beds, the cownose ray often digs there for food.

R. bonasus reaches a width of 7 ft. (2.1 m) in the south. It ranges north to Nantucket. In North Carolina's sounds, Chesapeake Bay, and other areas, large schools of these big rays consume great quantities of commercially valuable hard-shelled clams, scallops, and oysters. Because they are a good source of food (though unappreciated in America), rays themselves are a potential commercial fishery. Some restaurants have been known to serve "scallops" that have been cut from the wings of rays. Greater utilization of the rays could have a favorable effect on the state of the shellfish beds.

STINGRAYS. Several members of this family (Dasyatidae) feed over the flats. The **southern stingray** *(Dasyatis americana)* is a good-sized species found in estuaries from New Jersey south, mostly in the warmer seasons. It feeds on clams, shrimps, annelids, blue crabs, and small fishes, in shallow areas with both mud and sand bottoms. Measuring up to 7 ft. (2.1 m) long and 5 ft. (1.5 m) wide, it bears a barbed spine near the base of the tail.

The **Atlantic stingray** *(Dasyatis sabina)* is distinguished by its pointed snout. This "stingaree" is a small species, 2 ft. (0.6 m) or less in length, that does not dig pits but feeds in the shallows on crustaceans and fishes. It tends to run well up the estuaries, even to fresh water. A larger species, the **smooth butterfly ray** *(Gymnura micrura),* prefers sandy bottoms. It is found in the offshore waters from Cape Cod south, and in late spring and summer it goes into the estuaries to prey upon fishes, particularly the black sea bass, *Centropristis striata* (which, like the stingray, lives offshore in winter). *Gymnura* and *Centropristis* share the same range on the Middle Atlantic coast, and it may be that the ray is following the fish when it enters the bays and sounds. But *Gymnura* also feeds on mollusks, annelids, and small crustaceans, including shrimps. It reaches a maximum width of 4 ft. (1.2 m) and has the ability to change color to blend with its background. The *disc* (the broad, flat, main part of the animal) of this species is nearly twice as broad as long, and its tail is very short and lacking a spine, despite its classification with the sting-rays.

Unlike the skates, rays and stingrays do not lay eggs in leathery pouches; the young are hatched within the female's body, where they may remain for a time getting nourishment from the mother before birth. Skates, rays, and eagle rays all have teeth arranged something like paving blocks, rather than the rows of sharp, blade-like teeth of sharks.

One may never encounter a live ray in the estuary, but should watch for the telltale pits that result from their depredations on the shellfish beds. These clues appear even at the very upper edge of the intertidal zone, where at high tide the water is less than a foot deep. If one keeps a sharp eye for these distinctively shaped animals when walking along estuarine and lagoonal shores, it is quite possible to discover a ray in the shallows at the edge.

SHARKS. Most sharks of the temperate zone are oceanic species, but some occur in inshore waters. A few members of the requiem shark family (Carcharhinidae) and one each of the angel shark family (Squatinidae) and the hammerhead shark family (Sphyrnidae) come into the estuaries to feed. Only a handful are common enough in this habitat to be of significance. Table 7 provides basic data on their occurrence and their niche in the estuarine system.

BONY, OR TRUE, FISHES

The fin fishes of the estuaries and offshore waters are of importance to humans for several purposes: as food; as a resource for sport; for commercial purposes such as fertilizer and industrial products; as bait; for their value in controlling such pests as mosquitos; as biological indicators; as food for other animals appreciated by man for esthetic, sporting, or commercial reasons; and, at least to biologists, for their overall role in marine and estuarine ecosystems. Here we can deal with only a few species that illustrate these values. Some have already been described in Chapter Two under Animals of the Inshore Waters.

Table 7: Sharks Found in Estuaries

Family	Latin/Common Name	Occurrence	Estuarine Habitat
Carcharhinidae	*Rhizoprionodon terraenovae* Atlantic sharpnose shark	Outer Banks; accidental to Cape Cod	Brackish water, but not in intertidal zone
	Carcharhinus leucas Bull shark	North Carolina; strays to New York. Abundant.	Inshore, never far from land. Shallows, harbors, estuaries to fresh water.
	Negaprion brevirostris Lemon shark	North Carolina; strays to New Jersey	Shallow-water species. Young in schools in shallows.
	Carcharhinus plumbeus (C. milberti) Sandbar shark	Cape Cod to Cape Hatteras	Shallows and deeper estuarine waters. Usually near or on bottom.
	Carcharhinus obscurus Dusky shark	Cape Cod to Cape Hatteras	In shallows and over intertidal flats, as well as offshore
	Mustelus canis Smooth dogfish (not related to spiny dogfish, which occurs offshore to 200 fathoms)	Cape Cod to Cape Hatteras	Bays and estuaries, not in intertidal zone, occasionally to fresh water. Bottom dweller.
Sphyrnidae	*Sphyrna lewini* Scalloped hammerhead shark	New Jersey and south	Deeper waters
Squatinidae	*Squatina dumerili* Atlantic angel shark	Cape Cod to Cape Hatteras (most abundant in Virginia, Maryland and Delaware)	Lower estuarine reaches

Size & Weight	Food	Comments
3 ft. (1m)	Mainly fishes including pigfish, silversides, menhaden; hermit, blue, and fiddler crabs; mollusks; shrimp; annelids	Often seen in sounds of North Carolina. May stray far up rivers into fresh water.
8 ft. (2.4m), 300 lbs. (136 kg)	Sharks, stingrays, and bony fishes including shad, mackerel; a few benthic animals; scavenger on garbage	Has been known to attack bathers. Feeding is correlated with tidal movements. Ascends rivers.
11 ft. (3.4m) (lighter in weight than most sharks of similar length)	Mostly fishes, including mullets; also crustaceans; feeds mostly at night	Strictly an inshore species. Common around docks and in saltwater creeks.
8 ft. (2.4m), 200 lbs. (91kg)	Preys on fishes, including pinfish; mollusks, crustaceans; also scavenges	Feeds in eelgrass beds. Commonest in waters 10–30 ft. (3–9m) deep. Very common on Atlantic coast.
11 ft. (3.4m)	Fishes, including menhaden and butterfish	Often taken far from shore in deep water
5 ft. (1.5m) 2-ft. length common)	Crabs, lobsters, squids; fishes, including tautog and menhaden	Often in large schools. Reproduction in early July. Ten-month gestation; young 1 ft. at birth; sexual maturity at 3 ft. Normally in depths less than 60 ft. (18m).
10 ft. (3m) 1,000 lbs. (312kg)	Fishes, squids	Habits not well known. When in ocean, remains near surface. Attacks other hammerheads as well as people.
4 ft. (1.2m) (5 ft. reported) 60 lbs. (27kg)	Fishes and crustaceans	Winglike pectoral fins give this shark a skatelike form. Most are taken in shallow water.

The fishes occupy all levels of the estuarine food chain above that of primary producers. Some feed directly on algae or phytoplankton; some feed on detritus; some are predators on herbivores and detritivores; and some prey on lesser predators. Some are scavengers, or are semi-parasitic or parasitic on other fishes. A species of fish may occupy several trophic levels at various stages of its life history.

BAITFISHES. The most abundant of all estuarine fishes, **silversides** (*Membras* and *Menidia* spp.) are small, slender fishes that live in schools in shallow waters. The young feed principally upon small crustacean zooplankters, including copepods, amphipods, isopods, small shrimps, and *megalops* (larvae) of these animals. Adults, more omnivorous, feed on juvenile and and larval fishes; polychaetes, small shrimps, amphipods, and other small crustaceans; insects; small snails; and detritus and algae. Some of the baitfish species feed in the salt-marsh creeks and among the marsh grasses at high tide.

In summer the more highly saline reaches of the shallow bays of the East Coast become alive with great schools of **common**, or **Atlantic, silverside** *(Menidia menidia)* congregating to spawn. Beginning in April in Virginia waters, in May in New York, Connecticut, and Rhode Island coastal areas, and in June in Massachusetts, this fish lays spherical eggs about 0.05 in. (1.15 mm) in diameter, which mat in lumps by means of adhesive threads. In water 72° F (22° C) the eggs will hatch in 8 or 9 days. When the juveniles reach 0.6 in. (15 mm) in length, they begin to resemble their parents. Full-grown Atlantic silversides measure 6 in. (15 cm).

The **tidewater silverside** *(M. beryllina)* is a small (up to 3 in., or 75 mm) species that like *M. menidia* is found along the coast from Cape Cod to Cape Hatteras, but in less saline waters than the Atlantic silverside. The range of the **rough silverside** *(Membras martinica)* extends north only to New York. In size it is between the two *Menidia* species.

The abundance of *M. menidia* and *M. beryllina* in our eastern estuaries is suggested by the fact that it is not unusual for researchers who are sampling fishes to take from 50% to 95% of their total catch from the populations of one or the other of these two species, depending on the location. By virtue of their countless numbers and the multiple role they play in the food web, these two must be considered among the most important of marine animals. While too small to be of use to humans as food, they are valuable as baitfish. The terns seen diving into shallow estuarine waters are often taking these species; and they are fed upon by such other predators as drums, croakers, and flounders.

In the same size class as the silversides (family Atherinidae) and at times and places comparably abundant, are some members of the killifish family (Cyprinodontidae). The **mummichog** *(Fundulus heteroclitus)* ranges along the entire coast, in brackish to fresh waters, and especially those with mud bottoms; it may feed chiefly in salt marshes at high tide. Because of its strong preference for eelgrass habitats, it is discussed in Chapter Five, The Eelgrass Community.

The **banded killifish** *(F. diaphanus)* is about 3 in. (75 mm) in length; this is a freshwater species that enters the estuary from tributary streams. Smallest of all is the **mosquitofish** *(Gambusia affinis)*—only 2 in. (5 cm) in length but a voracious predator on mosquito wrigglers, and valued for that reason in areas of human habitation. The two aforementioned families of fishes account for a great share of the food of terns, herons and egrets, and grebes, when these birds frequent the estuaries.

MULLETS. Belonging to a mostly tropical family (Mugilidae), the **striped mullet** *(Mugil cephalus)* is a valuable commercial species. This abundant fish grows to 2 ft. (0.6 m) or larger and in warmer waters may exceed 15 lb. (7 kg) in weight. Great schools are seen along this entire section of coast, but only occasionally as far north as Cape Cod. A marine fish rather than a true estuarine fish, it is common in shallow lagoons, sounds, and estuaries, usually in the period of growth from juvenile to adult. Small schools in the shallows sometimes leap from the water in unison when pursued. In fall, many of the mullets form schools to migrate south.

In terms of tonnage, the striped mullet accounts for

one of the largest coastal fisheries. Most mullets are caught in nets, and they are generally smoked for the market. Spawning takes place in the sea in late fall when water temperatures are dropping.

The feeding habits of *Mugil* spp. have been studied extensively. The diet of *M. cephalus* is unusual for a fish of its size: even the adults feed chiefly on detritus and green plants. The striped mullet obtains much of its food from mud, which it sucks into its buccal (mouth) cavity and works about with its pharyngeal pads, which are covered with denticles (small toothlike structures). A sifting apparatus on the gill rakers filters out the detritus and other food particles. In summer these fish browse heavily on epiphytic algae, the minute green plants that form feltlike coatings on a variety of substrates in the upper estuary. In winter the mullets tend to move down-estuary. They also feed upon microalgae and vascular plants, and sometimes on small benthic animals. One investigator found 35,000 snails *(Turtonia minuta)* in the stomach of a mullet.

A curious fact is that nearly any mullet will be found to have a pair of isopods *(Meinertia* sp.) attached to its tongue. The male *Meinertia* is only about one-third the size of the female, which has been described as being almost as large as the end of one's thumb.

The **white mullet** *(M. curema)* is the only other member of the family found on the Middle Atlantic coast. It is not as common as the striped mullet, and is nearer in size to the baitfish previously described; it averages about 5 in. (12.5 cm) but sometimes more than doubles that length, reaching 2 lb. (0.9 kg) in weight. It has a novel life history, exhibiting an unusual functional change during development. The adults begin spawning in early spring, when the waters over the Continental Shelf are warming up. The young, which spend the first weeks of their lives as pelagic fish in great surface swarms, are so different in the juvenile stage that they were once thought to be a different genus of fish. Very young individuals feed on plankton, an easily assimilated food, and function well with a simple, short intestine. As they approach a length of 1 in. (25 mm) they move toward the shore and into the estuaries. And as they grow, the intestine progressively lengthens and becomes much convoluted, enabling the digestive system to accommodate the adult food, which is more-resistant plant material. (This process is the reverse of the changes that occur when a tadpole—which feeds on algae and so requires a long, convoluted intestine—changes into a frog, which feeds on more easily assimilated insects.)

When the white mullet reaches a length of 4 or 5 in. (10 or 12 cm), it moves out of the estuary to inshore waters of the outer beach. A primarily warm-water fish, this species ranges north to Woods Hole and, in smaller numbers, to Cape Cod. In the estuaries it is a detritivore and, like the striped mullet, a feeder on algae,

FLATFISHES. Wading in shallow water on the intertidal or subtidal flats, or in seagrass beds, you may be startled to see a small patch of the sandy bottom apparently dart away and as suddenly vanish. Watch closely while approaching the spot where the movement seemed to end: again a bit of bottom flits a few feet away, becoming immediately invisible. Indeed, it may take repeated attempts and much peering at the bottom before you can finally discern the outline of a more or less oval fish colored exactly like the sand on which it rests and so flat that it makes no bump on the surface of the substrate. The protective coloration, unusual body form, and feeding habits make the flatfishes, as they are collectively called, fascinating objects of study. Additionally, this group—consisting, in our coastal area, of members of three families of fishes—is an important human food resource.

Along with the rays and skates and the baitfishes, the flatfishes are the most characteristic vertebrates of intertidal flats. They are also found in seagrass beds, a habitat not so favorable for the rays (except for the cownose ray).

Though they are all modified in the same general way for their role as bottom dwellers, the flatfishes show considerable variation in their feeding habits. Flounders and their relatives are considered bottom feeders, but their technique is often more elaborate than that term conveys. With their flatness and their remarkable

Animals of the Estuarine Waters 275

ability to match the colors and patterns of the bottom on which they happen to lie, they rest unseen until a potential victim appears. That may be a crab on the bottom or a fish swimming above. The flatfish takes its victim by surprise with a sudden dart from its place of concealment.

Many species of flatfishes include polychaetes in their diet. The hogchoker (described below), for example, feeds chiefly on these annelids, extracting them from the sandy sediments. A.C. Steven gave an account of the feeding behavior of a related species, *Microstomus kitt,* termed a dab, in the intertidal zone of the Scottish coast. *Microstomus* feeds almost exclusively on polychaetes, which it catches visually.

When hunting, the fish rests in a characteristic posture with the front of the body raised well off the ground which is scanned with the extremely mobile eyes. Should the tentacles of a worm emerge from the sand, the dab leaps onto it arching its body so that the head descends almost vertically onto the prey . . . Incidentally, the worm often suffers no more than the loss of its tentacular crown which can be regenerated, a form of renewable resource with few parallels in other predator-prey relationships.

As its name indicates, *Microstomus* has a small mouth; its eyes are large, as well as mobile. Some flatfishes, however, feed at night, when good eyesight is of no great importance, moving slowly over the sediments grubbing for food.

A flatfish is not born that way. It hatches from an egg into a quite normal-looking larva. But it soon enough begins to go astray. The eyes migrate to one side of the head, and the fish begins to swim on the other side, which becomes its white or pale-colored bottom side. The top side, the one with the eyes, develops a color pattern peculiar to the species but alterable according to the bottom on which the fish lives. The members of the three flatfish families—including well over 100 species on the two coasts of the conterminous 48 states—go by various names bearing little or no relationship to their taxonomic position: flounder, fluke, halibut, turbot, dab, sanddab, whiff, sole, plaice, hogchoker, and windowpane. Table 8 is an attempt to put a little order into the picture of the flatfish species most likely to be encountered in the Middle Atlantic coastal waters. In particular, it provides basic information about the role of some common flatfishes in the estuarine community. The Atlantic halibut *(Hippoglossus hippoglossus)*, which is known in this region neither in our estuaries nor in the inshore waters of the ocean beach, is included here for comparison purposes. (See *A Sierra Club Naturalist's Guide to the North Atlantic Coast* by Michael and Deborah Berrill.)

Unlike the baitfishes described above, the flatfishes are not true estuarine fishes; they are marine fishes that spend part of their lives in the estuary. Some pay regular visits to the estuary, usually as adults; some use the estuary primarily as a nursery ground, spawning and spending much of their adult lives at sea; some do not need the estuary for any stage of their life history, but appear there irregularly. Table 8 indicates into which category each species fits.

According to fishermen's lore, the **winter flounder** *(Pseudopleuronectes americanus)* hibernates in mud. Its failure to bite on the angler's line during winter and early spring can be attributed to the fact that it is spawning then (January to May) and feeding little. Winter flounders may spawn only at night. The heavy,

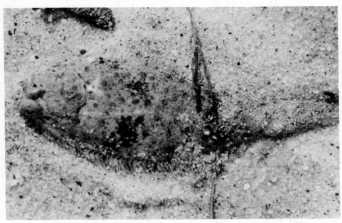

126. A small winter flounder on a sandy bottom at Fire Island National Seashore.

Animals of the Estuarine Waters

Table 8: Flatfishes of the Middle Atlantic/

Family	Latin Name	Regional Names	Occur-rence	Habitat
Soleidae	*Trinectys maculatus*	Hogchoker, American sole	Cape Cod to Cape Hatteras	Shallow, salt to fresh, mud or muddy sand bottom
Bothidae	*Paralichthys lethostigma*	Southern flounder	N.C.; juveniles year round, adults summer	Salt to brackish; bays, lagoons, and sounds; shallow mud bottoms
Bothidae	*Paralichthys dentatus*	Summer flounder, fluke, plaice	Cape Cod to Cape Hatteras; juveniles year round in N.C., adults summer	Summer: shallow, sand or sandy mud; in bays, harbors, estuary mouths. Winter: offshore, 150–300 ft.
Bothidae	*Scophthal-mus aquosus*	Windowpane, spotted flounder, brill	Cape Cod to Cape Hatteras	
Bothidae	*Etropus crossotus*	Fringed flounder	Cape Hatteras to Va. (abundant in N.C. sounds)	
Pleuro-nectidae	**Hippoglos-sus hippo-glossus*	Atlantic halibut	Cape Cod to Cape Hatteras (occasion-ally to Va.); a coldwater species	Deep water, 200–3,000 ft.
Pleuro-nectidae	*Pseudopleuro-nectes americanus*	Winter flounder, flatfish, mud dab, blueback flounder, sea flounder, blackback, snowshoe	Cape Cod to Cape Hatteras (common to Chesa-peake Bay)	Summer to 400 ft.; winter to high-tide mark; hard or soft bottom
Pleuro-nectidae	*Limanda ferruginea*	Yellowtail flounder, rusty dab	Cape Cod to Va. (common in northern part of range)	30–300 ft.; occasionally in shallower water; sand or sand-mud bottom

*Not an estuarine or inshore species; included here for comparison purposes

278   ESTUARINE COMMUNITIES

Size	Weight	Eyes	Food	Spawning
8 in.	8 oz.	Right	Annelids, small crustaceans including amphipods, detritus, insect larvae, algae, foraminifera	
20 in.		Left	90% fish: shad, anchovies, mullet, croakers, menhaden, pinfish, mojarra; mysids, shrimps, amphipods; blue, mud, and stone crabs; mollusks	Winter; in ocean at 18 mos.
36 in. (unusual)	2–5 lbs. (15 lbs. exceptional)	Left	Mostly fishes: silversides, anchovies, etc.; crabs, shrimps, mysids, *Gammarus;* small mollusks; squids; annelids; sand dollars	Late fall, winter, early spring
12 in.		Left	Mysids (young); small tomcods, smelts, hake, striped bass, pollock; herring; copepods, shrimp, amphipods, cumaceans, crabs; ascidians; annelids; snails	
		Left	Calanoid copepods, cumaceans, amphipods, mysids, shrimps, isopods, crabs; fishes; annelids; mollusks	
9 ft. (rare)	300 lbs. (700 lbs. exceptional)	Right	Cod, herring, ocean perches, mackerel, other flounders; lobsters, crabs; clams, mussels; skates	Spring through fall, at depths exceeding 1500 ft.; growth rate slow
15 in. (to 20 in.)	2 lbs. (to 6 lbs.)	Right	Shrimps and other crustaceans; small fish; mollusks; worms	Winter and early spring, usually at night; 10–24 ft.; eggs 1/32 in., hatch in 15 days at 39°F
22 in.	2 lbs. plus	Right	Mysids, shrimps, amphipods; mollusks; worms	March-Aug.; eggs pelagic, hatch in 5 days; young go to bottom at 0.5 in.

sticky eggs, to 1/32 in. (1 mm), hatch in 15 days at 39° F (9° C), and the flounder takes three years to mature. When young, winter flounders feed on small plants and crustaceans; later they eat worms, and eventually they take shrimp, mollusks, and fish.

This right-eyed flounder is well known to sport fishermen. It occurs up to the high-water mark, but larger specimens are more likely to be found in deeper water. Its preference is for a muddy-sand bottom, but it is also found over sand and clay substrates. Winter flounders sometimes go up-estuary almost to fresh water. They spawn offshore to depths of 240 ft. (73 m) as well as in shallows of the estuaries. Most large specimens of this species are found in the offshore waters, where they are called **sea flounders**. In Block Island Sound unusually large winter flounders, called **snowshoes**, are caught; one weighed 8 lbs. (3.6 kg).

The **summer flounder** *(Paralichthys dentatus)* belongs to the left-eyed flounder family. It is larger than the winter flounder, and it too is a popular game fish. It has been known to reach about 30 lbs. (14 kg), but most are less than 5 lbs. (2.3 kg). It is most common in summer in shallow water; medium-sized and larger fish move into offshore waters in winter. Spawning takes place at this time (or earlier or later according to latitude), and the young move into the estuarine-shallows nursery grounds. Many summer flounders are caught by fishermen from small boats, piers, bridges, and jetties, often with killifish as bait.

One member of the third flatfish family, the Soleidae, is the aforementioned **hogchoker** *(Trinectes maculatus)*, found from Cape Cod to Cape Hatteras but more common in North Carolina than in Massachusetts. The only sole that is often caught on this coast, it is too small —at up to 8 in. (20 cm) and 1/3 lb. (0.15 kg)—to be of commercial value. (The "fillet of sole" served in restaurants is likely some other flatfish.) It lacks pectoral fins, has small eyes placed close together, and has a small, twisted mouth. Its food (see Table 8) is about equally divided between detritus and small benthic animals, with a few algae and foraminifera thrown in. Because this fish ranges up the estuaries to fresh water, it includes insect larvae in its diet.

There is evidence that although the hogchoker is a feeder on the benthic infauna, it does not have a significant impact on the benthic infaunal community. It does not dig up the sediments in the manner of rays, skates, and blue crabs.

HERRINGS AND ALLIES. *Anadromous* fishes are marine species that migrate up rivers to spawn. They must use their time in the estuaries to adjust their *osmoregulatory* processes for the change from an environment with a higher concentration of salts to one with a lower concentration. Among the anadromous fishes found in estuaries of the Middle Atlantic coast are several members of the herring family, Clupeidae. Ten species of anchovies (family Engraulidae) swim in American Atlantic waters, and two of these are discussed below.

The binomial of the **Atlantic shad**, *Alosa sapidissima*, is Latin for "shad very good to eat," and that is just why this good-sized herring, about 2 ft. (o.6 m) long and 2 to 4 lb. (o.9 to 1.8 kg) in weight (sometimes much larger), is netted during its upstream migration in spring. Called poor man's salmon, the Atlantic shad was overfished and its streams were polluted to the point where it became scarce. In recent years, improvements in stream conditions have helped it recover enough to be again sought by throngs of fishermen for sport and food; but it has not regained its former status as an important commercial species. It is a strict planktivore (feeder on plankton) throughout its life cycle, which makes its niche in the estuarine community more clear-cut than that of most fish species.

The **alewife**, or **sawbelly** *(Alosa pseudoharengus)*, is a smaller fish than the Atlantic shad; it also is harvested as food, and is eaten fresh, salted, or smoked. It is commercially important also as a source of oil, fish meal, and fertilizer. In the estuary it feeds upon crustaceans, small fishes, diatoms, and copepods. The **blueback herring** *(Alosa aestivalis)* is similar in form and life history to the alewife but is less abundant and is of minor value as a food fish.

The **Atlantic menhaden** *(Brevoortia tyrannus)* is exceedingly important commercially despite not being a marketable table fish. An annual catch of hundreds of

127. *Top:* Atlantic menhaden; *bottom:* Atlantic herring.

millions of pounds (in 1969, 1.5 billion lb., or 680 million kg) goes into oil for the chemical industry, fish meal for animal foods, bait for fishermen, and fertilizer. This abundant species is of value in the human diet indirectly, because of the large numbers eaten by tuna, swordfish, cod, bluefish, and rockfish. Sharks, as well as porpoises and larger cetaceans, also prey upon it. It is largely a fish of coastal waters throughout the region, spawning in the sea but using the estuaries as a nursery. The young in estuaries feed primarily on phytoplankton, and to some extent also utilize zooplankton and resuspended detritus.

The **Atlantic herring** *(Clupea harengus)* is notable for the extreme range of salinity tolerance exhibited in its early life stages, despite the fact that it is only an adventitious visitor in the estuaries. The eggs of this species are able to develop and hatch at any salinity between 6 o/oo and 52 o/oo—a remarkable range. The newly hatched larvae can remain for a matter of hours in water as low as 1.4 o/oo or as high as 60 o/oo. Though the adults exhibit a somewhat narrower tolerance, their regulation of blood concentration is quite efficient, enabling them to penetrate far into the estuaries without difficulty.

The New England "sardine" boats and canning factories are in reality utilizing the young of this species of herring. True sardines are unknown on the Atlantic coast.

Related to the herrings but constituting another family, the Engraulidae, are the anchovies. They are baitfish-sized, and some are present in the estuaries in numbers comparable to the silversides and mummichogs. The **bay anchovy** *(Anchoa mitchilli),* only 3 in. (7.5 cm) in length, is found along our entire coast but is commonest in the South. (It is the most abundant fish in Chesapeake Bay and is abundant in North Carolina's sounds year round.) The bay anchovy comes in over the flats on the flood tide, feeding primarily on zooplankton but also consuming mysid shrimps, larval penaeid shrimps, small mollusks and crustaceans, detritus, and —despite its own diminutive proportions—fishes. It is an important forage species for larger fish such as the striped bass.

The **striped anchovy** *(A. hepsetus)* is larger than the bay anchovy; it grows to about 6 in. (15 cm), and is found from Cape Cod to Cape Hatteras (but most abundantly farther south). In summer the adults are common in more saline reaches of the estuaries, where they feed upon annelids, foraminifers, copepods, and small crustaceans and crustacean larvae. In the northern part of the range (Massachusetts), anchovies are only occasionally taken in sampling hauls in the estuaries; but in North Carolina they, along with silversides, are the most abundant of the smaller fishes.

OTHER BONY FISHES. Its nearly scaleless, slimy skin; its squirming, snakelike form; and its generally lampreylike appearance have combined to make some people think of the **American eel** as a primitive animal perhaps somewhere below the sharks on the evolutionary ladder. But *Anguilla rostrata* is a true fish, and as such is far advanced over the lampreys and sharks. Its order, Anguilliformes, is placed on the taxonomic scale above the tarpons and below the herrings and the salmon-trout family. It is a *catadromous,* not an estuarine, species—an essentially freshwater fish that migrates down to the sea to spawn. But it is found along protected outer beaches and, during its migration, in the estuaries. There it feeds on fishes that feed on the intertidal flats; so a few words about its ecology are in order.

The American eel was a mystery animal until this

Animals of the Estuarine Waters

128. An American eel on the exposed bank of the cordgrass marsh, Westport River estuary, Mass.

century, when it was discovered that it makes a long journey to the Sargasso Sea—southeast of Bermuda, hundreds or even thousands of miles from its home rivers—to breed. Part of the strange story of eel spawning, scientists believe, is that the adults die after breeding, thus they are known in the estuaries only on the way to the sea following several years of growth in fresh water. Many are captured in the mouths of the rivers at this time. (Although most Americans are squeamish about eating eels, there is a large market in Europe for them.) The estuary is more than a mere route from fresh water to the sea, for it is during their period in the brackish waters that eels change over from one type of osmoregulation to another. In fresh water, their blood is *hyperosmotic* to the medium—that is, it is more concentrated than the water—and osmoregulatory processes must work to prevent movement of water into the eel's cells. In the sea, the eels' body fluids will be less concentrated than the medium, and they must maintain osmotic pressure compatible with the salinity tolerance range of their cells. How long the eels remain in the estuary during this changeover period is not known; nor is there definitive information on their food habits.

The young eels—called *leptocephali*—are hatched in

the Sargasso Sea, and in their second year journey to the North American coast, ranging anywhere from Florida to Labrador. Arriving in the estuaries in late autumn, they undergo a metamorphosis. About 3 in. (76 mm) long at this time, they are flattened, leaflike, and colorless. They remain transparent, but soon they stop feeding and become shorter and cylindrical. They lose their sharp, needlelike teeth. In spring they start ascending the rivers, and at this time their skins begin to take on color. The former "glass eels" are now known as *elvers*.

The movement up the estuaries to the rivers may take several weeks. Once in fresh water the eels remain there for a long period—5 to 12 years if they are males, 10 to 24 if they are females. By the time they are ready to migrate to sea as breeding adults, the males may reach 3 ft. (0.9 m) in length, and the females up to 5 ft. (1.5 m). In the estuaries they feed upon crustaceans, annelids, fishes, echinoderms, mollusks, and carrion, and are also said to eat eelgrass. Their abundance in many of the region's estuaries—especially from Chesapeake Bay north—makes them an important part of the ecosystem.

Several members of the cod family (Gadidae) are found in Middle Atlantic estuarine waters, though none is a true resident of the estuaries. Most are cold-water fishes, known primarily on the northern sector of the coast. The **spotted hake** *(Urophysis regius)* occurs as far south as Cape Hatteras, where it feeds in spring and fall in the intertidal zone on small crustaceans, including shrimp, crabs, mysids, and amphipods; on small fishes; and upon annelids and mollusks. It ranges as far north as Cape Cod, but it is little known in the estuaries of that region, where the genus is represented chiefly by the **white hake** *(U. tenuis)* and the **red hake** *(U. chuss)*. The **Atlantic tomcod** *(Microgradus tomcod)*, the **Atlantic cod** *(Gradus morhua)*, and the **pollock** *(Pollachius virens)* are other members of the family in Middle Atlantic coastal waters. None of these fishes spends the entire year in the estuaries; but they use them seasonally, generally as a spawning ground.

The Atlantic tomcod is the commonest member of

the family in the southern New England estuaries. It is sometimes taken in beach-seine sampling, but occurs more commonly in subtidal waters, where it feeds on the bottom on shrimp, amphipods, worms, clams, squids, and small fishes. It uses its chin barbel (a slender sensory appendage) and its ventral fins to to detect prey. Part of the tomcod population migrates up-estuary to spawn in brackish water in winter. It is a fine table fish, and is taken even in fresh water in winter. The eggs adhere to bottom algae and rocks.

Only the young of the Atlantic cod are shallow-water fishes. Very young individuals feed near the surface on copepods and other small crustaceans. When a bit larger they feed on the bottom on shrimp, barnacles, and small worms.

We cannot pass over the cod family without mentioning their reproductive behavior. It is in stark contrast to that of true littoral animals, which must produce fewer eggs, ensure their fertilization, and sometimes provide parental care well beyond hatching. The Atlantic cod exemplifies the casual way in which pelagic fish reproduce—discharging great numbers of eggs and great quantities of milt into the sea and trusting to luck for the necessary follow-through. This species is something of a champion, for it is known to produce up to 4 million eggs at one time. Obviously, only a small percentage of these need to be fertilized. The eggs float on the surface and hatch quickly, and the fry, with very little yolk to sustain them, must feed very soon. The myriad fry are an important part of the plankton and suffer enormous predation before any make it into the estuaries.

In addition to the sharks listed in Table 7, some bony fishes come into the estuaries from their marine habitat to feed upon fishes in the shallows. Among the species described in Chapter Two under Animals of the Inshore Waters is the **weakfish**, which, when in the estuaries, preys upon anchovies, herrings, pigfish, and spot; mysids, crabs, and other crustaceans; *Nereis;* and mollusks. The young of the **bluefish** prey on anchovies, silversides, killifishes, and herrings; shrimps and crabs; snails;

and annelids. The **striped bass** feeds on crustaceans, annelids, and insects.

The Role of Birds in the Estuarine Community

A functional rather than a taxonomic classification of the birds that feed on the flats and shoals is adopted by Charles and Nancy Peterson in *The Ecology of Intertidal Flats of North Carolina: A Community Profile*. This grouping of the birds by basic feeding behavior is a sound framework for discussion, and will be followed here in part.

WADING BIRDS

Waders include herons and egrets, the glossy ibis, the black-necked stilt, the avocet, and one shorebird—the greater yellowlegs. Most often seen on these shores are the **great egret, snowy egret, great blue heron, black-crowned night heron**, and **greater yellowlegs**. All of these except the yellowlegs breed from Cape Hatteras to Cape Cod, and all winter at least as far north as Cape May, New Jersey. In recent years the **glossy ibis** has not only been extending its range north to include all of the Middle Atlantic coast, but has become so abundant that visitors to some estuarine and marshland habitats might easily get the impression that it is the dominant species.

The waders are commonly thought of as marsh birds; many of them are discussed in Chapter Four. They hunt in the estuaries by stalking through the shallows spearing or snapping up fish, crustaceans, and gastropods.

Wading birds account for much of the attrition on the large schools of baitfishes such as anchovies, mummichogs and other killifishes, top minnows, silversides, and small menhaden. The larger herons and egrets are frequently seen catching fish that seem much too big to swallow, but the birds are almost snakelike in their ability to handle this unwieldy prey.

The myriad small fishes taken by the waders when the flats are inundated are themselves present in this habitat as foraging visitors, feeding on minute crustaceans and other invertebrates, plankton, and detritus. The waders, rather than being depredators on the fisheries resource, are playing a vital role in maintaining a healthy balance.

The **American avocet** *(Recurvirostra americana)*, not a common but a striking sight on the Middle Atlantic coast, may be seen in winter in the estuarine shallows from Chincoteague National Wildlife Refuge south to Cape Hatteras (and also in southern Florida). Over the years it has been a rare sight north of Delaware Bay, and early in the century Arthur Cleveland Bent gave the northern limit of its winter range as "Carolina." It is unmistakable when spotted, with its bold black-and-white pattern; long, slender, upturned bill; and stiltlike legs that give it a standing height of 20 in. (0.5 m). It tends to feed in the open; and, aided by webbed feet, it walks easily on soft, muddy bottoms and swims when it it has occasion to do so.

The avocet has a unique feeding technique, described in 1891 by Frank M. Chapman (Bulletin of the American Museum of Natural History, vol 3):

The use of the avocet's recurved bill is clearly explained by the manner in which the bird procures its food. In feeding they wade into the water and drop the bill below the surface until the convexity of the maxilla probably touches the bottom. In this position they move forward at a half run and with every step the bill is swung from side to side sweeping through an arc of about 50° in search of shells and other small aquatic animals. The mandibles are slightly opened, and at times the birds pause to swallow their prey. It is evident that birds with a straight or downward curved bill could not adopt this method of feeding.

Despite its highly specialized bill, the avocet is said to be in part a scavenger, and also partly herbivorous. Its animal food is apparently found by the sense of touch in the water and the sediments, and includes a variety of small invertebrates—in coastal environments, chiefly crustaceans, mollusks, and clam worms. The seeds of marsh plants are prominent in the vegetable component of its diet. It probably takes fewer fish than any of the other waders.

ESTUARINE COMMUNITIES

The herons and egrets mentioned above, along with the greater yellowlegs, are discussed in Chapter Four, as are the green, little blue, and Louisiana herons. In addition to all the above-named, the wading guild of the estuarine shallows includes the **white ibis** *(Eudocimus albus),* which may reach as far north as the Outer Banks in summer, and the **yellow-crowned night heron** *(Nycticorax violaceus).*

SHALLOW-PROBING AND SURFACE-SEARCHING BIRDS

The shallow probers and surface searchers are almost exclusively an invertebrate-eating guild. With two exceptions (clapper rail and American oystercatcher) they are not permanent residents of the Middle Atlantic coast; but individuals of many species can be seen in both summer and winter. Most belong to the order of shorebirds (Charadriiformes); most nest in the far north; and many are seen on the northern part of this coast only in migration. Some of the species that normally winter in South America are seen here as irregular winter residents.

It is not unusual to see several species of these shallow probers feeding on the mud or sand flats in mixed groups. One might wonder at the lack of competitive behavior in such close association among different birds all feeding on invertebrates on the surface and in the

129. Dunlins *(Calidris alpina)* feeding on the intertidal flats.

upper few centimeters of the deposits. But a diversity of bill structures and foraging techniques accords with the fact that their diets differ in detail.

The **ruddy turnstone** *(Arenaria interpres)* and the **dunlin** *(Calidris alpina)*—the former with a short, stout bill and the latter with a long bill slightly downcurved at the tip—illustrate how structural differences are reflected by differences in feeding behavior. As its name suggests, the turnstone has a habit of turning over stones, shells, seaweed, and debris to find beach-fleas, snails, and other small invertebrates. It sometimes chases fiddler crabs, and has been seen using its bill as a hammer to extract barnacles from their armor plate.

The dunlin, smaller and less stockily built than the turnstone, uses its droop-tipped bill, slightly opened, to probe in the mud or sand for marine worms and amphipods. Sometimes this feeding activity goes on in water up to the bird's belly. It is amusing to watch the flocks of these birds rapidly probing as they move about without ever standing upright. This hunched-over stance when feeding is a helpful clue to their identity in the field.

Both the dunlin and the turnstone feed in company with other small shorebirds (as well as in the midst of geese and other larger water birds), and competitive behavior does occur at times. Bent, in Part One of his *Life Histories of North American Shore Birds* (1927), described how some turnstones digging holes in wet sand with their bills were savagely driving off intruding sanderlings. The smaller birds, which normally feed from the surface, and by sight rather than by probing, were attempting to eat the small snails tossed out by the vigorously digging turnstones.

Most of the other species of the shorebird family—except the deep probers, discussed in the following section—belong in this group and get their food primarily from feeding in the intertidal zone. **Sanderlings**, so characteristic of the swash zone of the outer beach (and discussed in Chapter Two under Life Between the Tides) also feed in the intertidal flats. Among the others are the western sandpiper, which winters on this coast

130. American oystercatcher *(Haematopus palliatus)*.

(only north to New Jersey), and also frequents the beaches; and the **least sandpiper** and **short-billed do-witcher** (both feeding sometimes in salt marshes but characteristic of mud flats).

The specialized feeding habits of the **American oystercatcher** *(Haematopus palliatus)* set it apart from the other birds in this guild. It alone (excepting the gulls that drop mollusks and crustaceans from the air to break the shells) can harvest the largest bivalves. Its bill is used not only in probing; it is inserted between the valves of an oyster or other bivalve and used like a chisel to sever the ligament that holds the shell together; it then serves to remove the mollusk from its shell. Oys-tercatchers feed also on fiddlers and other small crabs, shrimps, sea urchins, and marine worms. One has been seen catching a small flounder in the shallows. Among all the birds of the shallow-probing and surface-search-ing guild, the oystercatcher is the most exclusively in-tertidal in its foraging activities.

From the point of view of the shellfish industry, the oystercatcher's role in the estuarine community is less than healthful. Its efficient feeding on oysters and clams is sometimes considered significant in depleting the populations of these commercially important mollusks, though not all of its consumption is detrimental to the harvested species. The oystercatcher eats the Baltic macoma, a small, thin-shelled clam that lives on shallow

Animals of the Estuarine Waters

muddy bottoms with a minimum salinity of 5 o/oo, throughout the Middle and North Atlantic coasts of North America, by the thousands. *Mytilus edulis,* the blue mussel, a species of growing commercial value and less characteristic of muddy bottoms, is another preferred food. But unlike *Macoma, M. edulis* also lives to depths of several hundred feet offshore, where it is well out of reach of the oystercatcher.

DEEP-PROBING SHOREBIRDS

Only a few species on the Middle Atlantic coast are among the deep probers. The **marbled godwit** *(Limosa fedoa)* is seldom seen north of Cape Henry, Virginia; the **whimbrel** *(Numenius phaeopus)* is only a migrant on these shores. The **willet** *(Catoptrophorus semipalmatus),* however, is common along the coast, and winters and breeds almost to Cape Cod. All the above are large shorebirds of the family Scolopacidae. The **long-billed curlew** *(Numenius americanus),* largest of the order (Charadriiformes), can be included in the group for Cape Hatteras, where it is occasionally seen in winter. (It formerly was a transient on the northeastern U.S. coast.)

The very long bills of these birds enable them to probe for such deep burrowers as mud shrimps, but their diet is by no means limited to such animals. The marbled godwit feeds upon a variety of crustaceans, small gastropods, insects and insect larvae, and marine worms. The whimbrel feeds chiefly on mussels, clams, and other mollusks, and upon crustaceans; it sometimes captures small fish; it takes lugworms from their burrows; and it eats many insects.

The willet fits least neatly into a particular community, for it feeds in many coastal habitats—outer beach, bayshores, salt marshes, intertidal flats, shallow pools, tidal creeks, and wet meadows. Although willets probe for burrowing worms when on the sand and mud flats, they eat a variety of small mollusks, crustaceans, small fish, and insects that do not require the deep-probing use of the long bill. On the outer beach they are seen in the swash-and-backwash zone, where they feed on *Emerita,* the mole-crab; but in winter when the mole-

131. Willet *(Catoptrophorus semipalmatus)* in flight.

crabs have moved offshore they feed in large numbers on the flats. Drab in appearance when on the ground, and hard to distinguish at a distance from the greater yellowlegs, willets display a strikingly bold black-and-white wing pattern in flight. This, along with their large size and prominent bill, makes them among the more easily identified shorebirds.

AERIAL-SEARCHING BIRDS

The terns and gulls, black skimmer, fish crow, and (south of Cape Henry) brown pelican make up this primarily fish-eating fraternity. Terns and pelicans dive from the air for their prey, the terns seizing individual fish from near the surface while the pelicans swim underwater to scoop numbers of small fish into their capacious pouches. Contrary to popular belief, pelicans do not carry fish in their pouches. When they come to the surface with a pouch full of fish and water, they drain the water from their bills and then swallow the fish

Animals of the Estuarine Waters

before taking off on another aerial foray. The tern, if its catch is not intended for its young or its mate back at the nest, generally swallows the fish on the wing.

The feeding habits of **gulls** are described in Chapter Two. Their role in the food web of the intertidal flats is much the same as in other habitats. These opportunistic birds scavenge dead fish and invertebrates and also capture both kinds of food alive. Their chief impact on the intertidal community is probably as a predator on bivalves; they are often also seen taking crabs. On the Middle Atlantic coastal flats and marshlands, the laughing gull is by far the most conspicuous bird—noisy, active, and abundant.

Although the ranges of both the **American crow** and the **fish crow** embrace the Middle Atlantic coast, the latter species is the one identified with the seashore habitat. Identical in appearance, and with size ranges overlapping so that the largest fish crows are bigger than the smallest of the American crows, the two species are hard to differentiate. The chances are, though, that a crow you see feeding on the intertidal flats, particularly in summer, is the fish crow. Their voices do distinguish the two species. Instead of the familiar loud "caw" of the American crow, the fish crow utters a nasal "ca" or "ca-ha."

The **black skimmer** *(Rhynchops niger)*, classified here with the aerial-searching birds, actually does its feeding on the wing, at the surface of the water. Belonging to the same order as the shorebirds, gulls, terns, auks, and oystercatcher, it finds its food by a technique all its own. Sometimes it fishes in the surf zone of the outer beach, but it is more often found in the estuaries and sounds, where its feeding is facilitated by smooth water in the tidal creeks, over the tidal flats when they are inundated, in shallow pools and channels of the salt marsh, and in open-water shoal areas. For some reason, these birds are not found in brackish bays such as Chesapeake, where there would seem to be much of the quiet-water habitat favorable to this technique, as well as a good supply of fishes near the surface.

A skillful aerialist of great grace and beauty of form and pattern, the skimmer is not often seen flying high;

132. Black skimmer *(Rynchops niger).*

when searching for food, it flies low over the water. In actual feeding, it skims the surface, with its lower mandible, which is longer than the upper, slicing the water. The upper mandible is movable—a unique adaptation —and the skimmer snatches the fish by closing it onto the lower mandible.

With such a specialized bill, picking up food from the exposed flats would seem to be an impossibility; but skimmers have been seen to wade in water 3 in. deep, thrusting the bill forward and down to capture small fish. The skimmer often feeds at night, a habit that is probably related to its specialized foraging technique.

Skimmers are known on this coast only in summer, except along the Outer Banks. They are not year-round residents even in Back Bay, just north of Cape Hatteras. In the past, however, they nested primarily on open ocean beaches. Human activities have driven them away from most of these sites, but they are protected in nesting colonies on barrier beaches controlled by the U.S. Fish and Wildlife Service, as on Brigantine National Wildlife Refuge, New Jersey, and by the National

Animals of the Estuarine Waters

Park Service, as on Ocracoke Island, North Carolina. Even on some shores protected from extensive development by public ownership or park status, the presence of people and the heavy use of beaches by off-road vehicles often discourages nesting by colonial birds. Today much use is being made by the skimmers, as well as by other water birds, of dredge-spoil islands in estuaries and in the Intracoastal Waterway. They breed in rather loose colonies, with numerous subcolonies, which may be separated by nest-free zones ten meters or more wide.

FLOATERS

Because the birds in this group feed mostly in shallow water by floating on the surface and either tipping or utilizing a long neck to reach benthic invertebrates or plants, they have an impact on the estuarine environment somewhat different from that of the birds in the next group, which dive from the surface and may feed in water up to 30 ft. (8-10 m) depth. Included in the floaters are swans, geese, and the so-called dabbling ducks, or marsh ducks. The mallard, black duck, snow goose, and Canada goose are treated in Chapter Four, Salt Marsh Communities.

Few if any macrophytes grow on the intertidal flats; the floaters, which subsist primarily on vegetation, consequently spend little time in this environment. They are much more evident in the marshes, shallow intertidal ponds, impoundments, and tidal creeks. Free-floating sea lettuce may occur in the intertidal zone and in open water in quantities sufficient to attract the brant and the Canada goose. And some of the dabbling ducks may visit the intertidal flats on the rising tide to feed on invertebrates. The black duck, for example, eats quantities of snails, which are abundant in this zone.

SURFACE DIVERS

Diving birds here does not mean those that, like the osprey and the terns, search for their fishy prey while in flight and then plunge from aloft to seize it, but rather means those that alight on the water and pursue fish by swimming beneath the surface, or swim to the bottom to forage for mollusks or plant food. Of this group of birds, those most commonly seen in the estuaries include several species of fish eaters—cormorants, loons, grebes, and mergansers; and several species of mollusk-eating waterfowl. (Most of the primarily herbivorous waterfowl forage for food by tipping while floating on the surface; and while they feed mostly in shallow water they do not find the intertidal flats a source of food. These species frequent fresh ponds, impoundments, and tidal creeks for the most part.)

The **double-crested cormorant**, *Phalacrocorax auritus*, is a large piscivorous bird seen at some time during the year along the entire U.S. coast. Its summer range extends spottily to the Cape Henry area; along most of the coast between there and Cape Cod only nonbreeding birds are seen in summer. (When Bent wrote his *Life Histories* the southernmost breeding site was off the Maine coast.) In winter the cormorants are seen as far north as Long Island.

Although *P. auritus* is often seen flying in V-formation or in irregular groups, a more familiar sight is one of the birds perched on a buoy or pile, drying its outspread wings in the sun. It is not unusual to see a row of piles with a sunning cormorant on each. Adapted for underwater pursuit of fish, these divers would be handicapped by the well-oiled plumage of waterfowl; the drying process is probably a necessary prelude to flight. When swimming, the cormorant sits low in the water; buoyancy would of course not be an advantage for a bird that must be adept below the surface. The food of cormorants is exclusively fish; eels appear to be a major item in their diet, but herring, cod, and other coastal fishes are also eaten. These birds are often seen, on tidal creeks and the water-filled ditches adjacent to the dikes of impoundments in such management preserves as Chincoteague National Wildlife Refuge, swimming along with little but their heads and necks above water.

The **pied-billed grebe** *(Podilymbus podiceps)* is found along the entire Middle Atlantic coast throughout the year; at the northern end in winter when fresh waterways are likely to be frozen, it is most easily seen in the saline environments. Like the double-crested cormorant, it finds its food underwater; unlike the cormorant, its diet is varied; besides fish, it eats snails and other invertebrates, and to a lesser extent certain plant foods. This most aquatic of birds is rarely seen on land. On the water, it swims low, sometimes with only its head above the surface. It is agile under water, and has earned the nickname "helldiver" by its ability to disappear instantly beneath the surface when disturbed—to reappear a considerable distance away, or not to be seen again at all. It uses its wings as well as its webbed toes in swimming underwater.

The pied-billed grebe seems to prefer smaller, quieter waterways, including the narrowest of ditches and tidal creeks. Though it appears not to mind the proximity of humans, it is difficult to approach and is an elusive target for the wildlife photographer, diving rather than taking flight. When it does take to the air, it paddles along the surface before becoming airborne, then flies with rapid beats of its small wings, with neck and feet outstretched.

The **common loon** (*Gavia immer*), a large bird distantly related to the grebe, is also very much a bird of the water environment, with feet placed well back where they function well below the surface but are virtually useless on land. In fact, the loon can take flight only from the water surface, and then only after pattering for a considerable distance, beating the water with both wings and feet. It flies strongly once airborne, and indeed migrates long distances; it nests primarily in Alaska, Canada, and Greenland in this hemisphere, and winters (in the East) along the coast from Newfoundland to Texas. Although it is seen in the sounds and estuaries, it demands open water and is usually well offshore; it keeps at a distance from humans.

The common loon is chiefly a fish eater; it is a powerful underwater swimmer, catching and swallowing its prey under the surface. It feeds on such bottom fish as flounders; one loon was found to have 15 of these fish in its gullet. It also eats some mollusks and other invertebrates that it finds on the bottom.

The rest of the common feathered underwater hunters—mergansers and diving ducks—are members of the waterfowl family (Anatidae). The mergansers are fish eaters; the diving ducks are primarily feeders on mollusks. Several species are seen in coastal estuaries frequently enough to be discussed here.

Lesser scaups *(Aythya affinis)* breed in western Canada and Alaska, but most of them winter in the eastern half of North America. Although most migrate south through the Mississippi valley, many thousands fly to the Atlantic and spend the winter on the stretch of coast from Cape Cod to Florida. Large concentrations of the bluebills, as they are often called, sojourn on the waters in and adjacent to New Jersey's extensive coastal marshes, and even larger numbers winter on Chesapeake Bay.

Lesser scaups feed in water of various depths, primarily on animal life. At times their chief food consists of seeds and vegetative parts of aquatic and marsh plants. In North Carolina's sounds mollusks appeared to be the major item of their diet. An expert diver, this bird can remain a long time on the bottom grubbing for food.

On the water, the male of this smallish duck looks black on both ends and white in the middle. When it is close enough, the blue bill and purplish head help in identification. The female is dark brown and has a white facial mask.

The smallest of our diving ducks, the **bufflehead** *(Bucephala albeola),* breeds in Canada and Alaska and winters in part on the Middle Atlantic coast. The largest numbers are found from New Jersey south. Their food during this period on salt water is mostly invertebrates —crustaceans (isopods, amphipods, and shrimp) and mollusks. Fish are also eaten, along with some aquatic plants. Feeding in groups, with one or more birds remaining on the surface—apparently as lookouts for danger—the buffleheads pursue moving prey under water or search for benthic animals in the sediments. The little duck is itself food for larger predators such as the peregrine falcon.

The butterball, as this species is sometimes called, is

a most attractive bird, easily recognized by the male's striking black and white plumage, big round head with a white bonnet, and (in flight) large white wing patch; and by the female's dark plumage and white cheek patch.

One of the commonest ducks seen on tidal creeks and impoundment ditches in winter is the **ruddy duck** *(Oxyura jamaicensis)*. It is also seen on more open water, by ones or twos and in groups. At this time of year the male does not display the colorful plumage that gives the species its name. Both males and females are grayish, the male having a white cheek and the female a dark line across the cheek. The most distinctive trait of the duck is its spiky tail, which is often cocked in a vertical position.

The ruddy duck, almost as diminutive as the buffle-head, is also a good diver, but eats a higher proportion of plant food. One researcher found 22,000 seeds of a (freshwater) pondweed in the stomach of a ruddy duck. In the salt marshes and other marine environments it feeds on snails, fiddlers and other small crabs, small fish, and the seeds and vegetative parts of various marsh and aquatic plants.

Mergansers are diving ducks with a more exclusively piscivorous diet. They are well adapted, having spike-like bills with saw-toothed mandibles and superior diving ability, for overtaking and seizing their fishy prey. On land they are awkward, and take off from the water surface with considerable effort.

The **red-breasted merganser** *(Mergus serrator)* is among the handsomest of birds, on the water or in flight. The male, with his streamlined form; his glossy green-black, crested head; his white collar and colorful body plumage; and his coral-red bill and red feet, cuts a dashing figure as he swims or flies about. The female is more modestly attired, with a crested rusty head, grayish body, large white wing patch, and, like the male, red bill and feet.

Although sometimes considered strictly a fish eater, the red-breasted merganser also eats crustaceans and mollusks. Most of the fish it eats are small—sticklebacks and other bait-sized species, herrings, and sculpins.

Breeding in the western hemisphere principally in Canada, Alaska, and Greenland, the red-breasted merganser is known also to breed in the Long Island area. In winter it can be seen along the entire U.S. Atlantic and Gulf coasts. It is more common in open waters, but frequents the marshes and tidal waterways as well.

BIRDS OF PREY

The characteristic raptorial birds of estuarine environments are the **osprey** *(Pandion haliaetus)*; the **northern harrier**, less accurately called **marsh hawk** *(Circus cyaneus)*; the **bald eagle** *(Haliaeetus leucocephalus)*, now quite rare along the Middle Atlantic coast; the **peregrine falcon** *(Falco peregrinus)*, a rare migrant on the coast south of Delaware Bay, though seen quite frequently on Assateague Island in fall; and the **short-eared owl** *(Asio flammeus)*. The marsh hawk and short-eared owl, both of which hunt in the dunes, grasslands, and marshes, are discussed in Chapter Four; the peregrine falcon is discussed in Appendix III, Endangered Species.

Because of its exclusively piscivorous diet and its hunting techniques, the osprey might easily have been included under Aerial-searching Birds. With its extraordinarily keen eyesight and ability to dive-bomb its target, the osprey is an efficient predator on fish. It can be seen in all water environments where its prey (medium-to-large fish) can be found, including shallow impoundments and large sounds.

The breeding range of the osprey embraces all of the coast south of Cape Cod, though its distribution is spotty. It was formerly much more abundant. Having been depleted severely by the effects of DDT in the mid-twentieth century, it now appears to be on the road to recovery. It has had one advantage over most raptorial species: it is a great favorite of humans, and has often been provided with artificial nesting platforms near homes and in managed preserves. These are in many cases much more suitable for osprey nests than are natural sites; the nests so increase in bulk with

133. A pair of ospreys *(Pandion haliaetus)* building a nest on a channel marker, Assateague Island.

materials added over the years that they are often destroyed by storms or by the breaking of supporting limbs from the sheer weight. The list of items other than sticks that have been observed in osprey nests is endless, and includes such oddities as rag dolls, fruit baskets, plastic bottles, door mats, gull wings, cow dung, sheep skulls, rubber boots, trousers, and a straw hat.

The osprey has roughened pads on the soles of its powerful grasping feet that enable it to carry large, heavy, and slippery prey. As evidence of the sharpness of its eyesight, this raptor sometimes catches flounders, which closely match in color and pattern the bottom on

ESTUARINE COMMUNITIES

which they rest. It hovers on beating wings at surprising heights—as much as 200 ft. (61 m) when scouting for prey. Upon sighting a fish near the surface, an osprey plunges with half-folded wings, hitting the water with an impact sometimes great enough to injure the bird. It occasionally emerges with a fish too large to lift, and must abandon it to try again. The list of species is too long to include here; the osprey is probably indiscriminate in its choice of fish, and may even take snakes or turtles at times.

The bald eagle, revered as our national bird, is something else to the osprey. It is probably the chief natural enemy of the smaller "fish hawk," which is a more efficient hunter and is often highjacked by the eagle while on the way to its nest or a feeding perch with a fish it has caught.

The bald eagle is less discriminating in its diet than the osprey, being quite willing to scavenge on dead fish cast upon the beach—something no self-respecting osprey would stoop to. The author has observed a pair of bald eagles feeding on the carcass of a white-tailed deer on a frozen lake. (Deer sometimes perish when they slip spread-eagled on the ice and are injured.) While the bulk of their food is fish, bald eagles eat a considerable number of birds and mammals. Among the species taken in coastal environments are grebes, fish crows, coots, waterfowl, gulls, wading birds, muskrats, and foxes.

Like the osprey, the bald eagle was almost extirpated from the Middle Atlantic coast during the DDT era. It too is on the road to recovery, and in some areas such as the upper Potomac estuary it is now a fairly dependable resident. Better protection and declining use of the most toxic pesticides have helped in the restoration effort.

To all the above-described birds with roles in the ecology of the estuary can be added those discussed in Chapter Four, since salt and brackish marshes are a prominent feature of most estuaries. Few species, at any rate, limit their feeding activities to a single ecosystem. While most shorebirds derive the bulk of their food from the intertidal zone—the sand and mud flats in particular—they also feed on the upper beaches, in grassland habitats, and of course in freshwater ponds. A bird of prey such as the marsh hawk, primarily a hunter of small animals in the marsh and grass communities, may visit the estuarine intertidal zone to prey on shorebirds feeding there.

CHAPTER FOUR

Salt Marsh Communities

Wetlands

A *wetland* is land where the soil or substrate is at least periodically saturated with or covered by water, and where this condition is a major factor determining the nature of soil development and the types of plant-and-animal communities occuring in the soil and on its surface.

A *swamp* is a wetland—usually only intermittently covered by water—where the dominant plants are shrubs or trees or both. A swamp may also exist where the ground is never inundated but is saturated most of the time, or where it is inundated for only a short period each year. Salt or brackish swamps are rare on the Middle Atlantic coast. Mangrove swamps occupy much of the intertidal and subtidal belt in southern Florida, but nothing comparable is found farther north. The maritime forest communities dealt with in Chapter Two are upland ecosystems, though within them, as in Fire Island's Sunken Forest, small boggy or swampy enclaves may exist. The depressions between the wooded dune ridges on Cape Henry support baldcypress ponds, picturesque swamps in which the trees are festooned with Spanish moss *(Tillandsia usneoides)*, an epiphyte of the pineapple family.

A *marsh* is a wetland in which the dominant plants are grasses and sedges and other herbaceous plants. The cattail marsh is the classic example of a fresh marsh, as the cordgrass community is for the salt or brackish wet-

134. Cordgrass marsh community: *Spartina alterniflora* (on creek border), *S. patens*, northern harrier, clapper rail.

land. Where seepage creates near-fresh microhabitats along the upper edges of brackish marshes, cattails (*Typha* spp.) may form fingers or islands of fresh marsh within the limits of tidal influence.

An animal or plant not adapted for life in water or in soil that is often saturated experiences serious physiological problems in such an environment. And the problem is compounded in habitats where saline conditions exist, as in coastal marshes—particularly in those where the salinity level is constantly changing. Generally, mammals, birds, and reptiles, with their essentially impervious skins, are least inhibited by such factors in determining their habitat.

Salt Marshes and Salt Flats

The term *salt marsh* is applied to several kinds of vegetated habitats in a wide range of coastal saline and brackish areas. They are found in estuaries, nearly enclosed bays, lagoons, sounds, rivers, and sometimes in more open coastal areas protected by offshore islands. The character of these marsh systems varies with latitude, physical location, elevation, degree of exposure to water action, substrate, and other factors. The two types of coastal marshes described below are not distinct and separate. As often as not they exist together, with overlapping and intermingled stands and with varying degrees of mixture with nondominant plant species. The term salt marsh used alone includes both low marsh and salt meadow (high marsh). Salt meadow, on the other hand, refers only to high marsh.

SALT MEADOWS (HIGH MARSH)

Salt meadows occur on the landward side of salt marshes, or on the border of open water. They exist where the soil is waterlogged throughout the growing season but is inundated by only the highest tides. The vegetation may be an almost pure stand of **saltmeadow cordgrass** *(Spartina patens)* or a mixture dominated by **blackgrass** *(Juncus gerardii)*. Throughout the Middle Atlantic range, in areas where there is much freshwater input, **Olney threesquare** *(Scirpus Olneyi)* and **saltmarsh fleabane** *(Pluchea camporata)* may be prominent.

CORDGRASS SALT MARSH (LOW MARSH)

Low salt marsh exists where the soil is covered by the average tide (during the growing season) by a half-foot or more of water. Such marshes occur in most of the estuaries, lagoons, and sounds of the Atlantic coast; they appear as well on the open coast of the Virginia portion of the Delmarva Peninsula, spottily on the shores of Cape Cod Bay, and on other protected sites. Locally, beds of cordgrass growing on intertidal zones of beaches are often mistakenly called **eelgrass**—but true eelgrass beds are subtidal, and are dominated not by grass but by a marine flowering plant *(Zostera)* related to the pondweeds.

Because *Spartina alterniflora* (**saltmarsh cordgrass** or **smooth cordgrass**) is virtually synonymous with the low marsh habitat, biologists often refer to such marsh as *cordgrass salt marsh.* In this book, wherever the reference is simply to *cordgrass marsh,* it applies to both low and high marshes dominated by *Spartina.* A possible source of confusion is the fact that low marsh is dominated by a tall species of *Spartina (S. alterniflora),* while high marsh is dominated by a low, usually matted species *(S. patens).* Actually, "low" and "high" refer to the elevation and degree of inundation of the substrate.

Open water in the saltmarsh cordgrass habitat may support other marsh plants such as **widgeongrass** *(Ruppia maritima)* and **sago pondweed** *(Potamogeton pectinatus).*

OTHER WETLAND COMMUNITIES

In this book we are concerned primarily with the two kinds of coastal marshes identified above. But two other types of herbaceous saline communities existing above the low-tide mark should be mentioned.

Salt flats are located on the landward side of, and sometimes within, salt meadows and low cordgrass marshes, where the soil is almost always waterlogged during the growing season. Some of these sites are submerged only by occasional wind tides, while others are usually covered with a few inches of water at high tide. The sparse or patchy vegetation generally consists of **glassworts** *(Salicornia* spp.), **Atlantic seablite** *(Suaeda maritima),* or **saltwort** *(Salsola kali).* Soil conditions, including excess salt content, are apparently among the factors accounting for these sparsely vegetated sites.

Needlerush marsh exists in areas flooded irregularly by wind tides along the shores of nearly enclosed estuaries and in lagoons, sounds, and rivers from Maryland southward. Ponds within the **needlerush** *(Juncus roemerianus)* marsh, like those in the cordgrass marsh, often support growths of widgeongrass.

Wind tides, it should be noted, are tides enhanced or caused by winds, with the result that areas not normally flooded by the sun–moon tidal forces are inundated on an irregular basis. In some coastal basins wind tides may be the dominant tidal force. An example is Back Bay, Virginia, which is so isolated from the sea that lunar

135. The matted growth of *Spartina patens* contrasts with the erect form of *S. alterniflora* plants where the salt meadow and low salt marsh merge.

tides are of little consequence; but the shallow waters of the bay are pushed in the direction the winds blow, creating differential levels along the shores.

Origins of the Eastern Salt Marshes

To explain the beginnings of the marshes of the northern, glaciated, sector of the coast being treated here, we must go back to the Ice Age, when the seas were much lower than they are today. At that time the inner Continental Shelf was mostly coastal plain. What is now Georges Bank was a large, forested island, with salt marshes bordering its coastal embayments. Today that coastal plain is submerged, with only a few high points remaining above water. In relative terms, the sea is still rising, and parts of today's coast are holding their own only because deposition of sediments keeps pace with the water level. Where net erosion of beach materials is occurring, that combines with the forces of submergence to eat away at the land mass. Regardless of net effects, the shoreline is always changing, and this is no less true with salt marshes than with other coastal formations.

As the seas gradually (but not steadily) rose, the flooding of lower river valleys formed estuaries; and sand spits built by longshore currents and wave action closed off bays and sounds. Along the shallow edges of these protected areas certain grasses took root. During periods of slowed submergence, sediments were deposited around these marsh plants, and they tended to spread farther into the shallows. In periods of relatively rapid rise in sea level, the marshes tended to hold their own by building up a substrate of peat with their accumulated rootstocks, and at the same time to move inland as more of the coastal plain was flooded. Over the long haul, as the ancient coastal plain became the inundated Continental Shelf, the coastal marshes have migrated landward.

Borings into salt marshes show not only the long trend of events as the sea invaded the eastern seaboard but also the details of short-term events, such as the deposition of a deep layer of sand on a marsh by a major storm and, much later, formation of a new marsh as the rising sea catches up with it.

The nature of the vegetation of the coastal marshes varies according to a number of factors, including discharge of fresh water from the uplands, slope of the substrate, effects of tidal currents, variations in salinity, water temperatures, seasonal climatic conditions, and tidal range, which on the Middle Atlantic coast may be as little as a foot (30 cm), as at Nantucket, or as much as 6 1/2 ft. (2 m) just 40 mi. (60 km) away at Nauset Harbor.*

South of the Glaciated Coast, an almost uninter-

*The student of salt marsh ecology would do well to read the case history of Barnstable Marsh, on Cape Cod Bay, which was intensively investigated by Dr. Alfred Redfield of Woods Hole Oceanographic Institute. By studying the peat and sand deposits he has traced the story of this marsh back some 40 centuries, to a time when sea level was about 20 ft. (6 m) lower than it is today. Lacking access to this material or incentive to research the story, the amateur seashore naturalist might read the brief account of it in John and Mildred Teal's *Life and Death of the Salt Marsh.*

rupted band of salt marshes exists all the way to the mangrove swamps of Florida. On the open coast they form a broad zone behind the chain of barrier islands; these marshes are much more extensive than those of the Glaciated Coast—reaching a width of 9 mi. (14.5 km), for example, at Brigantine, New Jersey. The large estuaries and other embayments of this region are frequently bordered by salt marsh, too—particularly the western shore of Delaware Bay, the eastern shore of Chesapeake Bay, and the vast sounds behind the Currituck and Outer banks of North Carolina. (The salt marshes are even more extensive south of Cape Hatteras, beyond the scope of this book.)

The origins of these southern marshes are different from those of the marshes north of New Jersey. The rivers of this region, unlike the rivers of the hard-rock, glaciated Northeast, carry immense loads of sediment. Notable in this respect is the Roanoke River, which empties into Albemarle Sound. Not even the largest eastern river, the Susquehanna, which empties into Chesapeake Bay, carries as much sediment as does the Roanoke. From Pennsylvania south the eastern rampart of the Appalachian chain consists of sedimentary rock, which is relatively easily eroded; together with the stream-laced coastal plain it contributes a bountiful and continuous supply of sediment to feed the shallows of the seacoast. This erosion and deposition process was drastically speeded up when the Europeans came and cut the forests of the dissected coastal plain sediments to grow corn, cotton, tobacco, and other crops. So rapidly did the soils of this farmland erode, the harbors through which the farm produce was shipped became clogged with silt and one by one were abandoned—except where costly dredging has managed to keep them open and usable. Thus, formerly busy and important shipping points such as Joppatown, Maryland, and Dumfries, Virginia, are now obscure small towns inaccessible to marine vessels.

As the muddy rivers slowed down on reaching sea level, they dropped their loads of sediment. Wherever the mud bottom was built up to midtide level, *Spartina alterniflora* and other salt-resistant plants were likely to become established. Thus the shores of bays and estuaries were built out, and towns and farms that had been on open water became separated from it by broad belts of salt marsh. Large sections of some seaboard cities, such as Washington, D.C., have been built on land where formerly rivers flowed and tides lapped the shore. This new land was acquired simply by dredging and filling to bring the substrate of the former marshland above the reach of the highest tides. It is not surprising that storm tides and river floodwaters occasionally inundate these uplands stolen from the sea.

Here, on the Nonglaciated Coast, where the longshore currents, waves, and winds have a much greater supply of materials to work with than they do on the Glaciated Coast, the process of marsh building has been enhanced by the building of spits from headlands and capes. Breached by storms at various points, spits became chains of barrier islands. In the shallows on the landward side of these barrier beaches, marshes developed. And with the landward migration of many of these barriers, the marshes also marched inward.

Plants of the Salt Marsh

Cordgrass Communities

Salt meadows and low salt marsh are among the most important of all natural communities. Cordgrass salt marsh *(Spartina alterniflora),* in fact, is the most productive of all ecosystems in terms of biomass. Together the two *Spartina*-dominated marshes not only benefit many animals, including man, that obtain food from them, but provide the principal food base for other intertidal and subtidal communities. *S. alterniflora* in particular supports food chains that include many of the commercially valuable animals of coastal oceanic waters as well as estuarine species. (The full significance of this vital ecosystem and the intricacy of its functioning as a natural community are admirably communicated in the Teals' *Life and Death of the Salt Marsh*.)

The upper limit of cordgrass communities is the upper limit of the highest spring tides; the lower limit varies somewhat between locations up- and down-estuary, but is somewhere about the upper limit of the lowest neap tides. One of the factors preventing cordgrass establishment in the lower part of the intertidal zone is that the seedlings apparently must have a substantial number of days of emergence, free of the action of waves, to achieve solid anchoring in the substrate. In the lower reaches of the intertidal zone, which are flooded by most tides, there is no such extended period of emergence. Thus, between the salt marsh and low-water mark of the spring tides there is an unvegetated zone of sand or mud flats. In many areas, these flats occupy the entire intertidal zone.

Saltmarsh cordgrass and **saltmeadow cordgrass** define zones reflecting the frequency with which they are inundated by the tides. The former species, *S. alterniflora*, is a coarse, dark-green grass that ranges from knee-high to taller than an adult human and occupies the part of the marsh that is inundated by most high tides. It grows tallest (and in the densest stands) along the borders of tidal creeks and in drainage ditches, where its roots are always in water. *S. patens* is a much finer grass, with leaves 1/16 in. (1.6 mm) wide, in contrast to *S. alterniflora*'s 3/4-in.-wide (19 mm-wide) leaves. Though it sometimes grows to waist height, *S. patens* typically reaches no more than 2 ft. (0.6 m), and its slender leaves tend to bend in swirled, matlike clumps, called cowlicks, that give the salt meadow its distinctive appearance. Because of this matting effect, and the fact that in this high zone tidal currents have little effect, the grass accumulates as it dies off. One year's growth forms a protective mat that persists through the next year, providing shelter for myriad small animals and preventing the soil from drying out even where the marsh is flooded only a few times a month.

S. alterniflora marsh, producing up to 10 tons per acre dry weight of vegetation a year (less in the northern part of the Middle Atlantic coast), is quite different from *S. patens* marsh. The short span of its growth-and-decay process creates a rapid cycling of nutrients that is of enormous significance throughout the estuarine system. A fair number of invertebrates—snails, marsh crabs, grasshoppers, flies, bugs, beetles, and ants —feed upon cordgrass. But the production of biomass is so high in the *S. alterniflora* zone that this local consumption is of relatively slight importance in the overall food web. Here, instead of the accumulation and matting of previous years' growth that occurs in the *S. patens* marsh, the *S. alterniflora* plant parts are constantly dying, breaking off, and being carried by tidal currents out of the salt marsh and into other estuarine habitats. Bacteria and fungi having begun the decay process, the cordgrass plant fragments are further broken down by a combination of plant and animal action. Fragments small enough to be ingested by estuarine invertebrates constitute, en masse, that most important of nutriments, *detritus.* The plant tissues themselves, however, are not the essential food of detritivores. These animals —fiddler crabs, mullets, the Baltic macoma (a clam) and many others—ingest the particles; remove the bacterial colonies, which are a nutritious food; and pass out the remainder, now in yet smaller particles. New bacteria quickly attack the detrital fragments, and they again become available for animals that can ingest the new, smaller particles. After being further broken down and relieved of their burdens of bacteria, fungi, and algae, the even smaller particles are again ready for processing and ingestion. Most of the energy wrapped up in the original green plant material is thus gradually acquired, via the bacterial agents of decay, by the bacteriophagous invertebrates and vertebrates.

The detritus-feeding invertebrates, constituting a major component of the estuarine first-order consumers, are worms, crustaceans (including most shrimps and crabs), oysters, many gastropods, the larvae of marsh flies and mosquitoes, and others. The young and sometimes the adults of many fish species are also detritivores. Most notable of these are mullet and the Atlantic menhaden (the latter being, by weight of catch, the Atlantic coast's leading commercial fish). Others are bay anchovy, killifishes, silversides, grunts, porgies, drums, Atlantic croaker, and soles. That many of the detritus feeders are the young of game and commercial species or are fed upon by such species attests to the great significance of detritus as a food resource. Oceanic species that use the estuaries as nurseries, as seasonal habitat, or in migration owe much to the salt marsh. The implications of continuing destruction of our coastal marshlands are only too obvious.

Associated Plants

The overwhelming dominance of the cordgrasses in the low and high marsh zones sometimes causes us to overlook other plants adapted to this habitat. One group of plants that are often pioneers in establishing vegetative cover on a new mud bank, and that take over depressions in the marsh where evaporation creates conditions too saline even for *Spartina*, is the **glassworts** (*Salicornia* spp.). Belonging to the Chenopodiaceae, a family of edible plants that includes garden beets, chard, spinach, sugar beets, and pigweed (a weed in name but nonetheless edible), the glassworts are among those few herbaceous flowering plants that produce brown flowers. The flowers are tiny, and are hidden in the axils of the leaves, which themselves are mere fleshy sheaths appressed to the translucent, cylindrical stems.

There are three species of *Salicornia* in the Middle Atlantic region. An observer unfamiliar with this group might take these plants for members of the nonflowering horsetail family. Esthetically, glassworts are notable for the patches of red they add to the marsh scene in autumn. Where abundant they may be important as wildlife food; 28,000 seeds of *Salicornia* were found in the stomach of a single northern pintail (a marsh duck). Geese feed upon the fleshy plants. Wild-food gourmands, including the writer, add pieces of glasswort to their salads. These plants were formerly gathered for

Plants of the Salt Marsh

136. Dwarf glasswort *(Salicornia bigelovii)* forms dense patches in Nauset Marsh, Cape Cod National Seashore.

pickling, hence the alternative name pickle plant. Samphire, another alternative, may be a corruption of swamp fire.

From Cape Cod to Virginia, **blackgrass** *(Juncus gerardii)*—a rush, and thus a member of the sedge family (Cyperaceae) rather than the grass family (Poaceae) —often forms a landward border between the salt marsh and the upland. In upper Chesapeake Bay and other places diluted by freshwater inflow, blackgrass may be the dominant marsh plant. From Maryland to Cape Hatteras, *J. roemerianus,* or **needlerush,** may fill the same niche in the marsh. To discover the source of this plant's common name, you have only to walk through a stand of it.

Mixed in with *S. patens,* or occasionally growing in a pure stand, **saltgrass** *(Distichlis spicata)* is a true grass of the high marsh. It looks enough like saltmeadow cordgrass that it might easily be overlooked; but it is not as tall—growing to knee height at most—and does not form cowlicks.

In the lower reaches of the estuary, where salinity is high, very few vascular plants compete with *S. alter-*

SALT MARSH COMMUNITIES

137. Slender glasswort (*Salicornia europaea*) creates a
miniature forest in the high marsh at Hammonasett,
Connecticut.

niflora, and stands of it appear to be almost pure. But
close examination reveals, besides the highly salt tolerant glassworts, a growth of lower plants: algae, blue-
green algae, diatoms, and dinoflagellates. Their
presence may be detected by the characteristic colors
they lend to the surface of the mud. Except for the
blue-green algae, which are very primitive organisms—
lacking organized nuclei, they are sometimes even classified below the plant kingdom—all these require a fair
measure of sunlight and are thus found at the edges of
the stands or in the more sparse growths of the rooted
plants.

Blue-green algae, like legumes in upland habitats,
function as nitrogen fixers, capturing nitrogen from the
air and making it available in compounds for higher
marsh plants. Just below the surface of the mud, photosynthetic bacteria, which need light to function but
cannot live in the presence of oxygen, create purple
films that can be exposed by scraping away a very thin
layer of mud.

Phragmites. Common reedgrass (*Phragmites communis*), an unwelcome alien from the Old World, has

Plants of the Salt Marsh   317 managed despite the rarity of its ripe-seed production to spread into wet places throughout the country. Particularly, it is prominent in the Atlantic coastal areas. It spreads mainly by long, creeping rootstocks, and during recent decades the species seems to have been increasing its takeover of salt marshlands. This process may have been accelerated by man's drainage of marshes for mosquito control.

Phragmites, certainly a picturesque plant with its feathery panicles borne like banners on stems 13 ft. (4 m) high and its hues that change with the seasons, is of little value for wildlife. Red-winged blackbirds and other songbirds may sound off from its swaying stalks, but they get little food from it. Glossy ibis and black-crowned night herons often nest on the ground in dense stands of the reed on dredge deposition sites. But its net value is certainly negative, for *Phragmites* displaces more valuable marsh plants, such as cordgrass.

Managers of refuges and parks where *Phragmites* thrives have fought it with many control methods, including chemical sprays, mowing (as many as four clippings a season), burning, and simple, laborious removal by hand. One of the most effective herbicides tried so far is Dalapon; unfortunately, this chemical also reduces many desirable plant species.

138. Reedgrass *(Phragmites communis),* Chincoteague National Wildlife Refuge, Virginia.

SALT MARSH COMMUNITIES

Scrub-Shrub Wetland

Several woody plants are found in the transition zone from high salt marsh to the upland. Where the zone is dominated by woody shrubs it is classified as *scrub-shrub wetland*—a type of swamp. This community occurs independently of the salt marsh in many locations. Most unwelcome to humans of the plants of the upper marsh and scrub-shrub wetland is **poison-ivy** *(Rhus radicans)*, which often constitutes an unavoidable hazard to anyone walking to the marsh from the upland. But it is eaten by some animals that frequent this habitat, including the white-tailed deer.

Many herbaceous and woody plants of this habitat are appreciated for the bright touch their flowers lend to the scene. Most spectacular is the perennial, **swamp rose-mallow** *(Hibiscus palustris)*, which grows man-high and produces huge pink (or, in the southern part of its range, white and red-centered) hollyhocklike blossoms in late summer. Rose-mallow grows in clumps on the high marsh and scrub-shrub zone along the coast from Cape Cod to Cape Hatteras.

A closely related perennial, **seashore mallow** *(Kosteletzkya virginica)* is a small version of the rose-mal-

139. Swamp rose-mallow *(Hibiscus palustris)*, Chincoteague National Wildlife Refuge, Virginia.

Plants of the Salt Marsh   319

low, about 3 ft. (0.9 m) in height and with flowers 1 to 2 in. (25 to 50 mm) across and leaves shaped somewhat like those of maples. It is found from Long Island south in a wide range of salinities. A third pink-flowered member of the family, **marsh mallow** *(Althea officinalis)*, occurs in the middle of the range, from Connecticut to Virginia. It is similar in size to *K. virginica*, but has leaves shaped more like those of *H. palustris*.

The perennial herb **seaside goldenrod** *(Solidago sempervirens)* splashes yellow over the late-season landscape from high spots in the marsh to the adjacent uplands, including dunelands. Where salinity is low, **marsh thistle** *(Cirsium palustre)* bears colorful clusters of pink flowers with purple bracts—smallish blossoms like those produced by the Canada thistle.

The **groundsel-tree** *(Baccharis halimifolia)* produces showy flowers with snow-white fluffs of capillary bristles in autumn, along the upper edges of salt marshes and in scrub-shrub wetland habitats throughout the range. It is sometimes called, descriptively, the cotton-seed tree. Actually a shrub, it does not exceed 10 ft. (3 m) in height and is usually much shorter.

Much less interesting to the eye than the colorful shrubs described above, but very important because it is so often a dominant species in the marsh-upland transition zone, is marsh-elder *(Iva frutescens)*. This salt-tolerant, part-woody composite also sometimes invades the marsh proper. Where *S. patens* marsh borders a lagoon, *Iva frutescens* may grow to the water's edge. This perennial bears greenish-white flowers on spikes arising from the upper leaf axils. Not showy but adding a delicate violet tinge to the late-summer marsh is another, smaller (knee-high) perennial, **sea-lavender** *(Limonium nashii)*. It is an herbaceous plant and, like marsh-elder, is found from Cape Cod to Cape Hatteras.

The diversity of this shrubby transition zone is functionally important in the marsh ecosystem in that its plants attract swarms of insects, and because it provides food and nesting sites for many birds, including the **red-winged blackbird, yellow warbler, gray catbird, sharp-tailed sparrow,** and **clapper rail.** Some of these birds feed in the adjacent cordgrass marsh. The major factors determining how far into the marsh the plants of the scrub-shrub zone can venture are salinity and moisture.

Animals of the Salt Marsh

Visitors to the salt marsh are more diverse than its inhabitants. For the most part they need no specialized mechanisms for dealing with the saline conditions (exceptions are aquatic animals, including fish, that invade the marsh with the rising tide). Birds and mammals, with waterproof skins, have no physiological adaptations for osmoregulation. Some birds, such as gulls, do have special nasal glands for excreting excess salt taken in with their food. A few of these birds and mammals are residents, breeding in the salt marsh—generally in the salt meadow and upper transition zone. But most come to the marsh only to feed, and it is this that makes the marsh such a rewarding wildlife-watching habitat.

Relatively few species feed directly upon the growing *Spartina* plants, but other rooted plants associated with the cordgrasses attract many waterfowl, wading birds, and shorebirds. Spikerushes and bulrushes (*Eleocharis* and *Scirpus* spp.) are important wildlife food, being consumed by dabbling ducks, scaup, snow and Canada geese, the American coot, and rails; muskrats eat the vegetative parts. Widgeongrass *(Ruppia maritima),* a submerged aquatic plant that grows in marshland pools, is particularly valuable because all parts of the plant are edible; it constitutes a large portion of the diet of the brant, Canada goose, coot, and scaup, and of many dabbling ducks.

Distichlis spicata (saltgrass) is eaten by the Canada goose, the northern shoveler, and the blue-winged teal. The seeds of cordgrasses are important to the American black duck, seaside sparrow, and sharp-tailed sparrow; and the rootstocks of both species of *Spartina* are heavily consumed by Canada and snow geese in winter. But *Potamogeton pectinatus* (sago pondweed), growing in pools within the salt marsh, far outstrips *Spartina alter-*

niflora in acceptability to seashore birds. It constitutes as much as half of the diet of the canvasback, and represents a sizable part of the diet of the Canada goose and tundra swan, as well as a wide array of dabbling and diving ducks. The seeds are eaten by some shore and marsh birds, and the plants are eaten by muskrats.

Life Among the Plant Roots

Burrowing animals are not as common in the marsh muds as they are in the mud flats, where their activity is unimpeded by plant roots. One filter-feeding polychaete worm is not handicapped by the tangle of *Spartina* roots; only 1/10 in. (2.5 mm) long, it occurs in great numbers in places in the cordgrass marsh.

Most of the nonterrestrial marsh dwellers spend the early part of their lives in the sea and in subtidal estuarine waters, as free-swimming or drifting larvae. Even animals as completely adapted to a semiterrestrial existence as the air-breathing crabs (*Uca, Sesarma,* and *Ocypode* spp.) must return to the water when the eggs they carry are ready to hatch. The larvae that emerge develop as they drift about on the estuarine currents, and eventually some of those that survive predation settle on a suitable marsh or mud-flat substrate and begin life as fugitives from the sea.

Among filter feeders in the marsh, the **ribbed mussel** *(Modiolus demissus)* is conspicuous along the edges of the tidal banks, almost to the high-tide mark. It is also found on estuarine mud flats, and thrives even in polluted waters. Similar to the edible, or blue, mussel (described in Chapter Three under Intertidal-flat Benthic Epifauna) in size and shape, it differs externally in having rough, radiating ribs. Anchoring itself half-buried in the marsh mud among the cordgrass roots, it waits with valves tightly closed for the tide to cover it. Then it quickly opens and extends its intake and output siphons. Water pumped into the mantle cavity passes through the gills, which strain out the diatoms and finer detrital particles. Rejected material is bound together in a ribbon of mucus and mud. Where currents are too weak to carry away these *pseudofeces* they accumulate

140. Ribbed mussels *(Modiolus demissus)*, Assateague Island.

around the mussel, which must move upward to avoid being buried in its own garbage heap. This slow vertical migration has a top limit of the level at which the mussel will be covered by the tide enough hours of the day to allow sufficient intake of food. Most of the filter feeders require a longer period of submersion than does this mussel, which can move at least a gallon of water through its siphon-and-filter system in an hour.

The ribbed mussel is found throughout the Middle Atlantic coast. South of Virginia another, smaller filter feeder, the **Carolina marsh clam** *(Polymesoda caroliniana)*, lives in the intertidal marsh, but only in water with a salinity of no more than 15 o/oo.

Invertebrates Living on and Among Marsh Plants

MARSH SNAILS

Throughout the Middle Atlantic range, some gastropods, such as the **oval**, or **mouse-eared**, **marsh snail** *(Ovatella myosotis)* and the **salt-marsh snail** *(Melampus bidentatus)*, are much more abundant than their visibility would suggest. Measuring 0.25 in. (6 mm) and 0.4 in. (10 mm) respectively, they are easily overlooked. *O. myosotis* is found most commonly near the high tide line, generally hidden from view under vegetation, in crevices of jetties, or under boards or other objects. *M. bidentatus* lives on cordgrass and other marsh grasses and sedges and under debris. The easiest way to discover *Melampus* is to wade into the high marsh when the tide is in; the snails move up the grass stems to keep above the water, and sometimes bend the plants over with their combined weight. These snails belong to an order of small, air-breathing gastropods that are for the most part still tied to the ocean. They require a moist habitat but spend most of their time out of the water, and try to keep above the tide.

A larger snail, less particular about its habitat and more tolerant of being out of wet places, is the **common periwinkle** *(Littorina littorea),* a cold-water immigrant from Northern Europe now well established on the North Atlantic coast. It has managed to reach Maryland, but in the southern part of its range it does not attain its normal size of about an inch (25 mm). With its shell closed, *L. littorea* can live a long time out of water and without feeding; *Melampus,* in contrast, has no horny operculum with which to close itself off from its environment. *L. littorea* is widely eaten by Europeans. Euell Gibbons devotes three pages of his book *Stalking the Blue-eyed Scallop* to this modest denizen of the seashore.

All these snails are herbivores, feeding on algal films from the lower parts of the marsh plants or from the surface of the mud, and on the marsh grasses themselves. They rasp the plant material from the substrate with the *radula,* a ribbonlike tongue armed with horny teeth. The radula of *L. littorea* is twice the snail's own length.

Marsh snails are food for many birds and other intertidal predators. They are the chief item, along with snails of the mud flats, in the diet of the black duck, which breeds in the salt marshes throughout the snail's range in the United States. All of our estuarine dabbling and diving ducks partake of this bountiful food supply, but none to the degree that the black duck does. Other marsh animals that feed upon snails are the muskrat; fish crow; egrets; rails; plovers and ruddy turnstone; yellowlegs, willet, dowitcher, and other sandpipers; and long-billed marsh wren. The little wren apparently picks off smaller snails only directly from the marsh plants and is not seen on the muddy substrate at all.

Several small fishes that are year-round or seasonal dwellers of the estuarine shallows swim in with the tide and feed upon snails in the marsh creeks or among the grasses. The mummichog *(Fundulus heroclitus),* at 5 in. (13 mm) a rather large killifish, and the tidewater silverside *(Menidia beryllina),* a tiny fish found from New England south, are among the resident snail eaters. They do not always leave the marsh with the ebbing tide, but remain in ponds and depressions that hold water.

CRUSTACEANS

FIDDLER CRABS.   Picture a bass-fiddle player holding his oversize, unwieldy instrument aloft with one hand, waving it to and fro to attract attention or perhaps to intimidate an adversary. This is the image that might be called up when one first glimpses the aptly named fiddler crab. In their habitat fiddlers are encountered in greater numbers than any other members of the macrofauna. They live on the banks of tidal creeks and in cordgrass marshes and sometimes on mud flats, throughout the range covered by this book.

Fiddler crabs, here, refers to true crabs belonging to three species, all found from Cape Cod south, and all of the genus *Uca.* They belong to the family Ocypodidae ("swift-footed"), as does the ghost crab, which is limited to outer beaches and the backside of spits and barrier islands, from southern New Jersey south (see Chapter Two, under Animals of the Upper Beach).

You will inevitably first become aware of the presence of fiddlers *en masse,* for they are the most gregarious of crabs. But take the time to observe them individually and close up. They are amusing to watch, and their role in the estuarine food web makes them an important subject of study.

141. Sand fiddlers on the lagoon side of the barrier beach at West Dennis, Massachusetts.

Fiddlers invariably scurry for their burrows when approached. In their haste to find shelter, sometimes two or three will duck down into the same hole; but since the burrows are not communal property the rightful owner quickly ejects all intruders. Very soon all will have found haven and there will be stillness where confusion reigned. Sit quietly, and claws and stalked eyes will come into view as fiddlers check to see if the way is clear to resume feeding. If you have placed yourself belly-down on the mud, you will be able to watch and photograph the fighting, feeding, digging, and courting activities. Just avoid sudden movements, which will send the crabs scrambling again for haven.

One might wonder how the marsh can support such hordes of crabs as are encountered. The answer lies in their diet. Fiddlers are vegetarians, subsisting on detritus and the algae that grow in such abundance and so quickly on the surface of the mud, where moisture and solar energy provide ideal conditions for high productivity. The fiddlers' daylight feeding behavior may be

SALT MARSH COMMUNITIES

related to the fact that, at least in the north, some of the microflora migrate to the surface only during daytime low-tide periods.

The fiddlers' adaptations for existence in the marsh are chiefly related to their dietary and burrowing habits. Like all true crabs, they bear *chelae*, or pinching claws, on the first pair of legs. In the fiddlers, these chelae are spoonlike, and are used to scrape algae from the surface of the mud. The male, unable to use its oversize claw in this fashion—since it functions only in courtship and territorial display—must make do with just one spoon.

Watch the female crab as she uses her left and right spoons in rapid alternation, like a greedy child trying to stuff as much stolen candy as possible into her mouth before being caught. It's hard to see how a one-handed male fiddler can keep up with her. Perhaps, because he doesn't lay eggs, he can manage with much less food. At any rate, his 50% feeding ability is apparently no great disadvantage; there seem to be at least as many males as females to a colony.

Writing of *Uca minax* in the 1901 book *The Sea-Beach at Ebb-tide*, Augusta Foote Arnold describes a procedure that is more or less common to all three fiddler species mentioned here:

The crab makes its burrow by scraping up the mud or sand and forming it into pellets, which it carries under the three anterior walking-feet on the under side, using the legs on the side moving forward, and the fourth on the other side, to climb out of the hole. After peering cautiously about, the crab emerges, and carries its load four or five feet away before dropping it; then again looks about before quickly running back; and, finally, turning its stalked eyes, looks in all directions and suddenly disappears, soon to return with another load.

Each of the three species has its preferred habitat. But since two of them overlap you need to know how to distinguish them. *U. minax*, the **brackish-water fiddler**, barely qualifies for inclusion in a seashore book, for its home is a fresh or slightly brackish marsh at the landward border of the estuary. The **mud fiddler**, *U. pugnax*, and the **sand fiddler**, *U. pugilator*, inhabit

142. Male sand fiddlers *(Uca pugilator)* on Ocracoke Island living up to their combative name.

the tidal flats and marshlands. Look for the former in marshes and mud flats, the latter in sandier areas. The writer once captured a number of fiddlers on the flats beside the Ocean Highway at Cape May; upon examination they proved to represent a ratio of about two mud fiddlers to one sand fiddler—reflecting the approximate proportions of mud to sand in the substrate. On other, sandier flats the reverse situation was discovered. Where the two species are intermixed in this way, there is no apparent incompatibility.

U. minax can be identified by its fresh or near-fresh habitat. If you aren't sure of that, note the arched-over entrance to its burrow—a front porch from which the crab can survey its immediate surroundings, and possibly an adaptation for protection from the sun and from predators. Its burrow, too, is above the high-tide mark. The plant life can also be a good indicator of the low-salinity habitat of this crab.

Using an entrenching spade, you can—with care—excavate fiddlers with slight chance of harming them. With a bit of practice you can catch them on the sur-

SALT MARSH COMMUNITIES

face; but collecting a quantity for comparison will be quicker with digging. Though the burrows may extend 2 ft. (o.6 m) into the mud, at feeding time (low tide) the crabs tend to retreat only a short distance below the surface when disturbed. Turning over a single spadeful of mud will often unearth the occupant.

The fiddler crabs, which thrive on the renewable resource of the salt-marsh detritus and algae, are a rich source of food for predators. A relative, the marsh crab *(Sesarma reticulatum),* only slightly larger than the sand and mud fiddlers, digs burrows in the same marshes (see below). It is principally an herbivore, but it preys on the fiddlers at times. Among other predators on these crabs are the diamondback terrapin, raccoon, and mink. Various shorebirds and waders, including the clapper rail, yellow-crowned night heron, ruddy turnstone, whimbrel, willet, great egret, great blue heron, snowy egret, and little blue heron, take a heavy toll of the fiddler numbers. Feeding upon fiddlers at high tide are the Atlantic sharpnose shark, oyster toadfish (or oyster toad), pigfish, and bighead searobin.

MARSH CRABS. *Sesarma reticulatum,* of the family Grapsidae, is commonly called the mud crab, but is not to be confused with the black-fingered mud crabs *(Panopeus* spp.) or the white-fingered mud crab *(Rhithropanopeus harrisii),* which are members of the family Xanthidae. An alternative name, the **purple marsh crab,** should perhaps be used to avoid confusion. Crabs of the genus *Sesarma* are sometimes called square-backed crabs. The white-fingered mud crab and black-fingered mud crabs are characteristic of estuarine mud flats rather than marshland.

About the size of a fiddler, *S. reticulatum* is distributed spottily along the entire Middle Atlantic coast and is seen much less often than the fiddlers. The purple marsh crab digs burrows with several openings in the muddy part of the marsh, often amongst fiddler burrows. It tends to feed mainly at midtide, hiding in the mud at both low and high tides. It is one of the few animals that feed directly on *Spartina.* It prefers the older, outer leaves of the plant.

A close cousin of *S. reticulatum,* the **wharf crab** *(S.*

143. The purple marsh crab *(Sesarma reticulatum)*, measuring about 1 in. (25 mm), is at times predatory in its habits.

cinereum), is slightly smaller (growing to 1 in., or 25 mm). It lives in water of salinities ranging from that of the sea to fresh, and it is found on wharf pilings and under debris on muddy shores. In the marsh proper it occupies the upper zone, where it escapes the rising water by climbing to the tops of the *Spartina* plants as insects do. Sometimes it moves on land beyond the high-tide mark. It is found in this region from Maryland south.

ARACHNIDS AND INSECTS

SPIDERS AND ALLIES. The commonest arachnids in the marsh are spiders; a few members of the other two orders of this class, mites and pseudoscorpions, are also found here. Tiny red, globular mites may occur in large numbers in the creeks of brackish marshes, swimming about under the surface and feeding on minute animal life or plant material. Some pseudoscorpions, slightly larger than mites, are found in the beach-wrack above the normal high-tide mark. A surprising number of spiders occur in the marsh proper, at its higher levels. Web-builders usually spin above the reach of most tides. Spiders that forage in the intertidal zone during periods of emergence retreat as the water rises, climbing the

144. This black and yellow argiope spider *(Argiope aurantia)* has constructed her web in a bed of dwarf glasswort.

grass stems like the insects. Some small pirate wolf spiders *(Pirata* spp.), however, can run on the water surface.

A number of wolf spiders *(Lycosa* spp.) occur in salt marshes, along with some of the lesser known genera, *Eperia* and *Tetragnatha;* among these are species that can withstand submersion for long periods—up to 12 hours. During the day lycosids remain hidden near the high-tide line under debris or in burrows. At night, their reflective eyes can be located with a light.

The familiar orb-weaving spiders of the genus *Argiope* may be much in evidence on the upper edge of the marsh and in the scrub-shrub zone, where they feed on insects caught in their webs. But they are not identified with the marsh habitat, being characteristic of upland environments.

AQUATIC INSECTS. For many a visitor to the salt marsh, insects constitute an annoyance or a hazard rather than a natural resource. But in addition to the mosquitos and the biting flies that seem to delight in tormenting humans, there is an unexpected range of terrestrial arthropods occupying this habitat. There are few truly marine species; a genus of water striders, *Halobetes,* has oceanic forms; and a springtail, *Anurida maritima,* may occur in great numbers on the surfaces of tidepools and at tide line in the northern part of this range of coast. Only 1/8 in. (3 mm) long, these wingless insects would be unnoticeable if they did not form blue-gray patches on the water. **Water boatmen** (Corixidae) are aquatic bugs common in fresh water; they also dwell in brackish pools above the normal high-tide line, where they feed on algae. **Shore bugs** (Saldidae) are semiaquatic, on sea beaches, marshes, and tidal flats.

Other than the salt-marsh insects mentioned above, most either are terrestrial or are aquatic only in the larval stage. Of these the Diptera are the most important order represented. Three families of flies are notable—for their great numbers, their importance in the food web, and their relationship to humans, for whom they represent discomfort, disease, and expense. Most notorious are the Culicids.

CULICIDAE. This family includes the **salt-marsh mosquito** *(Aedes sollicitans),* which may become quite abundant in spring or in late summer and fall when rains and high tides wet the high marsh. Some mosquitos lay their eggs in rafts, but *A. sollicitans* deposits them singly on the surface of the mud, where they promptly begin development; they hatch only when a pool forms. The larvae rest just under the surface, breathing through a tube and feeding upon microscopic organisms. At this stage they are called wrigglers. The pupal stage (when they're called tumblers) is short lived and active, and within a very few days the hatchlings have become adults. Those mosquitos that go through the larval period in low marsh pools accessible

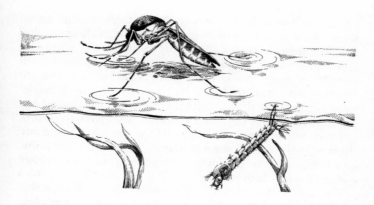

145. Salt-marsh mosquito *(Aedes sollicitans).*

to killifish, silversides, or the mosquitofish, *Gambusia affinis* (from New Jersey south), are preyed upon heavily by these fish. A mosquito population in a pool where *Gambusia* occurs is quite likely to be wiped out. Black ducks—particularly the ducklings—and other dabblers also feed upon the larvae. Enough generally survive, however, to feed upon humans and other warm-blooded creatures, to be eaten by dragonflies and swallows, and to produce another generation.

Because female Culicids must feed upon blood as a source of protein before laying eggs (the males being nectar eaters), the salt-marsh mosquito has always been a pest to humans. Mosquito-control measures over the years have altered more salt marsh habitat than has any other activity. The most obvious of the changes is construction of the drainage ditches that crisscross many thousands of acres of our eastern marshes. Impoundment also has been a technique used, although less frequently. In the effort to control mosquitos, much wildlife habitat has been destroyed or drastically altered. *Spartina* marsh has been converted to scrub-shrub wetland or *Phragmites* stands; the succession from low marsh to high marsh has been accelerated. Pesticides sprayed for mosquito control have killed other species.

Some ecologically sound mosquito-and-fly-control management methods are described in *Life and Death*

Animals of the Salt Marsh

of the Salt Marsh. Visitors to the eastern coastal marshes today see physical evidence of one of these in the swallow-nesting boxes placed in many of the national, state, and other public seashore areas. Nonpersistent pesticides have been tried with varying degrees of effectiveness and of harm to the ecosystem. Because mosquitos don't fly far afield, they can be avoided by putting a distance between you and the marsh—as boaters discover when they reach open water after wending their way through a coastal marsh. The marsh explorer can minimize the problem by visiting it on days when a strong wind blows.

CERATOPOGONIDAE. The **sand flies** (also called punkies, biting midges, or no-seeums) bite vigorously despite their size—less than 0.12 in. (3 mm). Unfortunately, they are most active during those hours that are most comfortable for people to be at the seashore during summer—early morning and evening. Sand flies lay their eggs in moist vegetation or in pools of the marsh. They are believed to be related to recent outbreaks of equine encephalitis in humans, on the New Jersey and Massachusetts coasts. Certainly, with their abundance and ferocity offsetting their small size, the no-seeums have a substantial role in both the environment of humans and the marsh food web. Our best defense against their tormenting attacks is probably use of an effective insect repellent rather than further tampering with the marsh community.

TABANIDAE. The third family of Diptera to be discussed is that of the **greenhead** and **deer flies**, which are not confined to the marsh environment. These are by no means "no-seeums"; most are in the range of 2/5 to 1 in. (10 to 25 mm) in body length. But their assault can be swift, silent, and merciless, and it is not always discouraged by liberal applications of repellent. They can make your dash from the bathhouse to the beach an ordeal. As with mosquitos, it is the female tabanid that seeks warm blood, without which she cannot produce viable eggs. The males feed upon plant nectar and juices. Greenhead eggs are laid upon vegetation; on hatching, the larvae drop into the mud or water. Adult tabanids, unlike mosquitos, range widely and may pur-

SALT MARSH COMMUNITIES

146. Greenhead fly (*Tabanus* sp.).

sue human targets far from the marsh.

OTHER INSECTS. Of particular interest, because they spend their entire life cycles in the salt marsh, are *Orchelium fidicinium*, a grasshopper, and *Prokelesia marginata*, a planthopper. The former eats the leaves of *Spartina alterniflora;* the latter sucks the juices of both *Spartina* species. In late summer the high marsh may be alive with hordes of field crickets (*Gryllus* spp.). Their chirping chorus increases in tempo and pitch with rising temperatures.

Marsh insects, mostly herbivorous, and spiders, which are all predatory, are a food source for a wide range of bird species, including swallows, ducklings, the red-winged blackbird, marsh wren, willet, clapper rail, common snipe, tricolored heron, and seaside sparrow. Small fish, which come into the marsh with the flood tide and are often trapped in depressions when the tide ebbs, feed on insects, too.

Salt Marsh Reptiles

Surprisingly few reptiles occupy the salt and brackish marshes of the Middle Atlantic coast. Most notable are the northern diamondback terrapin *(Malaclemys t. terrapin),* whose range coincides exactly with that of this book—and which is the only reptile limited to coastal habitats; the snapping turtle *(Chelydra serpentina),* which lives in many inland habitats as well as in salt and

147. Diamondback terrapin *(Malaclemys terrapin)*.

brackish marshes along the Atlantic coast; and the eastern cottonmouth *(Agkistrodon piscivorus),* found from
Cape Henry south. The spotted turtle *(Clemmys guttata)* is sometimes found in brackish water but is primarily a fresh water species and requires no discussion
here. Lizards, which are characteristic of some other
coastal habitats, are not dwellers of the marsh.

TURTLES

The **diamondback terrapin,** though it hardly rivals
the box turtle in popular esteem, is certainly one of the
favorites among aquatic turtles. Unfortunately, the high
regard in which it has been held is due, in large part,
to its desirability for the dinner table. It is not a large
reptile; males are about 4.8 in. (12 cm) long, and females
measure 8 in. (20 cm). Early in the century, when a
dollar was a lot of money and diamondback terrapin
soup was at the top of the gourmet's list, these turtles
commanded a price of $7 per inch and more on the
market. It is no wonder that they became scarce. They
are given a degree of protection today, but poaching
goes on.

The diamondback is not a scavenger, and perhaps its
status as a gastronomic delicacy is due partly to its fastidious diet of fresh snails, crabs, and other mollusks and
crustaceans; worms; and occasionally green plants. It
does not favor polluted water. Although it tends to inhabit marshes with muddy bottoms, it lays its eggs in

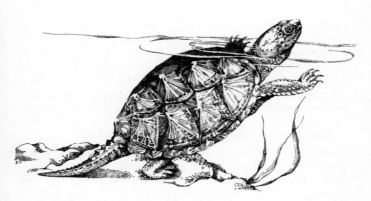

148. Snapping turtle *(Chelydra serpentina)*.

sand. In May or June the female comes out to seek a spot above the tides, digs a hole with her hind feet, and deposits from 5 to 12 eggs, about 1 2/5 in. (3.6 cm) long. Provided that skunks, raccoons, or mink do not excavate and eat them, the eggs hatch in about 90 days into young turtles with carapaces slightly more than 1 in. (2.5 cm) long.

Nobody loves a **snapping turtle**, it seems. This unhandsome, pugnacious, and rather smelly reptile is much more widely distributed than its cousin, the diamondback terrapin. But on the coast it occupies the same general habitat as the smaller and gentler turtle. It is less discriminating in its diet, which consists largely of animal matter—living or dead—of many origins, along with occasional large quantities of plant material. On this fare it grows to 1 1/2 ft. (0.46 m) in length and 70 lbs. (32 kg) in weight, though most individuals are much smaller and a few are considerably larger. Whether it's big or small, don't try to handle this creature as you might the docile diamondback. Anything but a very young snapper can give you a painful or severely injurious bite. The only safe way to pick it up is to hoist it by the tail, holding it well out to the side to prevent its reaching you with its powerful jaws. The lightning-fast speed with which it strikes out makes it about as easy to dodge as a rattlesnake.

Snapping turtles are considered palatable, if not an

epicure's delight. This writer has enjoyed a fine stew made from a large, fresh-killed snapper that was removed from a farm pond because of its depredations on the waterfowl. *C. serpentina* is indeed very destructive of ducklings and other water birds; but where there is a good population of skunks, the snapper's own depredations are kept in check by that animal's raids upon its nests.

Snapping turtles mate from midspring to midautumn. The female digs a hole in the ground somewhere near water, lays 24 to 30 spherical eggs—only 4/5 in. (2 cm) in diameter—which she covers with about 5 in. (13 cm) of soil. They hatch in 90 days (or, if laid in fall, the following spring); the young bear a yolk sac as long as their upper shell. Most discoveries of snapping turtle nests are made after a skunk, raccoon, mink, or fox has done its work and left an excavated hole with empty eggshells scattered about.

Snapping turtles are not sunbathers, so don't expect to see one napping on a log. They are often spotted as they lie just under the surface of the water with the tip of the snout protruding, and are frequently encountered as they lumber overland from one body of water to another.

SNAKES

The most notorious though probably not the most commonly seen snake of the salt marsh is the **cottonmouth**, or **water moccasin** (*Agkistrodon piscivorus*). Despite the insistence of many people who have "seen it with their own eyes" in the Middle Atlantic states, there is no record of its occurrence farther north than the very southern shores of Chesapeake Bay in Virginia. As far as venomous snakes are concerned, the seashore explorer north of the bay can feel safe. The cottonmouth is quite common in the vicinity of Knotts Island, on the Virginia–North Carolina border, and visitors to Back Bay and Mackay Island national wildlife refuges should be alert for it. It is often seen in this area sunning itself at the edge of the marsh or on water-control structures and other convenient resting places.

Take heed of the cottonmouth's readiness to strike,

149. Cottonmouth *(Agkistrodon piscivorus)*.

for this snake's venom is dangerous. As its Latin specific name indicates, it is a feeder upon fish; but it also eats frogs, snakes, lizards, small turtles, rice rats, and young muskrats. Full-grown cottonmouths probably have few enemies other than man, but younger ones are taken by the glossy ibis and great egret, and may fall prey to the snapping turtle.

The range of the **black rat snake** *(Elaphe o. obsoleta)* extends throughout the Middle Atlantic coast almost to Cape Cod, and it gives way to another subspecies of *Elaphe,* the **yellow rat snake** *(E. o. quadrivittata),* at Cape Hatteras. It is one of the most familiar of snakes, because of its size and visibility. (The black rat snake is active by daylight.) But it is often incorrectly called a black racer—a name properly applied to the slender, fast-moving *Coluber constrictor.*

A good climber and swimmer, and fast on the ground as snakes go (which is much slower than popular belief has it), the black rat snake is at home in the salt marsh. Its diet in the marsh is largely a matter of conjecture. This constrictor is known to feed primarily on birds and mammals; in the marsh it probably preys on small birds, deer mice, and rice rats. Young rat snakes eat cold-blooded vertebrates.

Rat snakes vibrate their tails rapidly when alarmed, and when this is done in contact with dry leaves or hard objects it may produce a buzz like that of a rattlesnake.

Animals of the Salt Marsh

But there is little to fear from this reptile, though it has been known to exceed 100 in. (2.54 m) in length, and though it sometimes stands its ground when threatened, rearing up and lunging at the intruder.

Black rat snakes are killed by great horned owls, red-tailed hawks, and, on rare occasions when it swims across open water, by the normally piscivorous osprey. Some are surely taken as well by snapping turtles, glossy ibises, and herons.

The water snakes (*Natrix* spp.) are a large group of widely distributed, primarily freshwater forms; a few species venture into brackish marshes. They feed primarily upon cold-blooded vertebrates, including fish, frogs, and salamanders (the latter two groups not occurring in saline environments). They are themselves prey for the usual roster of snake enemies. Except in the north of the range, where any water snake you see will be the **northern water snake** *(Natrix s. sipedon),* you will need a reptile guide for identification of snakes of this genus. A note of caution: from Cape Henry south, be sure of correct identity before picking up a snake from the water or shoreline. Some *N. sipedon* subspecies bear a close resemblance to the cottonmouth. To be on the safe side, avoid any heavy-bodied, rough-scaled snake in or near the water. Water snakes require fresh water to drink, and are seldom encountered in the coastal marshes.

Birds of the Salt Marsh

Many of the wading and shore birds seen in the estuarine system are associated with the salt marsh. In the case of perching birds, most species on the coast spend some time in the marsh, though few nest there. Many species that nest in the transition zone from marsh to upland, or in nearby upland habitats, move into the marsh to feed upon insects or seeds. The ubiquitous **red-winged blackbird** often nests in tall shrubs along the upper edge of the marsh. From spring to fall, one cannot visit the salt marsh without encountering this noisy, scrappy bird. It scolds human intruders as well as birds and mammals, especially near its nest. It is often seen

150. *Left:* sharp-tailed sparrow *(Ammodramus caudacutus); right:* seaside sparrow *(A. maritimus).*

chasing crows with persistent dive-bombing tactics. In the marsh redwings feed upon grasshoppers and other insects, spiders, snails, and small crustaceans, as well as upon grass seeds.

Other perching birds (Passeriformes) that are less conspicuous but that are often seen and heard in the salt marsh are several species of sparrows, the marsh wren, catbird, common yellowthroat, barn and tree swallows, eastern meadowlark, and yellow-rumped warbler. Three species among these (seaside sparrow, sharp-tailed sparrow, and marsh wren) nest in the marsh proper.

SONGBIRDS

The Atlantic and Gulf coastal marshes are the year-round and only home of the rather drab-looking seaside sparrow *(Ammodramus maritimus);* in this it is unique among our native birds. In winter it shares the salt marsh with the closely related sharp-tailed sparrow *(A. caudacutus),* similar in appearance but with a yellow face that gives it a bit more distinction. As with their general appearance, telling these two species apart by their songs in not easy, either, for they are closely similar. But the sharptail is a dweller of the high marsh, most likely to be seen in the saltmeadow cordgrass zone, while the seaside sparrow lives in the saltmarsh cordgrass habitat.

Animals of the Salt Marsh

Seaside Sparrow. This songbird breeds from Cape Cod to Texas (except for the southern part of Florida), and its winter range is virtually identical. Some of the birds in the northern sector of the range move down the coast when winter comes.

The seaside sparrow builds its nest in the relatively low-growing *Spartina alterniflora*, behind the tall grasses of this species that border the tidal creeks and drainage ditches. This is the habitat in which it feeds; its diet is chiefly animal life, especially in summer when it forages on the muddy ground amongst the cordgrass. There it finds small crustaceans—particularly young crabs, but also amphipods. It consumes many insects at this time of year, too; among these are leafhoppers, bugs, and flies and fly larvae. In fall, when the marsh grasses produce seed, the seaside sparrow behaves more like a typical sparrow, and cordgrass seeds become the major item in its diet, along with lesser quantities of saltbush (*Atriplex* spp.) and smartweed (*Polygonum* spp.) seeds. The animal component of its diet in spring is supplemented by *Atriplex* and bristlegrass (*Setaria* spp.) seeds where they are available.

Sharp-tailed Sparrow. The sharptail depends heavily on the seeds of *S. patens*, and favors amphipods over the young crabs that are the seaside sparrow's main animal food. Beach-hoppers are common at the base of the marsh grasses in the sharptail's habitat. The dead plants that form a dense groundcover in the salt meadow not only conceal a large population of the little crustaceans but also provide protection for the secretive sharptail as it forages. It has been described as being more like a mouse than a bird in its behavior. It runs through the grasses with head held low, and flies as little as possible.

The sharptail nests in small groups, often close to the ground in the soft grasses, but in higher marsh areas safely above normal high-tide limits. It breeds along the coast south to Cape Hatteras (and on the Canadian prairies) and shares the seaside sparrow's winter range, except for Cape Cod.

Marsh Wren. Formerly known as the long-billed marsh wren, *Cistothorus palustris* is a dweller of cattail

151. Marsh wren *(Cistothorus palustris).*

marshes and brackish marshes—an inland as well as a coastal bird. It has a clearly defined habitat in the salt marshes: it lives and nests in the tall *S. alterniflora* that borders tidal creeks and mosquito ditches, well above the reach of the tide. In summer it feeds almost exclusively on insects picked off the stems and leaves of the *Spartina* plants. When the tide rises, insects from the bases of the plants crawl up to keep above the water, and this tends to concentrate the wren's food supply. *C. palustris* would not deign to descend to ground level, in any event, as though having an aversion to dirtying its feet. It leaves that part of the habitat to the seaside sparrow. As H. W. Kale, in his paper "Ecology and Biogenetics of the Long-billed Marsh Wren," put it, "I have never collected a marsh wren with muddy feet or a seaside sparrow with clean feet."

The marsh wren breeds and winters locally on the coast from Rhode Island, and in winter some are seen on Cape Cod as well. Wintering wrens are commonest in the southern part of this range. The courtship and mating activities of this bird have a touch of both comedy and mystery, and are worth a few words here. At the appropriate time, the male wren stakes out a piece of the marsh as his territory and within it constructs many dummy nests. This is during a period of fast growth for *Spartina,* and the first nests are made partly of last year's dead leaves; these tend to break up as the plants grow. Later nests may last for a long time. In quality they range from something comparable in human terms to a child's ramshackle hut made from scrap to something that might be considered an unfinished summer cottage. But it is of little consequence to the female, who selects her own location within his territory and proceeds to build her own nest—a neat affair about the size of a softball, with a side entrance and an inside doorstep. She lines her little home with feathers, shredded grass, and mammal hairs; plugs the entrance with a door of shredded leaves; and lays 5 to 9 tiny eggs, which hatch in about 13 days.

The inconspicuousness of this nest is by no means a guarantee of safety from discovery by predators. The wrens have their share of enemies. The rice rat *(Oryzomys palustris)*, actually a large species of mouse related to deer mice, normally raises its young in grass nests. It climbs *Spartina* stems when overtaken by the rising tidewaters, and where its range coincides with that of the wren (from New Jersey south) this can result in an encounter between the rodent and the bird with its nestlings. The rice rat may eat the young and then take over the well-built nest to rear its own family.

As for the male's dummy nests, which may number a dozen or two, the marsh wrens may use them at times for temporary resting places. Beyond that, their function in the community is their use either as homes or as resting places for other animals. The herbivorous marsh crab, which digs burrows for itself, may climb the cordgrass stems when the water rises and use these nests as hiding places. Rice rats are known to make use of the dummies as well as nests they've raided; and vespid wasps sometimes build their paper nests in the wren's dummy nests.

The high marsh also is visited by a number of primarily upland-dwelling passerines. The song and savannah sparrows, one a bird of brushy edges and the other of meadows, are often seen here. The **song sparrow** *(Melospiza melodia)* nests in tall shrubs in the marsh-upland transition zone. It preys on a variety of insects, particularly when it is raising young; but its chief food

SALT MARSH COMMUNITIES

is seeds. *Setaria* and *Panicum* are among the seaside grasses that it is known to use. This species is the sparrow most likely to be seen in the marsh in winter. The **savannah sparrow** *(Passerculus sandwichensis)* ordinarily prefers upland meadows, but the *S. patens* high-marsh habitat is similar, and it nests on the edge of the marsh. The nest is in a hollow formed under the vegetation, for the savannah sparrow is a strictly ground-dwelling bird. It is perhaps most easily discovered by its manner of flight, which is undulating and zigzag and usually ends with a sudden drop into the grass.

Among the most commonly seen and perhaps the most numerous of perching birds of the salt marsh are the swallows, two species of which are particularly associated with this environment. Both are most welcome in the marsh from the human point of view, for they feed entirely on flying insects and are credited with destroying large numbers of greenhead flies and mosquitos. It is for this reason that nesting boxes are distributed about the marshes in many publicly owned seashore areas. The **tree swallow** *(Tachycineta bicolor)* adapts readily to these boxes, which are a satisfactory substitute for tree cavities. A familiar sight in late summer and early fall is the flocks of tree swallows circling and swooping about, weighting down shrub or *Phragmites* stands or telephone lines with their numbers. **Barn swallows** *(Hirundo rustica)* do not form such immense flocks prior to migrating south. The tree swallows winter from North Carolina south to Central America; the barn swallow's winter home is from Mexico to Brazil.

GULLS AND TERNS

One thinks of gulls and terns as creatures of the air —and so they are. They are not generally identified with the marsh habitat, yet one sees them there, sometimes in great numbers. One species in particular, the laughing gull, may be conspicuously present, often feeding in the midst of shorebirds and waders. Of course, the ubiquitous herring gull never surprises one with its presence anywhere. But it seems to belong to the ocean beach and the inshore waters, as well as the more open estuarine waters, and is less frequently found in the marsh.

Laughing Gull. *Larus atricilla* is familiar enough to beach-goers, but perhaps more than anything else it is a bird of the salt marsh. In that habitat this is often the most conspicuous animal species. These often numerous gulls are very active, flying back and forth most of the time, and noisy even when feeding and resting. Like many gulls, they are scavengers; but as predators in the marsh they eat small fish taken from the pools and creeks. Not being diving birds, they must get their prey at the surface. The laughing gull has been known to perch upon the head of a brown pelican after it comes to the surface with a pouchful of fish and to help itself to the larger bird's catch. Its depredations on the common tern and other terns are more rapacious, for it steals their eggs and occasionally kills and eats young terns in the nest.

The laughing gull sometimes nests in the marsh; but because it is a ground nester it must pick high spots beyond the reach of the tides. It often uses dune grasslands, mixed grass-shrub areas, and sand bars, and may share a small nesting island with herons, red-winged blackbirds, terns, and black skimmers. The nests range from crude to well made, and a variety of materials are used, including grasses, seaweeds, sedges, and debris.

RAILS AND SHOREBIRDS

Salt and brackish marshlands, because of the abundance of invertebrate life that occurs in the deposits, the water-filled depressions, the tidal creeks and muddy banks, and the vegetation, attract a greater variety of birds associated with the seashore than any other habitat. The marshlands are particularly attractive to the waders and probers and gleaners of the order Charadriiformes, which includes the shorebirds, gulls and terns, and skimmers. Most of the species in these groups are found in other habitats as well, but the wildlife watcher will find the marsh the most profitable in terms of both numbers and variety.

Clapper Rail. This big rail almost matches the seaside sparrow in its strict identification with coastal salt mar-

152. Clapper rail *(Rallus longirostris)*.

shes. Its range differs from the sparrow's in that it includes southern Florida, where instead of salt marshes
there are mangrove swamps. In the East the clapper
rail *(Rallus longirostris)* occurs from Cape Cod south.
But because of its secretive habits, it is seen by relatively few people. It is more often heard, calling "cha-
cha-cha"—beginning loudly and tapering off in volume,
tone, and frequency. Watch for it along the marsh
edges, where there are plentiful supplies of its food—
fiddler crabs, scuds, and other crustaceans, as well as
clams, snails, small fish, worms, and insects. Most of the
time the clapper rail is out of sight in the cordgrass,
where its laterally compressed body slips easily between the plant stems as it forages. This hen-sized bird
occupies the more saline marshes, building its well
camouflaged nest on the higher ground at the edge of
the marsh, where it is safe from all but extreme tides or
storms. If disaster strikes its first brood of the season, it
may raise another. Despite its secretiveness, it has enemies, among them the northern harrier—though that
predator is smaller than the clapper rail and in fact is
itself attacked by the rail when it flies low over the
marsh in search of prey. Against the red-tailed hawk,
however, such efforts by the rail would be useless, and
some rails are taken by these big buteos, which spy

Animals of the Salt Marsh

153. Northern harrier *(Circus cyaneus)*, formerly the marsh hawk.

them from high above and drop on them in the spectacular nose dive for which the species is famed.

Most certainly human beings have been this much hunted bird's greatest enemy. Audubon described the "uproar" from thousands of clapper rails when he visited the salt marsh a century and a half ago. No such experience can be hoped for in our time. Audubon himself played a small role in the rails' destruction; he once boasted of having collected 72 dozen rail eggs in one day.

Willet. Most of the shorebirds of the marsh are visitors during spring and fall migration. An exception is the willet *(Catoptrophorus semipalmatus)*, which both breeds and winters on the Middle Atlantic coast, although the population shifts north and south with the seasons. It summers throughout the range, and winters from New Jersey south. Northward migration begins in early spring (March) and reaches Cape Cod in May. Birds that nest on the cape begin to move south about the beginning of October.

Since the willet is one of the larger shorebirds, quite common on the marshes as well as mud flats, beaches, and coastal wet meadows, and has a bold pattern when in flight that makes identification unmistakable, it is sure to get on every birder's seashore species list. Owing to heavy hunting, in the early part of this century this member of the sandpiper family (Scolopacidae) was feared doomed to extirpation from our eastern marshes. Thanks to protective measures and the decrease in sport hunting of shorebirds, it appears now to be thriving over most of its range. In the East it is seldom seen away from the coast.

In the salt marsh the willet tends to feed along the banks of creeks, in mosquito ditches, and pools—areas less typical of the marsh than of the mud flats on which it is more commonly seen. In addition to the fish fry, small mollusks, and crustaceans it concentrates on when on the flats, it feeds on marsh insects and on some parts of the marsh grasses.

The willet rests near the marshes and flats in dry or damp, brushy or grassy spots. I have more than once been thoroughly convinced by the frenzied outcry that greeted my arrival in the high marsh or the scrub-shrub zone at its upper border that willets were nesting in the site. Yet despite careful searching, during which the birds continued their noisy dive-bombing passes at me, I have failed to locate nests. Apparently the mere appearance of humans is at times enough to incite a storm of protest. Man has certainly been the chief enemy of these birds in times past, and perhaps their hostility persists.

Yellowlegs. The greater and the lesser yellowlegs are closely related and so similar in appearance as to give some observers trouble in distinguishing them. They are quite different in their habits. The **greater yellowlegs** (*Tringa melanoleuca*) can logically be considered a wading bird, and it is so characterized in Peterson and Peterson's *The Ecology of Intertidal Flats of North Carolina*. The **lesser yellowlegs** (*T. flavipes*) behaves more like the shorebird it is, and it is often seen in company with smaller cousins such as dunlins, over which it towers on its long legs. Physical differences besides size help to distinguish the greater from the lesser yellowlegs. The bill of the greater is larger, stouter, and slightly upturned. The voice is the surest clue. The greater gives a loud, ringing "whew-whew-whew" when taking

Animals of the Salt Marsh

flight and often when passing overhead. The lesser's call is a softer, one- or two-syllabled "yew" or "yu-yu." The greater typically feeds by wading in water, sometimes up to its belly, catching small fish and crustaceans. It has been seen to take fish as large as the mummichog, which would seem more than a mouthful for this slender bird. The lesser also sometimes wades up to its belly (but for it that level would be shallower water) to get animal food from the surface, including small fry. It spends much time running about on the mud or flattened grass of the salt meadow, picking up grasshoppers and other insects, snails, small crustaceans, and worms.

Both yellowlegs nest in the far north. The greater yellowlegs winters from Cape Cod south; the lesser, from New Jersey south.

LONG-LEGGED WADERS

In the salt marshes of the Middle Atlantic coast, the long-legged waders include one member of the ibis family (Threskiornithidae) and several species of the heron family (Ardeidae), which includes birds of twelve genera that are variously called herons, night herons, egrets, and bitterns. These wading birds are actually representative of all water and wetland habitats of the seashore except the outer beaches and deep estuarine waters. They can and do utilize the marsh habitat whether the tide is low or high, and it is there that they can be seen in the greatest numbers and variety. Although they all are predaceous, their diets vary enough that they often feed in mixed groups without evident conflict.

Glossy Ibis. The status of *Plegadis falcinellus* as a North American bird has changed considerably since— more than a half-century ago—Arthur Cleveland Bent referred to its occurrence as very rare in a very limited breeding range. Then primarily an Old World bird, with a limited population in Florida, it has expanded its range northward and increased its numbers dramatically. It is common in the Brigantine marshes (New Jersey) and in Chincoteague National Wildlife Refuge (Virginia), for example, and now nests as far north as

SALT MARSH COMMUNITIES

154. Great egret *(Casmerodius albus)*.

Rhode Island. It generally breeds in the same colonies with egrets and herons (except the great blue heron), building its nest above the ground in shrubs and small trees. But glossy ibises have been seen to show intolerance for nests of herons in close proximity and may dismantle all those within 10 ft., driving off the other birds regardless of size. Since the glossy ibis is commonly seen foraging in the marsh in close company with great and snowy egrets, it is probably not in sharp competition with them for food. Its diet is almost entirely animal: in the marsh it feeds upon grasshoppers, crustaceans, snails, and fish. Despite its impressive instrument, it does not seem to probe deeply for burrowing animals. In some habitats, however, it feeds extensively on snakes, and for capture of such prey its bill is undoubtedly an effective tool.

With its distinctive coloring—rich, dark chestnut with metallic purple, bronze, and green iridescence (actually refractive colors) on the upper parts, depending upon the light—and its long, decurved bill, the glossy ibis is not easily mistaken for other marsh birds.

Animals of the Salt Marsh

155. *Left:* snowy egret *(Egretta thula); right:* tricolored heron *(E. tricolor),* formerly the Louisiana heron *(Hydranassa tricolor).*

In flight its long neck and long bill are outstretched (unlike those of herons), and its legs are extended backwards. At a distance it appears quite black. Its wingbeats are faster than herons', and it often flies in flocks.

Great and Snowy Egrets. These are among the most easily recognized birds of the salt marsh. Even when not seen together, the snowy egret *(Egretta thula)* and the great egret *(Casmerodius albus)* are fairly easily distinguished. In addition to the considerable difference in size, there are details and behavioral distinctions that help in identification. The great egret has a yellow bill; the snowy has yellow feet. And their stances when feeding are different. The snowy egret has a habit of dashing to and fro and shuffling its feet in the shallow water to stir up animal life. (Its "golden slippers" are said to attract fish.) The more stately, stalking gait of the great egret, with neck extended and poised for a strike, is in high contrast to the more erratic behavior of the snowy. Both egrets feed upon small fishes and crustaceans. The snowy is particularly fond of shrimp. It is known to consume large numbers of grasshoppers, and probably helps to control the populations of *Orchelium fidicinium*, a grasshopper that spends its entire life cycle in the cordgrass marsh. At times the snowy egret is seen to rush through the shallows with wings spread, in pursuit of small fry.

The great egret hunts more deliberately than the snowy, but its prey comes from the same groups. It is certainly capable of taking and swallowing larger fish, and it is more inclined to catch its fish by waiting. Though less active generally, it is also shyer and generally takes flight more quickly when approached by humans. Both these birds breed throughout the Middle Atlantic range and are commonly seen in winter from Cape May south.

Great Blue Heron. *Ardea herodias* is the largest wading bird of the region. Like the egrets, it is seen in all of the estuarine habitats. In the salt marsh it feeds upon

156. Great blue heron *(Ardea herodias)*, Chincoteague National Wildlife Refuge.

Animals of the Salt Marsh   353

157. Black-crowned night heron *(Nycticorax nycticorax)*, Chincoteague National Wildlife Refuge.

the same array of insect, crustacean, and fish prey, but it is more likely to hunt by standing patiently at the edge of a tidal creek or pond, content to spear the occasional fish that swims by. Even when hunting grasshoppers in the marsh grass, it may stand still, waiting for the insects to come within reach of its bill rather than searching for them. Sometimes, like the great egret, it will stalk with stately gait, neck tensed for a sudden downward thrust. Surprisingly large fish are captured in the formidable bill and gulped down the long neck.

Black-crowned Night Heron. *Nycticorax nycticorax,* somewhat taller and much stockier than the snowy egret, is also frequently seen in the salt marshes. De-

SALT MARSH COMMUNITIES

spite its name, it is often active in the day, and particularly in early evening and at dawn. Its food is largely fish, and it feeds upon small crustaceans, annelid worms (including *Nereis*), and insects. Its gull-like flight is unlike that of other members of the heron family. Breeding colonies occur locally along the entire Atlantic coast, and it can be seen in winter as far north as Cape Cod.

Cattle Egret. *Bubulcus ibis,* a recent immigrant to America from the Old World, must be given attention here because of its striking success story. Not even mentioned in Bent's classic *Life Histories* of North American birds—for the cattle egret arrived from Africa about 1952—it has worked its way north from Florida and is now the commonest wading bird in Delaware and one of the four most common in New Jersey. It has even strayed as far as Nova Scotia. Its nesting range extends to Cape Cod and a little beyond but is spotty on the Glaciated Coast.

A mostly white bird, the cattle egret is a little smaller than the snowy egret but stockier of build. It lacks the latter's black bill and golden slippers, and in breeding season it is washed with buff. It is more likely to be seen in upland fields and on impoundment dikes, where it feeds on insects. How competitive it is with the native herons and egrets may be in question, but it's a good bet that this bird, given to association with cattle in its upland habitats, feeds primarily on grasshoppers and other insects in the marsh.

Green-backed Heron. Formerly known as the green heron, *Butorides striatus* is, relatively speaking, the easiest of the heron family to approach. Like the great blue, it sometimes nests in its own colonies rather than in mixed heronries with other members of the heron family and with the glossy ibis. Unlike its relatives, it is known to plunge from a bank or a water-control device to capture a fish—though the writer has not observed this behavior. Besides small fish, the green-backed heron eats grasshoppers, crabs, and a variety of other crustaceans.

All of the heron tribe described above breed from Cape Hatteras to Cape Cod. Also found along this coast, but not seen so often in the salt marsh, are the yellow-crowned night heron, American bittern, and little blue heron. Collectively, the birds of this family and the glossy ibis (which often accompanies them) are perhaps responsible for the greater share of predation on marsh invertebrates and cold-blooded vertebrates.

WATERFOWL

Ducks, geese, and swans are much in evidence in the coastal marshes, particularly during migration periods, and, especially from New Jersey south, during the winter. A few species nest along this coast, although most normally fly to more northerly breeding grounds.

American Black Duck. None of the waterfowl species is as closely associated with the eastern coastal marshes as the American black duck *(Anas rubripes)*. It is the only one to breed in the salt marshes throughout the region covered by this book. (The **wood duck**—*Aix sponsa*—breeds along this coast, too, but it is not a marsh bird.) The black duck is said to be declining, in part owing to genetic competition with the mallard, with which it freely hybridizes, producing fertile offspring. It is still the duck most commonly seen with broods of young in the marshes and impoundments of wildlife refuges, such as Brigantine. The abundance of mud and marsh snails is surely one of the amenities of this environment, for the black duck feeds heavily on these gastropods. Among the other animal foods it takes in the marsh are bivalves, crustaceans, and a few fishes. It also eats a great deal of vegetable matter, including *Scirpus,* eelgrass, pondweeds, *Chenopodium,* cordgrass, and widgeongrass.

The black duck is notable for the skill with which it hides its nest, which may be in sites ranging from a recess among the roots of a tree to an abandoned crow's nest high in its branches. Because the drake abandons his mate as soon as the eggs have been laid, and the female is thus solely responsible for incubation and the care of the young, this obscurity is a crucial factor in survival. For a detailed and vivid account of the hatching of a black-duck egg, read that of Charles S. Allen in

SALT MARSH COMMUNITIES

Bent's *Life Histories of North American Wildfowl, Part One,* 1923 (now included in Dover reprints).

Other than by humans, black ducks in the marsh are preyed upon by red foxes, and northern harriers, and probably by short-eared owls and raccoons. Snapping turtles prey upon swimming ducks, and they take a heavy toll of ducklings in some locales.

Snow Goose. During the cold months of the year—the nonswimming season—nothing draws visitors to the Middle Atlantic seashore in greater numbers than do the wintering waterfowl, and particularly the snow goose *(Chen caerulescens)*. Spectacular in flight, noisily active when in the marshes and on the water, this bird keeps the wildlife watchers busy with binoculars and cameras. The contingent that winters on the Middle Atlantic coast is the major part of the population that breeds on the northernmost land masses—Ellsmere Island and the northwest coast of Greenland. (The former specific name of the snow goose was *hyperborea:* "far north.") In late summer the geese begin their long southward migration, most of them congregating in the Gulf of St. Lawrence before continuing on to New Jersey and beyond. They begin to arrive at Brigantine National Wildlife Refuge in early November; many stay here and in other areas of the South Jersey coast until the early-spring migration. From here on south, human visitors to the seashore brave the winter marsh winds to observe these geese. Large groups of the birds intermittently launch themselves with much noise from the ground or water to fly, apparently with purpose, in a direction that often suggests a resumption of the southward migration. But the constant comings and goings are motivated by other factors—one of which is their nervousness at the approach of human vistors. Few people actually see the geese in passage, for they fly at great heights when migrating.

The major wintering grounds of the snow goose on the Atlantic Coast are the marshlands of southern New Jersey, Delaware Bay (in and near Bombay Hook National Wildlife Refuge), Chincoteague Bay, Back Bay, Currituck Sound, and Pamlico Sound (particularly Pea

Island National Wildlife Refuge). Only a handful move on to South Carolina. A few strays are seen north of New Jersey in winter.

The remoteness of the snow goose's breeding grounds makes determination of its summer feeding habits difficult; but in the Atlantic coastal marshes its food is primarily the rootstocks and shoots of sedges (common threesquare, *Scirpus americanus;* Olney threesquare, *S. olneyi;* and saltmarsh bulrush, *S. robustus*), of *Spartina alterniflora,* and, to a lesser degree, of saltgrass *(Distichlis spicata).* Snow geese can be seen grazing in farm fields near Back Bay and Currituck Sound.

Early writers referred to the "immense numbers," "vast hordes," and "astounding abundance" of snow geese in America; but in this century their numbers must be stated in more moderate terms. It is estimated that the Atlantic coast population in recent years has fluctuated between 50,000 and 100,000 individuals, with the largest wintering congregations in North Carolina. The enormous toll inflicted on this species by hunters during the 19th century surely accounts for most of this decrease.

With its mostly pure-white plumage and black primary feathers, the snow goose is easily identified in the field. It is one of the most watchable of birds in the air. Many observers have written of the appearance and flight behavior of the snow goose. In 1898 *(The Wild Fowl of North America)* Dr. Daniel G. Elliott described it in these words:

[The snow geese] fly very high in a long, extended curved line, not nearly so angular as the V-shaped ranks of the Canada and other geese. With their snowy forms moving steadily along in the calm air, the outstretched wings tipped with black, glowing in the sun's rays with the faint blush of the rose, they present a most beautiful sight. Usually they fly silently with hardly a perceptible movement of the pinions, high above. . . . Occasionally, however, a solitary note like a softened "honk" is borne from out the sky to the ear of the watcher beneath. Should they perceive a place that attracts them, they begin to lower, at first gradually, sailing along on motionless wings until near the desired spot, and then descend rapidly

158. Canada geese *(Branta canadensis)*, stopping over at Blackwater National Wildlife Refuge, Maryland, on southward migration.

in zigzag lines until the ground or water is almost reached, when with a few quick flaps they gently alight.

For this writer no words can describe the clean, sheer beauty of a wedge of a few dozen snow geese flying overhead against a clear blue sky.

Canada Goose. *Branta canadensis* is the best known of America's wildfowl, with the possible exception of the mallard. Both the goose and the duck occur widely across North America, from Mexico to the Arctic. There are numerous subspecies or races of the Canada goose, which look alike but vary widely in size (males of the smallest race averaging 3.4 lb., or 1.5 kg, and those of the largest averaging 12.5 lb., or 5.7 kg—with an extreme of 18 lb., or 8.2 kg, which is nearly the upper limit of weight of the tundra swan).

Canada geese, unlike snow geese, migrate at low altitude, and are often heard on March nights passing over the eastern seaboard cities, their honking a true harbinger of spring (for these geese follow close behind the line of melting snow and ice as it moves northward).

The Canada geese that winter on the Middle Atlantic coast belong to two populations. One congregates in the

Animals of the Salt Marsh

bays and estuaries of the coast from Nags Head, just north of Cape Hatteras, all the way to Nova Scotia and southeastern Newfoundland; this group uses as its breeding ground Newfoundland, Labrador, and the eastern extension of Quebec on the north shore of the Gulf of St. Lawrence. The migration corridor of this population extends along the coast of the Labrador Peninsula, across the Gulf of St. Lawrence, through eastern New Brunswick, and down the U.S. coast to Pea Island National Wildlife Refuge, on the Outer Banks. Most winter from the Delmarva Peninsula north.

Another, larger population migrates south from Hudson's and James bays through New York and Pennsylvania to reach the coast at Maryland. This population, which formerly accounted for the huge concentrations of Canada geese on and near Mattamuskeet National Wildlife Refuge, North Carolina, now winters primarily on the Delmarva Peninsula, with small contingents moving on to Back Bay and North Carolina. This northward shift of winter concentrations has been attributed at least in part to the favorable conditions resulting from management of more northerly refuges such as Blackwater on the Delmarva Peninsula.

The Canada goose is not absent from these areas in summer, either. Although the normal southern limit of the breeding grounds for the eastern Canada goose is the Gulf of St. Lawrence, some nest in the various wildlife refuges and other suitable areas along the U.S. Atlantic coast. The summer visitor can always count on seeing Canadas in Chincoteague National Wildlife Refuge, and a few nest in Back Bay and the Outer Banks, remote indeed from Labrador.

Describing the nesting ground of Canada geese is difficult, for they utilize a greater diversity of sites than any other waterfowl species, including black ducks and mallards. The nest may be a mere depression in bare ground with a sparse lining of debris; it may be a bulky mass of marsh-plant material, or a bed of pine needles or pieces of pine bark. Some Canadas nest on muskrat houses or mats of sedge; some utilize abandoned heron and osprey nests; and (in other regions) some nest on rocky cliffs.

Besides the feed grains produced especially for them on national wildlife refuges and state preserves, and the waste corn and other grains gleaned from harvested farm fields, Canada geese feed on grasses, clovers, spikerush *(Eleocharis)*, *Spartina*, *Ulva lactuca*, and, to a small extent, glassworts, eelgrass, *Scirpus*, and saltgrass.

Man is by far the chief predator on this big, powerful, wary, and combative bird. At the same time, humans have probably devoted more land, time, money, and effort to conservation of this bird than to any other game species.

Salt Marsh Eatouts

An overabundance of marsh grazers such as snow geese, which remove the roots and rhizomes of marsh grasses and sedges including *Spartina*, *Distichlis*, and *Scirpus* to a depth of 20 to 25 cm, strips an area bare. The result is an *eatout*. Despite the fact that geese may consume only a small part of the plants they uproot, they may create an eatout hundreds of acres in extent. Much of the uneaten material is made available for transport by tidal waters to other parts of the estuary, where it is fed upon by herbivores and detritivores.

An eatout that remains flooded becomes populated by amphipods, corixids, diptera larvae, and other invertebrates that provide food for wading birds, shorebirds, waterfowl, and others. Unfortunately, this food resource is generally not available in winter, when it is most needed. The larger eatouts affect the availability of nesting cover and diminish the marsh's value for muskrats and other wildlife. Repeated denudation by geese, which sometimes happens in protected areas where the game species seek sanctuary, severely affects the ability of the cordgrass marsh to recover.

Salt Marsh Mammals

Because in general mammals require no special physiological adaptations to cope with the saline or

Animals of the Salt Marsh   361

brackish environment, needing only access to a source of fresh water, they do not exhibit behavioral or structural adaptations specifically to the salt marsh. In fact, there is no such thing as a salt marsh mammal. Muskrats, rice rats, and the alien nutria are all marsh-dwelling rodents; but the salt marsh animals are not different from the ones that live in fresh marshes except in respect to food and nesting habits. With the exception of the aforementioned species and a few smaller rodents that build their nests in the marsh vegetation above the reach of the tides, mammals are merely visitors to the salt marsh from upland habitats.

With skins that are virtually waterproof, mammals have no need for osmoregulatory apparatus. Salt marsh mammals are likely to ingest a large amount of salt with their food, of course. They cannot produce urine with a higher concentration of salt in it than there is in their blood, as do some animals, but they dispose of excess salt with their excreta. The smaller salt marsh mammals, which cannot easily travel to upland sources of fresh water, must fill their need for it in other ways. On windless mornings, for example, there may be enough dew on the grasses to supply their water requirement for the day. Some mammals have adaptations that conserve water, so do not have to drink as much as they otherwise would. Salt marsh mice have been found to produce a concentrated urine that removes a minimal amount of their systems' fresh water. They have this adaptation in common with some of the desert rodents.

RODENTS

As in most terrestrial habitats, the gnawing mammals are the most abundant and diverse terrestrial vertebrates in the marshland—if one excludes visiting birds. The members of the rodent order are primarily herbivorous, and the highly productive marsh grasses provide ample food for a good-sized population. Rodents constitute a major component in the second trophic level, functioning to convert green plants into flesh for consumption by the third trophic level: the first-order carnivores.

Muskrat. *Ondatra zibethica,* while it lives and

thrives in freshwater habitats and is said to attain its greatest size in cattail marshes, is common in coastal salt and brackish marshes as well. Here it may spend its entire life within the intertidal zone, building a lodge of plant materials with an underwater entrance and a dry chamber above the level of the high tide. In this chamber it raises its young; but it may build smaller feeding lodges at various locations in the nearby marsh, where it can eat in relative safety. It may alternatively make its nest in a burrow dug into the bank of a tidal creek. Where salt marshes have been diked for wildlife management purposes, this burrowing habit can become a vexing problem. To minimize the undermining of dikes by muskrat burrows, managers often allow controlled trapping by permit.

The muskrat's role in the salt marsh community is essentially that of primary consumer. This largely vegetarian animal eats stems, rootstocks, and leaves of a variety of marsh plants, including *Spartina, Scirpus, Phragmites* (unfortunately, only to a limited extent), and *Juncus*. It also eats some animal food, notably mollusks, insects, and crustaceans.

The prolific and abundant muskrat must constitute a large share of the diet of some of the marshland predators. Its host of enemies includes mink, river otters, great horned owls, marsh hawks (which take young muskrats), red-tailed hawks, red foxes, and snapping turtles. The mink is its most dreaded foe, for this agile carnivore, which weighs about the same as the muskrat (female minks, slightly less) is slender in build and easily invades the rodent's burrows and lodges. The muskrat is no match for the mink, which can wipe out an entire family of the rodents with ease. In its defense, however, it must be said that the mink kills not wantonly but only to feed itself and young.

In the face of such heavy predation, muskrats hold their own by breeding three to five times per year, sometimes beginning with a litter of four or five in early spring and perhaps finishing with a batch of nine offspring in fall (by which time most or all of the earlier young may have become part of a higher trophic level in the marsh food pyramid).

Besides providing much food for marshland predators the muskrat has other effects, good or bad according to the point of view, on the salt-marsh community. For example, the trails it keeps open in vegetation-choked waterways and in the marsh proper are possibly of aid to waterfowl and other birds and to four-footed predators.

Nutria. Also known as the **coypu,** *Myocaster coypus* is much larger than the muskrat; it weighs up to 20 lb. (9 kg), as against the 2 lb. (0.9 kg) of *Ondatra.* While it somewhat resembles the muskrat, the nutria belongs to a different family. It is related to *Aplodontia rufa,* a muskrat-sized rodent of the far West, where it is called, inappropriately, mountain beaver. But the nutria is from South America, where it lives in the Andean region from Peru southward. Imported to the United States a half-century ago for rearing as a furbearer, it accidentally spread to the wild and is now common in the Gulf states and on the southeastern Atlantic coast. It has adapted so well to the salt marshes that it has partially or wholly replaced the muskrat in some areas. It does not build a lodge like the muskrat, but burrows into banks—a habit that has not endeared it to refuge managers who have impoundment dikes to maintain. It is understandably now considered a pest in some situations.

The nutria's food is primarily the foliage, roots, seeds, and other parts of aquatic plants. It is said to be strictly herbivorous, unlike the muskrat. It is diurnal in its habits. The female may begin breeding at the age of six months, and may have three or four litters a year of about five young each time. The young are said to be able to swim within a few hours of birth, but a special adaptation enables them to remain with the mother even when nursing on the move. Her four or five pairs of teats are located high on her flanks, almost on her back, and thus the young can suckle while she is swimming. The females pay a price for their fertility: though they may breed during the very season in which they are born, they live only about two years—rarely more than three. Males live to the ripe old age of six or more.

The coypu (the preferred name, since nutria is really

SALT MARSH COMMUNITIES

the name of the animal's fur, widely but incorrectly applied to the animal itself) has not proven as yet to be a major pest; it is far from being the national scourge that another introduced rodent, the Norway rat, has become. But its impact on the coastal marsh ecosystem will almost surely increase as it becomes more abundant and more widely distributed.

White-footed Mouse. *Peromyscus*, the genus of white-footed mice, deer mice, and their close relatives, occupies a wide variety of habitats, from mountaintops to the edge of the sea. The species most commonly found on the Middle Atlantic coast is the abundant *P. leucopus* (*leucopus* means white foot). Monomoy Island once had its own subspecies of this mouse, a common situation when populations are isolated long enough—as they often are on islands—to become genetically different from the rest of the species. Intermittent connection of Monomoy with the mainland, however, reversed the process; the island subspecies was reabsorbed by the mainland population and its distinguishing characteristics were wiped out. (Martha's Vineyard also claims its own subspecies, but this is a woodland form not seen in the marshes.) One other species of *Peromyscus* is known on this coast: the **cotton mouse** (*P. gossypinus*) ranges from Cape Henry south.

Peromyscus is one of the most versatile of animals when it comes to diet. In winter its food is almost entirely plant material—the seeds, fruits, and roots of trees, shrubs, and herbaceous plants, much of which has been stored from summer harvest. Its choice in any season reflects in part the availability of various types of food in its habitat. The cotton mouse feeds upon sea oats, which is an abundant grass in its range. When insects are easy to come by, they constitute a large part of the white-footed mouse's diet. In the salt marsh, grasshoppers are a big item. This rodent also eats snails, groundbeetles, caterpillars, centipedes, and occasionally even small warm-blooded vertebrates.

The nocturnal habits of the white-footed mouse give it no protection from its chief enemy—owls. The short-eared owl is associated with the marsh habitat, and great horned owls also hunt there. Other marshland

159. Rice rat *(Oryzomys palustris).*

predators that make inroads on the white-footed mouse populations are red foxes, raccoons, northern harriers, black rat snakes, and probably the great blue heron, which is known to devour meadow voles. The last three predatory species, however, are diurnal in their habits.

Rice Rat. *Oryzomys palustris* belongs to that vast family of rodents (Cricetidae) that includes the white-footed mouse, wood rat, muskrat, harvest mouse, cotton rat, meadow vole ("field mouse"), pine mouse, and red-backed mouse. *Oryzomys* is larger than the closely related white-footed mouse but, at 5 in. (13 cm) in length, much smaller than the muskrat. It occupies a variety of habitats, but prefers wetlands. On the coast it is common in salt marshes from Cape May County, New Jersey, south. In the saltmeadow cordgrass zone it finds both the food and the cover it needs. It makes runways in the matted grasses, and may build a nest in a low shrub there or in the scrub-shrub wetland.

Other than the muskrat, which has webbed hind feet and a laterally compressed tail, the rice rat is the most amphibious of native rodents living in or frequenting the salt marsh. It is a strong swimmer, on the surface or underwater, and it uses this ability to escape predators. The presence of this mammal can be detected by floating mats of cut vegetation on the tidal creeks. The ani-

366   SALT MARSH COMMUNITIES

mal itself, being nocturnal in its habits, is not often seen, and it is much more abundant in the marsh than might be guessed. When the rice rat makes its nest, it chooses a spot above the high-water mark and constructs it under debris; or it weaves a nest into emergent plant stems out of reach of the tide.

Oryzomys feeds on plants (mostly the seeds) including cordgrass. It has the usual array of predatory foes suffered by rodents, including the northern harrier, mink, red fox, cottonmouth, and probably the snapping turtle. The rice rat is not as prolific as the other rodents described here but is probably more adept at avoiding capture. The cottonmouth, which is as aquatic as the rice rat and is known to reach 6 ft. (1.8 m) in length, shares its range from Cape Henry south; and in places where this snake is abundant, as in the Currituck marshes, it must exercise considerable control over the population of the rodent.

CARNIVORES

Some of the predatory mammals cited as hunters in the marshes are merely visitors from upland habitats that invade this habitat because of its herbivorous prey species. But two members of the order Carnivora play a major role in the ecology of the marsh. These are the mink and the raccoon, which are quite different in their habits and in the kind of impact they make on this environment.

The **mink** *(Mustela vison)* hunts, and sometimes dwells, in the salt marsh. This weasel preys on a variety of marshland vertebrates: fish, rodents (including small mice and muskrats), marsh birds, snakes, and young snapping turtles. It has few enemies other than humans, but young mink are taken by the red fox and the great horned owl.

An inveterate wanderer, the mink may not settle down even when it has a family. The mother does stay with her three to six young through the first summer, but she may move them from time to time, carrying them one by one by the scruff of the neck. She may take over a muskrat lodge—after feeding its occupants to

Animals of the Salt Marsh   367

160. Mink *(Mustela vison).*

her family—as a home in the marsh.

The **raccoon** *(Procyon lotor)* (discussed in Chapter Two under Animals of the Dune-and-Swale Zone) is the mammal whose presence in the salt marsh is most commonly detected. Although it is active chiefly at night, its easily recognized footprints are frequently found along the edges of tidal creeks, pools, and flats. Living in a wide range of upland habitats, it is an omnivore; but in the salt marsh it feeds almost exclusively on animal food. Its partiality for seafood is indulged here, as it forages for crustaceans, mollusks, and fish. It also preys upon rodents, including muskrats. The raccoon's depredations on marsh birds are the reason nesting boxes for

161. Raccoon *(Procyon lotor).*

swallows, wood ducks, and others must be made raccoon proof (note the inverted metal cones on the posts supporting wood duck boxes). Crickets, grasshoppers, and other large insects and insect larvae are not spurned by the raccoon, either.

Though the raccoon's home is a den or hollow tree in its upland habitats, at times it may remain in the marsh for a few days of uninterrupted feasting. It naps there in a nest it makes of *Spartina* stalks. The raccoon is so much at home in the water that rising tides create no problems for it.

CHAPTER FIVE

The Eelgrass Community

In subtidal shallows from South Carolina to the Arctic on the Atlantic coast, and from Baja California to the Arctic on the Pacific coast, as well as in many other parts of the world, a vitally important underwater community awaits exploration by the seashore naturalist. This community, the habitat of *Zostera marina*—misnamed eelgrass—and its close relatives, was largely neglected even by marine biologists until in the early 1930s a disastrous blight nearly wiped it out in many regions. The resulting decline in important animal species, notably the Atlantic brant (akin to the Canada goose) and the bay scallop, spurred research into this plant, so that today we know much of its biology and ecology. There is still much to be learned; but one thing is evident: a great array of plant and animal species are dependent in one way or another on *Zostera* and the habitat it creates.

Zostera marina is a member of a very small group of marine flowering plants called, collectively, *seagrasses*. The most widespread genus and, in the temperate zone, by far the most important, is *Zostera*.

Because it occupies a subtidal habitat, the eelgrass community is overlooked by many seashore visitors. It sometimes grows so densely as to impede the passage of motorboats; but it is easily accessible to the swimmer with snorkeling equipment. So equipped, the naturalist can observe a life community perhaps equalled in richness and diversity only by a healthy coral reef community. Virtually every phylum of the plant and animal

THE EELGRASS COMMUNITY

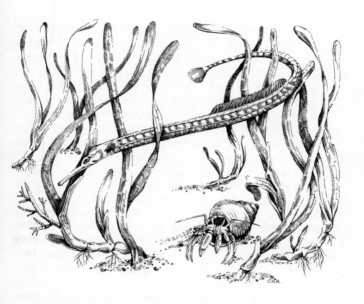

162. Profile of an eelgrass bed, showing *Zostera marina*, epiphytic algae, hermit-crab, and pipefish.

kingdoms is represented by residents of and visitors to the eelgrass habitat.

Seagrasses

The name applied, for convenience rather than to reflect taxonomic status, to this group of plants is a misnomer, for none of its members actually belongs to the grass family (Poaceae). Many of the species do have leaves that are slender and grasslike; but their relatives on land and in freshwater habitats are members of the pondweed family (Potamogetonaceae). (Eelgrass is sometimes placed in its own family, Zosteraceae.) There are also a dozen or so species of marine flowering plants in the obscure family Hydrocharitaceae, but we are concerned here with just two of the 38 species of the pondweed family that live in salt and brackish water.

Seagrasses are widespread, occurring in shallow waters of every coastal sea except the most polar. Only five species are found in temperate waters. **Turtlegrass** *(Thalassia testudinum)* grows in shallow bays, lagoons, and inlets from the Atlantic coast of Florida near Vero Beach around the Gulf coast to southern Texas. On the Middle Atlantic coast, only two species are common: Z. *marina* (**eelgrass**) and *Ruppia maritima* (**widgeongrass** or **ditchgrass**). *Ruppia* is found along the entire coast, even to Texas, well beyond the southern limit of eelgrass; but in this region most seagrass beds are dominated by *Zostera*. *Ruppia* is discussed later in this chapter under Plants Associated with *Zostera Marina*.

Except for their habitat, seagrasses have nothing in common with seaweeds. As marine macroalgae, seaweeds do not have roots and do not produce flowers. Seagrasses are *angiosperms*—plants having seeds enclosed by an ovary. They reproduce both vegetatively and sexually. They are the only true marine flowering plants, growing totally submerged (as do seaweeds) and producing their flowers and seeds underwater. The flowers are fertilized by waterborne pollen and the plants are anchored to the bottom by root systems. Seaweeds are attached to the substrate by holdfasts, but these structures do not function like roots in the plant's physiology.

Zostera marina is by far the most important of the seagrasses, including other eelgrasses of its genus. It is circumpolar in distribution in the Northern Hemisphere. It extends to the Bering Straits in the Pacific, and to southern Greenland, Iceland, and the North Cape in the Atlantic; it occurs in Arctic waters of the Barents Sea; and on the North American Atlantic Coast it is found from Labrador to South Carolina.

Zostera marina beds range in density from a few scattered plants or clumps of plants to extensive, homogeneous submerged meadows of eelgrass with up to 3,300 plants per square yard (4,000 per square meter). (This characteristic density of eelgrass beds is further discussed in this chapter under Growth and Reproduction.) Among marine angiosperms, *Zostera* is rivalled in density of growth only by *Thalassia testudinum,* turtle-

THE EELGRASS COMMUNITY

grass, which occurs in tropical and subtropical waters. The ranges of the two species do not overlap on the Atlantic coast.

Zostera grows on both sandy and muddy bottoms, mostly in the sublittoral zone (the upper intertidal waters). Some species are found in the lower intertidal zone, as high as the low-water mark of neap tides. *Z. marina,* however, doesn't tolerate much exposure, and occurs almost always below the low-tide mark. Rarely does *Zostera* border on salt marsh communities, which are generally found in the upper intertidal zone.

Zostera does not function as a beginning stage in a succession to a terrestrial system, as does salt marsh vegetation, though it does cause deposition of sediment that results in a raising of the bottom within the beds, and may increase deposition in the shoreward unvegetated zone by slowing water movement. Also, this buffering effect on currents and waves may inhibit erosion.

Among flowering plants, only the so-called seagrasses possess the necessary tolerances and adaptations for an underwater existence. In common with other seagrasses, *Zostera* is able to colonize shallow marine environments because it has the following faculties:

1. Tolerance for a salinity of up to at least 30 o/oo (this enables it to live in coastal shallows as well as estuaries, wherever water movement is not too great)
2. Ability to function in all life stages, including the generative cycle, when fully submerged
3. Ability to anchor itself on the bottom (by means of a root system)
4. Ability to compete with other plants—notably microalgae—in the suitable environment

In the marine and estuarine shallows, the seagrasses more than any other plants contribute to the stabilization of sandy and muddy bottoms. They also increase the amount of substrate for sessile organisms, particularly on bottoms that would otherwise be unsuitable habitat; in many areas, eelgrass is virtually the only available substrate for epiphytic organisms. They also provide shelter and nursery grounds for many invertebrates and fishes.

The seagrass bed's importance in the community is measured not by the biomass of the living plants, but by the vastly increased substrate, reflecting, in the case of *Zostera*, leaf area indexes as high as 20 square meters per 1 square meter of bottom; and by energy transfer through decomposition—the detritus cycle.

The Structure of Eelgrass Systems

The typical *Zostera* community is structured physically and biologically much like an upland forest dominated by a single tree species. It is perhaps best likened to the live-oak forest of the far southeastern United States with its drapery of Spanish moss, vanilla orchids, and other air plants scattered over the trunks and branches. In the eelgrass bed, the "forest canopy" consists of a single species, *Zostera marina*, with a heavy burden of algae growing on the surface of its leaves. Some eelgrass beds may contain other macrophytic species, but even these are often attached to the *Zostera* plants.

The algal epiphytes and the epifauna on the eelgrass leaves correspond to the lichens, air plants, mosses, and invertebrate animals that live on the surface and under the bark of forest trees. The forest understory is paralleled by the macroalgae attached to or entangled with the bases of the *Zostera* plants and to shells and other objects on the bottom. Comparable to the mosses of the forest floor are the diatoms and other microalgae growing on and in the upper layer of the deposits. The mobile epibenthos of the eelgrass community has obvious counterparts in the forest among the invertebrate and vertebrate grazers, browsers, and scavengers. The burrowing infauna, which in the eelgrass beds consists of invertebrates, in the forest includes insect larvae, earthworms, and other invertebrates, and such vertebrates as moles, shrews, and rodents. And ranging through the water column of the *Zostera* community are the free-swimming herbivores and carnivores, which have forest counterparts in the airborne birds and insects.

THE EELGRASS COMMUNITY

Epiphytes

The epiphytic component of the eelgrass community consists of diatoms and other algae, sessile animals, and, by some definitions of *epiphyte,* the grazing and foraging animals moving over the eelgrass plants. (Strictly speaking, *epiphyte* means a plant growing on another plant or object on which it depends for mechanical support; but *epiphytic* is often loosely used to describe any organism attached to or moving over the surface of a living plant.) Many kinds of algae grow attached to the *Zostera* blades, and the filaments of these algae trap diatoms and detritus that add to the food resource of the grazers. As many as 19,000 diatoms have been found living on a square inch of alga-coated *Zostera* leaf. Also living in the feltlike blanket are a micro- and meiofauna consisting of protozoans (ciliates, flagellates, foraminifers); free-living nematodes; rotifers (multicellular animals as small as protozoans—difficult to classify but sometimes put in the phylum Aschelminthes with the nematodes); and copepods and ostracods. The sessile macrofauna includes filter feeders and predators of several phyla: sponges such as *Haliclona loosanoffi,* cnidarians (stalked jellyfish, anemones, and hydroids), bryozoans such as *Membranipora,* annelids (tube-dwelling worms such as *Spirorbis*), arthropods (barnacles), and chordates (tunicates and sea squirts).

Most of the epiphytic plants and animals live on the eelgrass leaves. A different biota is attached to the stems and rhizomes. There are some sessile animals; there are tube-building amphipods *(Corophium* and *Erichthonius),* and there are polychaetes that build nests on the plants.

Grazers and Foragers

Moving over the surface of the *Zostera* leaves are both herbivores and secondary consumers. This group includes flatworms, nemerteans, gastropod mollusks, polychaete annelids, and crustaceans (tanaids, amphipods, and isopods). Of all these, one is most likely to discover the tiny snail *Diastoma varium* (sometimes classified as *Bittium varium)* or the equally small *Dias-toma alternatum (Bittium alternatum)*. The former is found from Maryland south, the latter from Virginia north.

Benthic Epifauna

Amongst the bases of the *Zostera* plants and on the muddy or sandy bottom are sedentary filter feeders, carnivores, and detritivores. This includes animals of the bottom that live on the surface of the deposits but are relatively immobile, attached bivalves, cnidarians such as the striped anemone, and mobile ostracods feeding on and in the upper layer of deposits but not ranging freely about the community. The bay scallop, while it is able to swim by a sort of jet propulsion, is essentially a member of the benthic epifauna, feeding while resting on the bottom. The oyster crab, a commensal in the bay scallop's mantle cavity, thus is part of the epifauna; when it lives in the tube of the parchment worm it is part of the infauna.

Mobile Epibenthos

The mobile epibenthos is distinguished from the rest of the benthic fauna by its ability to move freely over the bottom. It is dominated by gastropod mollusks and decapod crustaceans. The largest member of this fauna, however, is the horseshoe-crab, *Limulus*—not a permanent resident, admittedly, since it is present in great numbers only in late spring and summer. Most of the permanent residents of the mobile epibenthos, in fact, are small animals. In some eelgrass beds, at least, the long-clawed hermit-crab is the commonest species of the macrofauna. Among the true crabs are the blue crab, spider crab, and two species of black-fingered mud crabs. A few other arthropods, a number of mollusks, and several annelids appear prominently. The animal that is at once the most abundant and (with the exception of the horseshoe-crab) the best known of the

THE EELGRASS COMMUNITY

163. The horseshoe-crab *(Limulus polyphemus)*, ventral view.

larger epibenthic invertebrates is the blue crab *(Callinectes sapidus)*.

Infauna

There have been studies suggesting that the most densely populated portions of estuaries are muddy-sand bottoms in eelgrass beds. The silt component of such deposits is sufficient both to allow construction of permanent burrows and to provide ample detritus as a food resource for the deposit feeders. The infauna, however, is in some respects a relatively minor component of the *Zostera* system. Other than the hard-shelled clam *(M. mercenaria)* and some of the larger polychaetes, most of the animals in these deposits are very small, whether predators, detritivores, or filter feeders. The Cnidaria are represented by burrowing anemones, the Nematoda by a variety of worms, the Mollusca by the hard-shelled clam, the Annelida by diverse polychaetes, and the Arthropoda by sand shrimps. Most of the animals living in the deposits of the eelgrass beds are not limited to this environment, but are found in surrounding unvegetated sediments as well.

The Structure of Eelgrass Systems 377

Free-swimming Fauna

Living freely amongst and under the canopy of *Zostera* leaves are invertebrates and vertebrates ranging from the minute to the very large. Some of them behave much like epiphytic fauna, clinging to the *Zostera* leaves or resting alongside them; some are almost part of the benthos, lying half-covered by sand like the flatfishes.

Rather difficult to put into any of these spatial categories, the odd little amphipod *Caprella,* called skeleton shrimp, does not swim but moves freely about among the *Zostera* plants. Known for its habit of clinging inconspicuously to the eelgrass leaves in an attitude much like that of the praying mantis, *Caprella* moves when it wishes to new sites. Also, with mantislike voracity, it poises in waiting, ready to use its mantislike appendages to seize passing smaller crustaceans.

The northern pipefish *(Syngnathus fuscus)* has a somewhat similar way of life; it commonly rests on a *Zostera* blade in such a way as to seem a part of the plant. But the pipefish is a swimmer, and thus is much more mobile. This animal is discussed later in this chapter under Vertebrate Predators.

Many other crustaceans and fishes, not so near-sedentary or benthic in their habits, occupy the waters of the eelgrass community. Most of these free-swimming animals are predators. A variety of shrimps, amphipods, and ostracods are counted among them. The most prominent members of this fauna, however, are bony fishes of a great diversity of form and habits. The fish and the various invertebrate components of this habitat are characteristically more abundant and more diverse than those of adjacent waters. In fact, these neighboring communities owe much of their richness of fauna to their proximity to the *Zostera* community; for much of the nutrient and organic material derived from the eelgrass plants is carried into them by currents and tides.

The abundance and diversity of the vertebrates of

THE EELGRASS COMMUNITY

Table 9: Species Collected in the Greatest Numbers in
Lower Chesapeake Bay

Latin Name	Common Name	Number Collected
Leiostomus xanthurus	Spot	15,274
Syngnathus fuscus	Northern pipefish	3,308
Anchoa mitchilli	Bay anchovy	2,013
Bairdiella chrysoura	Silver perch	1,289
Menidia menidia	Atlantic silverside	475
*Syngnathus floridae**	Dusky pipefish	293
Apeltes quadracus	Fourspine stickleback	244
Hypsoblennius hentzi	Feather blenny	186
Fundulus heteroclitus	Mummichog	126
Orthopristis chrysoptera	Pigfish	123
Tautoga onitis	Tautog	99
Lagodon rhomboides	Pinfish	96
Paralichthys dentatus	Summer flounder	88

*The dusky pipefish chiefly occupies the deeper parts of the eelgrass beds, where collecting was not done; the northern pipefish occupies the shallower beds. Data for this table were obtained from "Structural components of Eelgrass Meadows in the Lower Chesapeake Bay—*Fishes,*" by Robert J. Orth and Kenneth L. Heck, Jr., in *Estuaries,* vol. 3, No. 4.

the eelgrass beds have been demonstrated by various investigators. One team sampled the fishes of the eelgrass beds of lower Chesapeake Bay by seining in three sites at depths of 3.2 to 5 ft. (1 to 1.5 m). They found 48 species of bony fishes present. Table 9 shows those collected in the greatest numbers. The team also seined in adjacent unvegetated shallows. (The table does not include the fishes captured in the nonvegetated areas.) The number of fish in the eelgrass beds was much higher, particularly during the daytime. It appeared that many fish left the *Zostera* beds at night for adjacent areas.

These researchers also collected fishes by trawling at night. Notable among those collected by this method were **sandbar sharks** *(Carcharhinus milberti),* in the stomachs of which they found large numbers of small, soft-shell blue crabs—reflecting the predominance of these crustaceans in the community, and indicating that the sharks' presence in the beds was not casual. The

The Structure of Eelgrass Systems

nighttime trawling turned up the following species of true (bony) fishes:

Strongylura marina	Atlantic needlefish
Sciaenops ocellata	Red drum
Cynoscion regalis	Weakfish
Pomatomus saltatrix	Bluefish
Brevoortia tyrannus	Atlantic menhaden
Micropogonius undulatus	Atlantic croaker
Mugil cephalus	Striped mullet

How the *Zostera* Community Functions

Eelgrass growing in favorable environments establishes a *gregarious* plant community—one in which individuals are closely spaced but not matted or densely clustered—and develops a dense root system. This enhances stabilization of the deposits and, by damping water movement, helps to protect the shore from erosion. *Zostera* does have difficulty in colonizing an area where wave action is strong or currents powerful. But if conditions normally are such that it can get a foothold on the bottom, the plant growth provides some buffering of the effect of storm waves. Observations made in areas where eelgrass beds existed before a wasting disease eliminated them often showed great changes in the bottom deposits and intertidal and subtidal beach contours in the years immediately ensuing. (See The Eelgrass Blight, below.)

The biomass of *Zostera* leaves, rhizomes, and roots may be equalled by that of the epiphytic plants, primarily diatoms and green algae, that utilize the leaf blades as a substrate for attachment, and by the epiphytic sponges, cnidarians, bryozoans, and other invertebrates that would find no satisfactory sites for attachment on an unvegetated sand or mud bottom. And for those organisms that can utilize either the surface of the deposits or the plants as a substrate, the eelgrass greatly increases the substrate area—by as much as 20 times what would exist if the bottom were unvegetated.

An obvious function of the *Zostera* community is the utilization of the plants as a food resource by a wide range of estuarine consumers. Among the invertebrates, few graze directly on the *Zostera* leaves; sea urchins are known to do so, but even they prefer to feed upon epiphytic algae and sessile animals such as bryozoans and barnacles. A few fishes feed sparingly on the *Zostera* leaves. The most important direct use of *Zostera* is by the Atlantic brant, other geese, and ducks, some of which feed on the plants only when they are exposed or nearly so by low tide. A far greater number of animal species feed on the epiphytic and benthic algae in the community, and on the organic detritus on the bottom.

A sometimes-overlooked energy pathway from *Zostera* to primary consumers is the wrack composed of eelgrass leaves cast up on beaches by the waves. Talitrid amphipods (*Orchestia* spp.), insect larvae, and adult insects often abound in these decaying windrows, which can be massive. Predators, from spiders and ghost crabs to songbirds and shorebirds, feed upon these scavengers.

Eelgrass beds are nurseries for a wide variety of organisms. Even among species that have no trophic relationship with *Zostera*, many are restricted to the eelgrass beds for completion of one or more early life stages. Worms, mollusks, and fishes attach eggs and egg capsules to the plants. Numerous invertebrate and vertebrate species survive the vulnerable juvenile stage by utilizing the shelter offered by the dense growth of eelgrass and algae. Among these are mollusks, shrimps, and fishes.

The eelgrass plants are also known to accumulate nutritive material from sea water; and by pumping nutrients, notably phosphorus, from the deposits, the eelgrass makes them available for organisms living in the water column and on the bottom. As for eelgrass photosynthesis and respiration, their net effect on the supply of oxygen in the community is not fully known. Respiration at night is assumed to be the same as during the day. Photosynthesis, of course, proceeds only when there is sunlight. One investigator measured oxygen in a *Zostera* bed during daytime at 260% of saturation; he was unable to detect any oxygen at night in the same bed. Studies in the Narrow River estuary and Ninigret Pond (a lagoon) in Rhode Island found net production of oxygen to be zero over a 24-hour period. All this may have a bearing on an observed shift made by bony fishes at night from the eelgrass beds to adjacent areas.

Within the eelgrass community, the major plant consumers of oxygen are not the macroflora (dominated by *Zostera*) but the microflora, mostly diatoms and bacteria. Plants that increase the supply of oxygen through photosynthesis during daylight hours consume it at night.

Night-day temperature rhythms appear to be less pronounced in eelgrass beds than in shallow waters lacking a dense benthic vegetation. This stabilizing effect is also a factor in seasonal temperature fluctuations, which tend to be greater in the unvegetated areas.

Many of the above-mentioned effects are related to the fact than an eelgrass bed, particularly one where the plants grow densely on the border, slows water movement caused by wind and sea currents by about 50%. This decreased movement increases the rate of deposition of suspended sediments and decreases the available supply of plankton, oxygen, and other waterborne requirements of organisms in the community.

In areas where tidal influence is minimal, an eelgrass bed may produce a pronounced difference in salinity between the water mass on the far side of the bed and that in the shallows between the bed and the shore, where more stagnant and brackish conditions exist because of decreased water movement and the runoff of fresh water from the land. Such a shallow, protected zone, on the other hand, may in summer attain a higher salinity than the zone on the far side of the *Zostera* bed, because of reduced runoff and increased evaporation.

General Biology of
Zostera Marina

Habitat

The habitat requirements for a healthy stand of *Zost-era* are not known fully, but following the eelgrass blight of the early 1930s much research has been devoted to just this; and much is going on to determine the causes of current problems such as the serious decline of the seagrasses in Chesapeake Bay. There is good reason to believe that *Zostera* does have certain requirements as to clarity of the water, freedom from pollution, and nature of the bottom sediments. Water that is too turbid, for example, will inhibit photosynthetic activity. Just which kinds of pollution have the most effect on eelgrass health is being studied. It is known that generally eelgrass grows best in sand or sandy-mud deposits. It does not easily colonize bottoms where wave action or tidal currents are strong, and because of this it is not likely to be found in barrier inlets where the currents are highest, or on unprotected shores. One study showed that *Z. marina* produced the highest standing crop where current velocity was about 0.625 knots/hr., indicating that moderate but not extreme water movement is favorable.

The depth range within which *Zostera* will grow is a function of light penetration and exposure. On the Middle Atlantic shore it seldom is found where falling tides leave it completely exposed; thus the lower intertidal zone of mud and sand flats is virtually devoid of macroflora, and there is seldom a conjunction of eelgrass and salt marsh systems. Where there is eelgrass growing above the level of the mean-low-water mark of spring tides, it is likely to consist of small and sparsely growing plants.

Habitat is also somewhat limited in terms of salinity range; but *Zostera* is a *euryhaline* species—widely tolerant in this respect—and occurs in coastal waters ranging from 5 o/oo to at least 30 o/oo salinity. It can be found both in the upper reaches of estuaries and in protected areas of the open coast such as Cape Cod Bay and the mouth of Delaware Bay. Its leaves are equipped with salt glands that remove sodium and chorine ions from the cell sap.

Freedom from pollution is another factor in habitat suitability for *Zostera*. A dense, thriving eelgrass community is said to be an indicator of good water conditions, and pollution has been the basis of some explanations of the near-disappearance of *Z. marina* from the Atlantic coast in the early 1930s. The bulk of research evidence, however, has not supported this explanation.

Temperature factors have been demonstrated to be a major determinant of *Zostera marina* distribution patterns. Apparently each race of the species has a narrow range of tolerance for temperature. The length of time the eelgrass is exposed to extremes within this range of tolerance is also a factor. For example, *Zostera* plants can survive high temperatures encountered on a summer day if cool nights give them respite. The species occurs on the Atlantic coast from South Carolina to Labrador; in northern waters the plants were found to be functioning in temperatures near 32° F (0° C), but in the sounds behind the Outer Banks the species would neither encounter nor be able to withstand such lows.

There are also ecologic biotypes of *Zostera* with different temperature tolerances. Plants growing in tide-pools and other shallow waters, and on sandier bottoms, tend to have shorter, narrower leaves, a low rhizome biomass, and flower stems; and these appear to have a greater tolerance for high temperatures. Plants growing in deep water and muddier deposits have longer and broader leaves and large rhizome biomass; these may lack a reproductive cycle and fail to develop flower stems. Such plants have less tolerance for high temperatures.

As further evidence of the correlation between water temperature requirements and leaf width, it should be noted that *Zostera* plants transplanted from shallow waters to deeper water develop broader leaves.

THE EELGRASS COMMUNITY

Growth and Reproduction

Zostera marina spreads vegetatively by rhizomes—horizontal perennial stems or "rootstocks"—from the under surface of which grow bundles of roots, and from the upper surface of which shoots are sent out. Under ordinary conditions the rhizomes are buried in the deposits. The stems are compressed and branching, and the leaves are very narrow and tapelike, 1/12 to 1/3 in. (2 to 8 mm) wide and 1 to 6 ft. (0.3 to 1.8 m) long. The bluntly round-tipped leaves are characterized by 3 to 11 principal nerves, are dark green, and are as flexible as ribbons, yielding readily to water movement or the passage of objects. A *Zostera* rhizome may send up several shoots, consisting either of a short stem, tubular 2-to-8-in. (5-to-20 cm) leaf sheaths, and leaves, or of a flowering spike. Of these shoots *(turions)*, the leaf shoots are much more abundant. The density of an eelgrass bed is stated in terms of turions per square meter of bottom.

A turion commonly has from four to six leaves. The growing leaves are buoyant, having air canals that are continuous from the roots to the leaves. When damaged and frayed, the leaves become waterlogged, sink, and die. As the rhizomes grow horizontally, they branch laterally and send up new shoots, while older parts of the plant decay and break off. The dead plant parts contribute to the detritus deposits in the bed or are carried by currents and deposited outside the beds, cast up by waves onto the shore, or carried to sea on tidal currents.

Under most conditions, it is likely that vegetative growth plays a more dominant role in eelgrass biology than does sexual reproduction. Vegetative growth can occur at lower temperatures, and consequently sexual reproductive growth lags behind vegetative growth in the growing season. There is evidence that in the same area reproductive shoots are produced earlier in shallow water than in deep water, suggesting that the role of sexual reproduction may be related to depth.

The branching reproductive turions, sometimes two

or three to a rhizome system, produce erect flower spikes bearing a number of *spathes* (sheathlike bracts). Enclosed in each spathe is a spadix 1 to 2 1/2 in. (2.5 to 6 cm) long, with about 20 anthers and ovaries alternately arranged. The anthers discharge glutinous, stringy pollen, and fertilization takes place underwater. (The stamens mature before the pistils; thus self-fertilization is avoided.)

Zostera flowering takes place along the Middle Atlantic coast in a northward progression, beginning in March and April in the Outer Banks and reaching Cape Cod in June or July. Seed dispersal takes place with the help of water currents, as the generative shoots break loose and float away. Germination in the south occurs at the time of falling temperatures in autumn, but in northern waters it may be delayed until spring or early summer.

Productivity

The most productive areas of the ocean are the upwelling regions of the continental shelves (the most famous of these, worldwide, being that off the coast of Peru); shallow, protected bays and sounds; salt marshes; coral reefs; and seagrass meadows. The production in eelgrass beds has been found to exceed that of the upwelling off Peru and that of coral reefs by close to 100%; and the densest eelgrass beds have few rivals even among cultivated crops.

Much of the production of the *Zostera* bed is the growth of epiphytic algae. In a particular bed, the algal flora is likely to be dominated by a very few species of diatoms and multicellular algae. In mass, a *Zostera* bed's algal flora may equal that of the leaves that serve as its substrate. (*Zostera* leaf sheaths and rhizomes are generally free of epiphytic algae.) Benthic micro- and macroalgae also account for a considerable part of the productivity of an eelgrass bed. It is the algae, more than the living *Zostera* plants, that account for most of the direct energy transfer to a higher trophic level. As has been noted, the chief path of energy transfer within the community from the *Zostera* plants themselves is by way of the detritus cycle. Visiting waterfowl are the major first-order consumers of *Zostera*.

Most epiphytic production appears to occur in seasonal cycles, with a period of low productivity in winter. It has been suggested that carbon and nitrogen from the water surrounding the roots (rather than that in the water column) find their way through the vascular plants (*Zostera*) to the diatoms on the leaf surfaces. There is also some evidence that phosphate and ammonia from the sediments are transferred to the water column through the *Zostera* plants, with the effect of increasing the productivity of all *primary producers* (plants) in the system and adjacent waters. Through such processes the nutrient pool of the sediments may be made available not only to the *Zostera* plants but to epiphytic flora and to some of the macroalgae.

The major factors controlling photosynthesis of *Zostera* plants are light and temperature; these conditions are understandably important in the global distribution of eelgrass and its distribution on the sublittoral slopes. Increasing depth means decreasing light, of course, and the plant's need for light for photosynthesis limits them to the upper few meters in most areas. In cases of exceptional light penetration, *Zostera* may grow to depths of about 50 ft. (15 m), which is also the approximate lower limit of brown algae, nonvascular plants that live in eelgrass beds.

Other limiting factors in productivity are the high nutrient demand of the plants and the dynamic cycling of trace metals and other compounds essential for growth. Through their root systems, seagrasses can absorb compounds from the sediments—an advantage denied to macroalgae anchored by holdfasts. Although the sediments are the major site of seagrasses' nutrient absorption, they are believed to have some ability to absorb nutrients from the water column through the surfaces of their leaves.

The Eelgrass Blight

The transatlantic catastrophe that struck *Zostera marina* in the 1930s was the greatest and most widespread of a number of puzzling setbacks to this important marine species. Because it affected both European and North American populations, it spurred extensive cooperative research programs aimed in part at getting information that will help prevent or deal with future outbreaks. Any comprehensive discussion of eelgrass or other seagrasses calls for an account of this ecological disaster.

CHRONOLOGY

A "wasting disease," as it came to be called, struck the eelgrass plants of the U.S. and Canadian Atlantic coast with catastrophic suddenness in 1931. Within a year the *Zostera marina* beds on the coasts of Great Britain, the Netherlands, France, and Portugal went into a similar decline; in 1933 it was reported to have reached Scandinavia.

Although the cause or causes of the mysterious blight were unknown—and they are still not fully understood—the symptoms, which appeared during the warm season, were the same everywhere. First, brownish-gray spots formed on both leaves and rhizomes. Spreading blackish-brown discoloration, destruction of tissues, loss of leaves, and the death of the plants ensued.

The violent decline took place over a very short period; in fact, by 1933 there were signs of beginning recovery in some localities. These resurgences during the 1930s were generally of a temporary nature. The first half of the 1940s was characterized by fluctuating growth of the beds. Over the last half of that decade there was noticeable improvement in many places, some of which had been devoid of eelgrass since 1932. The years 1951 to 1953 were a period of recovery—the greatest since the initial onslaught in the early 1930s. In many locales there was complete or nearly complete return of the eelgrass, though other places remained unvegetated. In the ensuing years the recovery trend proceeded with varying degrees of stability. Short-term and long-term fluctuations have occurred widely, and occasionally severe reversals have occurred. In Chesapeake Bay, for example, the 1970s saw a decline in *Zostera*, and by 1976 it had disappeared from most of the tidal river systems of the Maryland eastern shore. Currently, however, there is eelgrass in a few locations in the southern part of the Maryland eastern shore, as well as on both sides of the bay in Virginia. Along Maryland's western shore, including the Potomac estuary, rooted plants of any kind are scant, and no eelgrass is present.

North of Chesapeake Bay, the picture is brighter. Eelgrass has persisted to Labrador and Hudson's Bay, and no recent reversals such as that in Chesapeake Bay have been reported. In Long Island Sound and the lagoons behind Fire Island and other Long Island barrier beaches, *Zostera* seems to be doing particularly well. It is in this region, incidentally, that in 1966 the highest standing stocks of *Zostera* in temperate waters have been recorded. South of Chesapeake Bay, eelgrass beds occupy many suitable sites as far as Bogue Sound in North Carolina beyond the Outer Banks; and have been found in South Carolina waters.

CAUSES

Some scientists put the blame on a bacterial attack. Some have theorized that altered environmental conditions, such as changes in the solar and water-temperature regimes, were the cause. No single organism has as yet been proven to cause the disease and subsequent death of *Zostera*. But the greatest agreement to date has been on explanations attributing the decline and death of the plants to attacks by a fungus and a slime mold. Generally, in eelgrass plants with the characteristic symptoms of the blight, a mycelium of the fungus *Ophiobolus halimus*, along with a slime mold, *Labyrinthula macrocystis*, have been present.

Erik Rasmussen, in *Seagrass Ecosystems* (edited by McRoy and Helfferich), makes a strong case for water-temperature changes (warming trends) during the early 1930s as the primary cause of the mass destruction of *Zostera marina* on both sides of the Atlantic. (It should be kept in mind that populations of *Zostera* are adapted to the temperature regimes of their locale.) According to this theory, the higher temperatures affected the plants both directly, by destroying metabolism, and indirectly, by weakening them, so that the ever-present bacteria, slime molds, fungi, and other organisms could bring about complete degeneration.

EFFECTS

The most conspicuous result of the wasting disease (beyond the immediate effect: loss of the eelgrass itself) was the exposure of formerly vegetated bottom. For nothing comparable replaced the eelgrass plants. The loss of the vegetation was typically followed by a change in the nature of the deposits; without the binding action of the *Zostera* roots and rhizomes the finer materials were removed by water action, so that formerly muddy bottoms were succeeded by coarser deposits. On rocky coasts, formerly buried stones were exposed, and macroalgae such as *Fucus* were able to take hold. In such localities, the windrows of eelgrass leaves that had formed most of the beach-wrack were succeeded by the washed-up *thalluses* (plant bodies) of *Fucus*. New coarse materials such as shells and stones were actually transported by storm waves from deeper water to the upper slope of the beach, through the buoyant effect of *Fucus* plants on the materials to which they were attached by their holdfasts.

On nonglaciated shores, where stones were not available as a substrate for seaweeds, former *Zostera* beds were typically succeeded by broad, subtidal sandy shoals completely devoid of macroflora. In quieter waters with little current and minimal tidal action a few muddy bottoms persisted.

The detritus regime was drastically altered with the loss of the eelgrass because, along with *Spartina alterniflora* leaves from the salt marshes, *Zostera* had been the main source of organic material in estuaries and coastal waters. As indicated earlier in this chapter, eelgrass is a major factor in the composition of faunas not only where the beds exist but in adjacent waters. The blight's effect on many species was severe; on some, it was devastating. Most dramatically, the Atlantic brant, which when wintering and migrating on the Middle Atlantic coast had depended heavily on this plant, had to adapt to new food resources. This was a severe strain on the species; *Zostera* had constituted the great bulk

THE EELGRASS COMMUNITY

(upwards of 80%) of its diet. Not surprisingly, there was a great decline in the brant population—by 92%, in New Jersey—following the onslaught of the disease. Canada geese were also hit hard.

Fundamental changes also occurred in the fauna of the subtidal slope when the eelgrass beds were destroyed. The animal communities had been dominated by eelgrass epifauna, with a relatively poor infauna in the deposits, during the *Zostera* regime. After the destruction of the plant by the blight, the epifauna, where present, was characterized by organisms on stones and on macroalgae—chiefly *Fucus*. Where deposits had been muddy sand or mud, new sandier bottoms prevailed, with a less predominant epifauna and an infauna dominated by different species. The detritus feeders, in particular, found the new benthic habitat less favorable.

The most drastic decline of a resident species was the depletion or total disappearance of *Aequipecten irradians*, the bay scallop, an economically important species that, in its minute postveliger stage (reached after the second larval stage, when the mollusk has developed a shell), had depended on the eelgrass beds for survival. Scallops had been common in the Woods Hole, Massachusetts, area before 1931, on bottoms ranging from mud to hard sand and, most prominently, in dense beds of *Zostera*. They virtually disappeared from this area when the blight struck. In another example of the effect of the blight, a commercial scallop fishery on the eastern shore of Chesapeake Bay in Virginia was reduced to zero when the eelgrass disappeared.

In the period from 1935 through 1940, scientists from the Biological Laboratory at Cold Spring Harbor, New York, found only one scallop in Great South Bay at Fire Island State Park—an area formerly well populated with the bivalve and with *Zostera*. During those same years, no eelgrass whatsoever was found at the site.

There were occasional departures from this pattern. In the Niantic River (in Connecticut), for example, scallops for a time increased dramatically during the absence of *Zostera*—enough that a major local fishery was developed to exploit it in the mid-1930s. In a single season 60,000 bushels were harvested in the two-

164. Loosanoff's haliclona *(Haliclona loosanoffi)*.

square-mile scalloping ground. Yet there was little other plant growth to account for the resurgence of the scallop.

Many other organisms are affected in one way or another when *Zostera* declines. For example, *Haliclona loosanoffi*, a small encrusting sponge that is common on eelgrass, is at a big disadvantage in an area where suitable alternative substrates, such as stones or pilings, are limited. Unlike *Haliclona*, which can grow on eelgrass as well as on stones, blue mussels *(Mytilus edulis)* require a firm substrate. The populations of this mollusk have been known to increase dramatically when the bottom changed from muddy or sandy to stony following the demise of *Zostera*.

Some barnacles *(Balanus* spp.) also respond favorably to a new regime in which sandy bottoms are replaced by coarser materials, providing shells and stones for attachment. These crustaceans (and the mussel, *Mytilus,* as well) have a relatively high oxygen demand and are heavily dependent on plankton and suspended organic particles; thus they benefit from the increased water movement that follows the loss of *Zostera.* Where the sedentary bottom fauna had been dominated by burrowing deposit feeders, filter-feeding epifauna are likely to prevail in the absence of eelgrass.

Zostera had been more or less taken for granted before the blight. From the early 1930s on, there has been a worldwide effort on the part of scientists to learn more about its biology and ecology. If and when a similar widespread decline occurs, it will at the least be better monitored. One area of investigation that is receiving increased attention is the effects of pollution on eelgrass. The possible cause of the decline of *Zostera* in Chesapeake Bay in the 1970s is contamination of the bay's waters by agricultural chemicals, industrial wastes, and other toxicants. Among the worst offenders, according to studies of the response of *Zostera* to chemicals, is 2,4-D. Another possible cause is diminished clarity of the water, which has inhibited photosynthesis.

Plants Associated with *Zostera Marina*

Other Flowering Plants

The eelgrass system is unusual in the almost complete dominance of a single species. It is comparable in this respect to a cultivated cropland, such as a cornfield. Yet, as in the cornfield, with its weeds, fungi, and parasitic plants, the eelgrass community harbors many other plants, some of them playing important roles in the ecology of the system.

In most of the seagrass beds of the Middle Atlantic coast, *Zostera marina* is the only species of marine flowering plant present. South of the Virginia–North Carolina border, **shoalgrass** *(Halodule wrightii)*, which like *Zostera* is a pondweed, grows with it. Shoalgrass resembles the narrow-leaved forms of *Z. marina;* but examination of its leaf tips reveals that they are three-pointed, unlike those of eelgrass, which are rounded.

There are several other pondweeds associated with *Zostera* that do not qualify as seagrasses in the strictest sense of the word. **Widgeongrass** *(Ruppia maritima)* appears in salt and brackish waters all along the coast; and it does produce only submerged leaves. But its flowers are fertilized above the water. (After fertilization, the peduncle of *Ruppia* coils up and draws the fruit down below the surface.) It evidently has a high requirement for light. The presence of widgeongrass is said to indicate satisfactory turbidity conditions, as it will not grow in water lacking sufficient clarity to enhance photosynthesis.

Horned pondweed *(Zannichellia palustris)*, a primarily freshwater species, is sometimes found in brackish eelgrass beds. Occurring along the entire coast, it both flowers and ripens its fruit underwater. **Sago pondweed** *(Potamogeton pectinatus)* grows in fresh, brackish, and salt water along the whole coast, and it is sometimes associated with *Zostera*.

The pondweeds, most notably sago pondweed and widgeongrass, are outstanding wildlife foods. Most of the ducks that migrate through, breed in, or winter on this coast feed upon the seeds and vegetative parts of these plants. Many are heavily dependent on them. More than half of the canvasback's food is said to consist of *P. pectinatus*. Other water birds feeding heavily on the pondweeds include the brant, Canada goose, and tundra swan (which eat the seeds and plants), as well as the red knot, American avocet, and marbled godwit, which eat only the seeds.

Nonflowering Plants

With a few exceptions such as the aforementioned flowering vascular plants, the plant life occurring with *Zostera* in beds of the Middle Atlantic coast are thallophytes. The Thallophyta is a division—or, depending upon who is doing the classifying, a group of divisions—of the plant kingdom. It includes the lower nonflowering plants, which are generally classified as algae, fungi, and lichens. In the eelgrass beds, one group of fungi, the bacteria, plays an enormously important role in the transfer of energy from the primary producers to the consumers. Those groups lumped under "algae," however, are the most conspicuous of the plant associates of *Zostera*. Many are members of the phytoplankton resource that exists in all marine waters where light conditions are sufficient for photosynthesis and nutrients are available. Diatoms and dinoflagellates make up much of this life, and are an energy resource for animals that live on and among the eelgrass plants. But these minute organisms are incidental members of the *Zostera* community and are found as well in adjacent waters. Diatoms exist in great numbers also on the surfaces of the large plants and their epiphytes and in the upper layer of deposits.

Described below are some of the macroflora of the nonflowering component of the eelgrass community—mostly those algae called seaweeds that are most readily observed and that are common enough in *Zostera* beds of the Middle Atlantic coast to be of significance in the ecology of these systems. By no means can all of the seaweeds be included here; but in the Woods Hole area alone, 42 species of green, red, and brown seaweeds and of blue-green algae and algal mats were recorded in eelgrass communities.

Among the seaweeds are many epiphytes on the leaves of *Zostera* or on the thalluses of other seaweeds. (In all, there are at least 100 species of algae epiphytic on *Zostera*.) Some of these are *facultatively* epiphytic: they can exist attached to other substrates such as rocks, shells, and pilings; but they take advantage of the great area of substrate provided by the larger plants of the seagrass beds. Some species are *obligately* epiphytic; these grow only on the substrates provided by other plants. A few obligates are found only in *Zostera* beds. Some seaweeds normally epiphytic frequently break loose and become free-floating drifters.

The seaweeds, included with the diatoms, dinoflagellates, euglenoids, and others in the catchall category *algae*, belong to several groups: blue-green algae, red algae, brown algae, and the green algae and stoneworts.

BLUE-GREEN ALGAE. These are extremely simple, primitive organisms considered by some to rank below the plant kingdom. Others say they are related through common ancestry to the red algae. They are visible generally only in the aggregate—as films on mud flats, scum on the water surface, gelatinous masses, or

Plants Associated with Zostera Marina

filaments. One blue-green alga, **mermaid's hair** *(Lyngbya majuscula)*, is common in salt water on rocks and pilings, and may be seen in eelgrass beds. It grows as dark-green filamentous tufts. Blue-green algae are not known to be of great importance in the *Zostera* community.

RED ALGAE. *Polysiphonia denudata,* one of a number of species of the genus that are epiphytic, is found on the whole coast. This bushy "tubed weed" commonly occurs on *Zostera,* growing to a length of a foot (30 cm) or so. The generic name means "many tubes" or "many siphons," referring to the structure of the main axis of the thallus, which appears as if made of filamentous fibers bound together.

Melobesia, Lithophyllum, and *Fosliella* spp. are *crustose* (encrusting) forms of red algae epiphytic on eelgrass. They are found along the whole coast. They are generally white to rose or purple in color, and are encrusted with calcium carbonate. For identification, Kenneth Gosner *(A Field Guide to the Atlantic Seashore)* suggests placing a drop of hydrochloric or other strong acid on specimens as a test for the presence of calcium carbonate.

BROWN ALGAE. This plant division is associated mostly with relatively cold waters and with rocky shores. It is extremely varied in size, structure, and complexity. It is almost exclusively marine. There are microscopic filamentous forms measuring less than 1/16 in. (1.6 mm) and huge kelps 300 ft. (90 m) long. Some are found in eelgrass beds.

Ectocarpus dasycarpus. This species occurs in the northernmost part of the Middle Atlantic range, in Rhode Island and Massachusetts waters. The 3-in. (8 cm) light-brown colonies grow abundantly not only on eelgrass but on other macroalgae.

Ectocarpus confervoides. This is a tufted filamentous alga growing either as an epiphyte or attached to objects on the bottom. It is found throughout the region, often growing on the rhizomes of *Zostera.*

Endesme spp. The so-called brown slimeweeds are slender, stringy, gelatinous-textured algae lacking the substance of most brown algae. Dried on paper, they

THE EELGRASS COMMUNITY

leave little more than a stain. *E. virescens,* relatively thick (about 3/8 in., or 1 cm) and about 1 ft. (30 cm) long, is epiphytic on larger seaweeds and on *Zostera. E. zosterae,* also, as its name indicates, is characteristic of eelgrass beds. The former species is found from Long Island south; the latter grows throughout the Middle Atlantic coast.

Desmotrichium undulatum. Characteristic of eel-grass beds, this alga usually grows as an epiphyte on *Zostera* leaves. The spiral, paper-thin blades are some-what grasslike and about as wide as grass blades; but they are only a couple of inches long and are light brown in color, so they contrast with the dark-green ribbons of their host plant. In early summer *Desmotri-chium* may be abundant, enhancing the value of eel-grass as shelter for small animals and providing food for some.

Slippery Tangle Weed. *Sphaerotrichia divaricata* is an epiphyte commonly found in the northern half of the range (from New Jersey to Cape Cod). It is soft and slimy to the touch, is finely branched, and grows to a length of 20 in. (50 cm). In contrast, **rough tangle weed** *(Stylophora rhizoides),* though somewhat similar in ap-pearance, is coarser in form and rough to the touch. It is found throughout the range as an epiphyte or drifting free.

Delicate Ribbon Weed. *Punctaria latifolia,* also characteristic of eelgrass, is a very thin, light-brown epiphyte with a small, padlike holdfast, and is about 1 ft. (30 cm) in length. **Coarse ribbon weed,** *Petalonia plan-taginea,* is darker, thicker, and leathery in texture. It also can be epiphytic, but it is found more often at-tached to stones. The former is found from New Jersey north, the latter as far south as Chesapeake Bay.

GREEN ALGAE. Epiphytic green algae are espe-cially likely to be present in brackish-water eelgrass beds. Among the genera represented in this group are filamentous *Cladophora* and *Chaetomorpha. Clado-phora* ("twig-form") attaches itself to the eelgrass plant by means of branched, threadlike growths. Masses of these algae often break loose and are found as floating colonies in the community. They are eaten by some

165. Green fleece *(Codium fragile)* is an abundant green alga; while it is not particularly associated with *Zostera,* this specimen was found in an eelgrass bed in Ninigret Pond, Rhode Island.

fishes and invertebrates. *Chaetomorpha* ("bristle-form") is a coarser, bright green to yellowish filamentous alga that grows in tangled masses amongst the eelgrass plants from South Carolina to Nova Scotia. Less desirable as food for animals because of its texture, it is valuable for the shelter it provides for small fishes and invertebrates.

Enteromorpha intestinalis. This green alga, as its name ("intestine-form of the intestine") suggests, is characterized by tubular, saclike blades with numerous constrictions, which are filled with gas. Known as **link confetti,** it is attached by threadlike outgrowths from the base of the thallus to shells, rocks, and other objects. It occurs along the Middle Atlantic coast in a wide range of salinity levels and is tolerant of changes in salinity. Year-round this alga can be found in the intertidal and subtidal zones, including shallow eelgrass beds. It is an important food for crabs, fishes, and other marine animals.

THE EELGRASS COMMUNITY

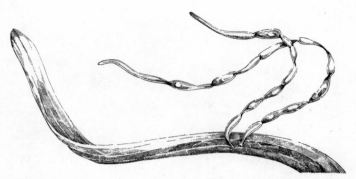

166. Link confetti *(Enteromorpha intestinalis)* growing on *Zostera* blade.

Ulva lactuca. The best known of the green algae is the aptly named **sea lettuce.** Found almost everywhere along the U.S. Atlantic coast, it is so abundant in some areas that it has been used for hog food, and it is an important energy source for marine animals and waterfowl. The Atlantic brant, which lost its chief food when the wasting disease struck the East coast eelgrass beds, turned to sea lettuce as a substitute. The plant thus helped save these geese from total disaster, and with eelgrass largely recovered, sea lettuce is still an important food for the brant, as well as for greater scaup and other ducks.

Ulva lactuca resembles leaf lettuce; further description is hardly necessary. (Cast on the beach, the thallus turns black as it dries.) Sea lettuce grows attached by a rhizoidal holdfast to objects on the bottom as well as to eelgrass plants. In coastal waters it commonly breaks loose and remains as a free-floating plant.

Sea lettuce is widely used as human food in the Orient. Peterson and Peterson (1979) recommend its use not only in salad but also (dried and powdered) as a saltlike seasoning. Note: this plant is tougher than it looks, so you may want to chop or shred it for use as a salad green. A further note of caution: dense concentrations of *Ulva lactuca* may indicate eutrophication due to sewage or other pollutants.

Caulerpa prolifera. This easily identified alga, with

Plants Associated with Zostera Marina

167. Sea lettuce *(Ulva lactuca)*.

its spatulate, erect, bright-green branches, favors the same habitat as *Zostera*—shallow sandy or muddy bottoms. Its growth form is similar, too, with green branches rising from horizontal, often buried *stolons* (basal branches that root at the nodes). The blades are flat, slightly wider than those of *Zostera,* and stalked rather than grasslike; and the plant is much smaller, with stolons about a foot in length and with 6-inch blades. In this range, it is found only in North Carolina.

Chara. This genus belongs to the stoneworts, a group of algae sometimes classified separately but considered here with the green algae. Freshwater stoneworts are among the very few coarse algae that are not seaweeds. The brackish-water forms sometimes grow in eelgrass beds, where they anchor themselves in the bottom by means of rootlike filaments. Their resemblance to vascular plants fools many people. *Chara* spp., called muskgrasses because of their skunky odor, are an important food for the American coot, for the greater scaup and other dabbling and diving ducks, and for the semipalmated sandpiper, which feeds on them in the shallowest eelgrass beds at low tide. Waterfowl seek

THE EELGRASS COMMUNITY

them especially during the reproductive period of the plants. The stomach of a single duck contained more than 300,000 of the tiny, sporelike oögonia of *Chara*.

Consumer Ecology of the Eelgrass Community

Herbivorous and Planktivorous Invertebrates

The consumers in the eelgrass beds of the Middle Atlantic coast belong to a wide range of animal phyla, from sponges to vertebrates; and they exhibit an equally wide range of life styles reflecting their means of capitalizing on the abundant food resource. The herbivores utilize the primary production of many non-flowering plants as well as that of *Zostera marina*. Among these are filter-feeding benthic epifauna that consume phytoplankton, grazers on the epiphytic algae that abound on the eelgrass plants, some herbivores that feed directly on *Zostera* leaves, and some that feed on the microalgae and diatoms growing on and in the upper layer of deposits.

SESSILE ANIMALS

The most primitive of the animals living on the *Zostera* leaves are the sponges. From Cape Cod to Cape Hatteras one can find **Loosanoff's haliclona** (*H. loosanoffi*), which grows to as much as 1 in. (25 mm) high in a chimneylike form, on shells, rocks, and pilings as well as on *Zostera*. The food of sponges is obtained by means of beating cilia that create water currents bearing particles of organic matter to the animal's cells through openings called *ostia*.

Other sessile animals of the eelgrass community that feed, with the aid of cilia, upon phytoplankton, zooplankton, detritus, and bacteria are bryozoans and ascidians. A number of these are listed in Table 10. Certain species are commonly associated with *Zostera*: **bushy bugula** (*B. turrita*); lacy crusts (*Membranipora*,

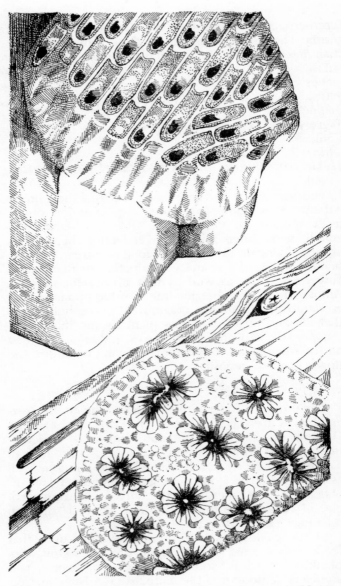

168. *Top:* lacy crust (*Membranipora* sp.); *bottom:* golden star tunicate *(Botryllus schlosseri).*

THE EELGRASS COMMUNITY

Electra, Tegella, Conopeum, and *Callipora* spp.); and panpipe bryozoans *(Tubulipora* spp.), notably *T. lilia-ceae.* These are colonial animals, minute individually but in the aggregate covering as much as several square inches of substrate. The sea squirts—primitive chordates with vase-shaped, grape-shaped, or walnut-shaped bodies—include white crust *(Didemnum* spp.), encrusting compound ascidians found abundantly along our coast; and the **golden star tunicate** *(Botryllus schlosseri),* found from Cape Cod at least to Chesapeake Bay. The larvae of these sessile tunicates are tadpolelike members of the zooplankton, and are thus eaten by various consumer organisms of the community.

There are even annelids—usually thought of as quite mobile animals—that live a sedentary existence on the leaves of *Zostera.* These "hard tube worms," members of the Serpulidae family, dwell in hard, limy tubes adhering to various substrata. The tubes of worms of the genus *Spirorbis* are coiled. Some are found only on hard substrates such as rocks and shells, some live only on seaweeds, and some are found on a wide range of surfaces. Occurring in great numbers on the leaves of *Zostera* in the northern part of our coast, *Spirorbis spirillum* and *S. borealis* can be distinguished by the

169. *Spirorbis borealis* on eelgrass leaf; note left-handed spirals.

Consumer Ecology of the Eelgrass Community   403

orientation of their coils. The tubes of the former are right-handed spirals; those of *S. borealis* are left-handed. You will need a strong hand lens to examine these pinhead-size worm tubes, which appear as white specks on the leaf surfaces.

Shells lying on the sediments in the eelgrass beds may have the much larger tubes of *Hydroides dianthus,* a close relative of *Spirorbis* annelids that does not form neat snail-like coils. The crustaceans are represented in the sessile community by barnacles. Some species of acorn barnacles *(Balanus)* are associated with *Zostera;* but this genus is noted for its adaptation to a wide variety of substrates, including rocks, ship bottoms, empty shells, the shells of hermit-crabs, horseshoe-crab carapaces, sea-turtle shells, and even the skin of cetaceans. Those found in the eelgrass community are not limited to it. An acorn barnacle feeds by trapping plankton and bits of detritus with feathery cirri that are waved about in the water and then withdrawn through the barnacle's trap door.

GRAZERS

The grazing component of the eelgrass community is dominated by the gastropods and crustaceans, with annelids making a strong showing. Hordes of tiny snails crawl over the *Zostera* blades feeding on the epiphytic algae and the diatoms on their filaments. Several of the more characteristic species are the **tortoiseshell limpet** *(Acmaea testudinalis);* **chink shell** *(Lacuna vincta);* **variegate miniature horn shell,** or **variable bittium** *(Diastoma varium);* **New England dog whelk** *(Nassarius trivittatus);* and **crescent mitrella** *(Mitrella lunata).* None of these is limited to *Zostera,* but all are common in the eelgrass beds. The first two range from Long Island north, and *D. varium,* from Maryland south; the others occur throughout the region covered by this book. The variegate miniature horn shell is so abundant on eelgrass in its range that it must be considered the major dominant of the epiphytic faunal community. This snail, measuring only to 1/5 in. (5 mm) in height, makes up in numbers what it lacks in size. From Virginia north, the comparably abundant **alternate miniature horn shell** *(Diastoma alternatum)* fills the same niche. Where the ranges of the two overlap you can distinguish them by the stronger sculpturing and larger size (to 1/4 in., or 6 mm, in height) of the latter species. The shell of each is narrow, high, and turreted, and is gray to blackish or reddish brown. (Note: in Kenneth Gosner's *A Field Guide to the Atlantic Seashore* they are *Bittium varium* and *B. alternatum.*) In areas where the **pinfish** *(Lagodon rhomboides)* is abundant, these snails may not be able to attain the numbers they reach where that predator is rare or absent. *Lagodon's* range embraces that covered by this book, but the pinfish is most common to the south.

The **eelgrass slug,** *Elysia catula,* found from Cape Cod to at least as far south as Chesapeake Bay, is a 1.1-in. (28-mm) shell-less gastropod characteristically found on *Zostera* plants. It is an herbivore, feeding on epiphytic algae as it creeps over the eelgrass blades.

Other grazing invertebrates of the epiphytic community are listed in Table 10. Some of them are swimmers able to move among the plants more readily than the gastropods and annelids, but nevertheless are essentially part of the epiphytic fauna.

EPIBENTHIC HERBIVORES

Bacteria, diatoms, and microalgae grow on and in the surface layer of the mud or sand in the eelgrass beds, and this food resource is utilized by invertebrates such as ostracods and sand dollars (and by fishes). From New Jersey north, the curious **common sand dollar** *(Echinarachnius parma)* occurs on sandy bottoms, mostly subtidally but also in the lower intertidal zone in the northern part of its range. It feeds by moving through the loose deposits, removing microorganisms from sand that it takes in with the help of its movable spines. Although diatoms and other microalgae make up a major part of its diet, the sand dollar is not so much grazer as deposit feeder. Sand dollars do not appear to be important links in the energy pathways from primary producers to higher trophic levels, but they are eaten to some extent by the summer flounder and other flatfishes. The structure and habits of those bottom-dwelling fishes seem well suited to utilizing this animal, which lives a half-buried existence in the sand.

Consumer Ecology of the Eelgrass Community

The **bay scallop**'s niche in the eelgrass community is less easily pinpointed. *Aequipecten irradians* (or *Argopecten irradians*) in the adult stage is a filter feeder leading a benthic existence—but with a considerable degree of mobility because of its capability for jerky, erratic jet propulsion that enables it to escape such enemies as Forbes' asterias. In the sedentary postveliger stage the bay scallop depends heavily on eelgrass as a substrate to which it can attach itself (by byssus threads) above the bottom, where it might otherwise be suffocated by silt. The adult scallop is often seen lying on the bottom, valves agape, with the 30 to 40 bright blue eyes presumably watching for enemies as it feeds on the plankton and organic particles it draws into its mantle cavity. A soft-bodied **oyster crab** may be visible in the opening between the valves, getting its own share of the food and taking advantage of the protection offered by the scallop's shell and swimming ability.

The bay scallop's status, like that of the Atlantic brant, has been closely tied to that of *Zostera*. Both the bird and the bivalve suffered severe reverses when the wasting disease struck the eelgrass beds of the North American Atlantic coast. Both species, however, have recovered substantially since *Zostera* made its comeback.

170. Bay scallop *(Aequipecten irradians);* note eyes on mantle edge and commensal pea crab (round object in right center).

Table 10: Some Invertebrate and Lower-Chordate Consumers of Middle Atlantic Eelgrass Communities

Phylum	Latin Name	Common Name (or descriptive name)*	Sessile epiphytes	Grazers and foragers	Benthic epifauna	Benthic infauna	Mobile epibenthos	Free swimmers
Annelida	Sthelenais boa	(Burrowing scale worm)				X		
	Glycera robusta	(Blood worm)				X		
	Podarke obscura	Swift-footed worm					X	X
	Nereis virens	(Clam worm)				X		X
	Platynereis dumerilii	Dumeril's clam worm		X				
	Diopatra cuprea	Plumed worm				X		
	Marphysa sanguinea	Red-gilled marphysa				X		
	Arabella iricolor	Opal worm				X		
	Lumbrinereis tenuis	(Thread worm)				X		
	Haploscoloplos fragilis	(Orbiniid worm)				X		
	Arenicola cristata	(Lugworm)				X		
	Clymenella torquata	(Bamboo worm)				X		
	Spio setosa	Mud worm				X		
	Chaetopterus variopedatus	Parchment worm				X		
	Amphitrite ornata	Ornate terebellid worm				X		
	Pherusa inflata	(Flabelligerid worm)				X		
	Spirorbis spp.	(Hard tube worms)	X					
	Phascolopsis gouldii	Gould's sipunculid				X		
Arthropoda	Limulus polyphemus	Horseshoe-crab					X	X
	Loxoconcha impressa	(Ostracod)		X	X		X	
	Sarsialla zostericola	(Ostracod)		X				
	Balanus spp.	(Acorn barnacles)	X					
	Harpacticoid copepods			X				X
	Tanais cavolinii	Pericarid crustacean		X				X
	Idotea baltica	Baltic idotea		X				X
	I. irrorata	(Isopod)		X				X
	Erichsonella filiformis	(Isopod)		X				X

*Names in parentheses are not common names of individual species but descriptive terms applied to organisms belonging to particular orders, families, or genera (or groups of genera with similar characteristics), or are simply loose descriptive terms.

Consumer Ecology of the Eelgrass Community

Table 10 *(continued)*

Phylum	Latin Name	Common Name (or descriptive name)*	Sessile epiphytes	Grazers and foragers	Benthic epifauna	Benthic infauna	Mobile epibenthos	Free swimmers
Arthropoda	E. attenuata	(Isopod)		X				X
	Edotea triloba	(Isopod)		X	X	X		X
	Gammarus mucronatus	(Scud)		X				X
	Ampelisca spp.	(Four-eyed amphipods)		X				X
	Byblis spp.	(Four-eyed amphipods)		X				X
	Erichthonius spp.	(Tubiculous amphipods)	X		X			
	Caprella spp.	(Skeleton shrimps)		X				
	Mysis stenolepis	(Bent mysid shrimp)		X	X			X
	Palaemonetes vulgaris	Common shore shrimp		X				X
	Crangon septemspinosa	Sand shrimp		X	X	X		X
	Hyppolyte pleuracantha	(Grass shrimp)		X				X
	H. zostericola	Eelgrass shrimp		X				X
	Pagurus longicarpus	Long-clawed hermit					X	
	P. pollicaris	Flat-clawed hermit					X	
	Polyonyx gibbesi	Parchment worm polyonyx[1]				X		
	Libinia emarginata	Common spider crab					X	
	L. dubia	Doubtful spider crab					X	
	Carcinus maenas	Green crab					X	
	Callinectes sapidus	Blue crab					X	
	Ovalipes ocellatus	Lady crab					X	
	Neopanopeus sayi	(Black-fingered mud crab)					X	
	Pinnotheres ostreum	Oyster crab[2]			X	X		
	P. maculatus	Mussel crab[3]			X	X		
	Dissodactylus mellitae	Urchin crab[4]			X			
	Pinnixa cylindrica	Lugworm crab[5]				X		

[1]Commensal in tube of parchment worm

[2]Commensal in oysters, scallops, mussels, or in parchment worm tubes

[3]Commensal in mussels, scallops, in parchment worm tubes, or tunicates; also can be free-swimming

[4]Commensal on underside of sand dollars

[5]Commensal in lugworm burrows; may live free in mud

THE EELGRASS COMMUNITY

Table 10 *(continued)*

Phylum	Latin Name	Common Name (or descriptive name)*	Sessile epiphytes	Grazers and foragers	Benthic epifauna	Benthic infauna	Mobile epibenthos	Free swimmers
Arthropoda	*P. chaetopterana*	Parchment worm crab[6]				X		
	P. retinens	Mud shrimp crab[7]						X
Echinodermata	*Sclerodactyla briareus*	Hairy cucumber				X		
	Leptosynapta inhaerens	Common white synapta				X		
	Arbacia punctulata	Purple sea urchin		X	X			
	Echinarachnius parma	Sand dollar			X			
Chordata	*Botryllus schlosseri*	Golden star tunicate	X					
	Dolichoglossus kowalevskyi	(Acorn worm)				X		
	Ciona intestinalis	Sea vase	X					
	Molgula manhattensis	(Sea grape)	X					
	M. provisionalis	(Sea grape)	X					
	Didemnum spp.	(White crusts)	X					
Porifera	*Haliclona loosanoffi*	Loosanoff's haliclona	X					
Cnidaria	*Gonionemus vertens*	Angled hydromedusa	X					
	Pennaria tiarella	Feather hydroid	X					
	Hydractinia echinata	Snail fur[8]					X	
	Obelia spp.	Bushy wineglass hydroids[9]	X					
	Cyanea capillata	Lion's mane jelly[9]	X					
	Aurelia aurita	Moon jelly						X
	Haliclystus auricula	(Stalked jellyfish)	X					
	H. salpinx	(Stalked jellyfish)	X					
	Craterolophus convolvulus	(Stalked jellyfish)	X					
	Lucernaria quadricornis	(Stalked jellyfish)	X					

[6]Commensal in parchment worm tubes; may live free in mud
[7]Commensal with mud shrimps; may live free in mud
[8]Commensal on *Pagurus* shell
[9]Polyps of sessile generation

Consumer Ecology of the Eelgrass Community 409

Table 10 (continued)

Phylum	Latin Name	Common Name (or descriptive name)*	Sessile epiphytes	Grazers and foragers	Benthic epifauna	Benthic infauna	Mobile epibenthos	Free swimmers
Cnidaria	Thaumatoscyphus atlanticus	(Stalked jellyfish)	X					
	Epiactis prolifera	Proliferating anemone				X		
	Actinothoe spp.	Burrowing anemones				X		
	Haliplanella luciae	Striped anemone				X		
Platyhelminthes	Bdellora candida	Limulus leech[10]					X	
	Euplana gracilis	Slender flatworm		X				
	Gnesioceros floridana	Florida flatworm		X				
Rhynchocoela	Cerebratulus lacteus	Milky ribbon worm				X		
	Tetrastemma spp.	(Four-eyed nemerteans)		X			X	
	Oerstedia dorsalis	(Four-eyed nemertean)		X				
	Amphiporus spp.	(Many-eyed nemerteans)		X				
	Zygonemertes spp.	(Many-eyed nemerteans)		X				
Bryozoa	Tubulipora liliaceae	Panpipe bryozoan	X					
	Membranipora membranaceae	(Lacy crust)	X					
	M. monostachys	(Lacy crust)	X					
	M. tenuis	(Lacy crust)	X					
	Conopeum truitti	(Lacy crust)	X					
	Tegella unicornis	(Lacy crust)	X					
	Callipora craticula	(Lacy crust)	X					
	Electra pilosa	(Lacy crust)	X					
	E. crustulenta	(Lacy crust)	X					
	Bugula turrita	Bushy bugula	X					
Mollusca	Acmaea testudinalis	Tortoiseshell limpet		X				
	A. alveus	(Limpet)		X				
	Lacuna vincta	Chink shell		X				
	Littorina littorea	Common periwinkle		X				
	Diastoma alternatum	Alternate miniature horn shell		X				

[10]Commensal on book gills and legs of horseshoe-crab

Table 10 (continued)

Phylum	Latin Name	Common Name (or descriptive name)*	Sessile epiphytes	Grazers and foragers	Benthic epifauna	Benthic infauna	Mobile epibenthos	Free swimmers
Mollusca	D. varium	Variegate miniature horn shell		X				
	Crepidula fornicata	Common slipper shell	X					
	C. convexa	Convex slipper shell	X					
	C. plana	Flat slipper shell	X					
	Ilyanassa obsoleta	Mud basket shell		X				
	Nassarius trivittatus	New England dog whelk		X			X	
	Haminoea solitaria	Solitary glass bubble					X	
	Mitrella lunata	Crescent mitrella		X			X	
	Anachis avara	Greedy dove shell		X				
	Elysia catula	Eelgrass slug		X				
	Solemya velum	Veiled clam				X		
	Mytilus edulis	Blue mussel			X			
	Modiolus demissus	Ribbed mussel			X			
	Aequipecten irradians	Bay scallop[11]	X		X			X
	Crassostrea virginica	Eastern oyster			X			
	Mercenaria mercenaria	Hardshell clam				X		
	Ensis directus	Common razor clam				X		
	Mya arenaria	Soft-shelled clam				X		

[11]Young scallops attach to *Zostera* plant

Vertebrate Herbivores

EELGRASS EATERS

The vast majority of vertebrates in the *Zostera* community are secondary and tertiary consumers. Some species feed principally or to a small degree on the algal epiphytes. A few feed on *Zostera* itself. *Zostera* leaves are part of the diet of the American eel, and bits of the green leaves are found in the stomachs of spot, pinfish,

Consumer Ecology of the Eelgrass Community   411

Atlantic silversides, bay anchovy, striped anchovy, and black sea bass. The species that feed most heavily on eelgrass, however, are visitors to the community such as the Atlantic brant.

GREEN-ALGAE EATERS

Striped mullet are both detritivorous and herbivorous; when in the eelgrass community, they feed primarily on green algae. The green algae, mostly epiphytic in this habitat, are utilized to an extent by many fishes whose principal diet is invertebrates, other fishes, or both. Among these are the oyster toad, mummichog, Atlantic silverside, pinfish, and spot.

Invertebrate Predators

CNIDARIANS

All classes of the phylum Cnidaria are represented in the *Zostera* community. Among the hydrozoans are the **angled hydromedusa** *(Gonionemus vertens)*, the medusa of which is characteristic of this habitat. (The polyp stage of this species is unknown.) *Gonionemus* has been much less prevalent since the eelgrass blight of the 1930s.

A number of hydrozoans are sessile on the eelgrass blades in the polyp stage; their free-swimming medusae may be present in the community in great numbers. One of these is the **feather hydroid** *(Pennaria tiarella)*, common on this stretch of coast in both stages. In the polyp stage it is large enough (with colonies reaching 6 in., or 15 cm) to be easily detected.

Perhaps the most readily discovered hydroid is **snail fur** *(Hydractinia echinata);* the polyps colony of this species encrusts gastropod shells occupied by hermit-crabs. The individual polyps may exceed 0.25 in. (6.4 mm) in height. There is no medusa stage in this species. While not an obligate member of the eelgrass community, it is common there because the environment is favorable for the hermit-crabs with which it associates.

171. Snail fur *(Hydractinia echinata)*, greatly enlarged.
Note three kinds of polyps: the long, flexible defensive
polyps without tentacles; the slender feeding polyps with
tentacles surrounding mouth; and shorter reproductive
polyps with saclike male or female organs.

Sooner or later when exploring shallow eelgrass beds
you will come across a hermit-crab *(Pagurus longicarpus* or *P. pollicaris)* moving about in its living fur coat.
The range of *Hydractinia* embraces those of both *Pagurus* and *Zostera* on the Atlantic coast. This commensal
relationship is further discussed in this chapter under
Epibenthic Scavengers.

Living a sessile existence on eelgrass are members of
another class of cnidarians, the Scyphozoa. These
stalked jellyfish are characteristic of the shallow eelgrass beds but are sessile also on seaweeds, rocks, and
some gastropods. The **eared stalked jellyfish** *(Haliclystus auricula)*, growing to 1.25 in. (32 mm) and the
horned stalked jellyfish *(Lucernaria quadricornis)*, to
2.75 in. (7 cm), are large enough to be easily seen. The
former (common on the south shore of Cape Cod) is
able to move about with the aid of adhesive structures
in the notches between the lobes; the latter is strictly
sedentary. These iridescent jellyfish, shaped like vases
or upside-down bells, are found also on rocky shores, on
Fucus. They are shallow-water forms, and they are

Consumer Ecology of the Eelgrass Community   413

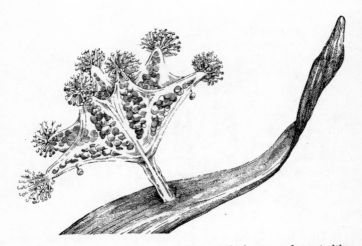

172. The trumpet stalked jellyfish *(Haliclystus salpinx),* like *H. auricula,* is not found south of the Cape Cod region; both species attach themselves to eelgrass leaves and prey on small crustaceans.

quite voracious predators despite the fact that they must wait for their victims to come to them. Among their prey are some rather large annelids. Both these species are northern forms, found in this range only in the vicinity of Cape Cod.

The third class of cnidarians is the Anthozoa. This group includes the sea anemones, one of which, *Cerian-theopsis americanus,* is found subtidally and sometimes in the lower intertidal zone, from Cape Cod south. This species swims about when young, and in the adult stage burrows into the mud, leaving tentacles and oral disc exposed. It forms about itself a tube of mucus that collects sand grains and detritus. Its food is small animals that come within reach of its tentacles. *Ceriantheopsis* reaches a length of 8 in. (20 cm).

The cnidarians of the eelgrass habitat, whether polyps or medusae, are predatory. *(Hydractinia*—snail fur—because of its special relationship to the hermit-crabs, obtains its food in unusual ways.) Stinging cells (nematocysts) are of help both in obtaining food and in defense against enemies—though some predators are immune.

ECHINODERMS

The short-spined **brittle star** *(Ophioderma brevis-pina)* represents the spiny-skinned tribe in the eelgrass community. This greenish-to-black predator, with arms about 2.5 in. (64 mm) long, is found on muddy-bottom *Zostera* beds throughout the Middle Atlantic range; but it appears to be common only from Long Island Sound to Cape Cod. *Ophioderma* lacks the red eyespot that **Forbes' asterias** *(A. forbesi)* has on the end of each arm; but it behaves as if light sensitive. *Asterias* is less common than the brittle star in the eelgrass habitat but is of special interest because of its depredations on bivalves. One young *Asterias* may eat 50 young clams in six days. This sea star is associated with bottoms that are sandy or rocky rather than muddy, and it occurs in deeper water as well as in the subtidal shallows and the intertidal zone. *Ophioderma*, a shallow-water form, is not as large and heavy bodied, and it probably is much less a threat to adult bivalves such as scallops and clams. The bay scallop is wary of any sea star. A good demonstration of the swimming ability of the scallop can be conducted by dropping either *Ophioderma* or *Asterias* into an aquarium containing the blue-eyed bivalve.

CRUSTACEANS

The class Crustacea of the phylum Arthropoda is made up predominantly of aquatic forms, both freshwater and marine. It includes the dominant invertebrate predators (and many scavengers) of the *Zostera* community. Members of the group occupy every level of the eelgrass jungle, living in the deposits, moving over the bottom, clinging to the vegetation, and swimming freely among the plants. They are omnivores, predators, and scavengers.

Blue Crab. *Callinectes sapidus*—"beautiful swimmer"—is King of the Benthos, excluding vertebrates such as selachians and flatfishes, which are bottom feeders. In addition to functioning as a consumer of living plants, providing a substrate for attachment of barnacles, harboring other barnacles in its gill chambers, carrying the parasitic barnacle *Loxothylacus texanus* and parasitic nemertean worms in its body, and also scavenging on dead animal matter, the blue crab is an active predator on many animals. There is no denying that its ecological niche in the eelgrass community is complex. This crab is a major link in an endless array of food chains, many of which culminate with humans—for whom this crustacean is a delicacy. For this reason the health of its habitat (which is not confined to the *Zostera* community) is of special concern to us. (The blue crab is also discussed in Chapter Three under The Mobile Epibenthos of the Intertidal Flats.)

An aggressive and formidably armed animal, the blue crab is nevertheless preyed upon by selachians (the sandbar and Atlantic sharpnose sharks); the oyster toad, tautog, black sea bass, and other bony fishes; and by the gulls and wading birds that capture it at low tide in shallow beds. Of course, the young crabs are most vulnerable. A true swimming crab (its last pair of legs being paddle shaped), it can be included in the free-swimming fauna as well as the mobile epibenthos. Most of its food is obtained on and in the bottom deposits. It excavates worms and other invertebrates from their burrows, but it will eat almost any animal food it comes across, dead or alive.

Because of the niches the blue crab fills in the ecology of the eelgrass beds, a case can be made for designating this habitat—from Cape Cod south—as the *Zostera-Callinectes* community.

SHORE AND SAND SHRIMPS. Surpassing the blue crab and virtually all other macrofauna species in sheer numbers, the caridean shrimps are a major group in this community. In a study of macroinvertebrates collected in the southern part of Chesapeake Bay, the fact that all 14 species found were crustaceans points up the complete dominance of the class Crustacea in the free-swimming and mobile epibenthic invertebrate fauna—even allowing for the lesser effectiveness of the collecting methods in capturing gastropods and other bottom crawlers.

OSTRACODS. An ostracod, *Sarsialla zostericola*, despite its diminutive size—0.05 in. (1.3 mm) long—belongs with the predators. As its name suggests, it is

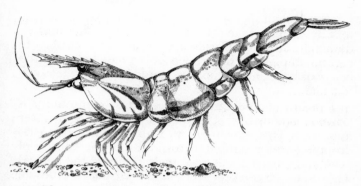

173. The common shore shrimp *(Palaemonetes vulgaris)*, can be distinguished from similar caridean shrimps by the two teeth on the crest of the carapace *behind* the eye stalk.

found on *Zostera* (though also on hydroids); it occurs on our coast from Long Island Sound to Cape Cod. It feeds on smaller animals. You may see this minute crustacean by putting a *Zostera* plant into a jar of water and holding it to the light. A magnifying glass will be needed to make out the form of this crustacean and other minute invertebrates in your sample. In fact, seeing many species requires a microscope.

An even smaller ostracod, *Loxoconcha impressa*, ranges from Cape Cod south. Only 0.03 in. (0.8 mm) long, it belongs to a group of crustaceans that generally live on the bottom, where they actively move about in search of prey; but *Loxoconcha* is found more often on and amongst the eelgrass plants in relatively shallow waters. It is also found on hydroids. Each second antenna of this crustacean is armed with a poison gland, which is associated with a pair of curved claws at the end of the antenna.

Vertebrate Predators

There is abundant evidence that, although the populations of fishes in eelgrass beds are predominantly juveniles and small species, the community is richer in vertebrate biomass than others where larger fishes may be dominant. In North Carolina, for example, according to certain studies the difference in biomass between the eel-grass beds and the nonvegetated adjacent areas was fourfold.

The fish component of the eelgrass community is largely made up of species that move into deeper water in winter. This movement probably is in response to dropping water temperatures and a lower density of vegetation in the eelgrass beds. During the period when such larger predators as the weakfish, bluefish, and sandbar shark occupy the *Zostera* community, they probably have greater impact, through their feeding activities, on the populations of the macroinvertebrates of the mobile epibenthos than do predators that are residents in the community.

The food habits of the selachians and true fishes of the *Zostera* community are summarized in Table 11.

CARTILAGINOUS FISHES

The cartilaginous fishes of the eelgrass beds are members of orders that as a group are sometimes referred to as selachians—a term with little taxonomic meaning. The most prominent species in the *Zostera* community are the cownose ray, the bluntnose stingray, and the sandbar shark. Other estuarine residents or visitors that probably feed in the eelgrass beds include the **Atlantic sharpnose shark** *(Rhizoprionodon terraenovae)*, a small species (to 3 ft., or 0.9 m) that frequents the North Carolina sounds and is occasionally found farther north; the **southern stingray** *(Dasyatis americana)*, to New Jersey; **Atlantic stingray** *(D. sabina)*, not usually found north of the Outer Banks; **smooth butterfly ray** *(Gymnura micrura)*, north to Chesapeake Bay, sometimes to Long Island Sound; **dusky shark** *(Carcharhinus obscurus)*, north to Cape Cod; and **smooth dogfish** *(Mustelus canis)*, north to Cape Cod. Some of these species are discussed elsewhere in this book. (See Index.)

Table 11: Some Cartilaginous and Bony Fishes of Middle Atlantic Eelgrass Communities

Class	Latin Name	Common Name	Food
Chondrichthyes	*Carcharhinus milberti*	Sandbar shark	Pinfish and other fishes; blue crabs
	Rhizoprionodon terraenovae	Atlantic sharpnose shark	Fishes (pigfish, silversides, menhaden); blue crabs, fiddlers, hermit-crabs, shrimp, mollusks, annelids
Osteichthyes	*Anchoa hepsetus*	Striped anchovy	Plankton
	A. mitchilli	Bay anchovy	Small shrimps, detritus; also zooplankton; small benthic gastropods, bivalves, crustaceans
	Synodus foetens	Inshore lizardfish	Fish, shrimp
	Anguilla rostrata	American eel	Crustaceans, annelids, fishes, echinoderms, mollusks, eelgrass; also carrion
	Strongylura marina	Atlantic needlefish	Anchovies, mullets, silversides; shrimps, amphipods; annelids; heart urchins (young eat detritus)
	Fundulus heteroclitus	Mummichog	Small crustaceans, detritus, fecal pellets, polychaetes, small bivalves, algae
	Apeltes quadracus	Fourspine stickleback	Amphipods, mysids, and other small crustaceans
	Gasterosteus aculeatus	Threespine stickleback	Amphipods, mysids, and other small crustaceans
	Hippocampus erectus	Lined seahorse	Small crustaceans and other minute animals
	Syngnathus fuscus	Northern pipefish	Amphipods, mysids, and other crustaceans; fish, shrimp

Table 11 (continued)

Class	Latin Name	Common Name	Food
Osteichthyes	*S. floridae*	Dusky pipefish	Amphipods, small fishes, shrimp
	Centropristis striata	Black sea bass	Crustaceans (small blue crabs, isopods, caprellids, penaeids); eelgrass leaves; pipefish
	Orthopristis chrysopterus	Pigfish	Crustaceans (barnacles, shore shrimps, isopods, gammarids); gastropods, polychaetes, detritus, *Molgula*
	Bairdiella chrysoura	Silver perch	Mysids, amphipods, baitfish, shrimp
	Cynoscion nebulosus	Spotted seatrout (weakfish)	*Palaemonetes, Crangon septemspinosa,* eelgrass leaves, herrings, pigfish, spot, crabs, annelids, mollusks
	Leiostomus xanthurus	Spot	Detritus, eelgrass leaves, ampeliscids, caprellids, ostracods, polychaetes, mollusks, plankton
	Lagodon rhomboides	Pinfish	Crustaceans (barnacles, isopods, shore shrimps); gastropods, limpets; polychaetes; detritus; eelgrass and epiphytic fauna
	Tautoga onitis	Tautog	Blue crabs, penaeids, isopods; young tautogs eat worms and small crustaceans
	Stathmonotus stahli	Eelgrass blenny	Small crustaceans
	Chasmodes bosquianus	Striped blenny	Detritus, amphipods, isopods
	Hypsoblennius hentzi	Feather blenny	Detritus; caprellids and other amphipods

Table 11 (continued)

Class	Latin Name	Common Name	Food
Osteichthyes	*Mugil cephalus*	Striped mullet	Organic detritus, epiphytic algae, littoral diatoms
	Menidia menidia	Atlantic silverside	Crustaceans (copepods, mysids, amphipods); gastropods, polychaetes, detritus
	Paralichthys dentatus	Summer flounder	Fishes, squid, crustaceans, annelids, sand dollars, gastropods, bivalves
	P. lethostigma	Southern flounder	Mainly fishes, including herrings, pinfish; crabs, mysids, mollusks, shrimps, sand dollars
	Scophthalmus aquosus	Windowpane	Mainly fishes; also squid, shrimp, crabs, mysids, small mollusks, sand dollars, annelids, amphipods
	Hippoglossoides platessoides	American plaice	Young eat caprellids and other amphipods, mysids, decapods; adults eat sand dollars, worms, mollusks, shrimps, sea urchins, brittle stars
	Pseupleuronectes americanus	Winter flounder	Small crustaceans, worms, small fishes, shrimps
	Trinectes maculatus	Hogchoker	Annelids, small crustaceans, detritus; algae, foraminifers
	Sphaeroides maculatus	Northern puffer	Small crustaceans, small bivalves and gastropods; annelids, urchins, bryozoans, ascidians, sponges, algae

Table 11 (continued)

Class	Latin Name	Common Name	Food
Osteichthyes	*Opsanus tau*	Oyster toadfish	Crustaceans (small blue, spider, stone, mud, and fiddler crabs; hermit-crabs; shrimp, isopods, amphipods); mollusks (small snails, scallops, clams); fishes (gobies, silversides); annelids, anemones, urchins, vegetation

Cownose Ray. *Rhinoptera bonasus* is a shallow-water species, found in the inshore waters of the outer beach as well as in the estuaries. Its impact on estuarine ecology is discussed in Chapter Three under Estuarine Chordates. Its pit-digging activities, in search of clams and other infauna, damage and destroy large areas of eelgrass habitat. It is common in Chesapeake Bay, and is found throughout the Middle Atlantic coast.

Bluntnose Stingray. *Dasyastis sayi,* a small species— average width 1 ft. (30 cm)—is known throughout the Middle Atlantic coast. It can be abundant in North Carolina waters at times. This species invades the estuaries in schools, and in the eelgrass beds feeds on worms,

174. *Top:* sandbar shark *(Carcharhinus milberti); bottom:* Atlantic sharpnose shark *(Rhizoprionodon terraenovae).*

amphipods and other crustaceans, and small clams and other mollusks.

Sandbar Shark. *Carcharhinus milberti,* one of the commonest sharks of the coastal waters, averages about 6 ft. (1.8 m) in length. It is both predator and scavenger, feeding on many fishes, including pinfish, which are common in eelgrass beds. Since pinfish eat *Zostera* leaves and algae that grow on them, the sandbar shark may in one respect have a beneficial effect on the community, offsetting to some degree the destruction of eelgrass by the cownose ray.

BONY FISHES

The bony, or true, fishes are diverse and abundant in the eelgrass habitat as well as in open estuarine waters. There are so many species that only a small representation of this group can be discussed here. Among those most closely associated with *Zostera* are spot, Atlantic silverside, fourspine and threespine sticklebacks, northern pipefish, dwarf seahorse, dusky and northern pipefishes, bay and striped anchovies, menhaden, pigfish, and summer flounder and other flatfishes. No estuarine fishes are strictly limited to the seagrass beds, but many forage in that habitat, and several—pipefishes, seahorses, and sticklebacks—have special relationships to *Zostera.*

The species described below are grouped taxonomically by orders rather than by their roles in the eelgrass community. Many of their kin are also important in this ecology. The Bibliography includes publications that can be consulted for more information about this subject.

BATRACHOIDIFORMES.   This is a small order, with only one family and four fish species on the U.S. Atlantic coast. Best known is the **oyster toadfish** *(Opsanus tau),* sometimes called **oyster toad, mud toad,** or **sapo;** it is found from Cape Cod south. It is characteristic of the intertidal zone but also inhabits eelgrass beds and other shallow subtidal waters. It is unusual in that it often spawns above the low-tide mark. In early summer the oyster toadfish lays its eggs, in a single layer, in a cavity (sometimes the concave surface of a mollusk valve).

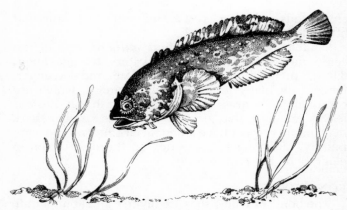

175. Oyster toadfish *(Opsanus tau).*

Each egg is attached to the substrate by an adhesive
disk. The larva that hatches remains attached by its
ventral surface to the disk, until the yolk is absorbed. In
the meantime, the male toadfish has taken over from
the female. He guards the nest diligently, preventing
silt from settling on the eggs. His instinct for the role of
protective father is so strong that he will remain with
the nest even when it is exposed by the falling tide.

With no close relatives on the Middle Atlantic coast,
the oyster toad is easily recognized. It has a distinctive
structure and pattern, with a stout body, large head,
and scaleless, loose, and wrinkled skin. It is depressed in
front, and the flattened head bears many flaps, or cirri.
It is blackish or dull brownish green, with dark, vermiform markings. The male grows larger than the female, reaching a length of 18 in. (46 cm) and a weight
of a little more than a pound (about a half-kilogram).
The male also lives longer—to 12 years, as compared
with the female's 7-year life span.

The oyster toad is a carnivore, with a wide-ranging
diet of both invertebrate and vertebrate prey. Its chief
food is crabs, including fiddlers, mud crabs, and the
spider, stone, and blue crabs; other crustaceans, including shrimps, isopods, amphipods, and hermit-crabs;
mollusks, including scallops, clams, and small gastropods; fishes, including gobies and silversides; the eggs of

its own species (despite the parental care); annelids; anemones; and the purple sea urchin. It also eats some vegetation. The toadfish itself has enemies; the young are prey for other carnivorous fishes, and adults are eaten by bald eagles and ospreys, and probably by large skates and sharks. This unprepossessing fish is good human food, too; but handle it carefully, for the dorsal and opercular spines are poisonous. It is most common in rocky and weedy locations.

ANTHERINIFORMES. The needlefishes and their kin include many species of baitfish size, some of which, including the **mummichog** *(Fundulus heteroclitus)*, were treated briefly or at length in Chapter Three, under Animals of the Estuarine Waters. These species, along with those of other orders, including silversides and herrings, may be found in a wide varity of estuarine habitats, even the upper, freshwater reaches of tidal action. Some venture into the salt marshes at high tide. Some species—the mummichog, the rainwater killifish *(Lucania parva)*, the bay anchovy, and the fourspine and threespine sticklebacks—show a strong preference for the eelgrass community.

Atlantic Needlefish. *Strongylura marina* is abundant as far north as Cape Cod. Its relationship to the flying fishes is reflected in its unsymmetrical tail with a much longer lower lobe. Although it does not fly like its cousins, the needlefish flees predators by skipping over the surface. It grows sometimes to 4 ft. (1.2 m) but generally reaches less than half of that length.

The needlefish's name derives from its extremely slender shape, with elongate, toothed jaws. Young needlefish an inch or two long resemble floating twigs as they rest at the surface.

Needlefishes live mostly at the surface, where they feed upon small fishes: notably anchovies, mullets, and silversides. They also eat shrimps, amphipods, annelids, and, in North Carolina, heart urchins. Young needlefishes consume quantities of detritus. These fish go upestuary into fresh water at times. They are sometimes found in the littoral zone, but more characteristically they feed in subtidal waters.

Although it is the adults that most commonly enter

Consumer Ecology of the Eelgrass Community   425

estuaries (and ascend rivers), needlefish young may be plentiful in such coastal lagoons as Great South Bay. They are apparently absent from well-protected Wellfleet Harbor on the bay side of Cape Cod but present in Pleasant Bay—a lagoon—on the east side and also in the Westport River estuary (Buzzards Bay).

Mummichog. *Fundulus heteroclitus* is a true estuarine fish; generally it moves in winter from the shoals and shallow eelgrass beds into deeper water. In the southern part of this range (North Carolina) some mummichogs are resident year round in deep tidepools in the estuaries. It is extremely abundant in places. Researchers in Great South Bay collecting eelgrass-community fishes found mummichogs in every haul of the seine; it was far more numerous than any other species except the fourspine stickleback. Other collections from shallow waters of the Atlantic coast estuaries show the mummichog to be a dominant species in much of its range.

The mummichog measures only 5 in. (12.5 cm) long, but it includes other fishes in its diet. Its diet is most notable, however, for the mummichog's effectiveness in controlling mosquitos. It also eats small crustaceans, including amphipods, isopods, and copepods; polychaete worms; crabs; snails; insects; and algae and detritus.

GASTEROSTEIFORMES. This order of oddly shaped and armored fishes includes some species that are nicely adapted to life in the eelgrass community. Most are small fishes, but the **bluespotted cornetfish** *(Fistularia tabacaria)*, which lives in seagrass meadows, feeding on shrimps and small fishes, has been said to reach 6 ft. (1.8 m). It is not frequently seen.

Fourspine and **Threespine Sticklebacks.** *Apeltes quadracus,* the fourspine stickleback, is at home in fresh water but is primarily a marine species. Found principally in the *Zostera* community, it is sometimes incredibly abundant there. As noted above, it far exceeded in numbers any other species in the Great South Bay studies. Investigations in Rhode Island and Connecticut revealed a similar dominant position. Of estuarine resident fishes taken in 17 Massachusetts estuaries, *Apeltes* frequently was among the three or four most abundant.

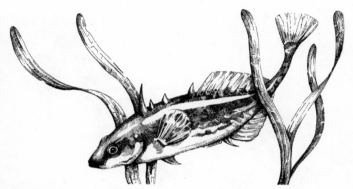

176. Fourspine stickleback *(Apeltes quadracus)*.

A member of the Gasterosteidae, a family of 1.5- to 4-in. (6- to 10-cm) fishes, the fourspine stickleback at 2 in. is one of the smaller species. The threespine stickleback (fasterosteus aculeatus), at 4 in., is one of the larger. It, too, strongly prefers the eelgrass habitat and is among the most abundant species in many Atlantic-coast estuaries. *Apeltes* ranges south to Maryland; *Gasterosteus* on this coast is a New England fish.

The sticklebacks are famous for their nesting habits and for the care they give their young. Despite their small size, because of their great numbers they are important in estuarine ecology; they consume great quantities of small crustaceans, and are themselves preyed upon by larger fishes as well as by wading birds.

Dwarf Seahorse. The image of a seahorse as a quaint creature in an upright posture with its tail coiled about a blade of eelgrass is not at all fanciful, for this fish has a habit of holding just such a position while it awaits its prey. Of the three species of *Hippocampus* in the waters of the U.S. Atlantic Coast, the dwarf seahorse, *H. zosterae,* is the one most often seen in the eelgrass beds. It is well suited for life in this environment, where water movement is subdued, where the green vegetation provides protective cover and resting places, and where the minute animal life on which it feeds is abundant.

Clinging by its tail to a *Zostera* blade, the dwarf seahorse waits for its food to come to it. A small crustacean

Consumer Ecology of the Eelgrass Community   427

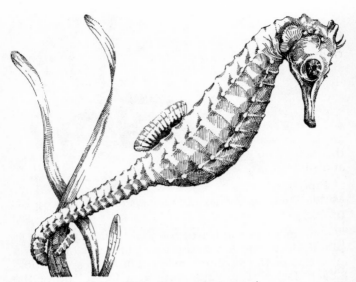

177. Dwarf seahorse *(Hippocampus zosterae).*

or fish larva that approaches within range is sucked into the fish's gullet through the long snout. Much of the seahorse's time is spent in this manner; but this unfish-like fish can swim. It travels in an upright attitude, by oscillations of its dorsal fin. (The prehensile tail has no fin.)

The female seahorse deposits some 200 eggs in a pouch the male bears on its ventral (forward) side. There they remain for 40 to 50 days, until hatched. The young seahorses, less than 1/3 in. (8 mm) long, are ex-pelled one by one from the pouch. For a time, the young swim in a horizontal position, even after they have developed the elongated snout.

Cape Cod is the practical northern limit for this genus of a family of primarily warm-water fishes, but seahorses have been found as far north as Nova Scotia.

Northern Pipefish. *Syngnathus fuscus* is the most common of the pipefishes in the Middle Atlantic range. Like the seahorse, it is structurally adapted to life in the eelgrass beds; and it shows—in its odd, bony-plated form—its kinship to the seahorses. Both pipefishes and seahorses belong to the family Syngnathidae. The pipefish are more fishlike in appearance than the sea-horses in several ways: they have less prominent horny rings about the body; they lack the horselike head set at right angles to the body; they swim horizontally; and they have a tailfin. But they have the same tubelike snout, the same habit of lying almost invisible alongside a *Zostera* leaf, like a plant fragment, and the same unusual breeding habits. Their feeding habits are similar, too. After hatching, young pipefish may retreat to the father's pouch in time of danger. (Female seahorses and pipefishes have no pouches.)

Pipefishes are among the most abundant fishes in Middle Atlantic coast eelgrass beds. They show a strong preference for this habitat; unvegetated bottoms offer little concealment and protection for these poor swimmers. Not surprisingly, the syngnathids prey upon *Caprella*, the little skeleton shrimp (actually an amphipod). *Caprella*'s own habits are quite similar to those of the relatively large pipefishes and seahorses; but it cannot swim at all. Other small crustaceans, along with crustacean and fish larvae, are taken by the seahorses and pipefishes. In turn they are eaten by blue crabs and by fishes larger than the syngnathids.

The pipefishes and seahorses were struck hard by the eelgrass blight, almost disappearing along the Middle and North Atlantic coast in some areas.

PERCIFORMES. This is an enormous order of bony fishes—in fact, it is the largest of all vertebrate orders. Not surprisingly, it is represented in the *Zostera* community by many species. Among those described in other chapters there are many that live in this habitat as young or come into it as adults to feed. A few of the fish of this order that play roles in the eelgrass ecology are described below.

Black Sea Bass. *Centropristis striata* is a bottom-dwelling species that lives offshore in winter. It is a marine fish, and does not enter rivers. Even in the bays it prefers water up to 50 ft. (15 m) in depth, over hard bottoms. But some of the smaller fish feed in the eelgrass beds on crustaceans, fishes, and urchins, and upon the leaves of *Zostera*. It is found throughout the Middle Atlantic range.

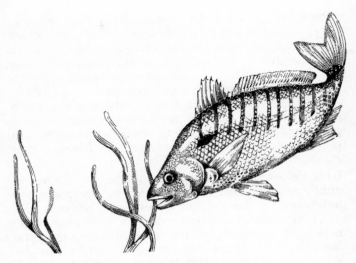

178. Spot *(Leiostomus xanthurus)*.

Spot. *Leiostomus xanthurus* is extremely abundant in some of the Middle Atlantic eelgrass beds. This fish feeds upon a wide range of invertebrate prey, and it is worth noting that detritus and green *Zostera* leaves are important items in its diet. No species of predator with a specialized animal diet would be expected to occur with the abundance that the spot maintains on its broad diet.

Red Drum. *Sciaenops ocellatus,* known in some areas as **redfish** or **channel bass,** is a good-sized fish; the record, caught in North Carolina, was 90 lb. (41 kg). It is a bottom fish, and feeds mostly on mollusks and crustaceans. It is the young fish of this species that come into the eelgrass beds; the adults are not shallow-water fish, and tend to remain in the deeper channels when in the estuaries.

Eelgrass Blenny. *Stathmonotus stahli* is a small shallow-water fish often found in eelgrass, as are the **striped blenny** *(Chasmodes bosquianus)* and **feather blenny** *(Hypsoblennius hentzi)*. These fishes are hard to identify; even the taxonomists can't agree on their status, but presently *S. stahli* is placed in the family Clinidae, and the other two are placed in the Blenniidae.

The blennies, small fish themselves (to 4 in., or 10 cm) feed on minute animal life. The striped blenny, which prefers eelgrass beds on sandy bottoms, also frequents oyster bars; it sometimes lays its eggs in empty shells. The feather blenny's name derives from the two branching tentacles over its head.

OTHER BONY FISHES. Several members of the Gadidae (cod family) are discussed in Chapter Three under Animals of the Estuarine Waters. One, the **spotted hake** *(Urophycis regius)*, which occurs from Cape Cod to Cape Hatteras, can be found in the eelgrass beds. It feeds in the shallows in spring and fall on small crustaceans, small fishes, annelids, and mollusks. This is a small cod, measuring only 12 in. (30 cm).

The **inshore lizardfish** *(Synodus foetens)*, a member of a southern family of fishes, ranges to Cape Cod. A bottom dweller, it feeds on smaller fishes and shrimp in eelgrass beds with sand bottoms. It measures to 16 in. (41 cm).

Epibenthic Scavengers

The sanitary department of the eelgrass community is dominated by crustaceans—amphipods, true crabs, and hermit-crabs. The feeding habits of several species in the first two groups have been discussed earlier in this book. The hermit-crabs are particularly characteristic of the *Zostera* habitat, though they are by no means limited to it. Their niche in the community is much more than that of mere removers of garbage, for their relationships with other animals are complex. Furthermore, from the human point of view, they are the clowns of the community. This writer has found them so entertaining to watch that he has sometimes been distracted from more serious observations by their antics.

HERMIT-CRABS. The hermit-crabs *(Pagurus* spp.) belong to an infraorder (Anomura) of the decapods that contains more than 700 species. The hermits lack the reduced and reflexed abdomen of true crabs. (One must turn over a crab to see this modified abdomen, which is well protected by the ventral shell.) The hermit's abdomen is long, soft, and vulnerable, and thus requires the special protection that the hermit's residence in an old snail shell provides. As the hermit grows, its rigid shell becomes a tighter home; eventually the shell is outgrown, and the hermit must vacate. But first it must find a new, better-fitting domicile. (A shell too large also has disadvantages: it may be an additional burden to carry around; and the extra space provides opportunities for commensals to complicate the hermit's life.)

Whenever more than one hermit-crab is present at the same spot, there is likely to be combat—or at least belligerent behavior—for these animals seem unable to live together peacefully. The quarrelsomeness is undoubtedly related to the competition among these crustaceans for the available empty gastropod shells. As a hermit-crab grows, it must seek larger quarters, and sometimes the nearest shell of the desired size is already occupied. One of the best places to look for this activity is the *Zostera* beds near the low-tide mark, when it is covered by only a few inches of water. Or you might capture two or three hermit-crabs and transfer them to a small water-filled depression on the lower beach. If you can find some empty snail shells, add them to spice up the situation.

The search for a new shell sometimes entails a struggle with another hermit-crab that is also house hunting, or with one that is perfectly content with its present quarters and quite ready to defend itself from eviction. When the desired empty shell is finally at hand, the hermit tries it on for size by backing up to it and inserting its elongate, asymmetrical, spirally twisted abdomen. (Observation shows how carefully the hermit moves the new shell into position and then places itself in just the right position to make a remarkably quick switch—minimizing the length of its exposure to predators.)

Sometimes the new shell doesn't suit, and the hermit moves back into its old shell to resume the search. During the brief period out-of-doors, of course, the hermit is highly vulnerable not only to predators but to other hermit-crabs that may want its shell. When attacked by

THE EELGRASS COMMUNITY

a larger enemy, a hermit retreats into its own shell, closing off the opening with its closely fitting chelipeds. Most species of hermit-crabs have a smaller left claw that is shaped so as to fit the part of the opening not covered by the right.

Rasplike devices on the hermit's abdomen secure it to the inside of the shell. Trying forcibly to remove *Pagurus* from its shell usually results in either breaking off the claws or separating abdomen from cephalothorax.

Pagurus pays a price for inhabiting a home made for another tenant rather than growing its own hard exoskeleton like most decapods. It harbors commensals of various kinds in the excess inner space, as well as carrying others that attach to the surface of the shell it occupies. Of particular interest is *Hydractinia echinata,* a hydroid that often forms a velvety, pinkish blanket that completely hides the gastropod shell in which the hermit lives (except the ventral surface on which its drags itself when traveling). **Snail fur,** as this hydroid is called, lacks a medusoid stage. Undoubtedly the crustacean not only provides a substrate for the colony but, in carrying it about, helps it to get food and oxygen. The hydroid's paralyzing stinging cells are of service to the hermit in discouraging other would-be commensals and in making it less appetizing to predators. Also, a certain flatworm that eats hermit-crab eggs is killed by the *Hydractinia* colony when it comes to rest on the hermit's shell. But the arrangement is a mixed blessing. Sometimes, *Hydractinia* itself eats eggs of the hermit that come within reach of the food-getting polyps. This may be more a case of scavenging than of predation, however, for the eggs eaten are those that have become dislodged from the female hermit's pleopods, where they are carried until hatching; and it is doubtful that any of these detached eggs would survive

In this species of *Hydractinia* the defensive members of the colony are slender, tall (growing to more than 3/8 in., or 1 cm) and very mobile—almost snakelike; they lack tentacles. The colony also includes nutritive and reproductive polyps. Each colony is of a single sex; those composed of males are a lighter pink. This hydroid is most often discovered growing on *P. longicarpus*, the long-clawed hermit-crab, but it also occurs on shells, rocks, and pilings in shallow water.

The array of commensals on and in the hermit-crabs' shell homes includes anthozoans, polychaetes, bivalves, gastropods, barnacles, anemones, sponges, bryozoans, tunicates, amphipods, and other decapods. Among them are some that, like *Hydractinia*, may eat the hermit's eggs: *Palaemonetes pugios*, a shore shrimp; *Panopeus turgidus*, a mud crab; *Porcellana sayana*, a porcelain crab; some amphipods; and *Diastoma varium*, the little snail that is so abundant on eelgrass leaves. As many as 32 of these gastropods have been found on a single hermit-crab shell.

Long-clawed Hermit-crab and **Flat-clawed Hermit-crab.** *Pagurus longicarpus*, the species most likely to be encountered in the shallow eelgrass beds of the Middle Atlantic coast, is surely one of the best known of estuarine animals. It is exceedingly abundant in many locations. It is distinguished from the flat-clawed hermit-crab *(P. pollicaris)* by its narrow, smooth major claw, which has a dark longitudinal stripe on the front surface. Its preferred shells are those of periwinkles, mud snails, and oyster drills.

Although *P. longicarpus* is the characteristic hermit-crab of the *Zostera* community, *P. pollicaris*, the flat-clawed hermit-crab, which is normally an inhabitant of somewhat deeper waters, is sometimes found there. *P. pollicaris* can be recognized by its broad, flat claws (the left one smaller) covered with tubercles. It reaches a much greater size than *P. longicarpus*, and it chooses the shells of whelks and moon snails for its home. Maximum carapace sizes of the two species are, for *P. longicarpus*, 3/8 in. (9 mm); and for *P. pollicaris*, 1 1/4 in. (31 mm). Both use their second and third pairs of legs for walking and the first pair for fighting and getting food. The role of both species in the ecology of the eelgrass community is significant not only in the food chains of which they are part, but in their function as a means of housing and transport for commensals.

179. Long-clawed hermit-crab *(Pagurus longicarpus)*.

Hermit-crabs, like many true crabs, are chiefly sca-vengers. They themselves are eaten, shell and all, by fishes and wading birds.

Detritivores

An endless web of food chains in which detritivores are links make the detritus cycle of major importance in eelgrass-bed ecology. Deposit feeders of the infauna and epibenthos, and even free-swimming detritus eat-ers such as the striped mullet, partake of the nutritious burdens of bacteria and fungi on the fragments of *Zost-era* and other plants that are constantly accumulating on the bottom. This pathway for energy transfer is equalled in the community only by the epiphytic-grazer route. Much detrital material is transported out of the *Zostera* community by water currents to supply other estuarine habitats. Along with *Spartina alter-niflora*, *Zostera* also contributes to the ecosystems of coastal waters, by means of detritus carried out on tidal river currents and through inlets of lagoons, or from eelgrass beds in shallow bays.

Some lesser sources of detrital material in estuaries

are *Typha* (cattails), *Scirpus* (sedges), and *Phragmites,* from brackish and near-fresh zones; and *Salicornia, Juncus,Ruppia,* and *Enteromorpha* and *Polysiphonia* (the last two, filamentous algae), from more marine environments.

A wide array of consumers utilize the microalgae and microfauna that occur in great abundance in the eelgrass detritus. The detritivorous community includes amphipods, gastropods, bivalves, polychaetes, and oligochaetes of the benthic infauna and mobile epibenthos. Zooflagellates by the millions on and amongst the detrital particles feed, probably exclusively, on bacteria; in turn, the zooflagellates are eaten by the smaller secondary consumers. Suspension feeders such as *Mya arenaria,* the soft-shelled clam, take in detritus with planktonic organisms. The lugworm, *Arenicola* spp., utilizes suspended material by driving water through its burrow so that particles are trapped in the sand lying in front of the worm's head; but it also takes in much settled detritus.

Because of the time delay in the utilization of the slowly disintegrating plant fragments by the bacteria and fungi, there is a more constant source of energy for *heterotrophic consumers* (those feeding on organisms of more than one trophic level, such as fishes that feed on detritus, green algae, and amphipods) than would exist if only primary (photosynthetic) production were available. At times, algal (primary) production is at a low level; detritus, which derives from earlier primary production, serves as stored energy to be released and utilized at such times. It is thus a buffer against seasons of low primary production, and helps prevent undue fluctuations in consumer populations.

This secondary production based on decomposition of *Zostera marina* can be very high—from 17 to 34 oz. per square yard (500 to 1,000 grams per square meter) of carbon per year. Two types of degradation of the *Zostera* plants occur: a mechanical one and a biochemical one. First, soluble constituents of the dead leaves leach out and become part of the dissolved organics of the system. Some of this is utilized by bacteria in the sediments. The leached leaves are broken down by a

number of mechanical processes: wave action, disturbance of the deposits by macrofauna, and browsing and
chewing of increasingly smaller particles by a series of
detritivores.

Biological decomposition is brought about by bacteria; by protozoans feeding on bacteria; by detritus-feeding mollusks such as *Hydrobia ventrosa* and *Macoma
balthica;* and by amphipods such as *Parhylalella whip-
pleyi* and *Corophium volutator* that assimilate only a
small portion of the organic carbon and pass on fecal
pellets with decreased carbon content but increased
organic nitrogen. These species have assimilation effi-
ciencies of more than 90% for bacteria and protozoa
and of 50% to 80% for microalgae, but the detrital
fragments pass through the digestive system nearly intact and are then available for more bacteria and protozoa to grow on them. The invertebrates living in *Zostera* beach-wrack apparently function in a similar way to
process the dead plants.

There is some evidence that, owing to the bacterial
action, the absolute amount of protein in detritus
greatly increases during decomposition, while that of
carbohydrate decreases somewhat.

More detailed presentations of the detrital cycle in
eelgrass beds can be read in some of the references
listed at the end of this book. Particularly recom-
mended is T. Fenchel's *Eelgrass Systems,* Chapter
Four.

Coastal Access Areas

The following areas on the Middle Atlantic coast are open to the public and offer easy access to the natural habitats described in this book. The location of each area and its outstanding features are noted; where full addresses are provided (in parentheses), the reader can write to the managing agency for additional information.

Sandy Neck and Great Marshes
Barnstable, Mass.
Major spit and dune development; sandy beach and extensive salt marsh.

Town beaches
Brewster and Orleans, Mass.
Extremely broad, sandy intertidal flats on protected shore of Cape Cod Bay.

Cape Cod National Seashore
(South Wellfleet, MA 02663)
Wide variety of coastal ecosystems including extensive mainland and barrier beaches, both bayside and ocean-side; spit and hook formation; major dune system, including active dunes; salt ponds; many freshwater lakes and ponds of glacial origin; tidal creeks and estuaries; rich eelgrass communities; fresh and salt marshes; northern white-cedar swamp south of its normal range.

Horseneck Beach State Reserve
Westport, Mass.
Sandy and rocky beaches; Westport River estuary with salt marshes, rocky islets, eelgrass beds, nesting ospreys; wading birds and waterfowl.

Sachuest Point to City of Newport, R.I.
Rocky coastline features including cliffs, embayed-shoreline beaches, and coastal ponds with waterfowl; marine algae and intertidal life. Famous Cliff Walk enhances observation of rocky shore geomorphology.

Ninigret Conservation Area
and Ninigret National Wildlife Refuge
Charlestown, R.I.
(Dept. of Environmental Management,
83 Park St., Providence, RI 02903)
One of the richest lagoons ("salt ponds") of the Rhode Island coast; rich eelgrass beds and intertidal flats; barrier beach on Block Island Sound.

Rocky Neck State Park
(Box 676, Niantic, CT 06357)
Brackish marsh and tidal creek with waterfowl, wading birds, ospreys; beach, adjacent rocky headland.

Hammonasett Beach State Park
(Box 271, Madison, CT 06443)
Extensive salt marsh and salt meadow; sandy and rocky beaches; intertidal flats; shorebirds, wading birds, waterfowl, including sea ducks; sandy and rocky beach on Long Island Sound; large variety of upper-beach and marsh plants, marine algae.

Hither Hills State Park, Long Island
(Montauk, NY 11954)
Occupies a section across neck separating Atlantic Ocean from Napeague Bay; 50-ft. sand cliffs; heavily vegetated hilly terrain (mostly scrubby oak–pine growth); mammals include red fox, whitetail deer, raccoon, muskrat; many migratory and wintering water birds; freshwater pond and marsh.

Coastal Access Areas

Fire Island National Seashore, Long Island
(120 Laurel St., Patchogue, NY 11772)
Classic example of barrier-beach maritime forest; extensive shrub-thicket development; broad spectrum of dune-and-swale vegetation; active high dunes in Fire Island Wilderness Area; salt and fresh marsh; red fox, muskrat, whitetail deer, wading and shorebirds. Access by ferry.

Jamaica Bay National Recreation Area and Jamaica Wildlife Refuge
(Floyd Bennett Field, Brooklyn, NY 11234)
13,000-acre preserve within sight of New York City skyscrapers; extensive marshes, shallow bay waters, fresh ponds, dunes; breeding herons, glossy ibis, waterfowl, intertidal life.

Sandy Hook National Recreation Area
Highlands, N.J.
(Floyd Bennett Field, Brooklyn, NY 11234)
Active barrier spit development; bay and ocean beaches, well-developed holly maritime forest, shrub thickets; salt marsh and mud flats; more than 300 bird species, including breeding rails.

Great Bay Boulevard Wildlife Management Area
Tuckerton, N.J.
(Division of Fish, Game, and Shellfisheries, P.O. Box 1809, Trenton, NJ 08625)
Vast salt-marsh system easily seen along road from Tuckerton to bay; abundant waterfowl, wading birds, and shorebirds; skimmer, oystercatcher, osprey, northern harrier; extensive tidal creeks.

Brigantine National Wildlife Refuge
(P.O. Box 721, Oceanville, NJ 08231)
Large refuge encompassing part of broadest salt marsh on Middle Atlantic coast; mecca for birders during migration; teeming with bird life, especially waterfowl, wading birds, and shorebirds; photo blinds available for use; auto trail; skimmer nesting colony on barrier beach of Hogate Unit.

Wetlands Institute
(Stone Harbor Blvd., Stone Harbor, NJ 08247)
Visitor center at edge of marsh with view of nesting ospreys; Absecon Wildlife Management Area adjacent; nearby water-bird sanctuary with concentration of wading birds in middle of town of Stone Harbor.

Cape May Point State Park
(Box 107, Cape May Point, NJ 08212)
Fall-migrating birds and monarch butterflies congregate on point prior to crossing Delaware Bay; famous for migrating hawks; sand beach, small maritime forest, fresh marsh; muskrats, nesting waterfowl.

Bombay Hook National Wildlife Refuge
(RFD 1, Box 147, Smyrna, DE 19977)
Major Atlantic Flyway stopover and wintering area; extensive brackish marshes and fresh impoundments; wide variety of water birds, red and gray foxes, deer, otter, muskrat, opossum.

Cape Henlopen State Park
(Lewes, DE 19958)
Accreting spit opposite Cape May at mouth of Delaware Bay. Active and stabilized dunes with low-shrub to pine forest cover; fresh ponds, salt marsh, ocean and bayside beach; tern nesting colony; mass concentration of breeding horseshoe-crabs in May and June. Nearby areas: Prime Hook National Wildlife Refuge, Delaware Seashore State Park, and Assawoman Wildlife Area.

Assateague Island National Seashore (Maryland sector)
(Rte. 2, Box 294, Berlin, MD 21811)
Prime area for observation of barrier-beach dynamics: active dunes, periodic washover, accelerated landward retreat; shorebirds, peregrine falcons in fall migration; eelgrass beds in lagoon.

Chincoteague National Wildlife Refuge (Virginia sector of Assateague Island National Seashore)
(P.O. Box 62, Chincoteague, VA 23336)

Abundant, diverse wildlife all year; auto-bike-walking loop trail for observation of marsh and wading birds, waterfowl, nesting ospreys, whitetail deer and sikas; ocean beach, salt marsh, forest, fresh impoundments, active hook development. Sanctuary for endangered Delmarva fox squirrel.

Blackwater National Wildlife Refuge
(Rte. 1, Box 121, Cambridge, MD 21613)
Important Atlantic Flyway refuge; Canada and snow geese, ducks, wading birds; important bald eagle nesting area; golden eagles in winter; ospreys, rails, gallinules, harriers; sika, whitetail deer, red fox, otter, Delmarva fox squirrel; auto loop trail through forest and brackish marsh.

Eastern Neck National Wildlife Refuge
(Rte. 2, Box 225, Rock Hall, MD 21661)
Brackish marsh and forest; bird and mammal life similar to that of Blackwater, including Delmarva fox squirrel; Canada goose, whistling swan, hawks during migration.

Point Lookout State Park
(P.O. Box 48, Scotland, MD 20687)
Of primary interest for migrating birds, including hawks; wintering waterfowl; nesting bald eagles; brackish marsh, loblolly pine forest.

Seashore State Park
(2500 Shore Drive, Virginia Beach, VA 23451)
A National Landmark, notable for diversity of plant life; hiking trail through forested dunes with boardwalks crossing picturesque baldcypress ponds; northernmost habitat of Spanish moss.

Back Bay National Wildlife Refuge
(Suite 218, 287 Pembroke Office Park, Virginia Beach, VA 23462)
Barrier beach, brackish and fresh marsh, maritime forest; sanctuary for wintering waterfowl; northern limit of regular nesting of loggerhead turtle; osprey nesting. Nearby areas: Mackay Island National Wildlife Refuge and False Cape State Park.

Jockey Ridge State Park
Nags Head, N.C.
Highest dune on the Atlantic coast (110 to 140 ft.); mostly unvegetated, it changes shape daily; here sea-oat replaces marram as principal stabilizer of active dune.

Cape Hatteras National Seashore
(Box 457, Manteo, NC 27954)
Preserves much of greatest barrier-beach system, the Outer Banks; great diversity of ecosystems, including dunelands, maritime forest, shrub thicket, salt marsh, fresh marsh and ponds, eelgrass, tidal creeks, mud and sand flats, ocean and bayside beaches; brown pelican, osprey, bald eagle, peregrine falcon; loggerhead turtle nesting; Ocracoke Island accessible only by ferry from mainland or Hatteras Island.

Endangered Species

Many species on the official lists of rare and endangered plants and animals are native to the Middle Atlantic seashore. The most publicized of these is the peregrine falcon *(Falco peregrinus);* its distribution was wide until pesticides extirpated it from most of its range in the 1950s. Brought to near extinction by the use of DDT, it has been the object of a vigorous and intensive restoration effort coordinated by Cornell University. Today, during the fall migration period, a visitor to Assateague Island can with a little persistence see this splendid bird as it stops over on its way south.

Two vertebrates on the official endangered species list can be seen in the Middle Atlantic region only on the coast. One is a mammal, the other a reptile. The former is found nowhere else but in one small sector of this region.

Delmarva Peninsula Fox Squirrel

Fox squirrels are larger versions of the more familiar gray squirrels. They weigh about twice as much as gray squirrels and show more color variation among the subspecies. The endangered form, the Delmarva Peninsula fox squirrel, is the subspecies *Sciurus niger cinereus.* It is bluish-gray above and on the sides, with interspersed black hairs tipped with white; on the squirrel's nose and underside the hairs are white; there are pronounced black stripes on the sides of the tail. Since *S.n. cinereus* tends to occupy the same habitats as does the gray squirrel, these differences should be kept in mind when observing in the field.

The known range of the Delmarva fox squirrel once

extended from southeastern Pennsylvania and central New Jersey to embrace the entire Delmarva Peninsula. The range has shrunk so that it now includes only parts of Kent, Queen Anne's, Talbot, and Dorchester counties in Maryland and a small area in Accomac County, Virginia. The largest populations are located in national wildlife refuges and on state-owned or controlled lands. Most stable of these are the populations on Eastern Neck and Blackwater national wildlife refuges, both in the Maryland part of the peninsula.

The decline of the Delmarva fox squirrel has been attributed to major alterations of its habitat by humans and by various other stresses brought on by increasing human population in its range. The habitat requirements for this squirrel are: (1) mature trees that produce a dependable mast (nut) crop, (2) a mixture of tree species adequate to insure against food shortages arising from failure of one or more species, and (3) denning sites—hollow trees—usually in short supply where forests are cut periodically. Like gray squirrels, fox squirrels will adapt to nesting boxes provided by humans. Fox squirrels are more terrestrial in their habits than gray squirrels. They frequently venture into open fields, and may even come down out of trees to escape danger. They get most of their food, however, from trees. Their diet is chiefly the mast of oaks, hickories, beech, walnut, and loblolly pine. They also eat tree buds and flowers, fungi, insects, and occasionally bird eggs or young.

The Delmarva fox squirrel historically met all of its needs in parklike woodlands with minimal growth of underbrush, forests bordering rivers and streams, and small open woodlots. The clearing of forests for agricultural purposes and the cutting of timber for forest products destroyed most of this habitat in the squirrel's range. Where the forests were allowed to return after cutting, the dense undergrowth that prevailed at least during the early stages of regrowth made them inhospitable to the fox squirrel. The forests were generally cut again before they were mature enough to develop the open, parklike aspect suitable for the squirrels.

By the turn of the century the Delmarva fox squirrel had disappeared from southern New Jersey and Pennsylvania; it is now confined, in its limited range, to mixed stands of hardwoods (often with mature loblolly pines), generally in groves of trees along bays and tidal streams, and in small woodlots.

A management plan being implemented largely by the U.S. Fish and Wildlife Service is aimed at restoring the Delmarva fox squirrel to a secure status in as much of its former range as is feasible, by preserving and managing suitable denning and feeding habitats; by transplanting colony-sized groups of squirrels from areas such as the Blackwater and Eastern Neck refuges to designated habitats from which they are now absent; and by protecting existing squirrels through legislation and public education. There is also an effort to identify threatened populations and to rescue them for release in more secure locations.

Although the Delmarva fox squirrel's habitat requirements do not limit it to seashore and estuarine environments, its present range is virtually restricted to woodlands adjacent to salt and brackish waters. Thus it is the only terrestrial animal on the endangered species list that is confined to the environments with which we are here concerned. Fortunately, the mere presence of human beings is apparently not a deterrent to the squirrel where the habitat fully meets its biological requirements.

Atlantic Loggerhead

The large seagoing turtles, most species of which are at home in tropical and subtropical waters, often straggle north to the Middle Atlantic coast; some even make it to Nova Scotia. Six of the seven species are in great danger of early extinction. We are concerned here with the one species that nests at Cape Hatteras and the shores to the immediate north.

The perilous state of sea turtles around the world is due entirely to human activities: predation by humans and their dogs; destruction of nesting habitat through development and erosion-control structures on the barrier islands; death by drowning in fishing nets; compacting of beach sands by off-road vehicles and litter-removal machines; even artificial lighting, which

446   ENDANGERED SPECIES

disorients hatchlings attempting to make it to the sea. Much of the blame can be laid at the doorstep of state and federal officials and agencies that have encouraged development and urbanization of barrier islands by building bridges from the mainland and by subsidizing flood-insurance programs for owners of barrier-island second homes and resort facilities, and that have opened federally owned beaches to vehicular traffic.

The Endangered Species Office of the U.S. Fish and Wildlife Service has developed programs for saving the sea turtles from extinction. But in the mid-1980s there seems to be a lack of enthusiasm on the part of many highly placed officials for efforts on behalf of endangered wildlife, even for enforcing the existing protective laws. A reversal of this attitude could prevent a serious setback, but time is critically short. Because the recovery and survival of depleted sea-turtle populations is of necessity an international affair, the leadership role that American know-how warrants is at stake. Much of the current work is being done by nongovernment scientists with volunteer help from private citizens.

The one turtle species that normally inhabits temperate waters is the Atlantic loggerhead *(Caretta caretta caretta)*. Its only ecological significance in seashore ecology relates to its nesting habits. The female visits the beach at egg-laying time, for only a few hours. Sea turtles rarely come to land for any other purpose.

The loggerhead nests as far north as Virginia. At Chincoteague National Wildlife Refuge an egg-transplant program is aimed at extending the breeding range. Farther south, on the Currituck and Outer banks, miles of protected beach—state and federal lands—are loggerhead nesting habitat. Monitoring and guarding turtle nesting is a task that requires many person-hours during the breeding period. Some programs have entailed placing protective barriers over nests to prevent raccoon predation; some have involved digging up the eggs and incubating them artifically. The young turtles are either returned to the nesting site to imprint the locale before they enter the sea, or are released at another site where future nesting will be adequately protected.

Endangered Species

Handle with Care

Many animals of the seashore will be unfamiliar to persons exploring these ecosystems for the first time. In addition to those notorious for being risky to handle, such as stingrays, cottonmouths, and red jellyfish, there are many less known creatures that can cause serious injury or troublesome skin reactions, or that are poisonous to eat; and a fair number can and do occasionally cause death. More comprehensive and detailed treatment of these animals can be found in *Dangerous Marine Animals* by Bruce W. Halstead, and (for jellyfish) in *Common Jellyfish and Comb Jellies of North Carolina* by Frank J. Schwartz. (See Bibliography.) The following list includes the species most likely to be encountered in the intertidal and shallow subtidal habitats of the Middle Atlantic coast.

INVERTEBRATES

Red beard sponge, *Microciona prolifera.* Common on Middle Atlantic coast; chemical substances on external surface of sponge cause painful dermatitis.

Cnidarians: *Physalia, Cyanea, Chrysaora,* and *Tamoya haplonema* (sea wasp). Stinging tentacles may extend 50 ft. or more from jellyfish; avoid contact; for *Physalia* and *Chrysaora* stings, get medical attention.

Bloodworm, or **beakthrower,** *Glycera dibranchiata.* Found on entire Middle Atlantic coast; poisonous fangs on proboscis; bite is comparable to bee sting.

Echinoderms. Sea urchins with elongate needlelike spines must not be handled; spines difficult to remove.

Mollusks: *Ensis, Mya, Cardium, Spisula, Donax, Mytilus.* Human poisoning generally caused by dinoflagellates in food chain—the notorious "red tide"; paralysis and death may result.

VERTEBRATES

Spiny dogfish, *Squalus acanthias.* Venomous spine on front of each of two dorsal fins; severe pain, reportedly some deaths.

Dusky shark, *Carcharhinus obscurus.* Enters estuaries, feeds in intertidal and subtidal zones; has been known to attack humans; reaches 12 ft.

Bluntnose stingray, *Dasyatis sayi.* Found in estuaries from New Jersey south; lies almost buried in muddy or sandy shallows, where unwary waders step on its poisonous spine.

Cownose ray, *Rhinoptera bonasus.* Range includes most of Middle Atlantic coast; more dangerous than bluntnose stingray, and no known antidote.

Atlantic needlefish, *Strongylura marina.* A good food fish, but has a habit of leaping from the water, inflicts wounds by plunging sharp beak into flesh; has killed by piercing brain.

Oyster toadfish, *Opsanus tau.* Two venomous dorsal-fin spines and two gill-cover spines. Painful wounds but no known fatalities.

Common trunkfish, *Lactophrys trigonis.* Inhabits entire coast to Cape Cod; flesh at times is toxic from occurrence of a certain dinoflagellate in the food chain. *Never* eat the liver of this fish or of species of Tetraodontidae (puffers, porcupinefish, etc.).

Bibliography

Coastal Geomorphology

Bascom, Willard. *Waves and Beaches—The Dynamics of the Ocean Surface.* Garden City, N.Y.: Doubleday & Co., 1964.

Kaufman, Wallace, and Pilkey, Orrin. *The Beaches Are Moving.* Garden City, N.Y.: Anchor Press/Doubleday, 1979.

Komar, Paul D. *Beach Processes and Sedimentation.* Englewood Cliffs, N.J.: Prentice-Hall, Inc., 1976.

Leatherman, Stephen P. *Barrier Island Handbook.* Amherst, Mass.: University of Massachusetts Press, 1979.

Leatherman, Stephen P., ed. *Environmental Geologic Guide to Cape Cod National Seashore.* Amherst, Mass.: University of Massachusetts Press, 1979.

Shepard, Francis P., and Wanless, Harold R. *Our Changing Coastlines.* New York: McGraw-Hill, 1972.

Strahler, Arthur N. *A Geologist's View of Cape Cod.* Garden City, N.Y.: Natural History Press, 1966.

———. *Physical Geography.* New York: John Wiley & Sons, 1945.

Yasso, Warren E., and Hartman, Elliott M., Jr. *Beach Forms and Coastal Processes.* MESA New York Bight Atlas Monograph 11. Albany: New York Sea Grant Institute, 1975.

Seashore Ecology

Amos, William H. *Assateaque Island: A Barrier Island Natural History.* National Park Handbook 106. Washington, D.C.: National Park Service, 1980.

Amos, William H. *Life of the Seashore.* New York: McGraw-Hill, 1966.

Arnold, Augusta Foote. *The Sea-beach at Ebb-tide.* 1901. Reprint. New York: Dover Publications, Inc., 1968.

Art, Henry Warren. *Ecological Studies of the Sunken Forest, Fire Island National Seashore, New York.* Washington, D.C.: National Park Service, 1976.

Barnes, R.S.K. *Coastal Lagoons—The Natural History of a Neglected Habitat.* Cambridge: Cambridge University Press, 1980.

Berrill, Michael, and Berrill, Deborah. *A Sierra Club Naturalist's Guide to the North Atlantic Coast—Cape Cod to Newfoundland.* San Francisco: Sierra Club Books, 1981.

Berrill, N.J., and Berrill, Jacquelyn. *1001 Questions Answered About the Seashore.* 1957. Reprint. New York: Dover Publications, Inc., 1976.

Carson, Rachel. *The Edge of the Sea.* Boston: Houghton Mifflin Co., 1955.

Crosland, Patrick D. *The Outer Banks.* Arlington, Va.: Interpretive Publications, 1981.

Crowder, William. *Seashore Life Between the Tides.* 1931. Reprint. New York: Dover Publications, Inc., 1975. (Originally published as *Between the Tides.*)

Eltringham, Stewart K. *Life in Mud and Sand.* New York: Russak & Co., 1971.

Godfrey, Paul J., and Godfrey, Melinda M. *Barrier Island Ecology of Cape Lookout National Seashore and Vicinity, North Carolina.* Washington, D.C.: National Park Service, 1976.

Hay, John. *The Great Beach.* New York: W. W. Norton & Co., 1980.

———. *The Sandy Shore.* Chatham, Mass.: The Chatham Press, Inc. 1968.

Lauff, George H., ed. *Estuaries.* Publication No. 83. Washington, D.C.: American Association for the Advancement of Science, 1967.

Lippson, Alice Jane, ed. and illustrator. *The Chesapeake Bay in Maryland—An Atlas of Natural Resources.* Baltimore: Johns Hopkins University Press, 1973.

Bibliography

Lippson, Alice Jane, and Lippson, Robert L. *Life in the Chesapeake Bay.* Baltimore: Johns Hopkins University Press, 1984.

McRoy, C. Peter, and Helfferich, Carla, eds. *Seagrass Ecosystems—A Scientific Perspective.* New York: Marcel Dekker, Inc., 1977.

Perry, Bill. *Discovering Fire Island: The Young Naturalist's Guide to the World of the Barrier Beach.* Washington, D.C.: National Park Service, 1978.

Peterson, Charles H., and Peterson, Nancy M. *The Ecology of Intertidal Flats of North Carolina: A Community Profile.* Washington, D.C.: U.S. Fish & Wildlife Service, Office of Biological Services, 1979.

Petry, Loren C., and Norman, Marcia G. *A Beachcomber's Botany.* Chatham, Mass.: The Chatham Conservation Foundation, 1963.

Phillips, R. *Ecological Life History of Zostera marina L. (Eelgrass) in Puget Sound, Washington.* Ann Arbor: University Microfilms International, 1972.

Pomeroy, L.R., and Wiegert, R.G., eds. *The Ecology of a Salt Marsh.* Ecological Studies 38. New York: Springer-Verlag New York, Inc., 1981.

Reid, George K. *Ecology of Intertidal Zones.* New York: Rand McNally, 1967.

Simon, Anne W. *The Thin Edge: Coast and Man in Crisis.* New York: Avon Books, 1978.

Steele, J. H., ed. *Marine Food Chains.* Berkeley: University of California Press, 1970.

Sterling, Dorothy. *The Outer Lands: A Natural History Guide to Cape Cod, Martha's Vineyard, Nantucket, Block Island, and Long Island.* New York: W. W. Norton & Co., 1978.

Teal, John, and Teal, Mildred. *Life and Death of the Salt Marsh.* New York: Ballantine Books, 1969.

General Ecology and Biology

Buchsbaum, Ralph, and Buchsbaum, Mildred. *Basic Ecology.* Pittsburgh: Boxwood Press, 1957.

Carson, Rachel. *Silent Spring.* Boston: Houghton Mifflin Co., 1962.

Krutch, Joseph Wood. *The Great Chain of Life.* Boston: Houghton Mifflin Co., 1977.

Martin, Alexander C., Zim, Herbert S., and Nelson, Arnold L. *American Wildlife and Plants: A Guide to Wildlife Food Habits.* 1951. Reprint. New York: Dover Publications, Inc., 1961.

Odum, Eugene P. *Ecology.* Modern Biology Series. New York: Holt, Rinehart & Winston, 1963.

Perry, Bill. *Our Threatened Wildlife.* New York: Coward-McCann Inc., 1969.

Smith, Robert L. *Ecology and Field Biology.* New York: Harper & Row, 1966.

Storer, John H. *The Web of Life.* New York: Devin-Adair, 1960.

Field Identification Manuals

Abbott, R. Tucker. *A Guide to Field Identification: Seashells of North America.* New York: Golden Press, 1968.

Angier, Bradford. *Field Guide to Edible Wild Plants.* Harrisburg: Stackpole Books, 1974.

Borror, Donald J., and White, Richard E. *A Field Guide to the Insects of America North of Mexico.* Boston: Houghton Mifflin Co., 1970.

Brockman, C. Frank. *Trees of North America.* New York: Golden Press, 1968.

Burt, William H., and Grosenheider, Richard P. *A Field Guide to the Mammals.* Boston: Houghton Mifflin Co., 1974.

Conant, Roger. *A Field Guide to Reptiles and Amphibians.* Cambridge, Mass.: The Riverside Press, 1958.

Emerson, William K., and Jacobson, Morris K. *The American Museum of Natural History Guide to Shells: Land, Freshwater, and Marine, from Nova Scotia to Florida.* New York: Alfred A. Knopf, 1976.

Gosner, Kenneth L. *A Field Guide to the Atlantic Seashore: Invertebrates and Seaweeds of the Atlantic Coast from the Bay of Fundy to Cape Hatteras.* Boston: Houghton Mifflin Co., 1979.

————. *Guide to Identification of Marine and Estuarine Invertebrates: Cape Hatteras to the Bay of Fundy.* New York: John Wiley & Sons, 1971.

Hillson, C. J. *Seaweeds: A Color-coded, Illustrated Guide to Common Marine Plants of the East Coast of the United States.* University Park: The Pennsylvania State University Press, 1977.

Levi, Herbert W., and Levi, Lorna R. *Spiders and their Kin.* New York: Golden Press, 1968.

McClane, A. J., ed. *McClane's Field Guide to Saltwater Fishes of North America.* New York: Holt, Rinehart & Winston, 1965.

Meinkoth, Norman A. *The Audubon Society Field Guide to North American Seashore Creatures.* New York: Alfred A. Knopf, 1981.

Murie, Olaus. *A Field Guide to Animal Tracks.* Boston: Houghton Mifflin Co., 1954.

Peterson, Lee. *A Field Guide to Edible Wild Plants of Eastern and Central North America.* Boston: Houghton Mifflin Co., 1977.

Peterson, Roger Tory. *A Field Guide to the Birds East of the Rockies.* Boston: Houghton Mifflin Co., 1980.

Peterson, Roger Tory, and McKenny, Margaret. *A Field Guide to Wildflowers.* Boston: Houghton Mifflin Co., 1968.

Shuttleworth, Floyd S., and Zim, Herbert S. *Non-flowering Plants: Ferns, Mosses, Lichens, Mushrooms and Other Fungi.* New York: Western Publishing Co., 1967.

Zim, Herbert S., and Ingle, Lester. *Seashores: A Guide to Animals and Plants Along the Beaches.* New York: Simon & Schuster, 1955.

Guides to Natural Areas

The following titles are books designed to help the amateur naturalist locate places accessible to the public for birdwatching, photography, and nature study; they provide brief descriptions of major natural features, along with logistical information.

Kulik, Stephen. *The Audubon Society Field Guide to the Natural Places of the Northeast—Coastal.* New York: Pantheon Books, 1984.

Covers Connecticut, Maine, Massachusetts, New Hampshire, New York, and Rhode Island.

Lawrence, Susannah. *The Audubon Society Field Guide to the Natural Places of the Mid-Atlantic States—Coastal.* New York: Pantheon Books, 1984.

Covers Delaware, Maryland, New Jersey, Pennsylvania, and Virginia.

Perry, John, and Perry, Jane Greverus. *The Random House Guide to Natural Areas of the Eastern United States.* New York: Random House, 1980.

A comprehensive listing of public lands and recreational access.

Riley, Laura, and Riley, William. *Guide to the National Wildlife Refuges.* New York: Anchor Press/Doubleday, 1981.

Covers all American National Wildlife Refuges.

Tilden, Freeman. *The National Parks.* 1951. Rev. ed. New York: Alfred A. Knopf Inc., 1970.

Interpretive treatment; includes Assateague, Cape Cod, Cape Hatteras, Fire Island.

Miscellaneous

Bellrose, Frank C. *Ducks, Geese, and Swans of North America.* Harrisburg: Stackpole Books, 1976.

An updating of the classic work by F. H. Kortright, first published in 1942 by the Wildlife Management Institute.

Bent, Arthur Cleveland. Life Histories of North American Birds. 20 vols. including *Marsh Birds, Diving Birds, Wild Fowl, Birds of Prey, Gulls and Terns, Petrels and Pelicans,* and *Shore Birds.* 1919–1958. Reprints. New York: Dover Publications, Inc., 1962–1964.

Bent's life histories were originally published as U.S. National Museum Bulletins by the U.S. Government Printing Office and the Smithsonian Institution.

Gibbons, Euell. *Stalking the Blue-eyed Scallop.* New York: David McKay Co., 1964.

Halstead, Bruce W., M.D. *Dangerous Marine Animals.* Centreville, Md.: Cornell Maritime Press, 1980.

A thoroughgoing treatment of seashore and other marine animals that bite, sting, shock, or are inedible.

Schwartz, Frank J. *Common Jellyfish and Comb Jellies of North Carolina.* Morehead City: Institute of Marine Sciences, University of North Carolina, 1979.

Stone, Witmer. *Bird Studies at Old Cape May: An Ornithology of Coastal New Jersey.* 2 vols. 1937. Reprint. New York: Dover Publications, Inc., 1965.

A reissue of a classic first published by the Delaware Valley Ornithological Club.

Warner, William W. *Beautiful Swimmers: Watermen, Crabs, and the Chesapeake Bay.* Boston: Little, Brown & Co., 1976.

This 1977 Pulitzer Prize winner is also available in paperback from Penguin Books.

INDEX

Page numbers in italics refer to illustrations, including maps; numbers followed by *t* refer to tables; numbers followed by *n* refer to footnotes.